THE SAGA OF
TANYA THE EVIL

06

Carlo Zen

Tojo

Shinobu Shinotsuki

COUNTRIES AT WAR
REGIONS OF CONFLICT
NEUTRAL COUNTRIES

100 0 100 200 300

REGADONIA
ENTENTE ALLIANCE

RUSSY
FEDERATION

IMPERIAL NORDEN
(IN DISPUTE)

COMMONWEALTH

IMPERIAL OSTLAND
(POTENTIAL DISPUTE)

EMPIRE

FRANÇOIS
REPUBLIC

IMPERIAL
DACIA

PRINCIPALITY
OF DACIA

KINGDOM
OF ILDOA

WALDSTÄTTE
CONFEDERACY

UNRECOVERED ILDOA
(POTENTIAL DISPUTE)

Die Zeiten

DIE KRIEGSGESCHICHTE EINES KLEINEN MÄDCHEN No.005

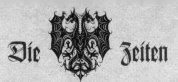

The battle log so far...

Our protagonist, a coolheaded salaryman in contemporary Japan, dies after being pushed off a train platform by a resentful man he fired.

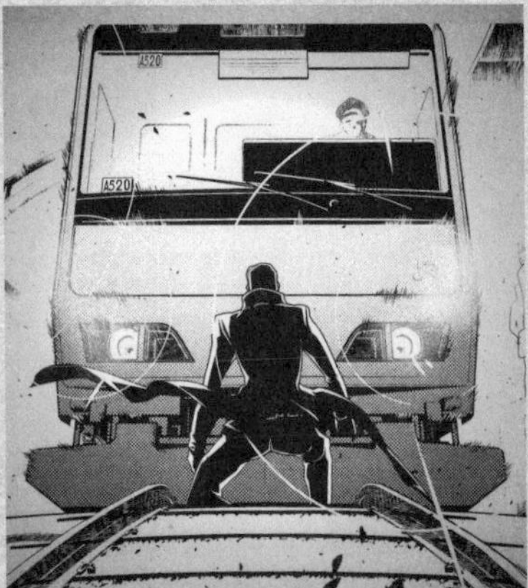
A520
A520

In the world beyond death, he encounters Being X, who claims to be the Creator. His lack of faith angers the being, and he is reborn in another world where gunfire and magic intermingle in combat. "You will be born into an unscientific world as a woman, come to know war, and be driven to your limits!"

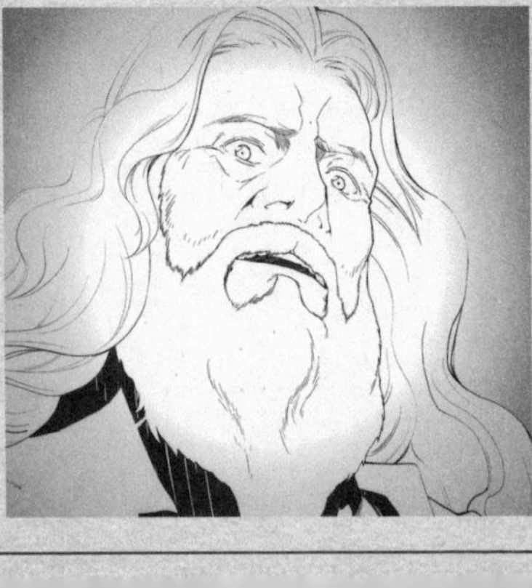

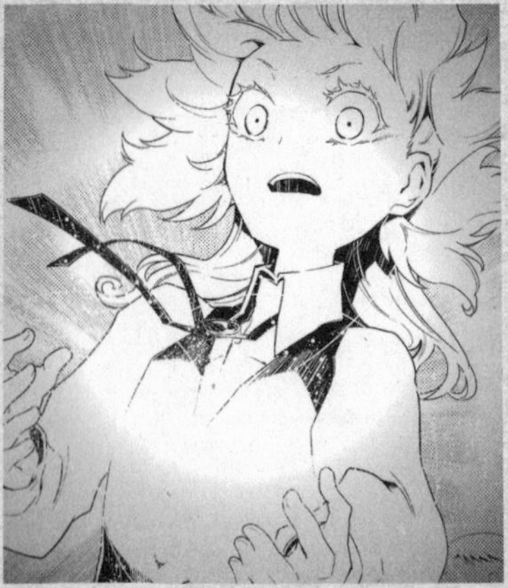

In the other world, he is reincarnated as Tanya Degurechaff. Upon recognition of her magic aptitude, she is sent to the battlefield at the age of nine.

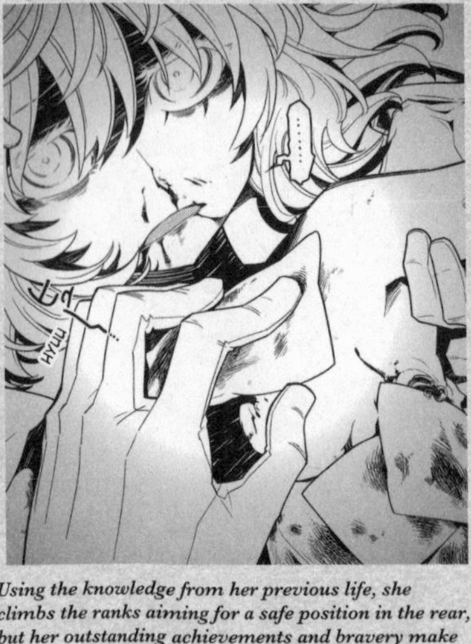
HYUU

Using the knowledge from her previous life, she climbs the ranks aiming for a safe position in the rear, but her outstanding achievements and bravery make such a good impression on her superiors that she is, on the contrary, repeatedly sent to the front lines...

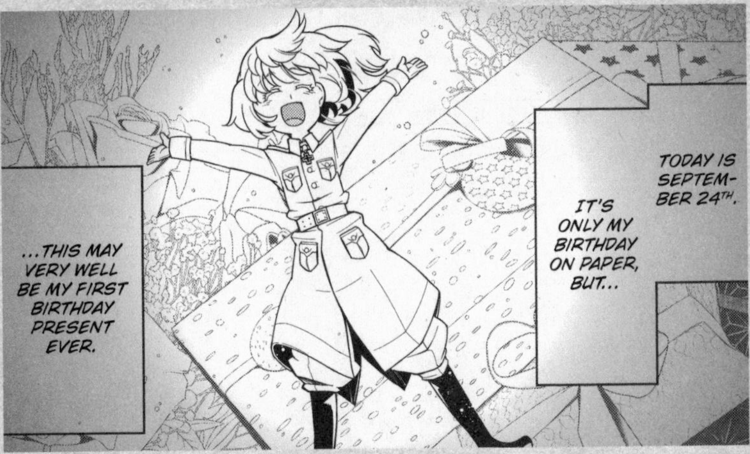
TODAY IS SEPTEMBER 24TH.
IT'S ONLY MY BIRTHDAY ON PAPER, BUT...
...THIS MAY VERY WELL BE MY FIRST BIRTHDAY PRESENT EVER.

On September 24, Unified Year 1925—oddly enough, Tanya's birthday—Principality of Dacia declares war on the Empire despite being much weaker.

Tanya's 203rd Aerial Mage Battalion is deployed to delay the enemy. Much to the major's delight, the reconnaissance aircraft reports that the sky is devoid of enemy air cover. Thrilled that her battalion's first live-combat mission will be fought with such an advantage, she exclaims, "You can call this my first birthday present ever!"

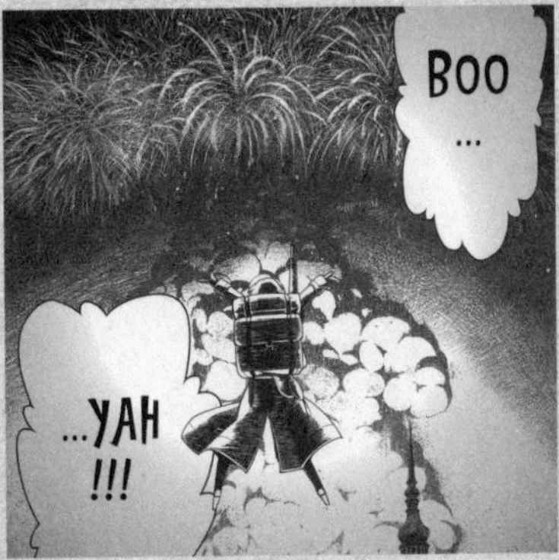
BOO ...
...YAH !!!

The 203rd Aerial Mage Battalion promptly engages the Dacian Army and achieves an overwhelming victory over its anachronistic infantry tactics.

The next morning before dawn, the battalion arrives at the Dacian capital. They pull off the first night attack on a city ever in that world, making their first real battle a spectacular success.

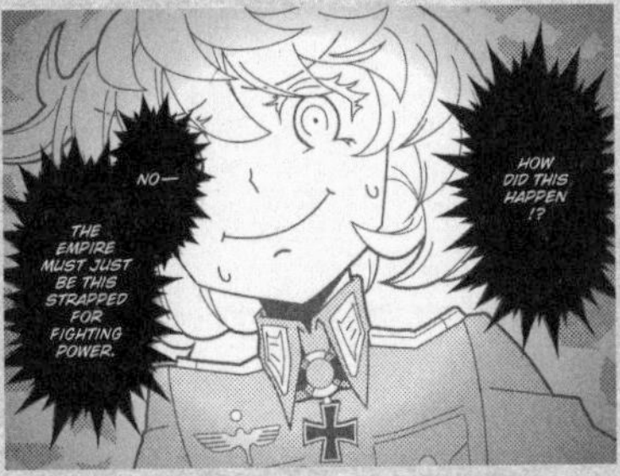
HOW DID THIS HAPPEN !?
NO—
THE EMPIRE MUST JUST BE THIS STRAPPED FOR FIGHTING POWER.

Having exhausted her efforts in the invasion of the Dacian capital, Tanya expects to be given the chance to spend a few months in the rear, but instead, her battalion is sent straight to Norden. She complains to Colonel von Lergen but in the end has no choice but to go.

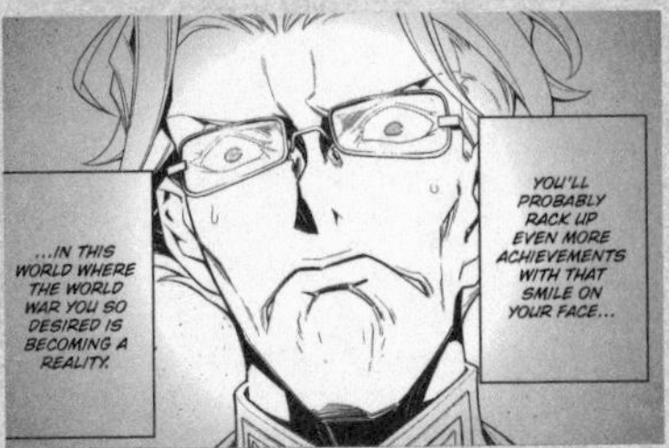
YOU'LL PROBABLY RACK UP EVEN MORE ACHIEVEMENTS WITH THAT SMILE ON YOUR FACE...
...IN THIS WORLD WHERE THE WORLD WAR YOU SO DESIRED IS BECOMING A REALITY.

Thus, about a year and a half into the war, White Silver is sent back up north...

The Saga of
Tanya the Evil

06

Original Story: Carlo Zen   Art: Chika Tojo
Character Design: Shinobu Shinotsuki

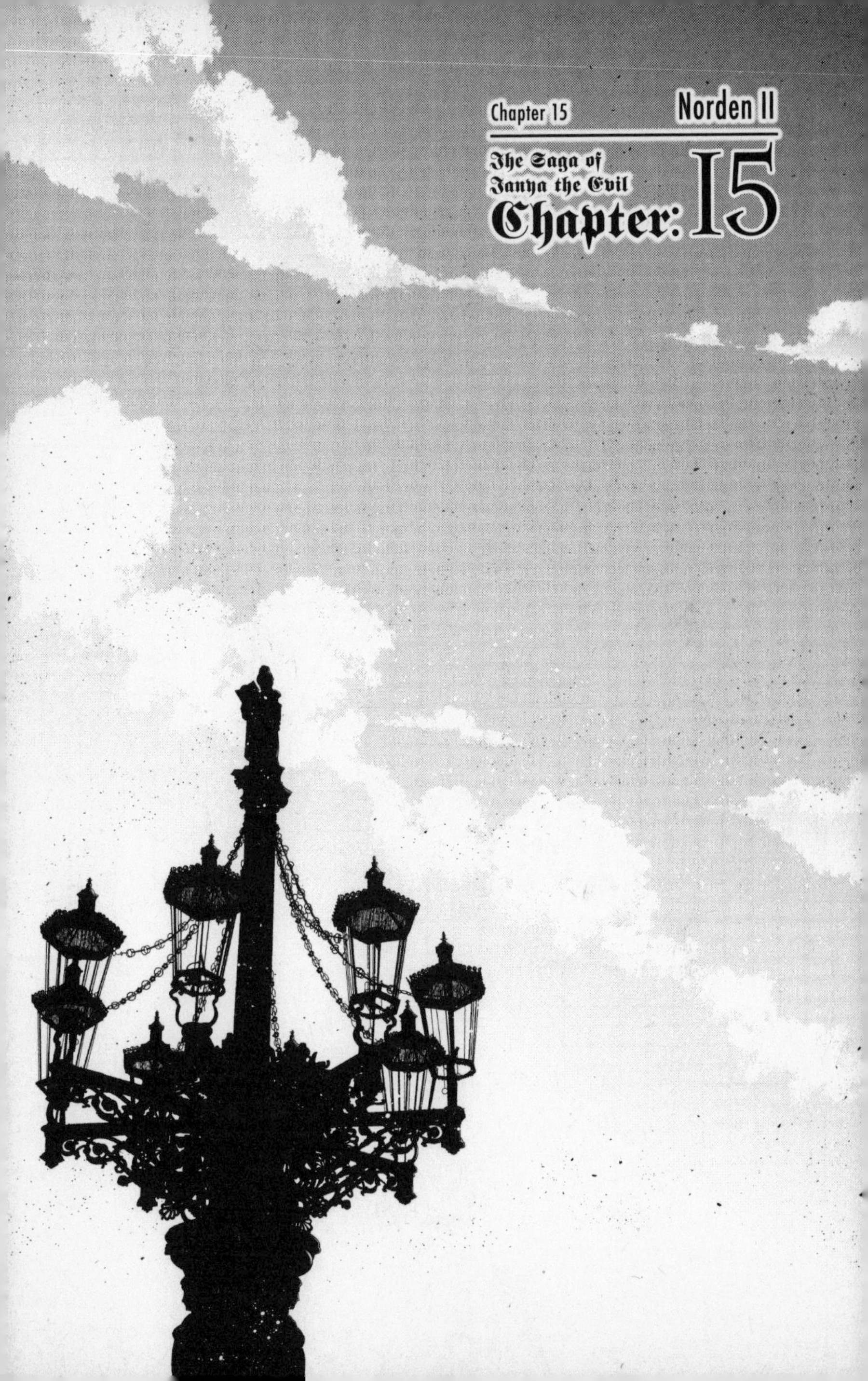
Chapter 15
Norden II
The Saga of Tanya the Evil
Chapter: 15

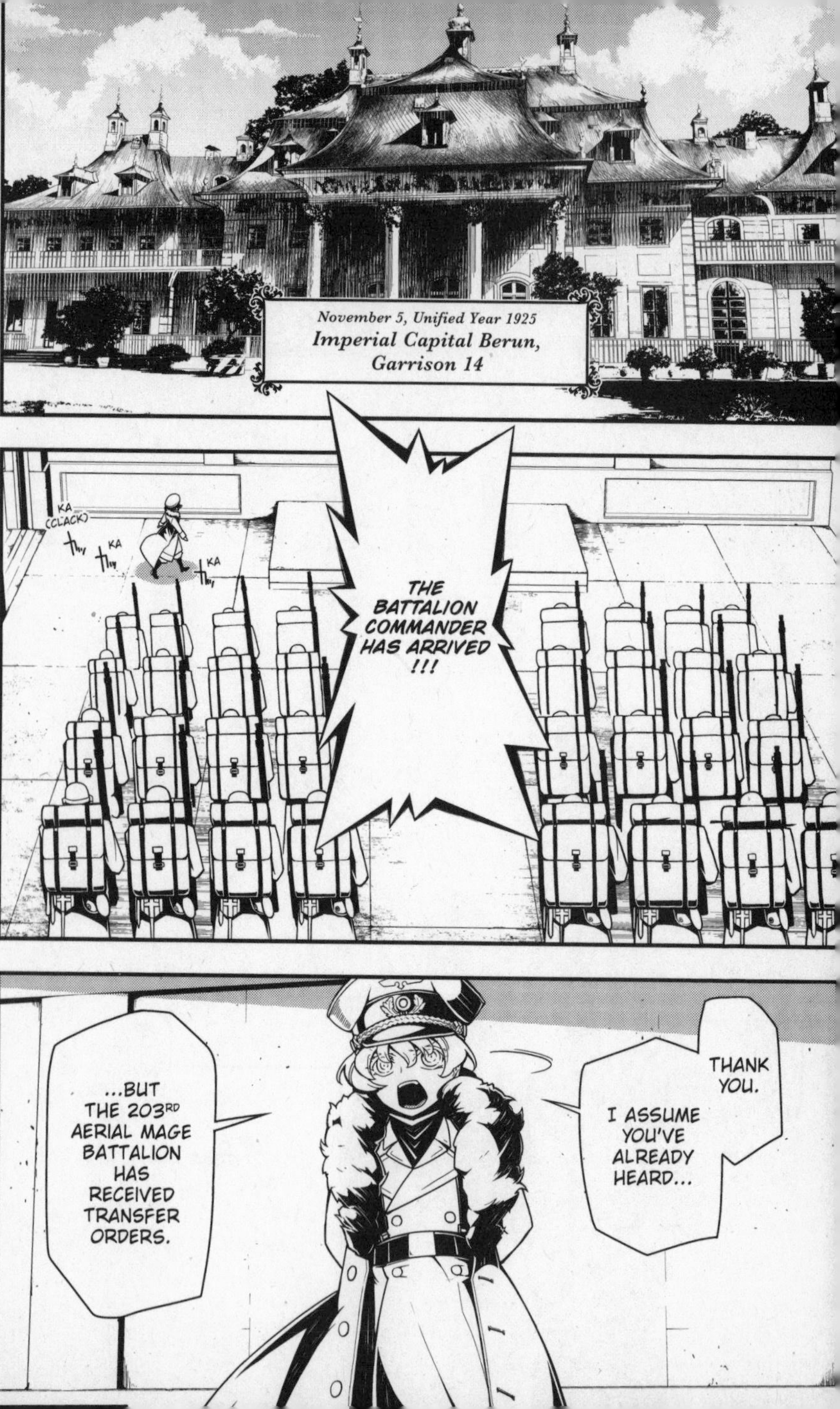
November 5, Unified Year 1925
Imperial Capital Berun, Garrison 14
THE BATTALION COMMANDER HAS ARRIVED !!!
KA (CLACK)
KA
KA
THANK YOU.
I ASSUME YOU'VE ALREADY HEARD...
...BUT THE 203RD AERIAL MAGE BATTALION HAS RECEIVED TRANSFER ORDERS.

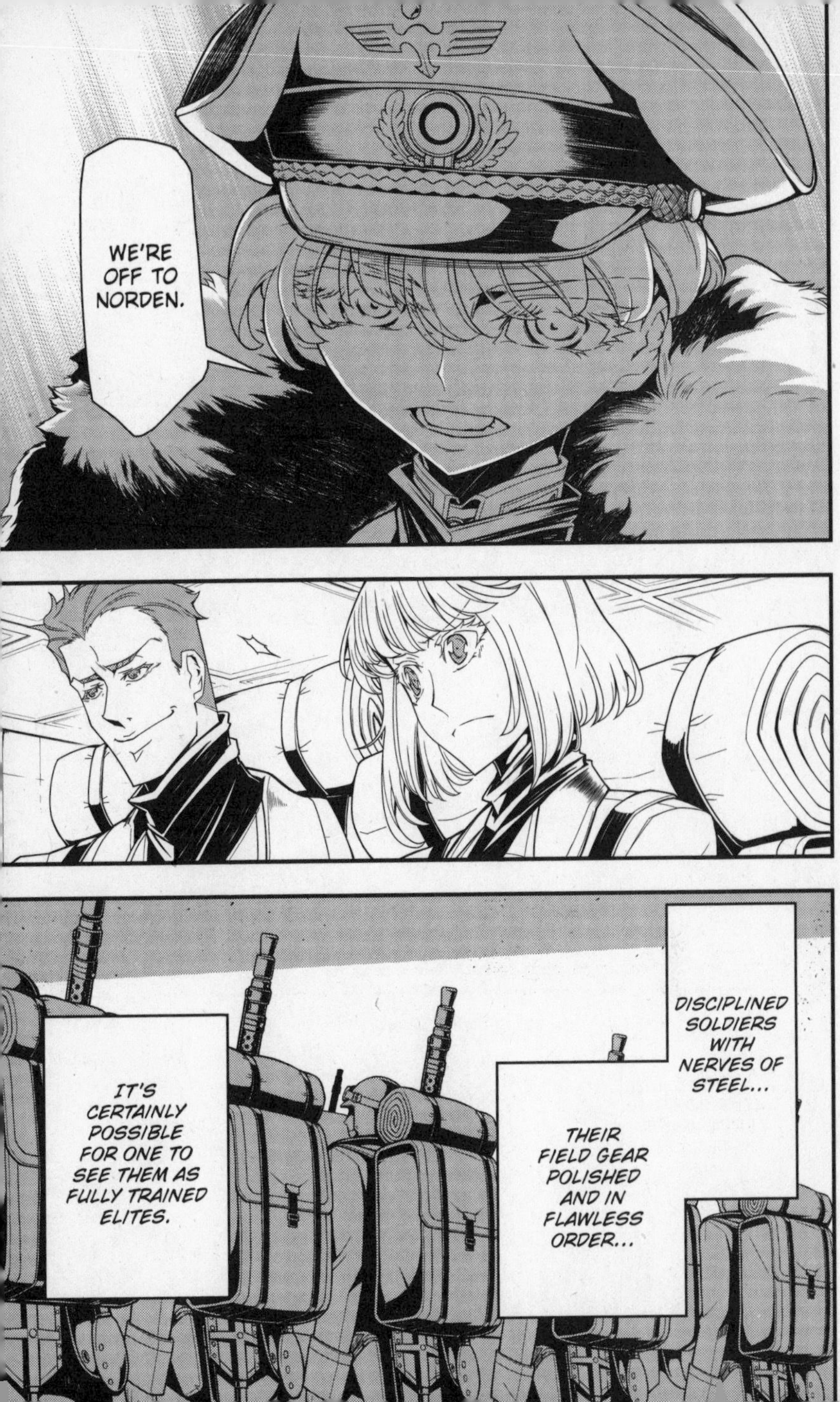
WE'RE OFF TO NORDEN.
DISCIPLINED SOLDIERS WITH NERVES OF STEEL...
THEIR FIELD GEAR POLISHED AND IN FLAWLESS ORDER...
IT'S CERTAINLY POSSIBLE FOR ONE TO SEE THEM AS FULLY TRAINED ELITES.

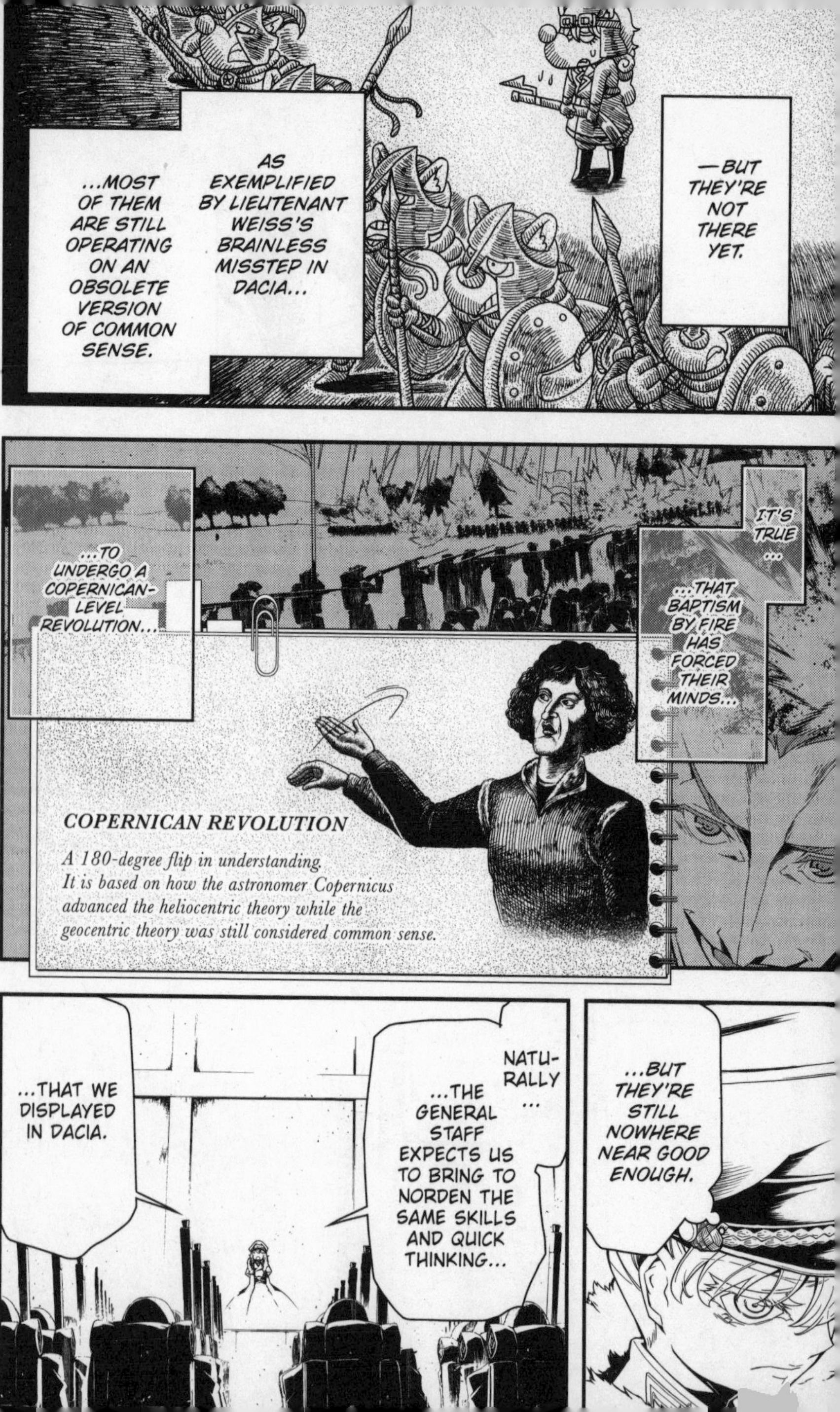
—BUT THEY'RE NOT THERE YET.
AS EXEMPLIFIED BY LIEUTENANT WEISS'S BRAINLESS MISSTEP IN DACIA...
...MOST OF THEM ARE STILL OPERATING ON AN OBSOLETE VERSION OF COMMON SENSE.
IT'S TRUE...
...THAT BAPTISM BY FIRE HAS FORCED THEIR MINDS...
...TO UNDERGO A COPERNICAN-LEVEL REVOLUTION...
COPERNICAN REVOLUTION
A 180-degree flip in understanding. It is based on how the astronomer Copernicus advanced the heliocentric theory while the geocentric theory was still considered common sense.
...BUT THEY'RE STILL NOWHERE NEAR GOOD ENOUGH.
NATURALLY...
...THE GENERAL STAFF EXPECTS US TO BRING TO NORDEN THE SAME SKILLS AND QUICK THINKING...
...THAT WE DISPLAYED IN DACIA.

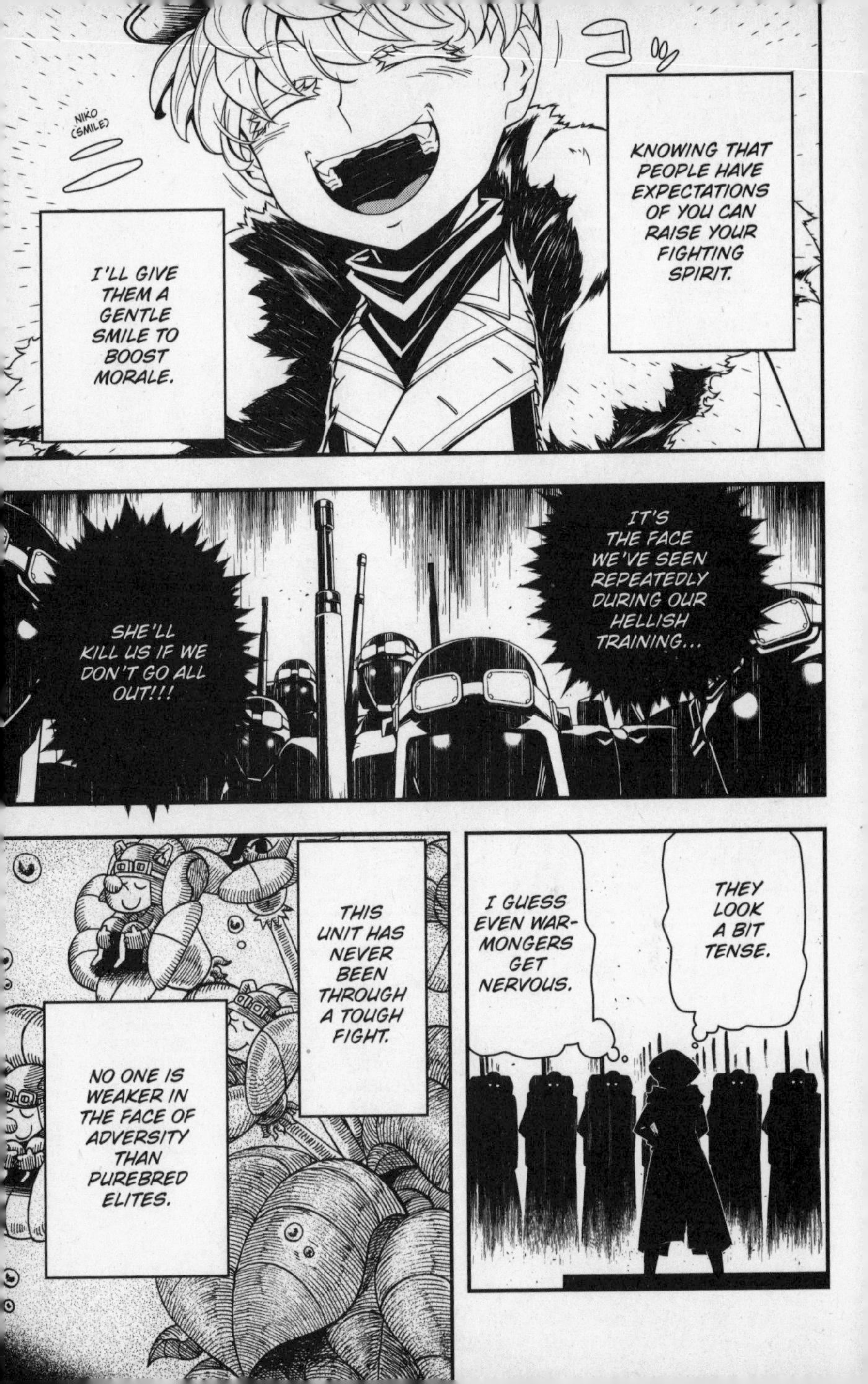
KNOWING THAT PEOPLE HAVE EXPECTATIONS OF YOU CAN RAISE YOUR FIGHTING SPIRIT.
NIKO (SMILE)
I'LL GIVE THEM A GENTLE SMILE TO BOOST MORALE.
IT'S THE FACE WE'VE SEEN REPEATEDLY DURING OUR HELLISH TRAINING...
SHE'LL KILL US IF WE DON'T GO ALL OUT!!!
THEY LOOK A BIT TENSE.
I GUESS EVEN WAR-MONGERS GET NERVOUS.
THIS UNIT HAS NEVER BEEN THROUGH A TOUGH FIGHT.
NO ONE IS WEAKER IN THE FACE OF ADVERSITY THAN PUREBRED ELITES.

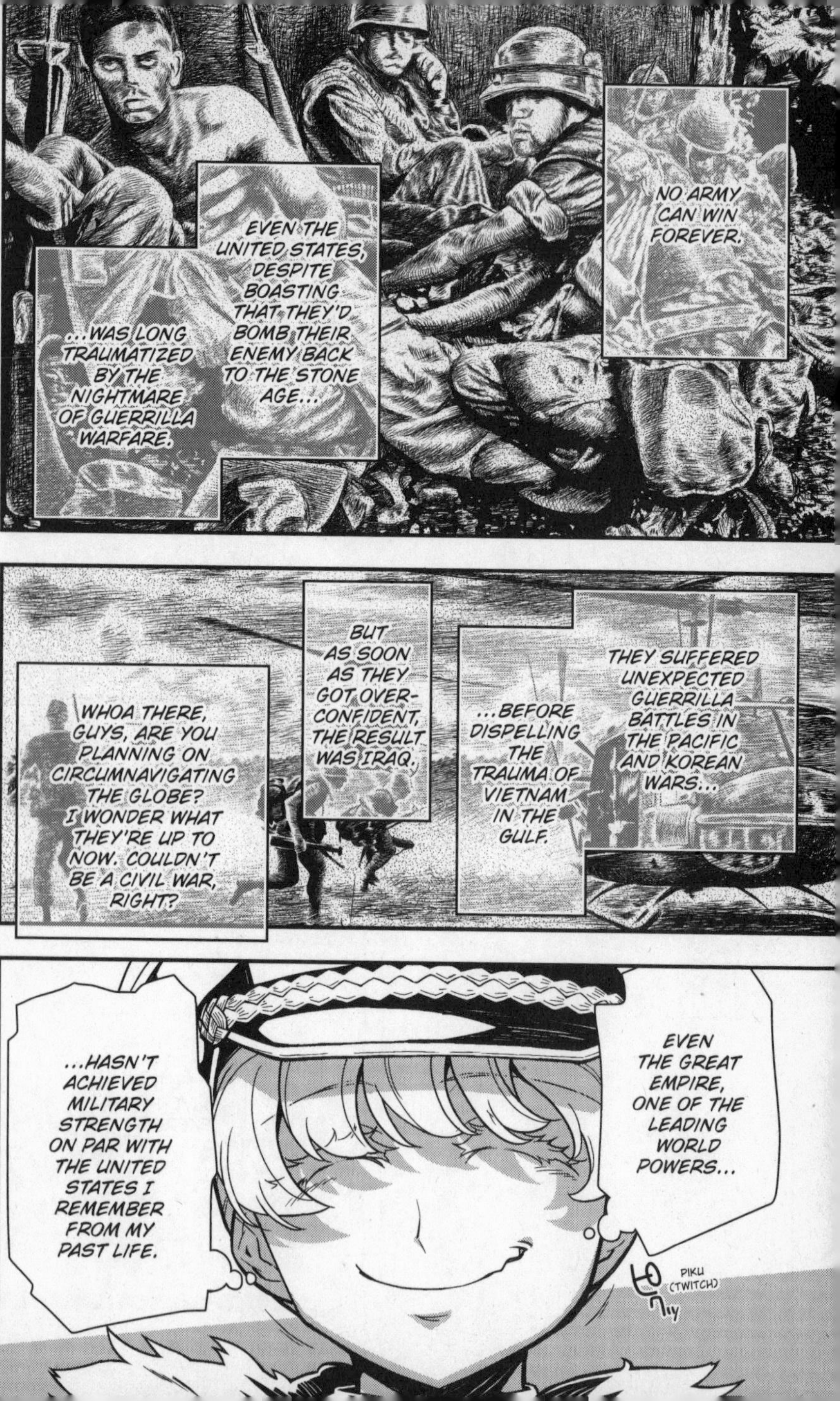
NO ARMY CAN WIN FOREVER.
EVEN THE UNITED STATES, DESPITE BOASTING THAT THEY'D BOMB THEIR ENEMY BACK TO THE STONE AGE...
...WAS LONG TRAUMATIZED BY THE NIGHTMARE OF GUERRILLA WARFARE.
THEY SUFFERED UNEXPECTED GUERRILLA BATTLES IN THE PACIFIC AND KOREAN WARS...
...BEFORE DISPELLING THE TRAUMA OF VIETNAM IN THE GULF.
BUT AS SOON AS THEY GOT OVER-CONFIDENT, THE RESULT WAS IRAQ.
WHOA THERE, GUYS, ARE YOU PLANNING ON CIRCUMNAVIGATING THE GLOBE? I WONDER WHAT THEY'RE UP TO NOW. COULDN'T BE A CIVIL WAR, RIGHT?
EVEN THE GREAT EMPIRE, ONE OF THE LEADING WORLD POWERS...
...HASN'T ACHIEVED MILITARY STRENGTH ON PAR WITH THE UNITED STATES I REMEMBER FROM MY PAST LIFE.
PIKU (TWITCH)

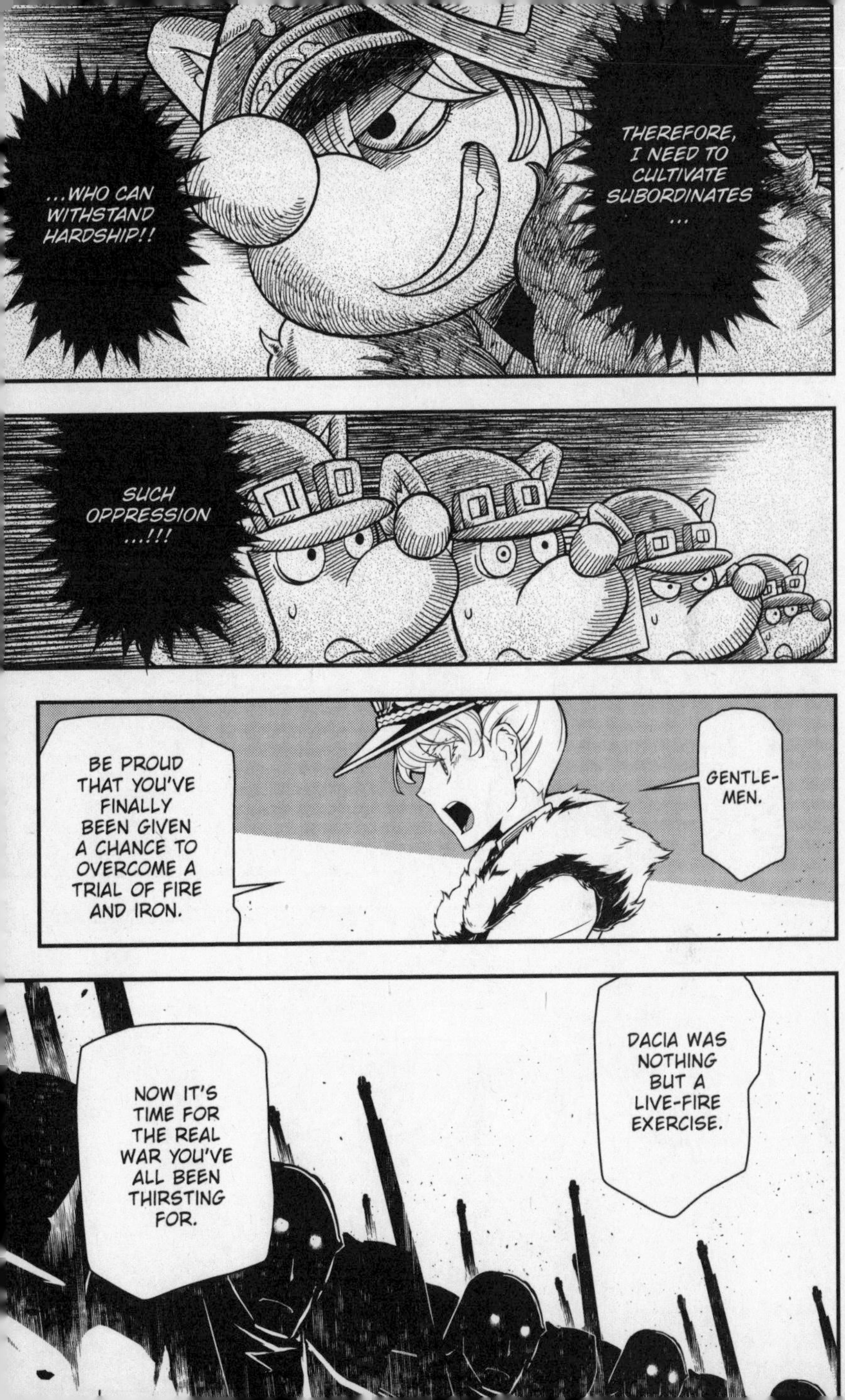
THEREFORE, I NEED TO CULTIVATE SUBORDINATES ...
...WHO CAN WITHSTAND HARDSHIP!!
SUCH OPPRESSION ...!!!
GENTLE-MEN.
BE PROUD THAT YOU'VE FINALLY BEEN GIVEN A CHANCE TO OVERCOME A TRIAL OF FIRE AND IRON.
DACIA WAS NOTHING BUT A LIVE-FIRE EXERCISE.
NOW IT'S TIME FOR THE REAL WAR YOU'VE ALL BEEN THIRSTING FOR.

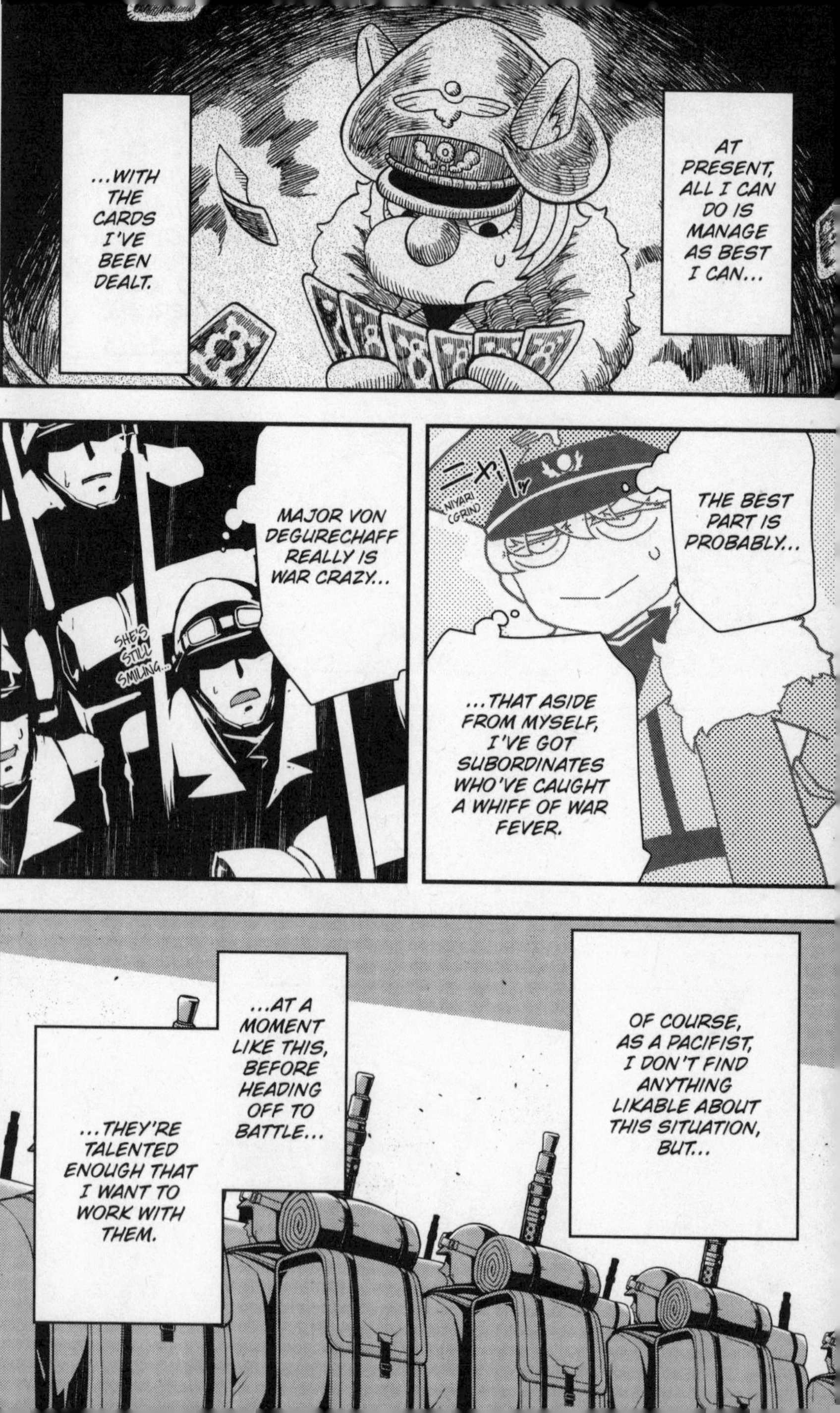
AT PRESENT, ALL I CAN DO IS MANAGE AS BEST I CAN...
...WITH THE CARDS I'VE BEEN DEALT.
THE BEST PART IS PROBABLY...
NIYARI (GRIN)
...THAT ASIDE FROM MYSELF, I'VE GOT SUBORDINATES WHO'VE CAUGHT A WHIFF OF WAR FEVER.
MAJOR VON DEGURECHAFF REALLY IS WAR CRAZY...
SHE'S STILL SMILING...
OF COURSE, AS A PACIFIST, I DON'T FIND ANYTHING LIKABLE ABOUT THIS SITUATION, BUT...
...AT A MOMENT LIKE THIS, BEFORE HEADING OFF TO BATTLE...
...THEY'RE TALENTED ENOUGH THAT I WANT TO WORK WITH THEM.

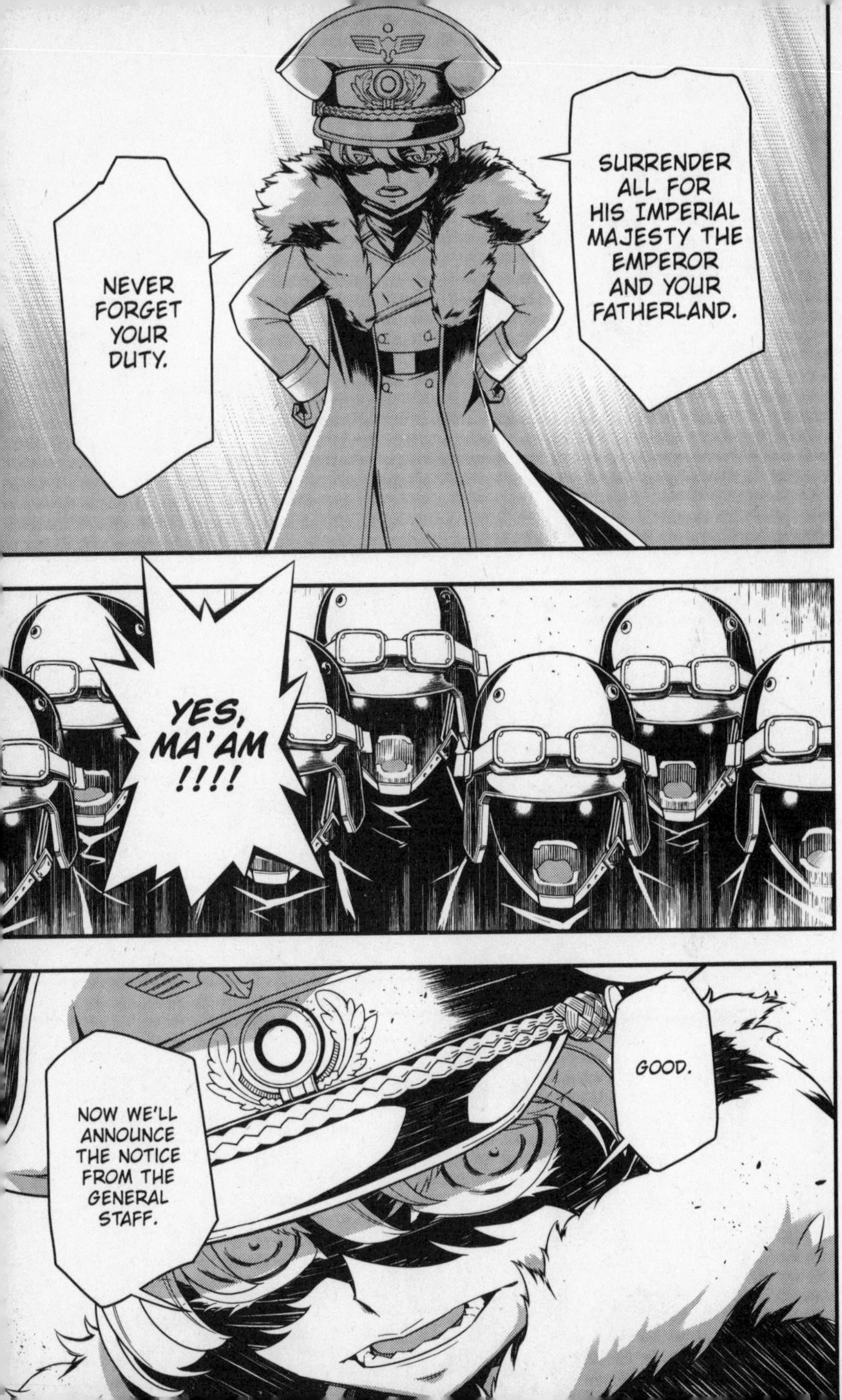
SURRENDER ALL FOR HIS IMPERIAL MAJESTY THE EMPEROR AND YOUR FATHERLAND.
NEVER FORGET YOUR DUTY.
YES, MA'AM !!!!
GOOD.
NOW WE'LL ANNOUNCE THE NOTICE FROM THE GENERAL STAFF.

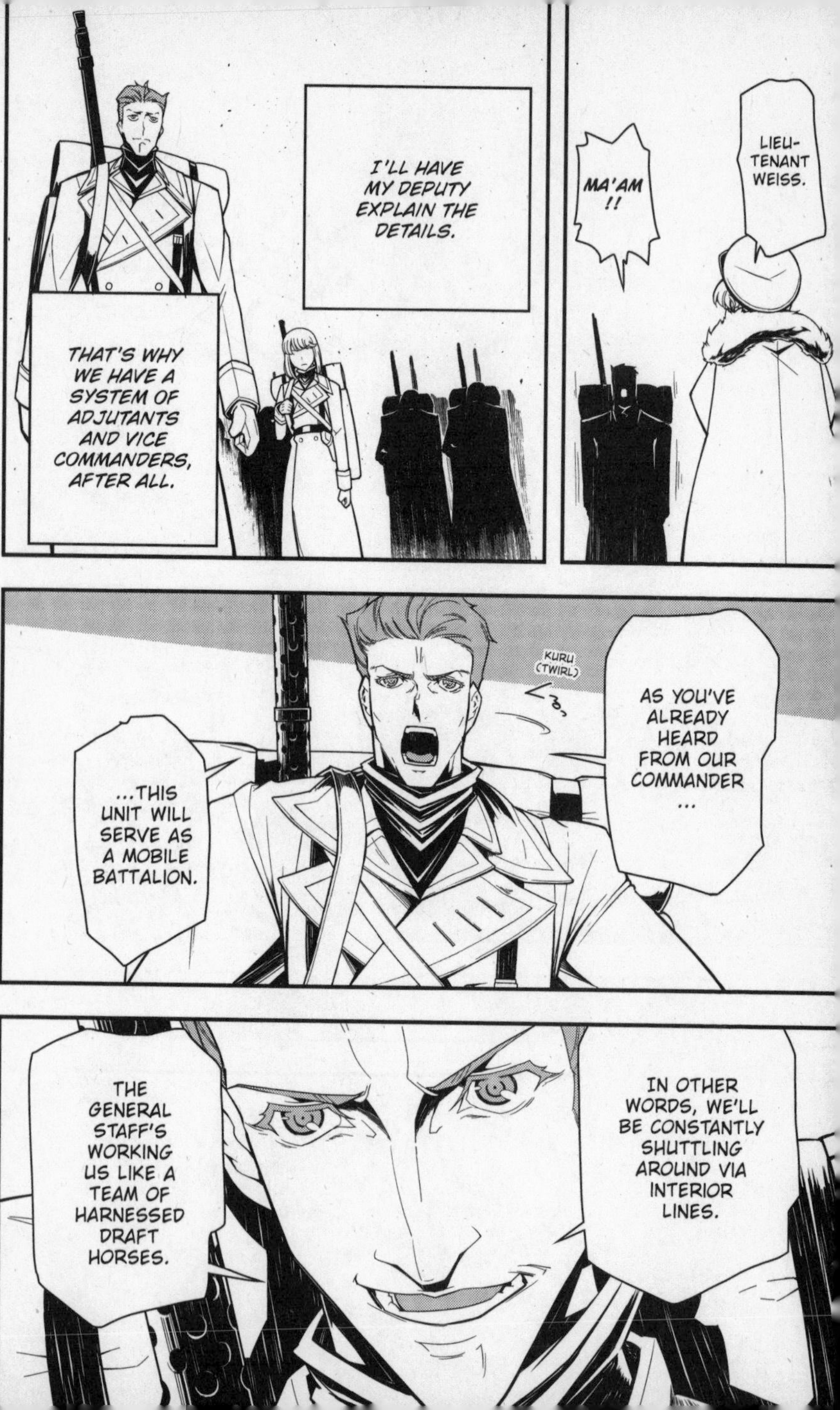

LIEU-TENANT WEISS.
MA'AM !!
I'LL HAVE MY DEPUTY EXPLAIN THE DETAILS.
THAT'S WHY WE HAVE A SYSTEM OF ADJUTANTS AND VICE COMMANDERS, AFTER ALL.
KURU (TWIRL)
AS YOU'VE ALREADY HEARD FROM OUR COMMANDER ...
...THIS UNIT WILL SERVE AS A MOBILE BATTALION.
IN OTHER WORDS, WE'LL BE CONSTANTLY SHUTTLING AROUND VIA INTERIOR LINES.
THE GENERAL STAFF'S WORKING US LIKE A TEAM OF HARNESSED DRAFT HORSES.

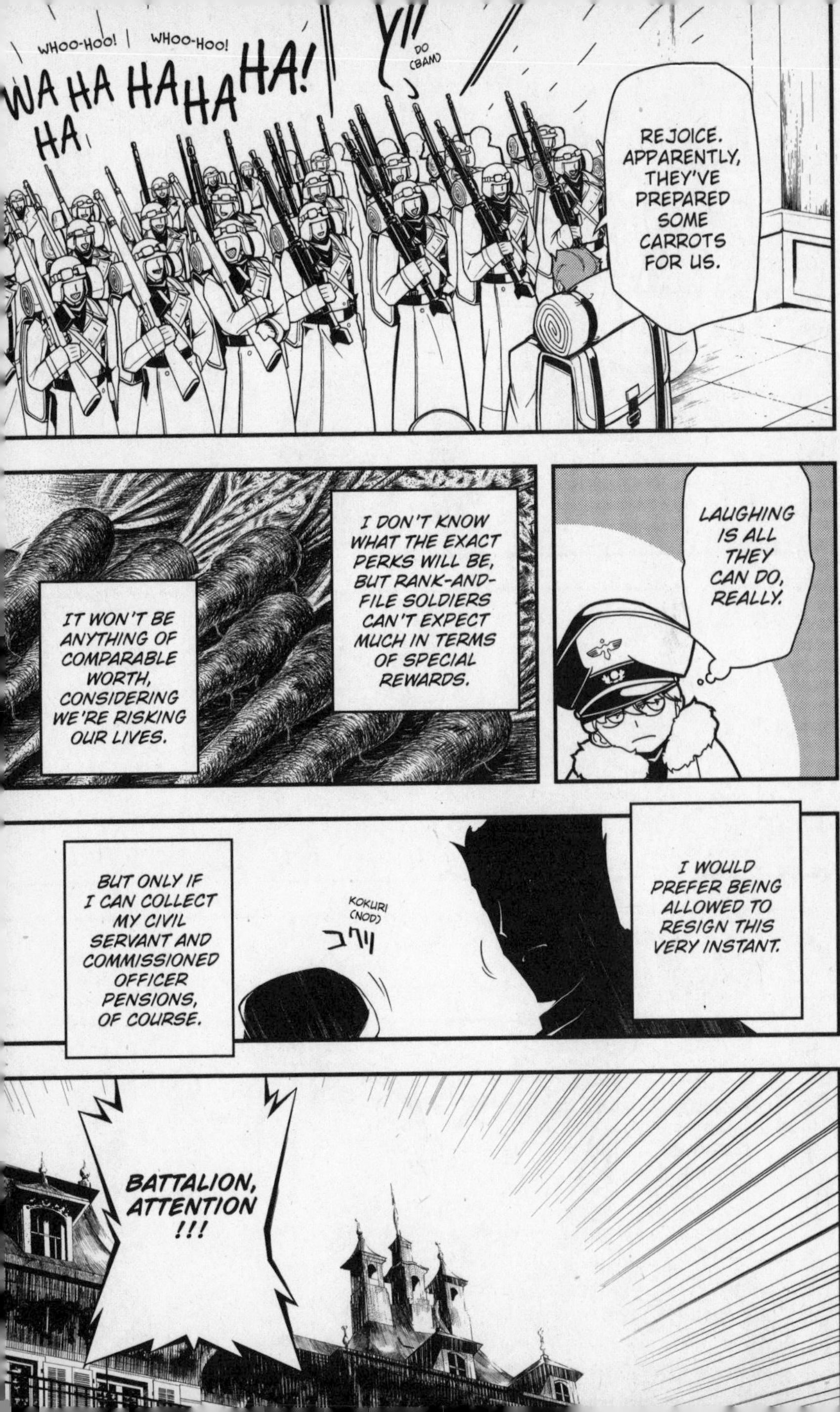
REJOICE. APPARENTLY, THEY'VE PREPARED SOME CARROTS FOR US.
DO (BAM)
WHOO-HOO! WHOO-HOO!
WA HA HA HA HA HA HA!
LAUGHING IS ALL THEY CAN DO, REALLY.
I DON'T KNOW WHAT THE EXACT PERKS WILL BE, BUT RANK-AND-FILE SOLDIERS CAN'T EXPECT MUCH IN TERMS OF SPECIAL REWARDS.
IT WON'T BE ANYTHING OF COMPARABLE WORTH, CONSIDERING WE'RE RISKING OUR LIVES.
I WOULD PREFER BEING ALLOWED TO RESIGN THIS VERY INSTANT.
KOKURI (NOD)
コクリ
BUT ONLY IF I CAN COLLECT MY CIVIL SERVANT AND COMMISSIONED OFFICER PENSIONS, OF COURSE.
BATTALION, ATTENTION !!!

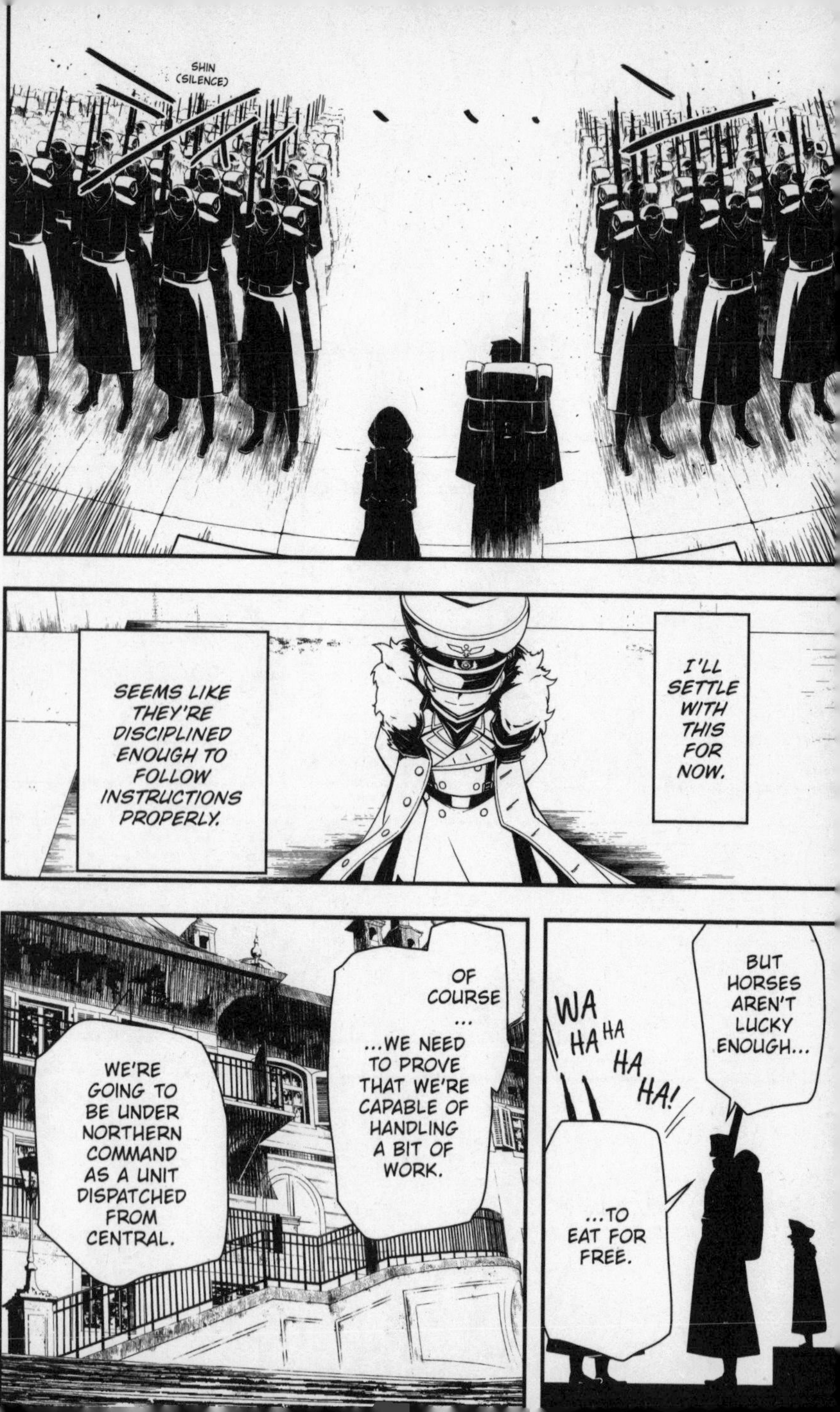
SHIN (SILENCE)
. . .
I'LL SETTLE WITH THIS FOR NOW.
SEEMS LIKE THEY'RE DISCIPLINED ENOUGH TO FOLLOW INSTRUCTIONS PROPERLY.
BUT HORSES AREN'T LUCKY ENOUGH...
WA HA HA HA HA!
...TO EAT FOR FREE.
OF COURSE...
...WE NEED TO PROVE THAT WE'RE CAPABLE OF HANDLING A BIT OF WORK.
WE'RE GOING TO BE UNDER NORTHERN COMMAND AS A UNIT DISPATCHED FROM CENTRAL.

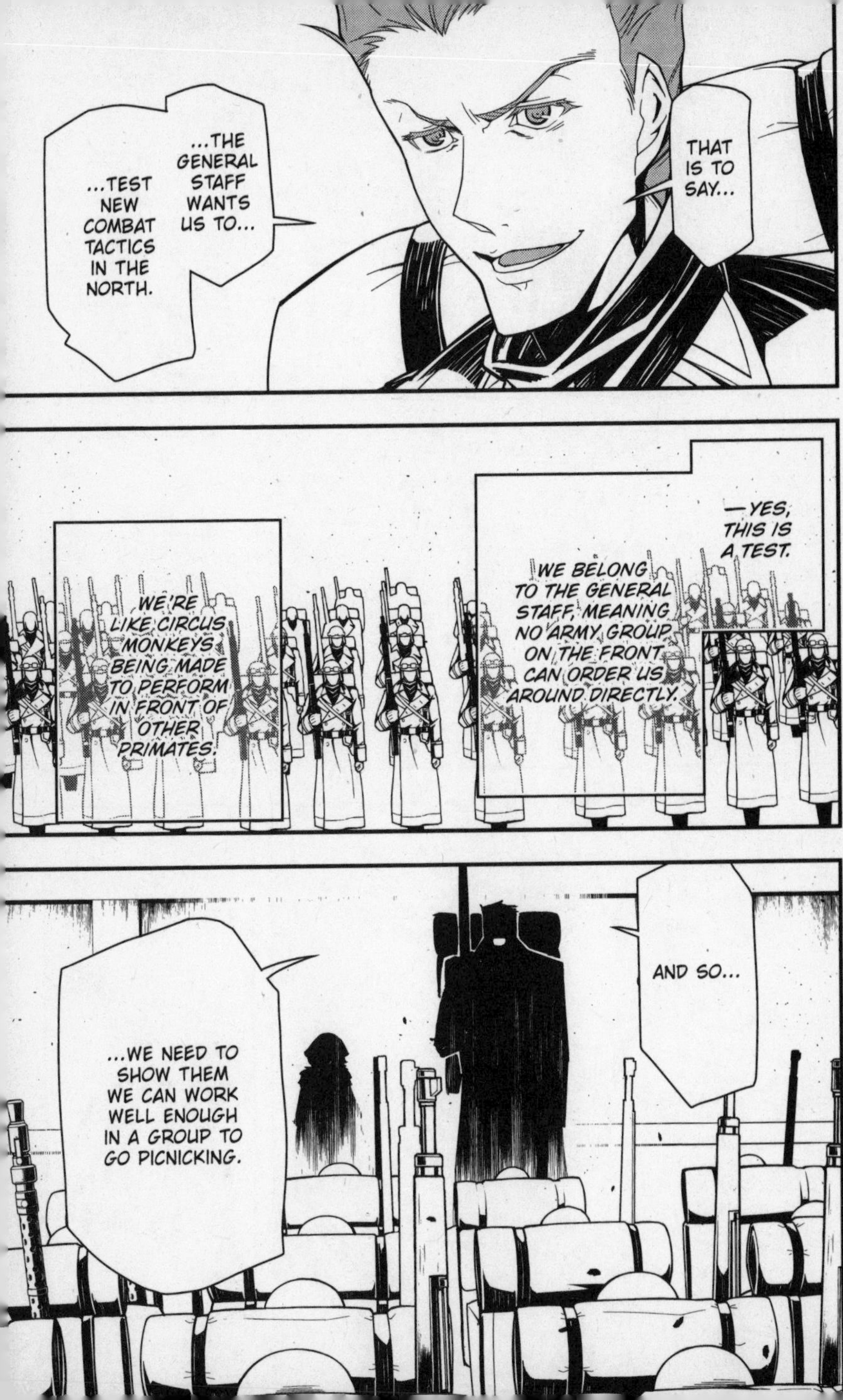
THAT IS TO SAY...
...THE GENERAL STAFF WANTS US TO...
...TEST NEW COMBAT TACTICS IN THE NORTH.
—YES, THIS IS A TEST.
WE BELONG TO THE GENERAL STAFF, MEANING NO ARMY GROUP ON THE FRONT CAN ORDER US AROUND DIRECTLY.
WE'RE LIKE CIRCUS MONKEYS BEING MADE TO PERFORM IN FRONT OF OTHER PRIMATES.
AND SO...
...WE NEED TO SHOW THEM WE CAN WORK WELL ENOUGH IN A GROUP TO GO PICNICKING.

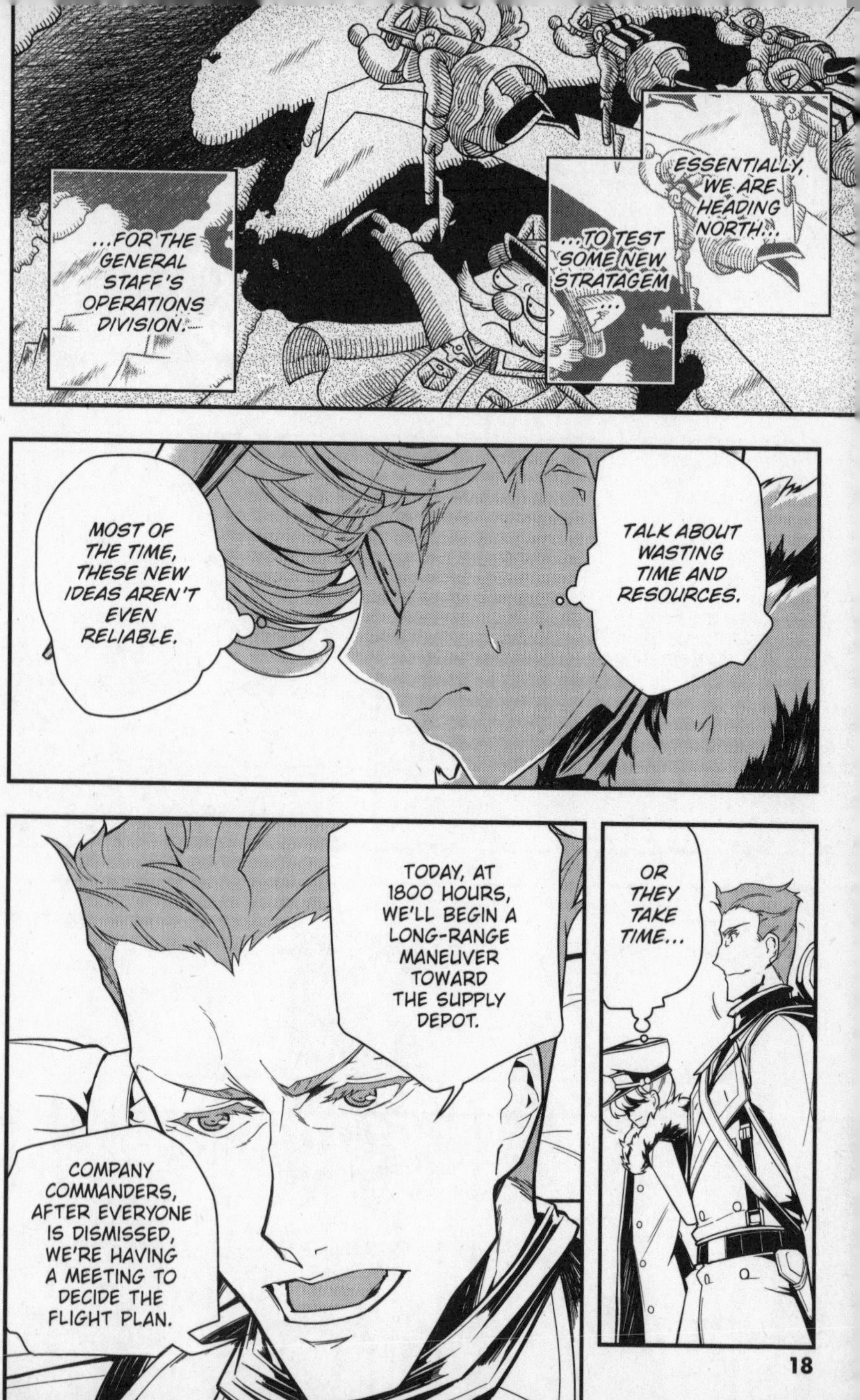
ESSENTIALLY, WE ARE HEADING NORTH...
...TO TEST SOME NEW STRATAGEM
...FOR THE GENERAL STAFF'S OPERATIONS DIVISION.
TALK ABOUT WASTING TIME AND RESOURCES.
MOST OF THE TIME, THESE NEW IDEAS AREN'T EVEN RELIABLE.
OR THEY TAKE TIME...
TODAY, AT 1800 HOURS, WE'LL BEGIN A LONG-RANGE MANEUVER TOWARD THE SUPPLY DEPOT.
COMPANY COMMANDERS, AFTER EVERYONE IS DISMISSED, WE'RE HAVING A MEETING TO DECIDE THE FLIGHT PLAN.

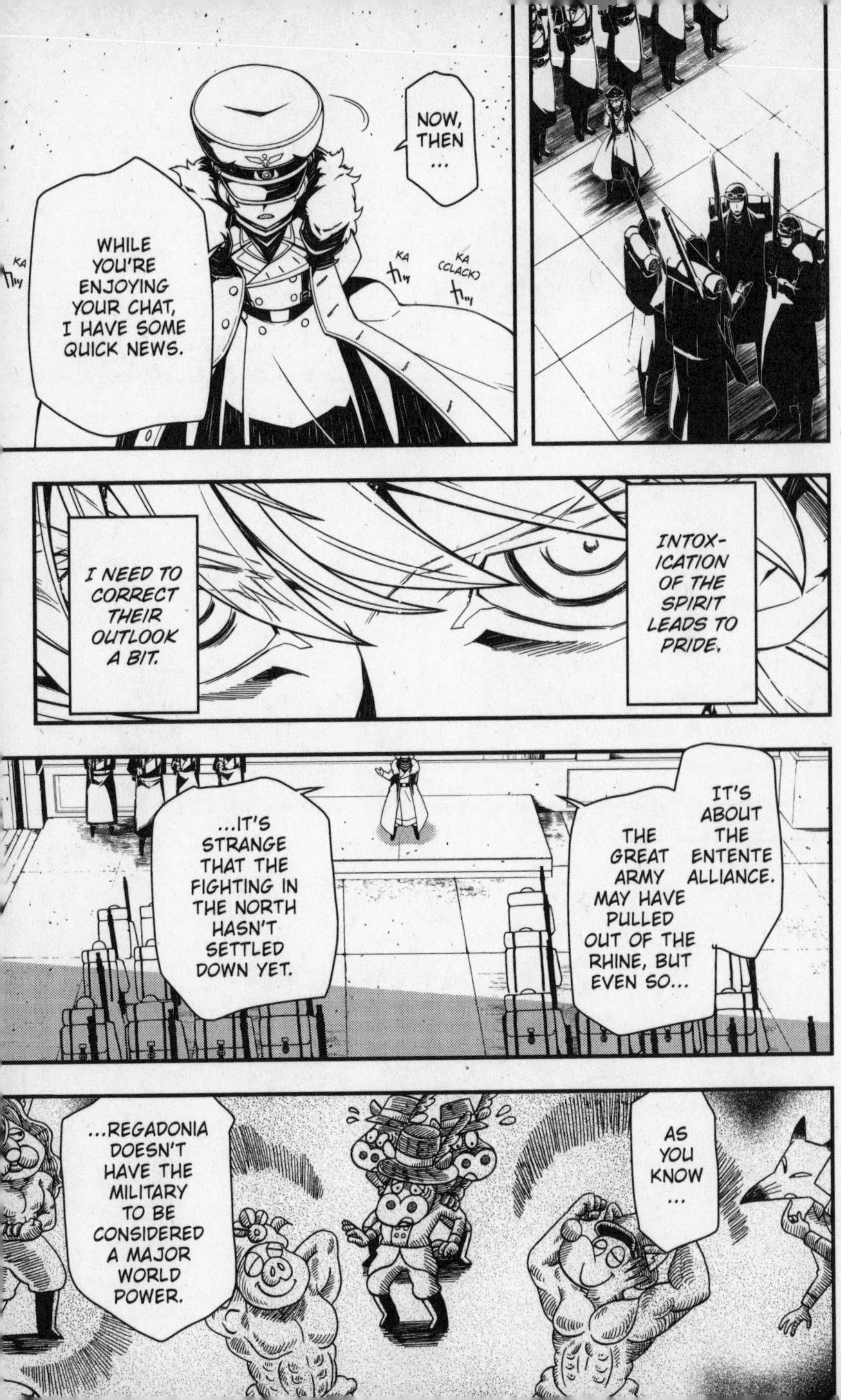
NOW, THEN ...
KA (CLACK)
KA
KA
WHILE YOU'RE ENJOYING YOUR CHAT, I HAVE SOME QUICK NEWS.
INTOX-ICATION OF THE SPIRIT LEADS TO PRIDE.
I NEED TO CORRECT THEIR OUTLOOK A BIT.
IT'S ABOUT THE ENTENTE ALLIANCE.
THE GREAT ARMY MAY HAVE PULLED OUT OF THE RHINE, BUT EVEN SO...
...IT'S STRANGE THAT THE FIGHTING IN THE NORTH HASN'T SETTLED DOWN YET.
AS YOU KNOW ...
...REGADONIA DOESN'T HAVE THE MILITARY TO BE CONSIDERED A MAJOR WORLD POWER.

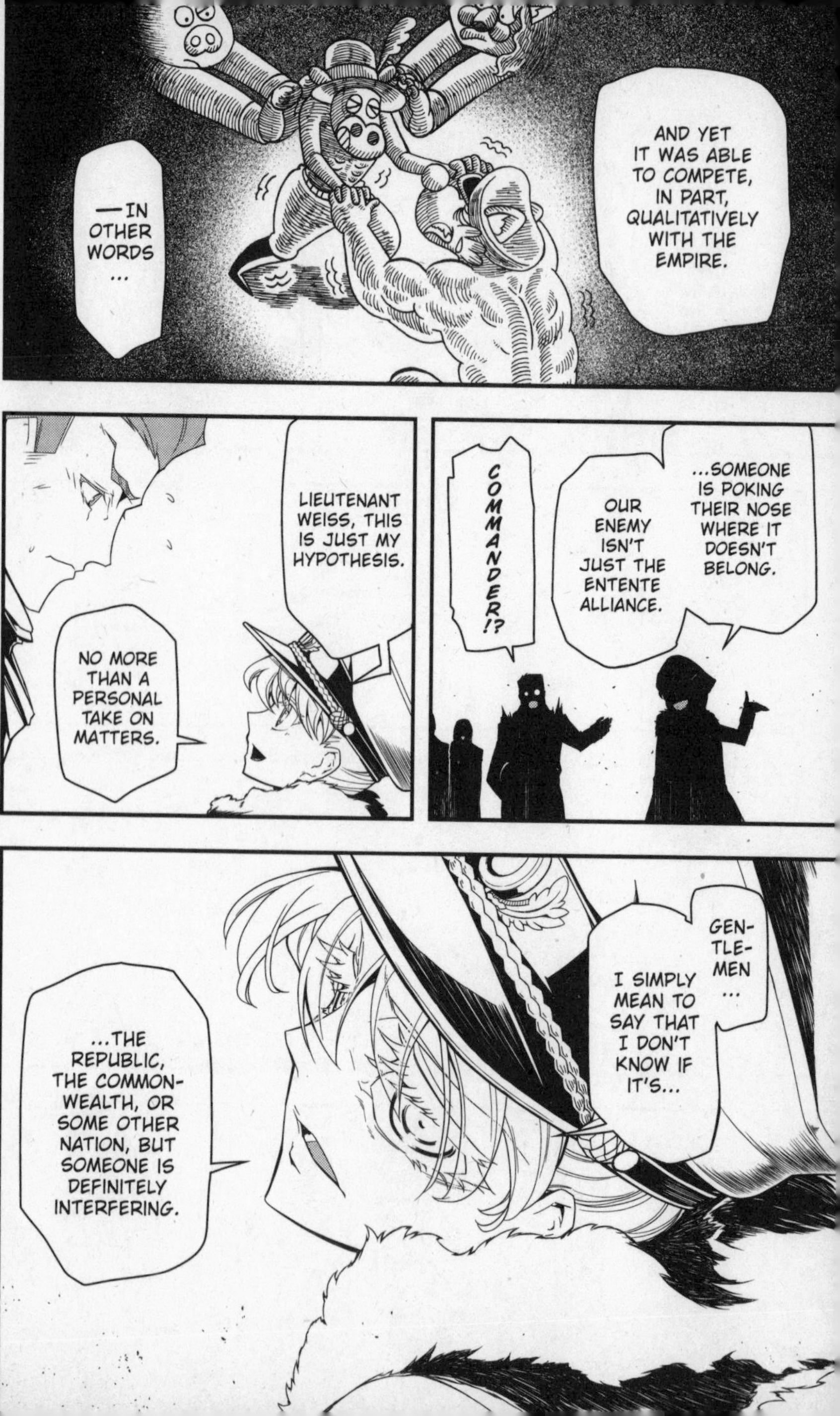
AND YET IT WAS ABLE TO COMPETE, IN PART, QUALITATIVELY WITH THE EMPIRE.
—IN OTHER WORDS ...
...SOMEONE IS POKING THEIR NOSE WHERE IT DOESN'T BELONG.
OUR ENEMY ISN'T JUST THE ENTENTE ALLIANCE.
COMMANDER!?
LIEUTENANT WEISS, THIS IS JUST MY HYPOTHESIS.
NO MORE THAN A PERSONAL TAKE ON MATTERS.
GENTLEMEN ...
I SIMPLY MEAN TO SAY THAT I DON'T KNOW IF IT'S...
...THE REPUBLIC, THE COMMONWEALTH, OR SOME OTHER NATION, BUT SOMEONE IS DEFINITELY INTERFERING.

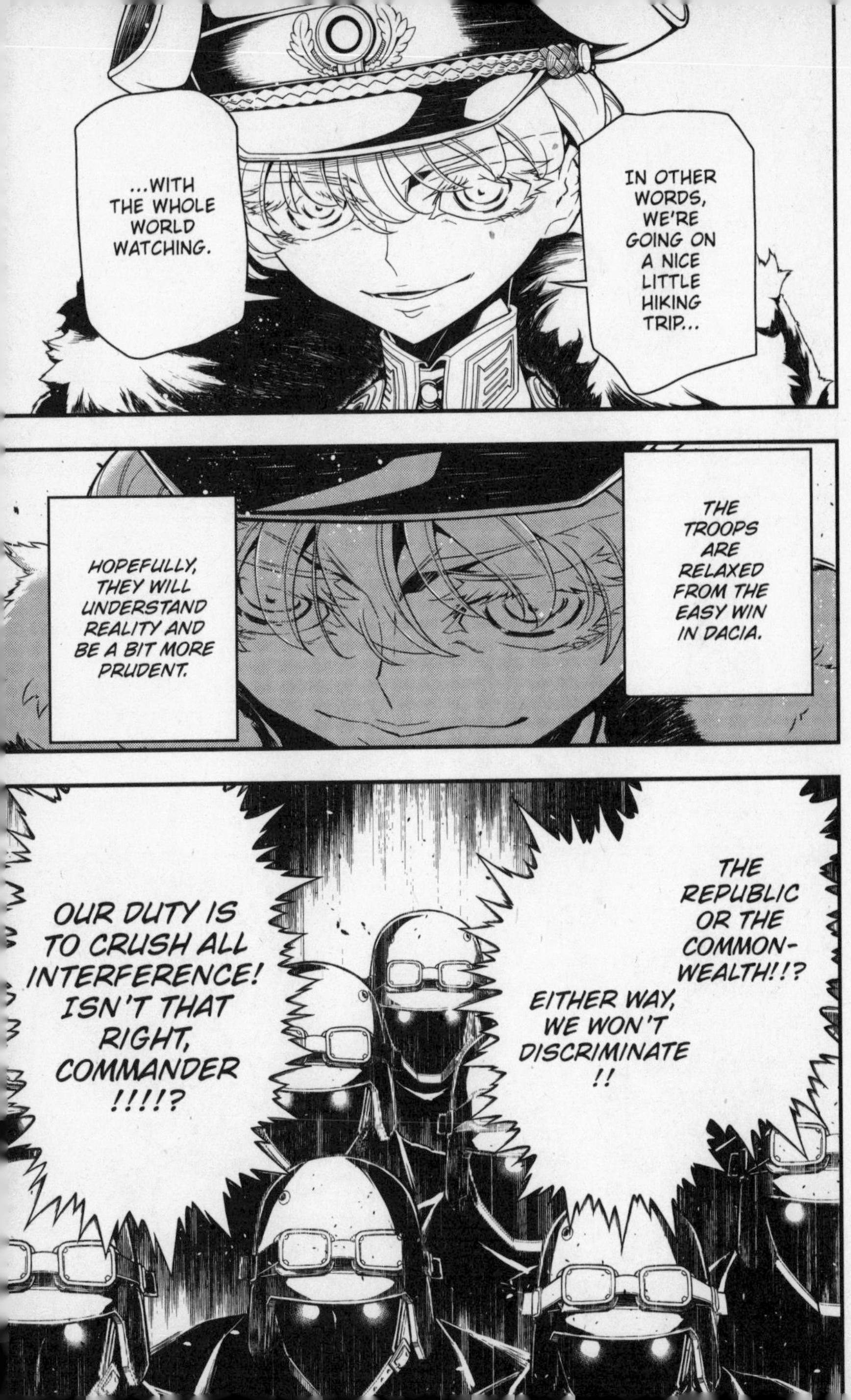
IN OTHER WORDS, WE'RE GOING ON A NICE LITTLE HIKING TRIP...
...WITH THE WHOLE WORLD WATCHING.
THE TROOPS ARE RELAXED FROM THE EASY WIN IN DACIA.
HOPEFULLY, THEY WILL UNDERSTAND REALITY AND BE A BIT MORE PRUDENT.
THE REPUBLIC OR THE COMMON-WEALTH!!?
EITHER WAY, WE WON'T DISCRIMINATE!!
OUR DUTY IS TO CRUSH ALL INTERFERENCE! ISN'T THAT RIGHT, COMMANDER!!!!?

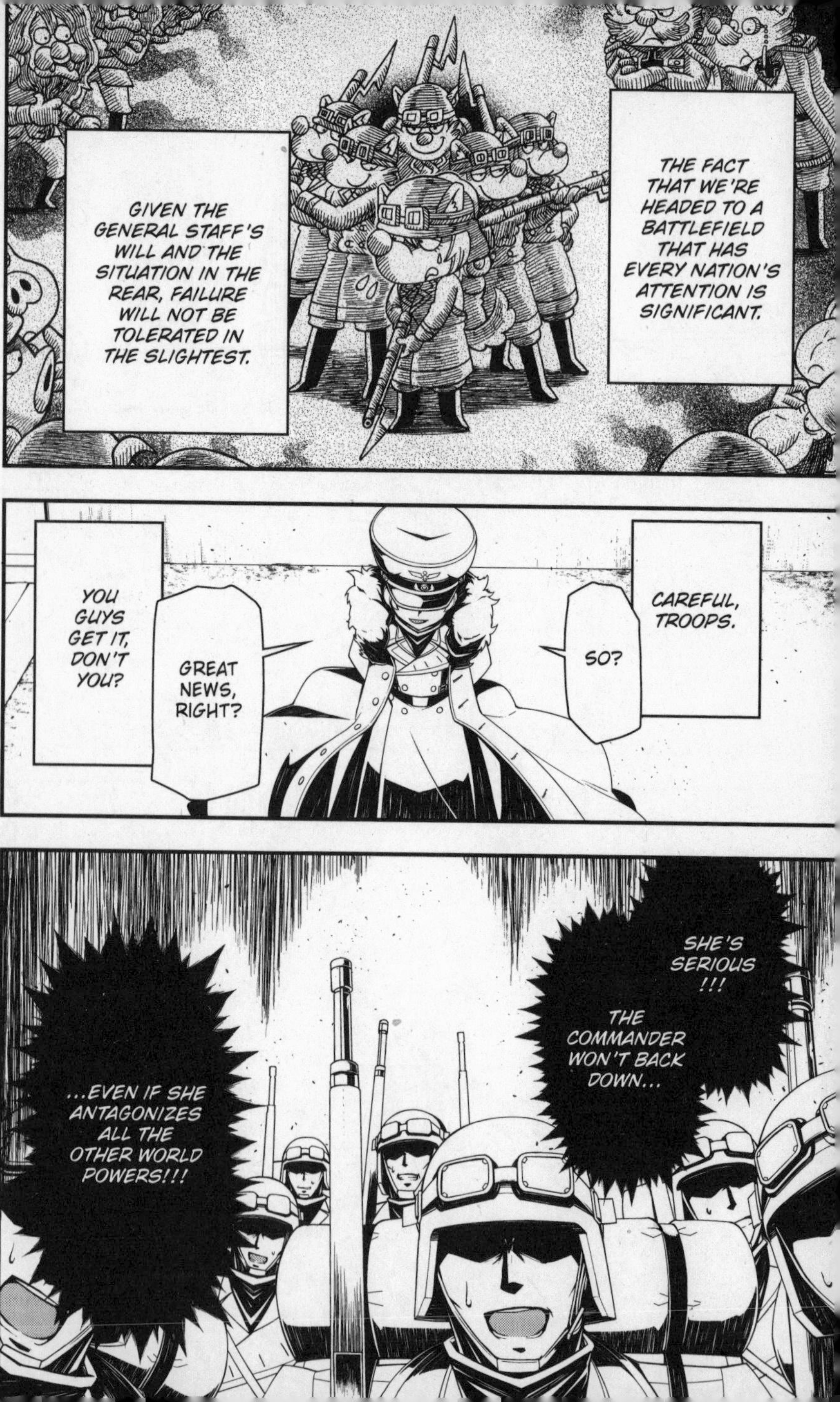
THE FACT THAT WE'RE HEADED TO A BATTLEFIELD THAT HAS EVERY NATION'S ATTENTION IS SIGNIFICANT.
GIVEN THE GENERAL STAFF'S WILL AND THE SITUATION IN THE REAR, FAILURE WILL NOT BE TOLERATED IN THE SLIGHTEST.
CAREFUL, TROOPS.
SO?
GREAT NEWS, RIGHT?
YOU GUYS GET IT, DON'T YOU?
SHE'S SERIOUS!!!
THE COMMANDER WON'T BACK DOWN...
...EVEN IF SHE ANTAGONIZES ALL THE OTHER WORLD POWERS!!!

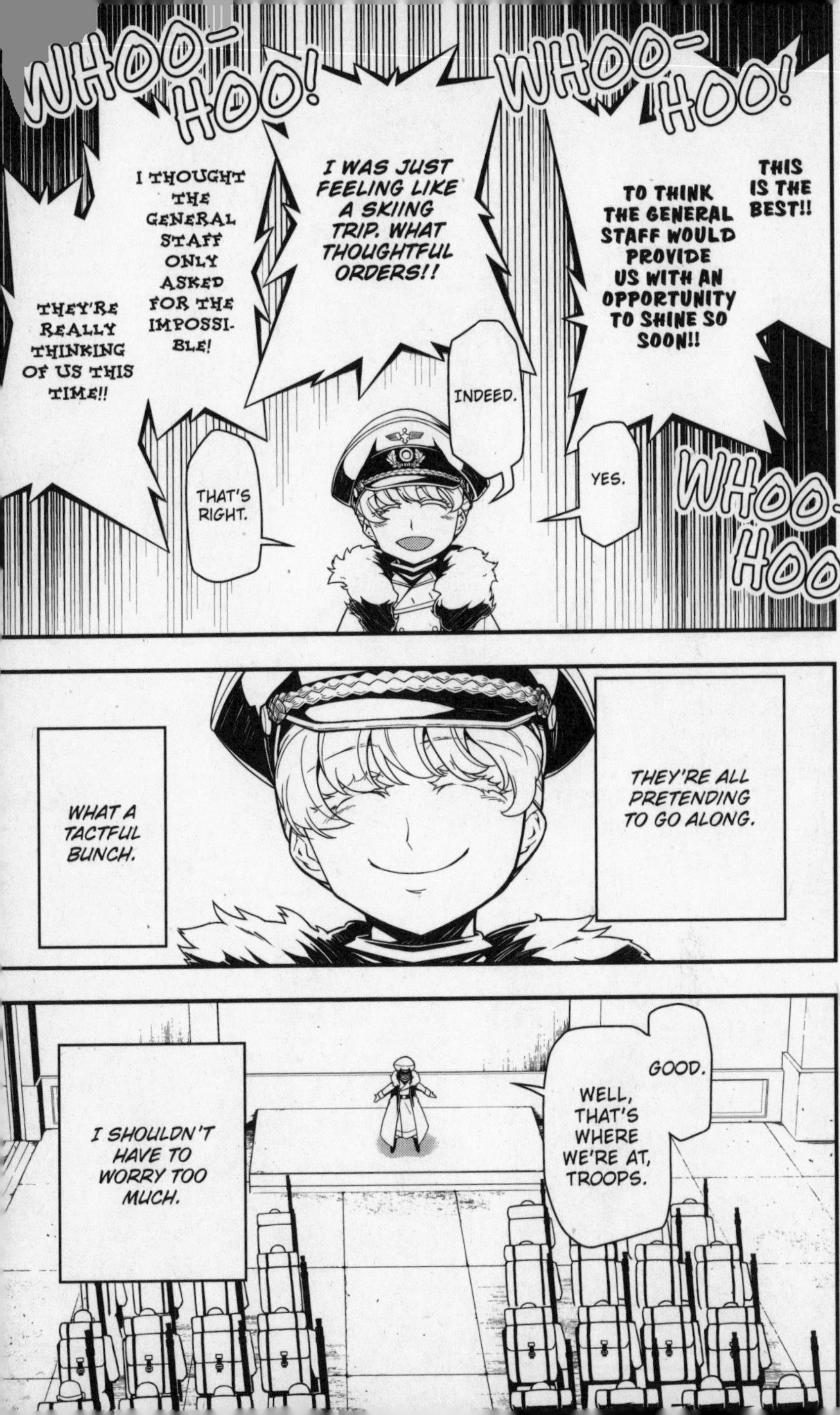
WHOO-HOO!
WHOO-HOO!
THIS IS THE BEST!!
TO THINK THE GENERAL STAFF WOULD PROVIDE US WITH AN OPPORTUNITY TO SHINE SO SOON!!
I WAS JUST FEELING LIKE A SKIING TRIP. WHAT THOUGHTFUL ORDERS!!
I THOUGHT THE GENERAL STAFF ONLY ASKED FOR THE IMPOSSI-BLE!
THEY'RE REALLY THINKING OF US THIS TIME!!
WHOO-HOO!
YES.
INDEED.
THAT'S RIGHT.
THEY'RE ALL PRETENDING TO GO ALONG.
WHAT A TACTFUL BUNCH.
GOOD.
WELL, THAT'S WHERE WE'RE AT, TROOPS.
I SHOULDN'T HAVE TO WORRY TOO MUCH.

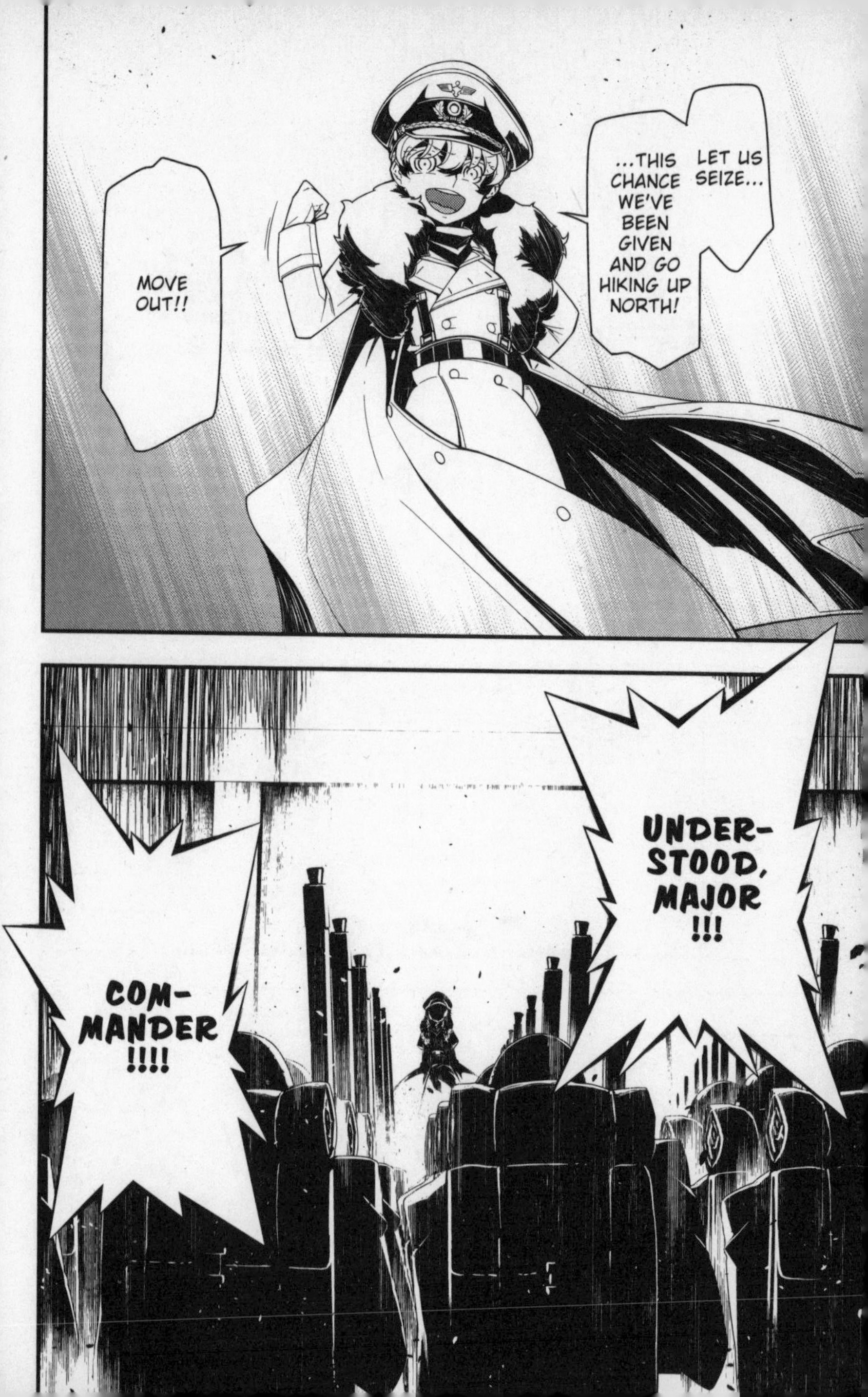
LET US SEIZE... ...THIS CHANCE WE'VE BEEN GIVEN AND GO HIKING UP NORTH!
MOVE OUT!!
UNDER-STOOD, MAJOR !!!
COM-MANDER !!!!

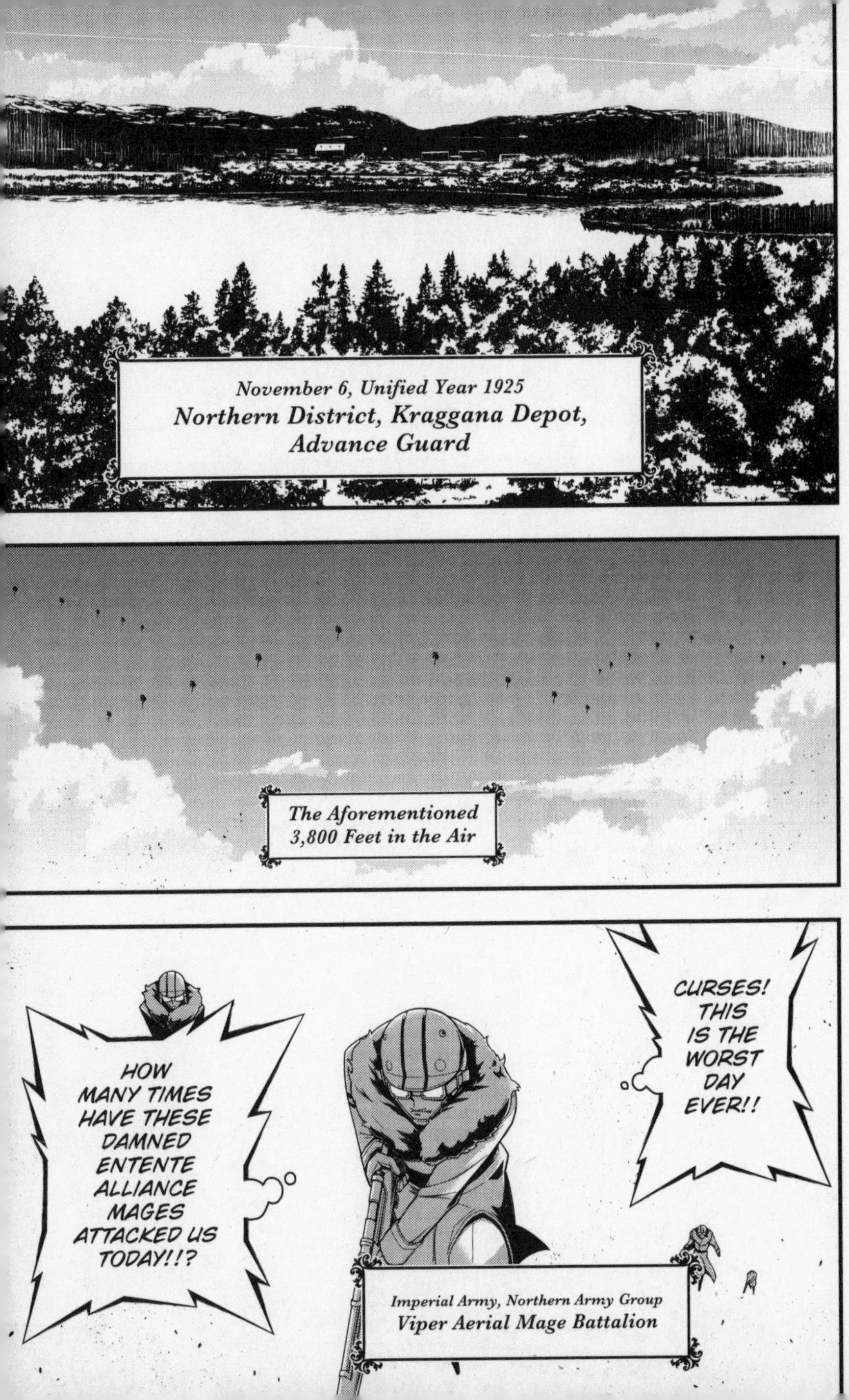
November 6, Unified Year 1925
Northern District, Kraggana Depot, Advance Guard
The Aforementioned 3,800 Feet in the Air
CURSES! THIS IS THE WORST DAY EVER!!
HOW MANY TIMES HAVE THESE DAMNED ENTENTE ALLIANCE MAGES ATTACKED US TODAY!!?
Imperial Army, Northern Army Group
Viper Aerial Mage Battalion

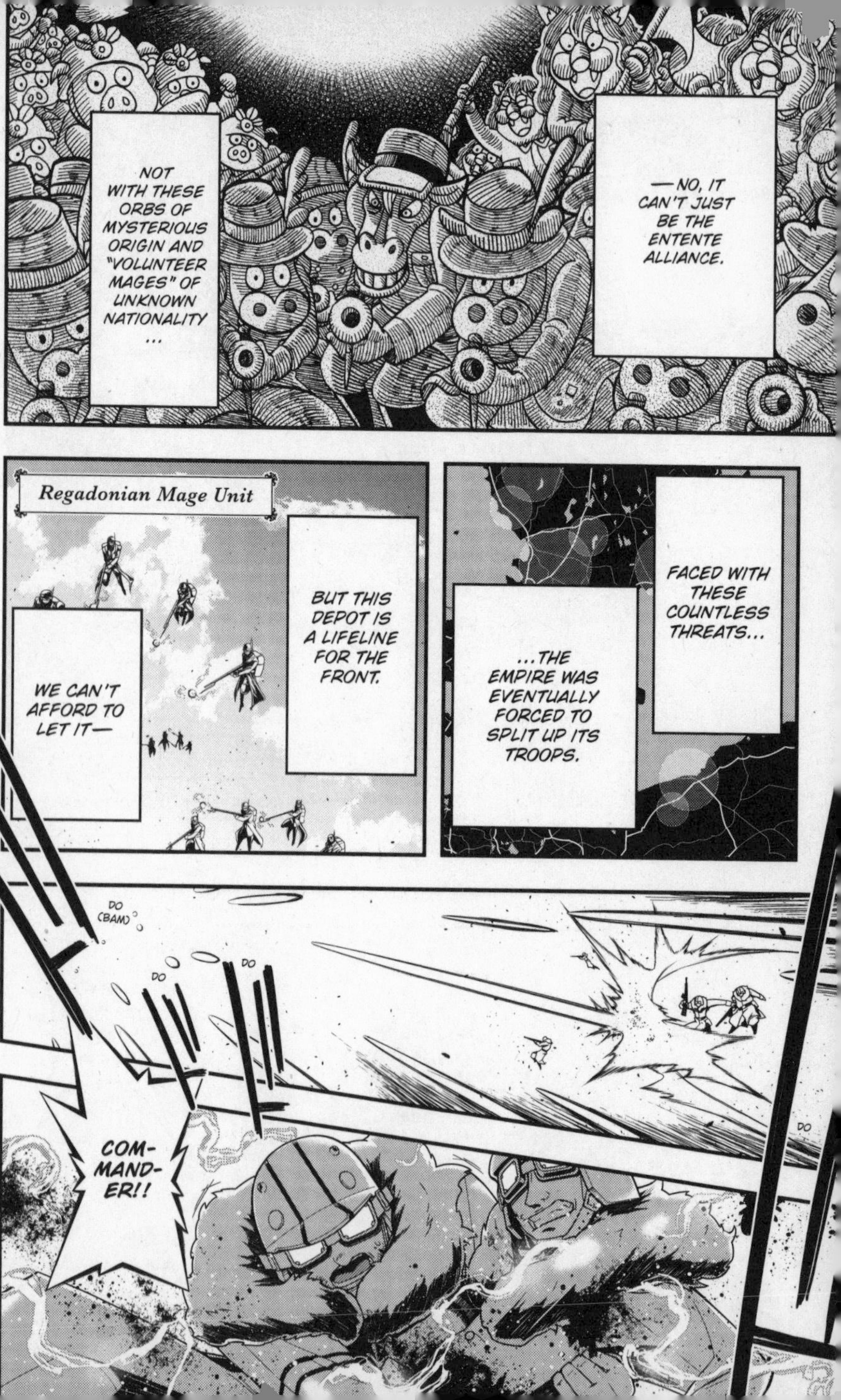
—NO, IT CAN'T JUST BE THE ENTENTE ALLIANCE.
NOT WITH THESE ORBS OF MYSTERIOUS ORIGIN AND "VOLUNTEER MAGES" OF UNKNOWN NATIONALITY...
FACED WITH THESE COUNTLESS THREATS...
...THE EMPIRE WAS EVENTUALLY FORCED TO SPLIT UP ITS TROOPS.
Regadonian Mage Unit
BUT THIS DEPOT IS A LIFELINE FOR THE FRONT.
WE CAN'T AFFORD TO LET IT—
DO
DO (BAM)
DO
DO
COM-MAND-ER!!

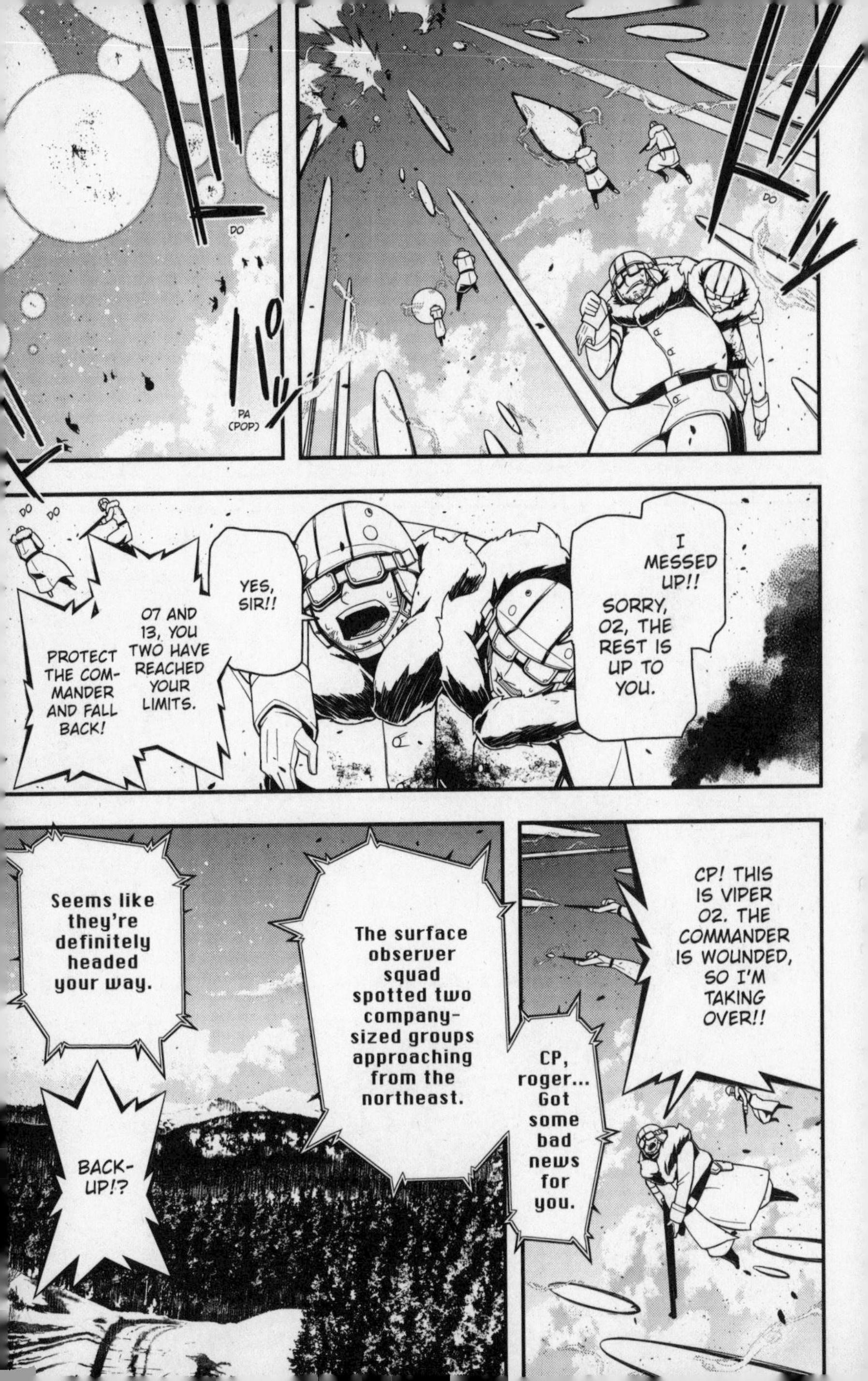
DO
DO
PA (POP)
I MESSED UP!! SORRY, 02, THE REST IS UP TO YOU.
YES, SIR!!
07 AND 13, YOU TWO HAVE REACHED YOUR LIMITS.
PROTECT THE COMMANDER AND FALL BACK!
DO
DO
CP! THIS IS VIPER 02. THE COMMANDER IS WOUNDED, SO I'M TAKING OVER!!
CP, roger... Got some bad news for you.
The surface observer squad spotted two company-sized groups approaching from the northeast.
Seems like they're definitely headed your way.
BACK-UP!?

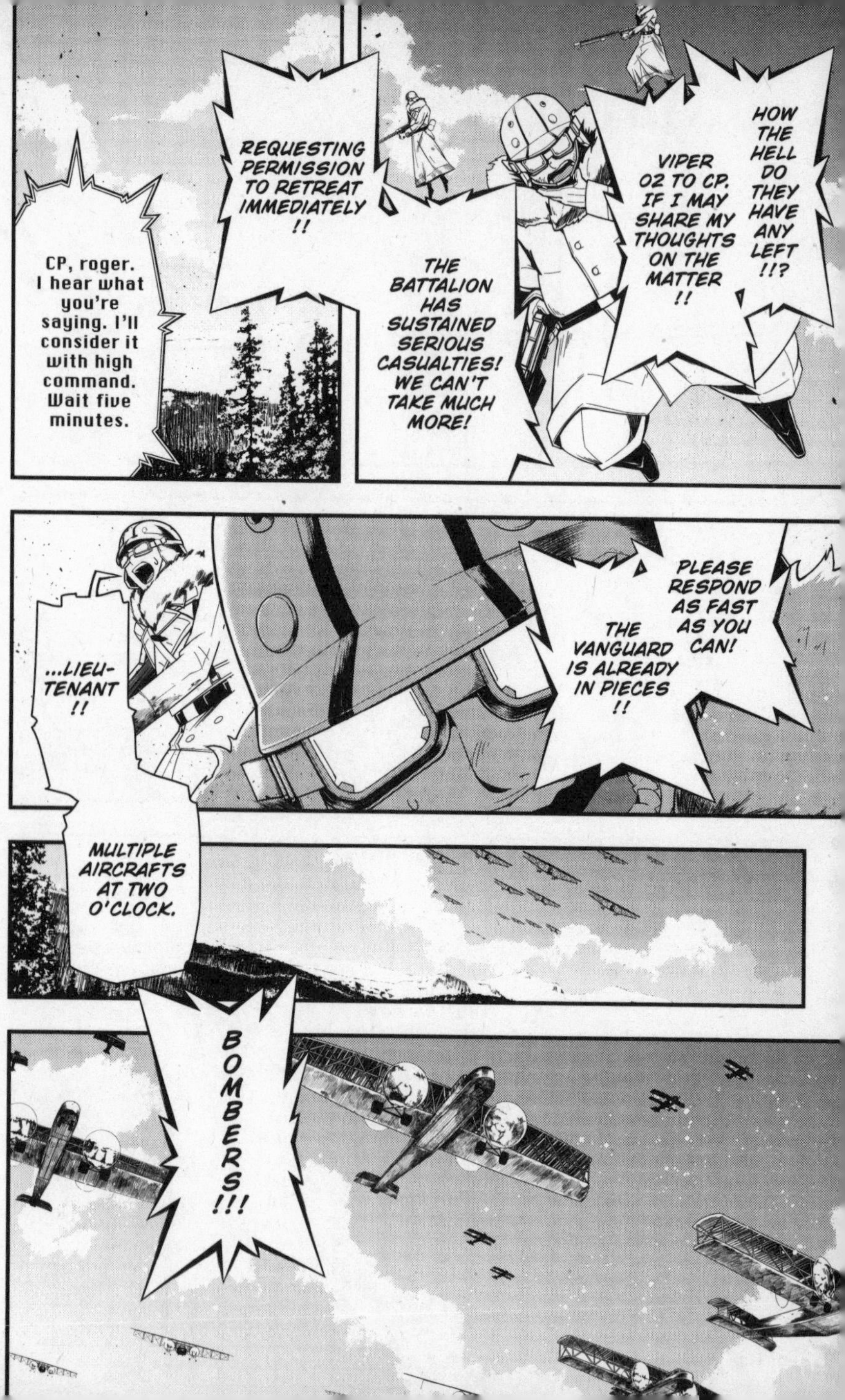
HOW THE HELL DO THEY HAVE ANY LEFT!!?
VIPER 02 TO CP. IF I MAY SHARE MY THOUGHTS ON THE MATTER!!
THE BATTALION HAS SUSTAINED SERIOUS CASUALTIES! WE CAN'T TAKE MUCH MORE!
REQUESTING PERMISSION TO RETREAT IMMEDIATELY!!
CP, roger. I hear what you're saying. I'll consider it with high command. Wait five minutes.
PLEASE RESPOND AS FAST AS YOU CAN!
THE VANGUARD IS ALREADY IN PIECES!!
...LIEU-TENANT!!
MULTIPLE AIRCRAFTS AT TWO O'CLOCK.
BOMBERS!!!

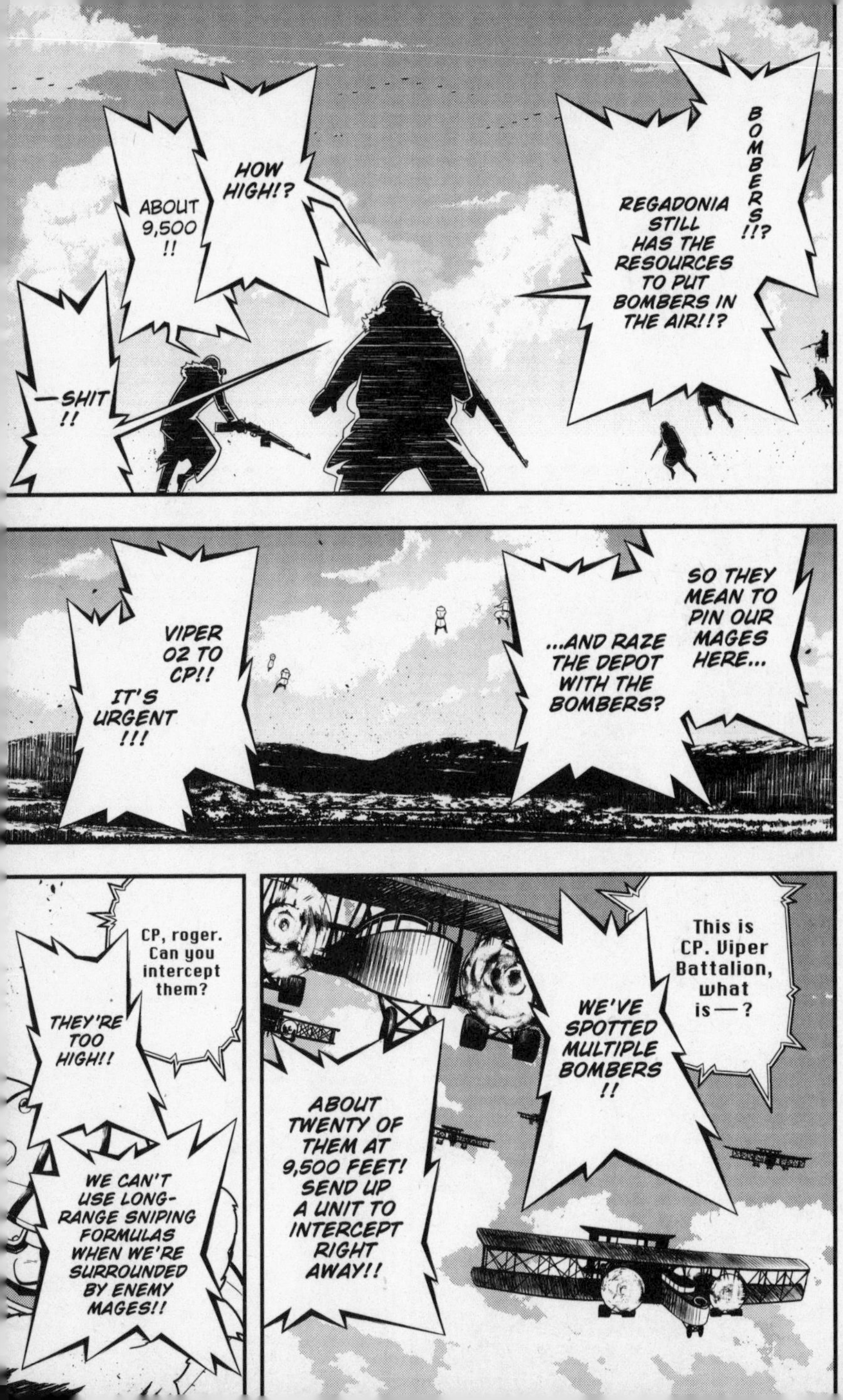
BOMBERS!!?
REGADONIA STILL HAS THE RESOURCES TO PUT BOMBERS IN THE AIR!!?
HOW HIGH!?
ABOUT 9,500!!
—SHIT!!
SO THEY MEAN TO PIN OUR MAGES HERE...
...AND RAZE THE DEPOT WITH THE BOMBERS?
VIPER 02 TO CP!!
IT'S URGENT!!!
This is CP. Viper Battalion, what is—?
WE'VE SPOTTED MULTIPLE BOMBERS!!
ABOUT TWENTY OF THEM AT 9,500 FEET! SEND UP A UNIT TO INTERCEPT RIGHT AWAY!!
CP, roger. Can you intercept them?
THEY'RE TOO HIGH!!
WE CAN'T USE LONG-RANGE SNIPING FORMULAS WHEN WE'RE SURROUNDED BY ENEMY MAGES!!

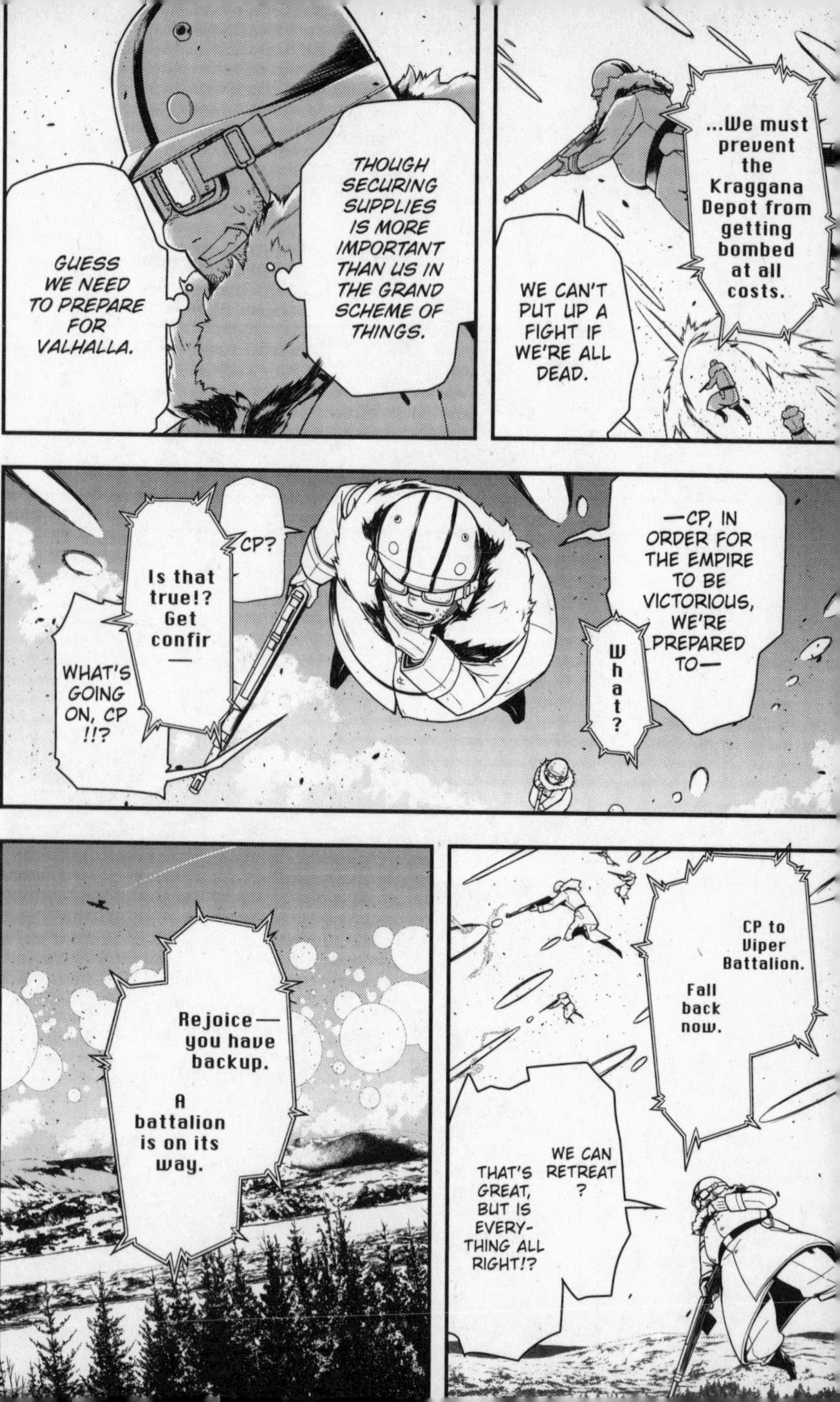
...We must prevent the Kraggana Depot from getting bombed at all costs.
WE CAN'T PUT UP A FIGHT IF WE'RE ALL DEAD.
THOUGH SECURING SUPPLIES IS MORE IMPORTANT THAN US IN THE GRAND SCHEME OF THINGS.
GUESS WE NEED TO PREPARE FOR VALHALLA.
—CP, IN ORDER FOR THE EMPIRE TO BE VICTORIOUS, WE'RE PREPARED TO—
What?
CP?
Is that true!? Get confir—
WHAT'S GOING ON, CP!!?
CP to Viper Battalion.
Fall back now.
WE CAN RETREAT?
THAT'S GREAT, BUT IS EVERY-THING ALL RIGHT!?
Rejoice—you have backup.
A battalion is on its way.

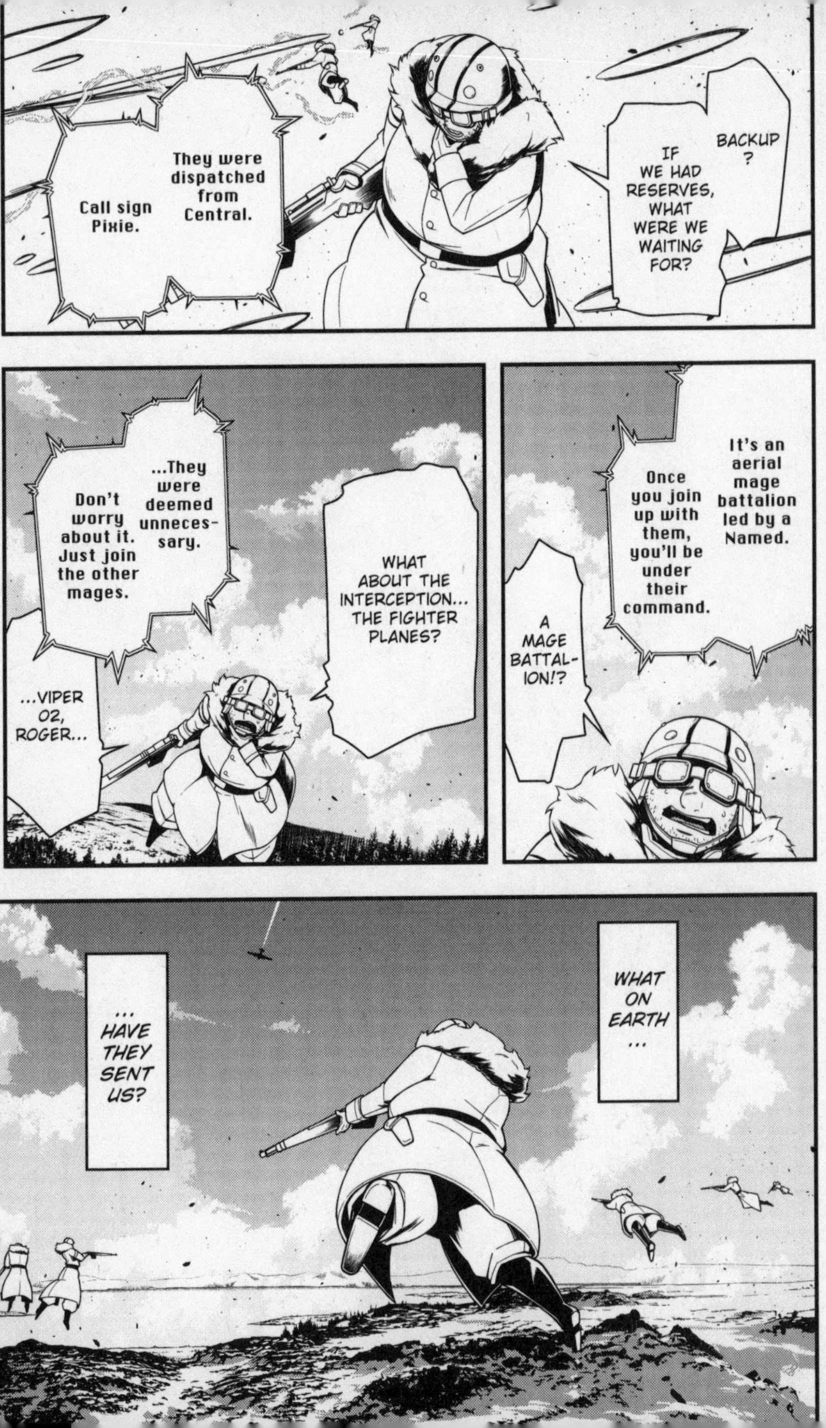
BACKUP?
IF WE HAD RESERVES, WHAT WERE WE WAITING FOR?
They were dispatched from Central.
Call sign Pixie.
It's an aerial mage battalion led by a Named.
Once you join up with them, you'll be under their command.
A MAGE BATTALION!?
WHAT ABOUT THE INTERCEPTION... THE FIGHTER PLANES?
...They were deemed unnecessary.
Don't worry about it. Just join the other mages.
...VIPER 02, ROGER...
WHAT ON EARTH...
...HAVE THEY SENT US?

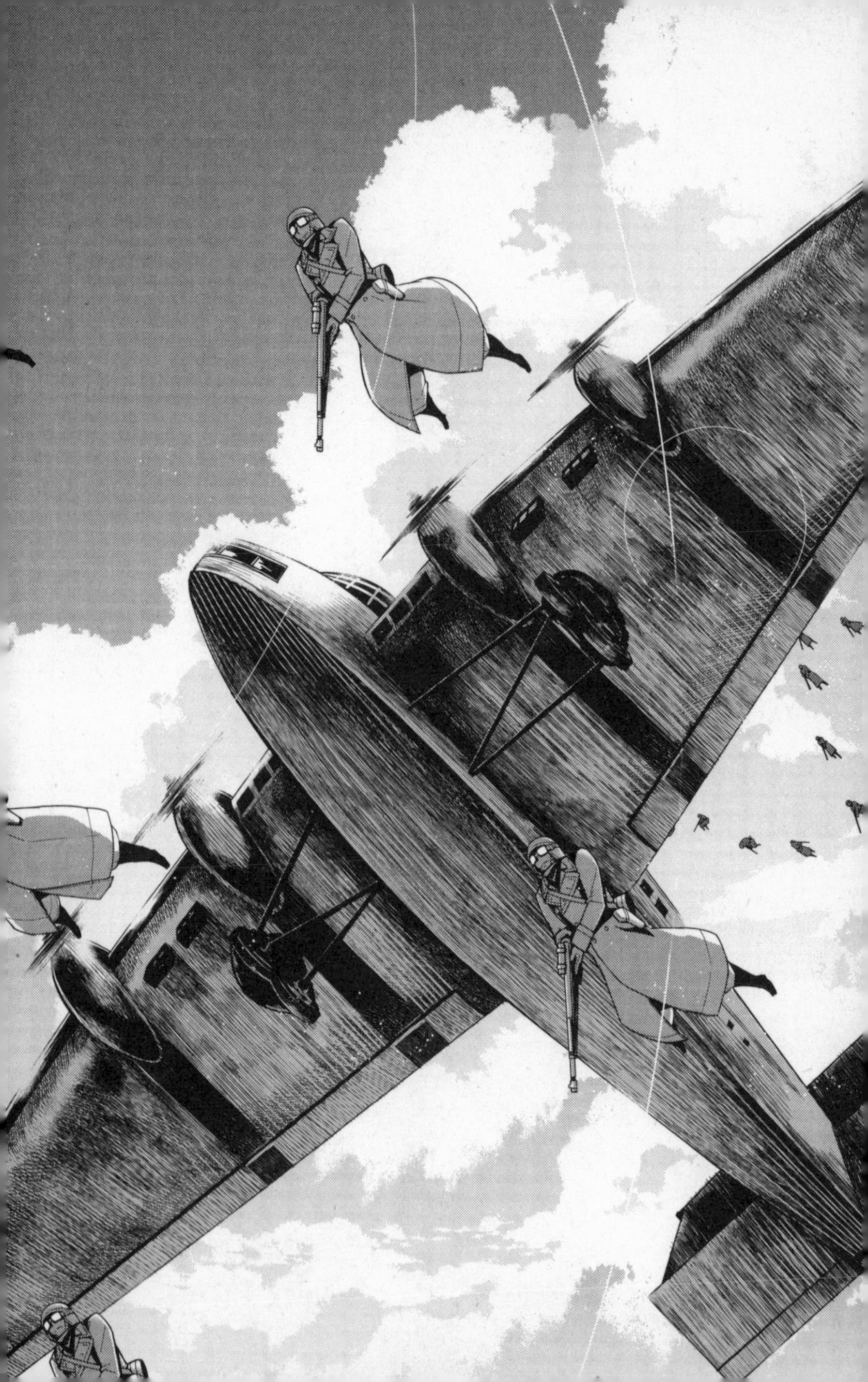

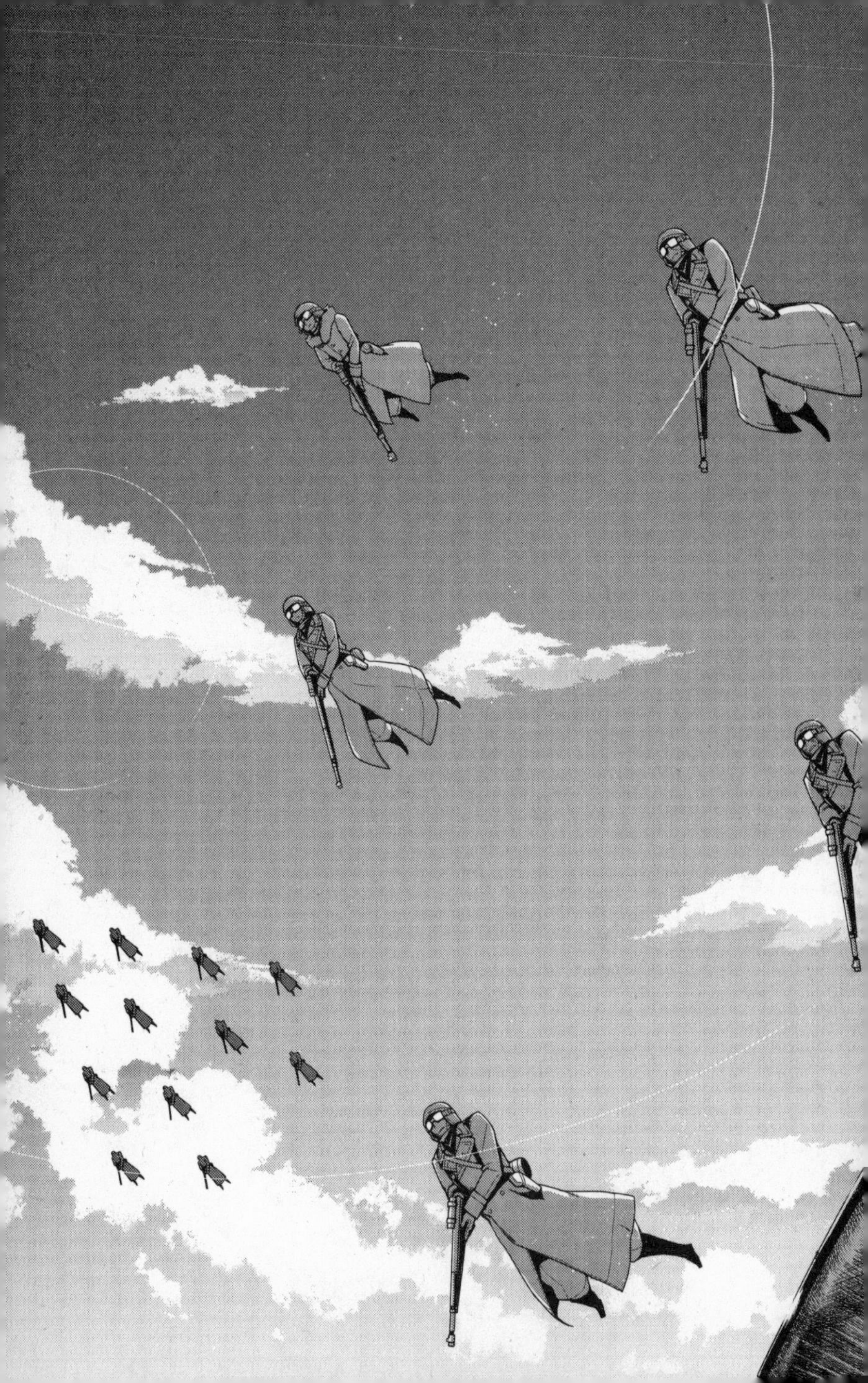

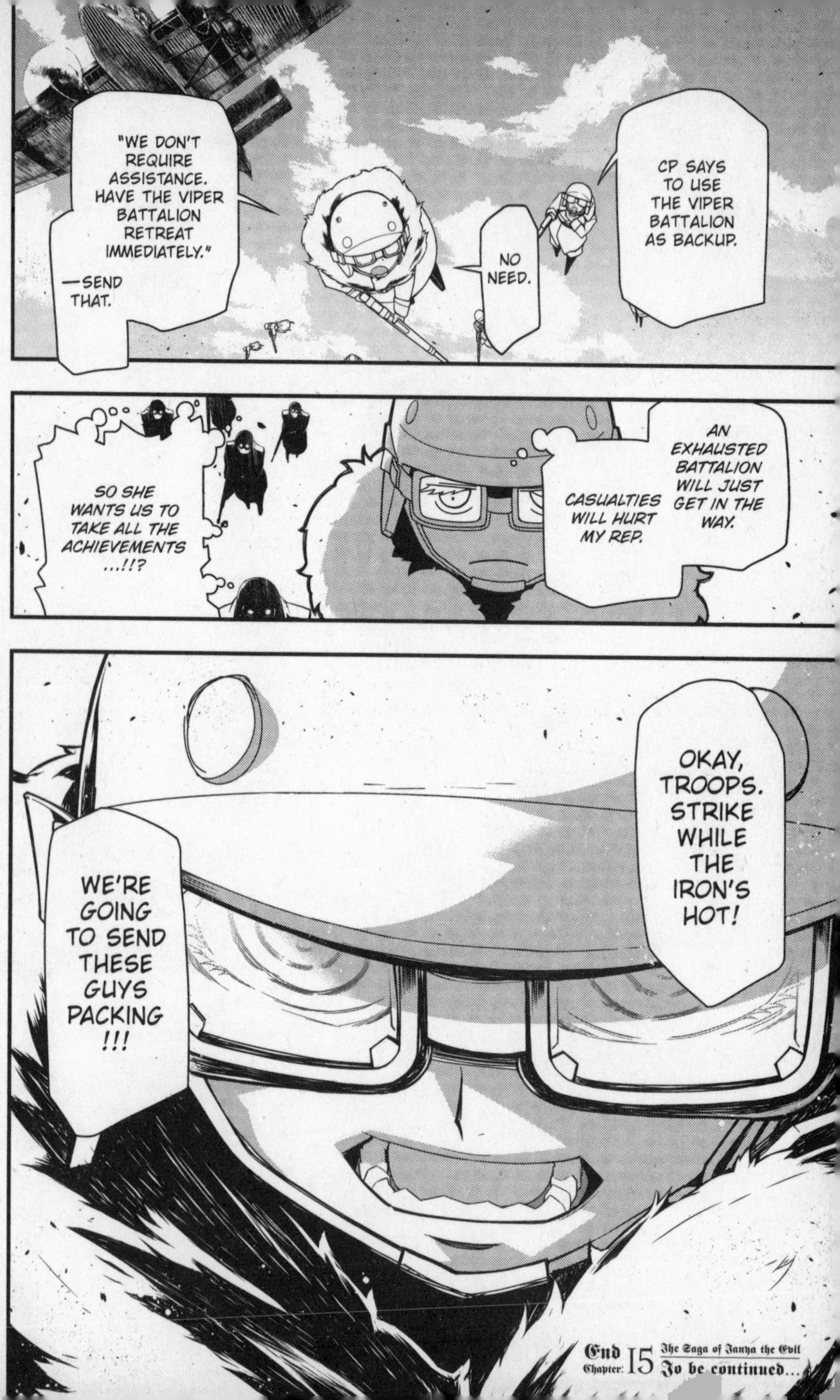
CP SAYS TO USE THE VIPER BATTALION AS BACKUP.
NO NEED.
"WE DON'T REQUIRE ASSISTANCE. HAVE THE VIPER BATTALION RETREAT IMMEDIATELY."
—SEND THAT.
AN EXHAUSTED BATTALION WILL JUST GET IN THE WAY.
CASUALTIES WILL HURT MY REP.
SO SHE WANTS US TO TAKE ALL THE ACHIEVEMENTS ...!!?
OKAY, TROOPS. STRIKE WHILE THE IRON'S HOT!
WE'RE GOING TO SEND THESE GUYS PACKING!!!
End Chapter: 15 The Saga of Tanya the Evil
To be continued...

Glossary Chapter 17

Guerrilla Warfare

When a less powerful force opposes an advancing army by attempting to tire them out with small-scale ambushes, sneak attacks, and destruction of rear supply facilities.

It's the opposite of regular armies fighting large-scale battles along a front. With no attack objectives set in advance, it's a repetition of splitting off troops and then attacking and fleeing. Attacks have a tendency to be carried out in places like forests or dense urban areas where a large army would have trouble flexing its numbers. For that reason, it's mainly a tactic or strategy that the militarily inferior side employs.

Unlike battles among regular armies, imbalanced struggles between a regular army versus guerrilla units often risk noncombatants getting caught up in the fighting. At the same time, volunteers from occupied territory join the ranks of the guerrillas of their own accord, or they join the suppressors for personal or ideological reasons, making it easy for the violence to escalate.

Deputy Commander

The officer who takes over command of the unit if the commander is injured, killed, or otherwise unable to lead.

In the chain of command, they come next after the commander and are often called "vice commanders." They are distinct from adjutants, who assist the commander.

1800

1800, or 6 p.m. sharp. It's read as "eighteen hundred," and it is the military way of transmitting numbers. Each number is pronounced in a way that is easy to understand through radio noise or even during a bombardment.

In Japanese, the pronunciation is "hito-hachi-maru-maru." Instead of using tens and hundreds, they pronounce each digit individually and omit units like hours or minutes. This way, it takes fewer syllables, and it makes it easier to envision the numbers as characters rather than amounts.

Glossary Chapter 18

Supply Depot

A place where food and ammunition is stored. Also called a logistics base.

Before military supplies are delivered to the front lines, they are stockpiled and divided several times. Specifically, supplies are initially transported from the main depots to the staging areas of local logistics districts or other related organizations. Then, after passing through a branch of command, they are sent to the logistics bases on the front.

Additionally, logistics bases are classified according to their function as strategic, operational, or tactical areas. Strategic logistics bases are established during peacetime as hubs of production and transport, operational logistics bases are set up by army groups in operational districts, and tactical logistics bases are set up as tactically necessary near the front lines.

Setting up logistics bases is a cornerstone of mobile strategy and is carried out according to the Service Corps' meticulous plans.

Bomber

An airplane that specializes in carrying and dropping bombs. They are mainly used to bomb targets from the sky in missions that are divided broadly into strategic and tactical strikes. The former targets the foundations of the enemy's war making, while the latter weakens the enemy's combat capabilities by attacking units on the front lines, hitting the enemy's communication lines in the rear, and providing support to friendly ground or navy forces.

However, since their air battle capabilities are limited, they are vulnerable to fighter planes specialized in dogfighting.

Fighter

A plane equipped with machine guns and specialized in battling enemy aircraft.

They originally developed out of reconnaissance planes. Early recon planes weren't very advanced aeronautically and had zero combat ability, so enemy pilots were said to have occasionally greeted each other when they crossed paths. But as the recon capabilities grew more advanced, it became necessary to eliminate enemy aircraft, so after a period of pilots throwing rocks and firing pistols at each other, planes were outfitted with machine guns, and the fighter was born.

Their main missions include shooting down enemy bombers, escorting friendly bombers, running interceptions to protect bases and navy fleets, and fighting air battles to secure command of the sky.

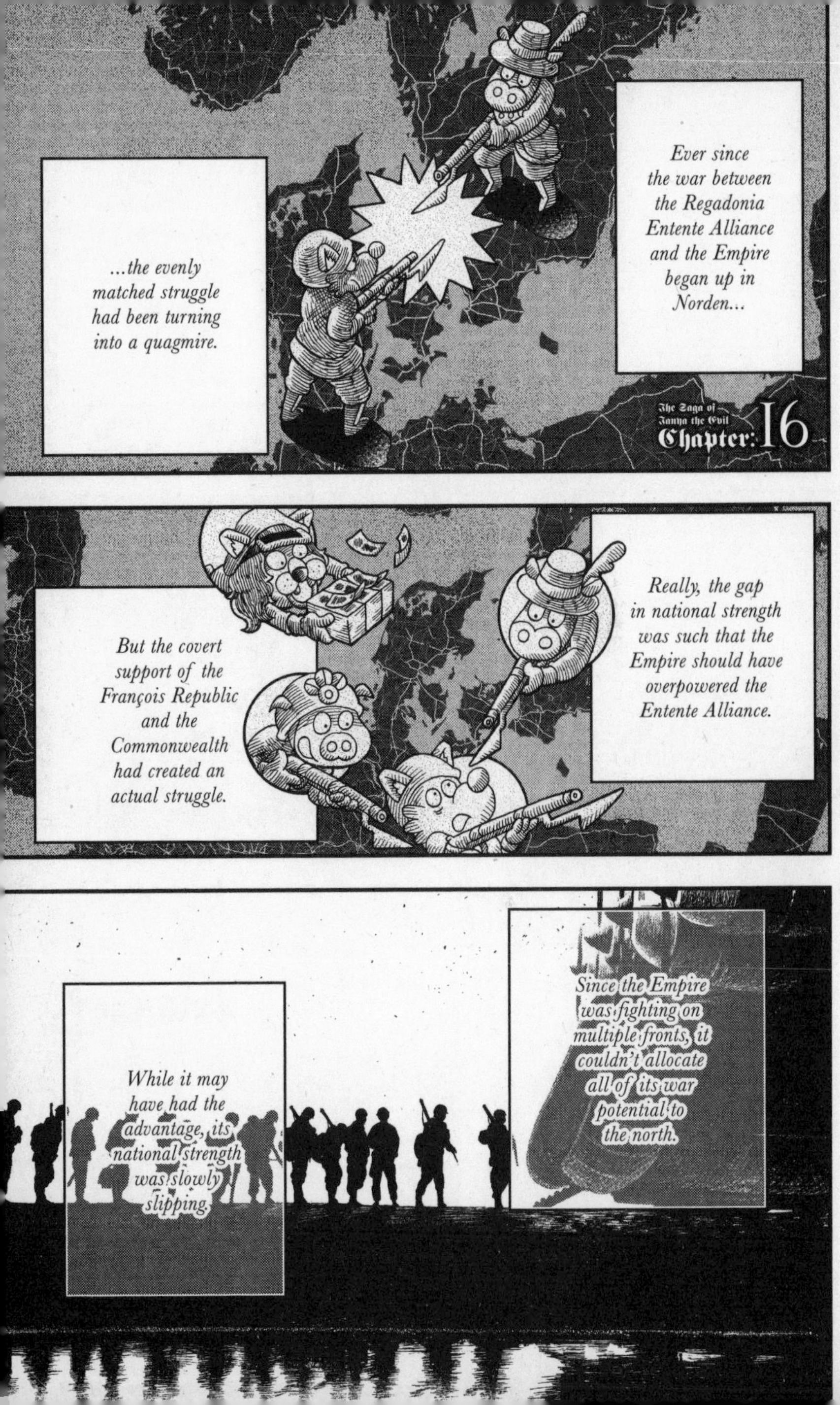
The Saga of Tanya the Evil
Chapter: 16
Ever since the war between the Regadonia Entente Alliance and the Empire began up in Norden...
...the evenly matched struggle had been turning into a quagmire.
Really, the gap in national strength was such that the Empire should have overpowered the Entente Alliance.
But the covert support of the François Republic and the Commonwealth had created an actual struggle.
Since the Empire was fighting on multiple fronts, it couldn't allocate all of its war potential to the north.
While it may have had the advantage, its national strength was slowly slipping.

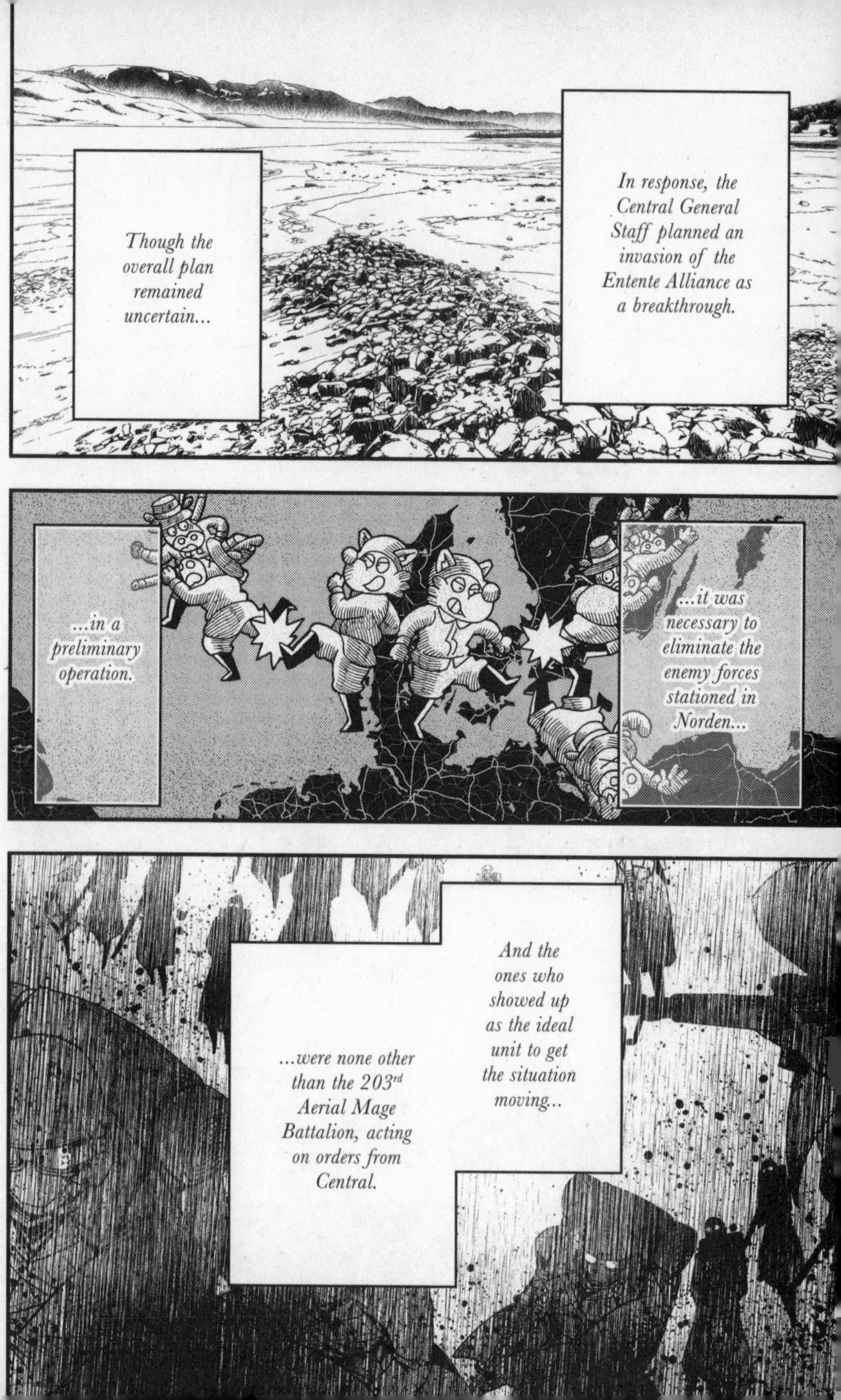
In response, the Central General Staff planned an invasion of the Entente Alliance as a breakthrough.
Though the overall plan remained uncertain...
...it was necessary to eliminate the enemy forces stationed in Norden...
...in a preliminary operation.
And the ones who showed up as the ideal unit to get the situation moving...
...were none other than the 203rd Aerial Mage Battalion, acting on orders from Central.

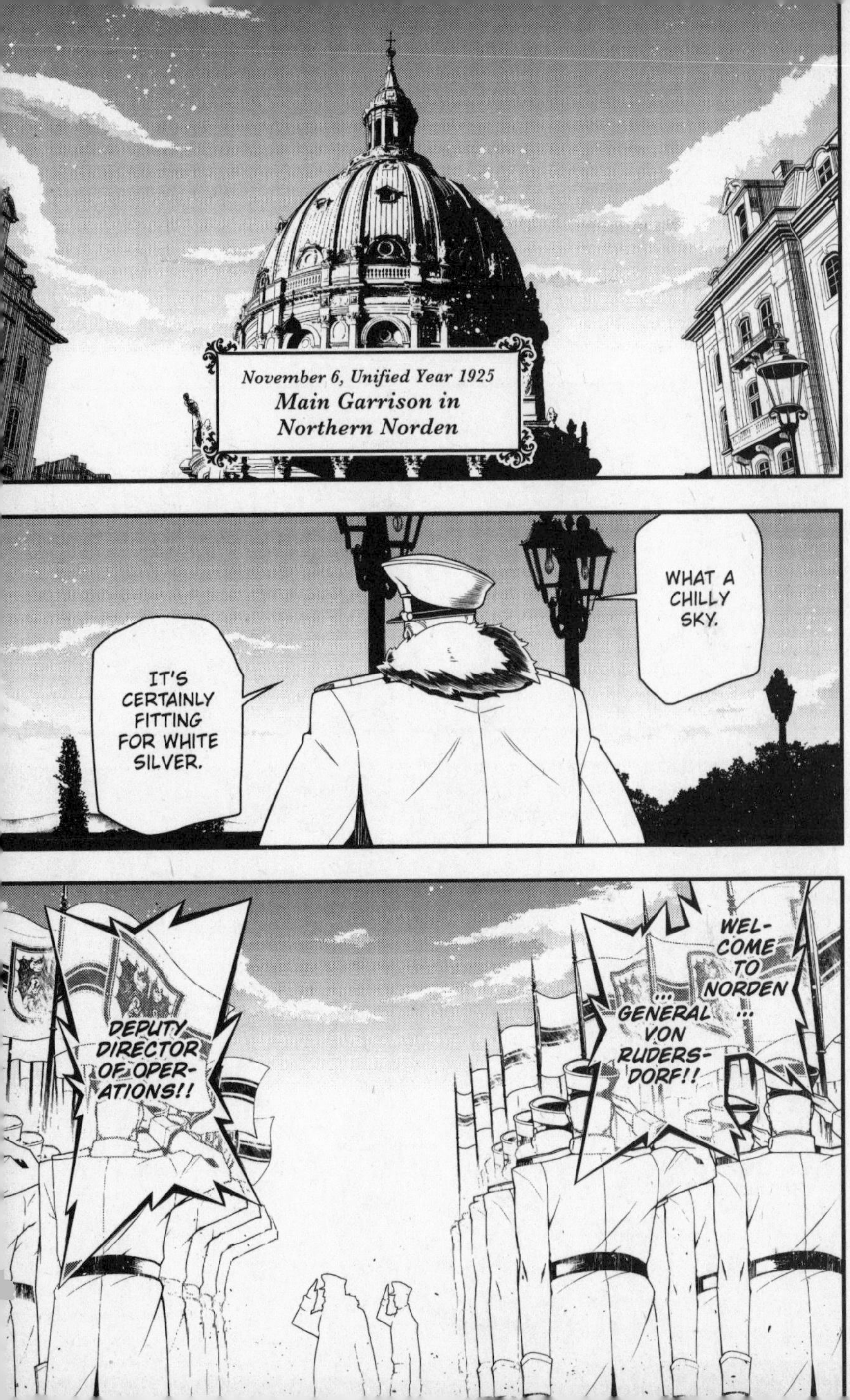
November 6, Unified Year 1925
Main Garrison in Northern Norden
WHAT A CHILLY SKY.
IT'S CERTAINLY FITTING FOR WHITE SILVER.
WEL-COME TO NORDEN...
...GENERAL VON RUDERS-DORF!!
DEPUTY DIRECTOR OF OPER-ATIONS!!

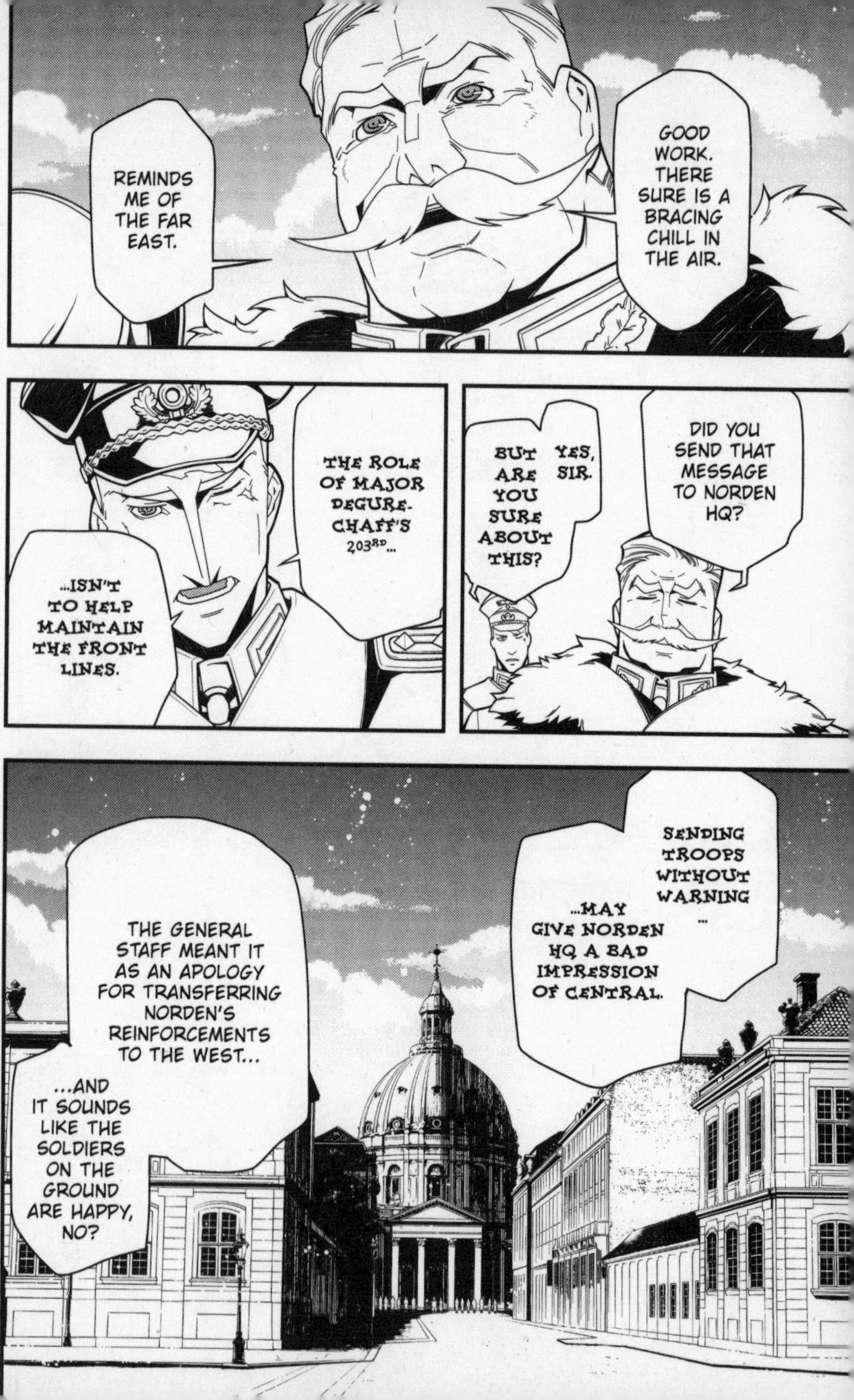
GOOD WORK. THERE SURE IS A BRACING CHILL IN THE AIR.
REMINDS ME OF THE FAR EAST.
DID YOU SEND THAT MESSAGE TO NORDEN HQ?
YES, SIR.
BUT ARE YOU SURE ABOUT THIS?
THE ROLE OF MAJOR DEGURECHAFF'S 203RD...
...ISN'T TO HELP MAINTAIN THE FRONT LINES.
SENDING TROOPS WITHOUT WARNING...
...MAY GIVE NORDEN HQ A BAD IMPRESSION OF CENTRAL.
THE GENERAL STAFF MEANT IT AS AN APOLOGY FOR TRANSFERRING NORDEN'S REINFORCEMENTS TO THE WEST...
...AND IT SOUNDS LIKE THE SOLDIERS ON THE GROUND ARE HAPPY, NO?

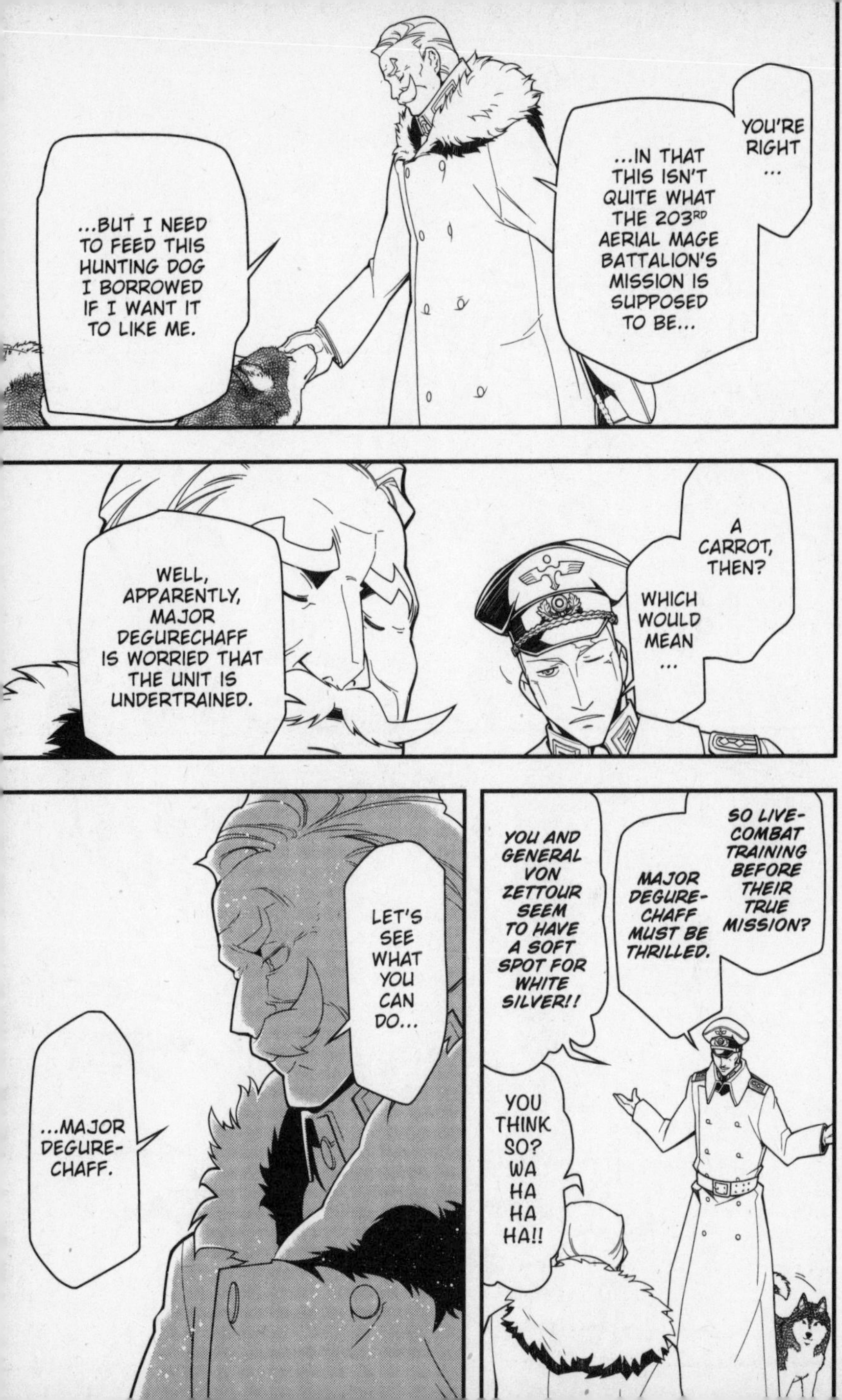
YOU'RE RIGHT...
...IN THAT THIS ISN'T QUITE WHAT THE 203RD AERIAL MAGE BATTALION'S MISSION IS SUPPOSED TO BE...
...BUT I NEED TO FEED THIS HUNTING DOG I BORROWED IF I WANT IT TO LIKE ME.
A CARROT, THEN?
WHICH WOULD MEAN...
WELL, APPARENTLY, MAJOR DEGURECHAFF IS WORRIED THAT THE UNIT IS UNDERTRAINED.
SO LIVE-COMBAT TRAINING BEFORE THEIR TRUE MISSION?
MAJOR DEGURE-CHAFF MUST BE THRILLED.
YOU AND GENERAL VON ZETTOUR SEEM TO HAVE A SOFT SPOT FOR WHITE SILVER!!
YOU THINK SO? WA HA HA HA!!
LET'S SEE WHAT YOU CAN DO...
...MAJOR DEGURE-CHAFF.

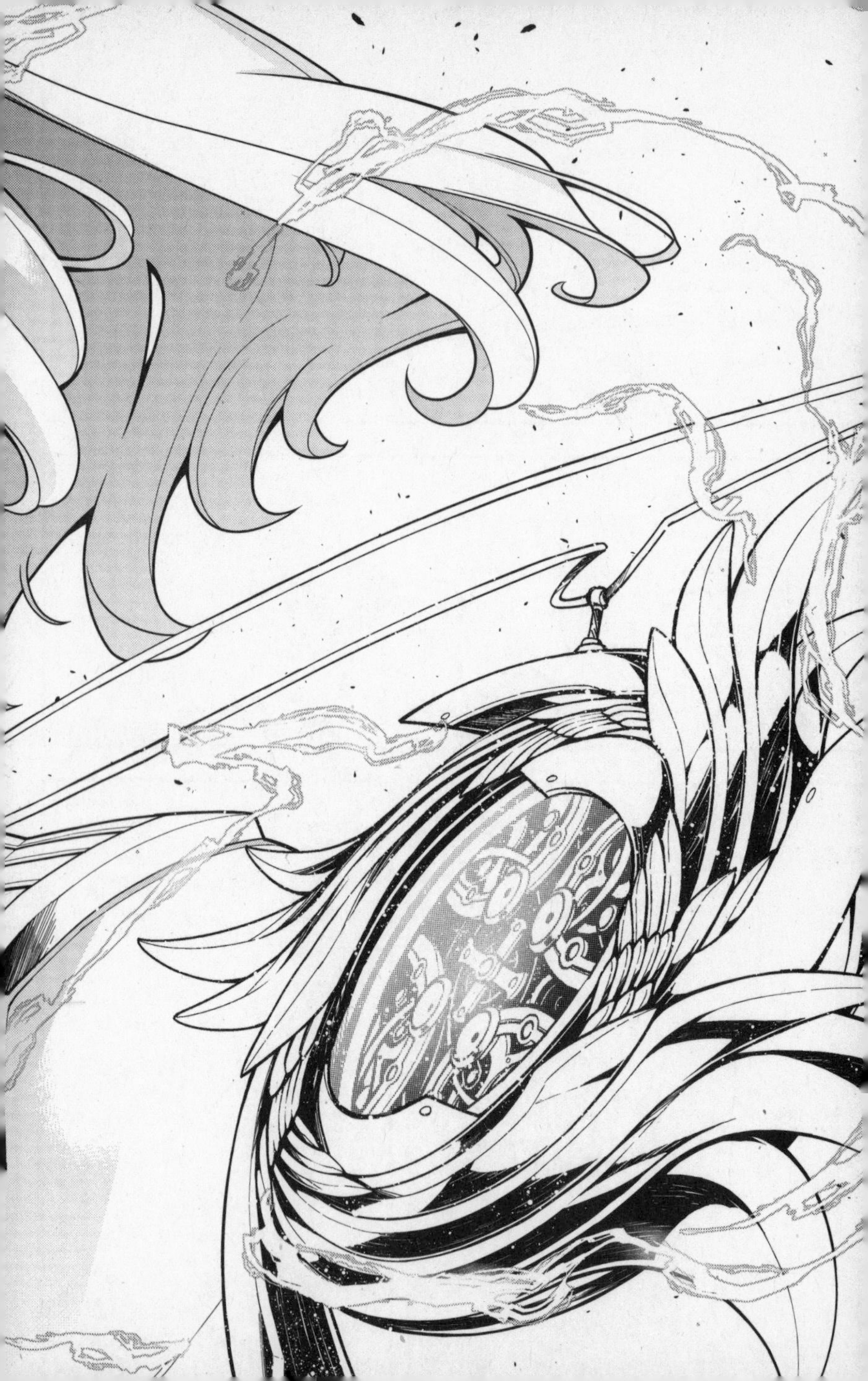

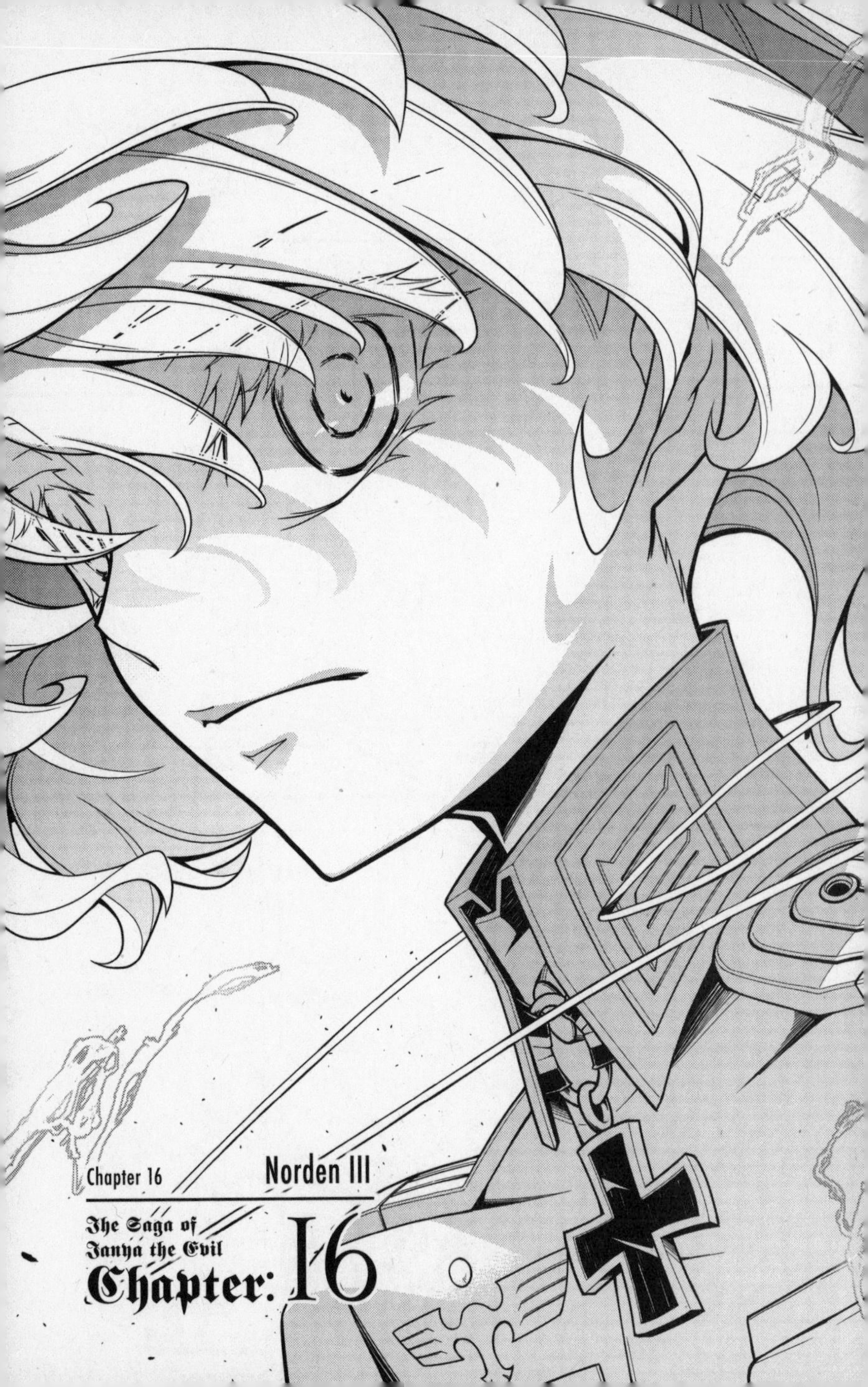
Chapter 16
Norden III
The Saga of Tanya the Evil
Chapter: 16

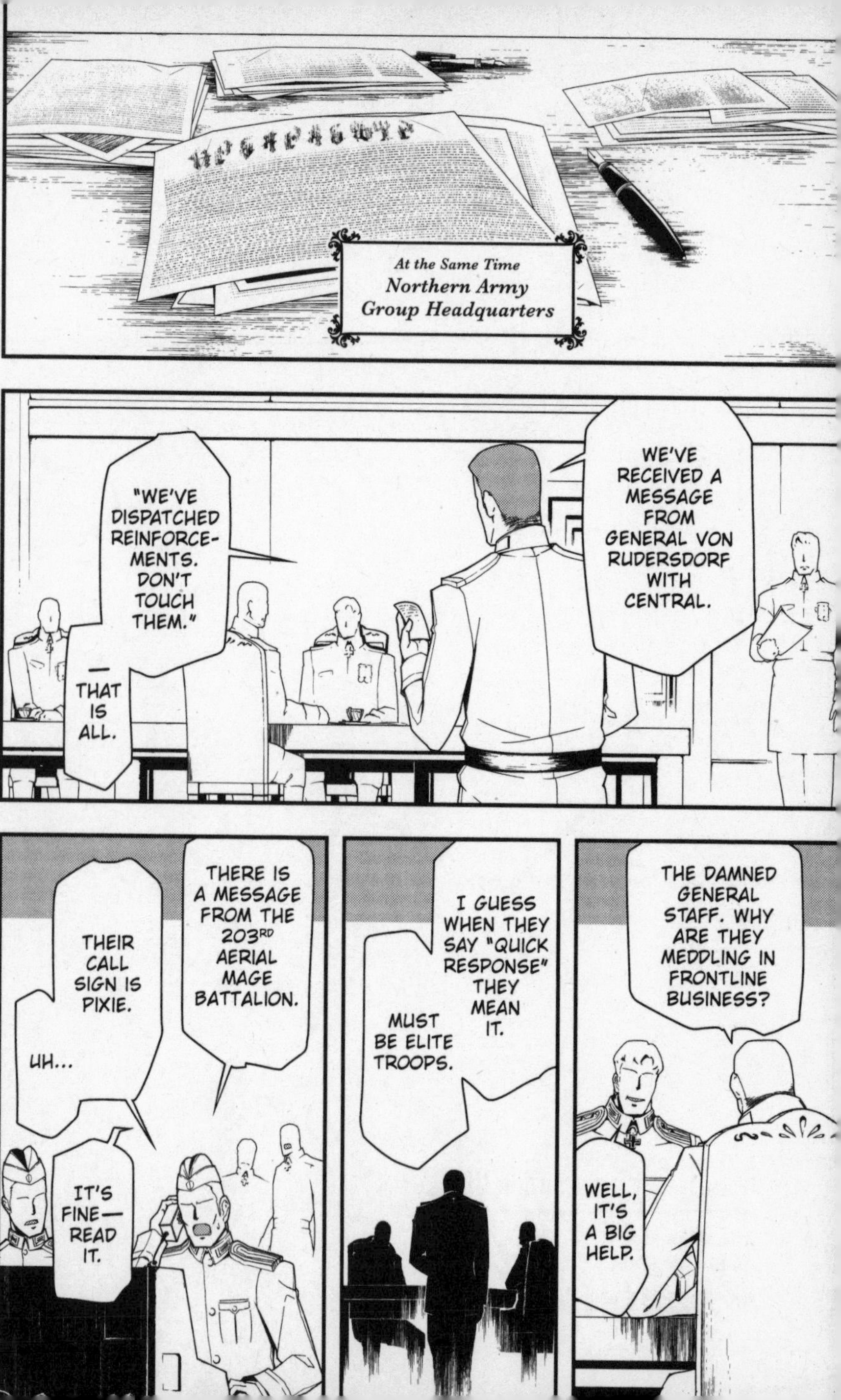
At the Same Time
Northern Army Group Headquarters
WE'VE RECEIVED A MESSAGE FROM GENERAL VON RUDERSDORF WITH CENTRAL.
"WE'VE DISPATCHED REINFORCE-MENTS. DON'T TOUCH THEM."
—THAT IS ALL.
THE DAMNED GENERAL STAFF. WHY ARE THEY MEDDLING IN FRONTLINE BUSINESS?
WELL, IT'S A BIG HELP.
I GUESS WHEN THEY SAY "QUICK RESPONSE" THEY MEAN IT.
MUST BE ELITE TROOPS.
THERE IS A MESSAGE FROM THE 203RD AERIAL MAGE BATTALION.
THEIR CALL SIGN IS PIXIE.
UH...
IT'S FINE—READ IT.

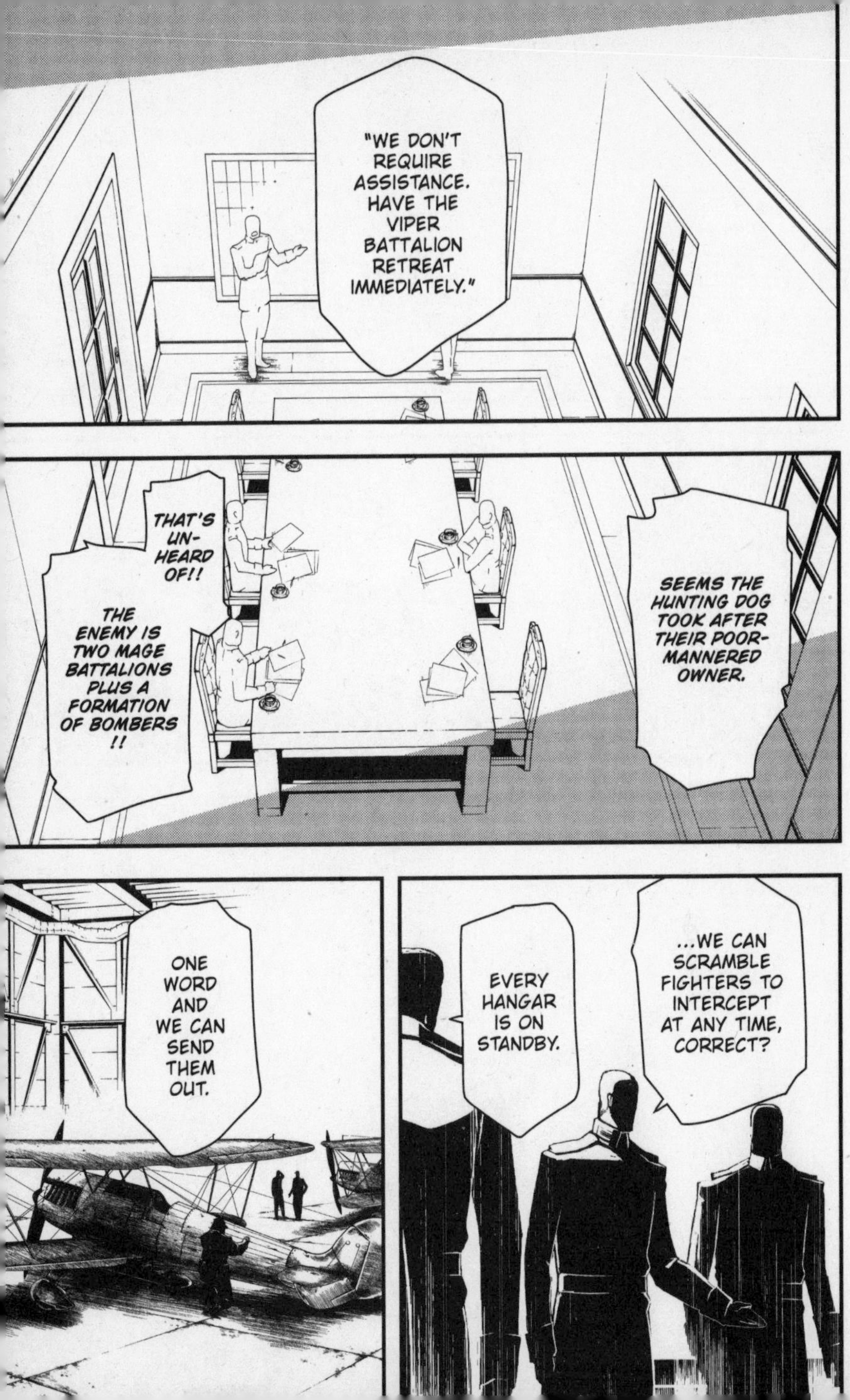
"WE DON'T REQUIRE ASSISTANCE. HAVE THE VIPER BATTALION RETREAT IMMEDIATELY."
SEEMS THE HUNTING DOG TOOK AFTER THEIR POOR-MANNERED OWNER.
THAT'S UN-HEARD OF!!
THE ENEMY IS TWO MAGE BATTALIONS PLUS A FORMATION OF BOMBERS!!
...WE CAN SCRAMBLE FIGHTERS TO INTERCEPT AT ANY TIME, CORRECT?
EVERY HANGAR IS ON STANDBY.
ONE WORD AND WE CAN SEND THEM OUT.

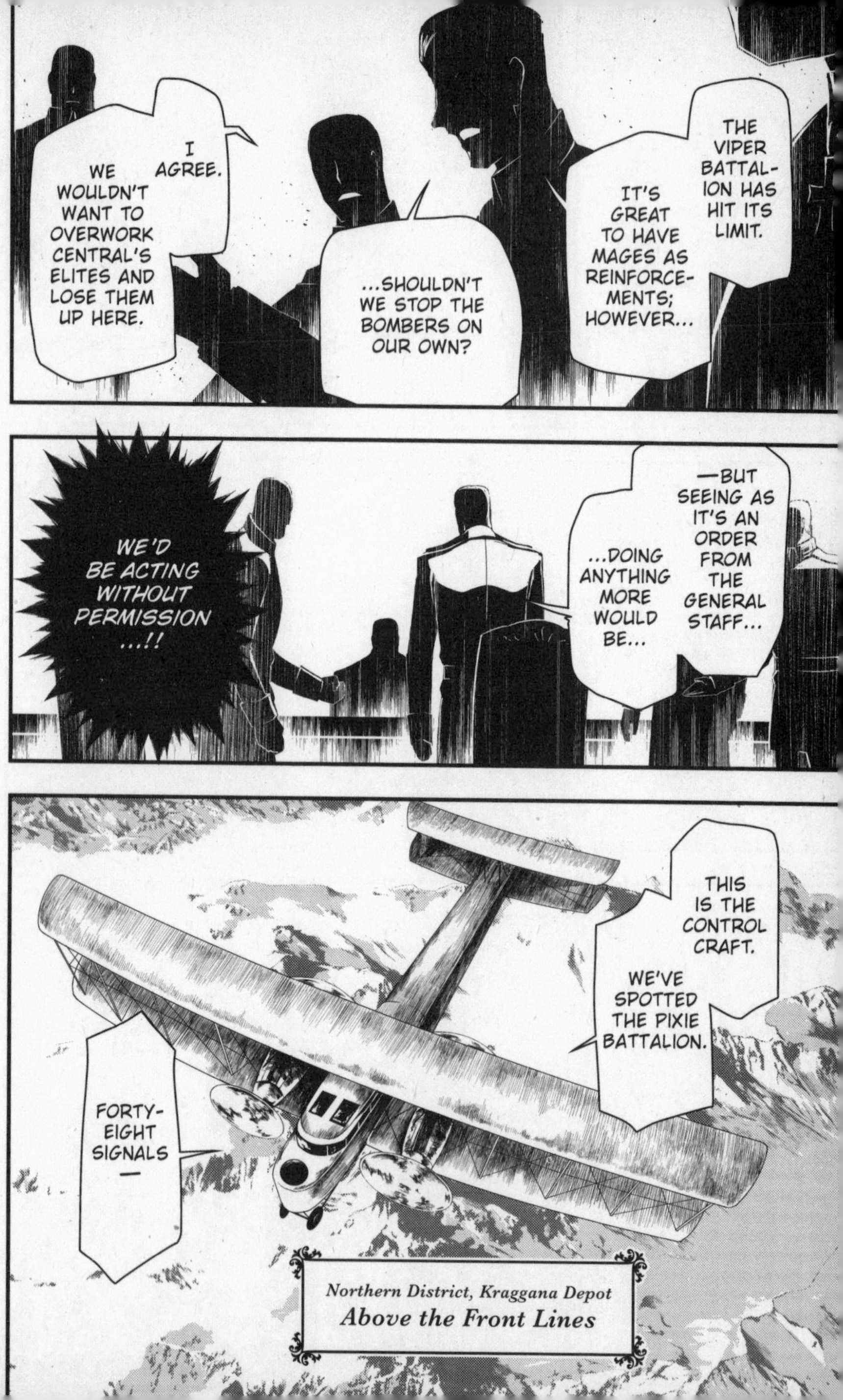
THE VIPER BATTALION HAS HIT ITS LIMIT.
IT'S GREAT TO HAVE MAGES AS REINFORCEMENTS; HOWEVER...
...SHOULDN'T WE STOP THE BOMBERS ON OUR OWN?
I AGREE.
WE WOULDN'T WANT TO OVERWORK CENTRAL'S ELITES AND LOSE THEM UP HERE.
—BUT SEEING AS IT'S AN ORDER FROM THE GENERAL STAFF...
...DOING ANYTHING MORE WOULD BE...
WE'D BE ACTING WITHOUT PERMISSION...!!
THIS IS THE CONTROL CRAFT.
WE'VE SPOTTED THE PIXIE BATTALION.
FORTY-EIGHT SIGNALS—
Northern District, Kraggana Depot
Above the Front Lines

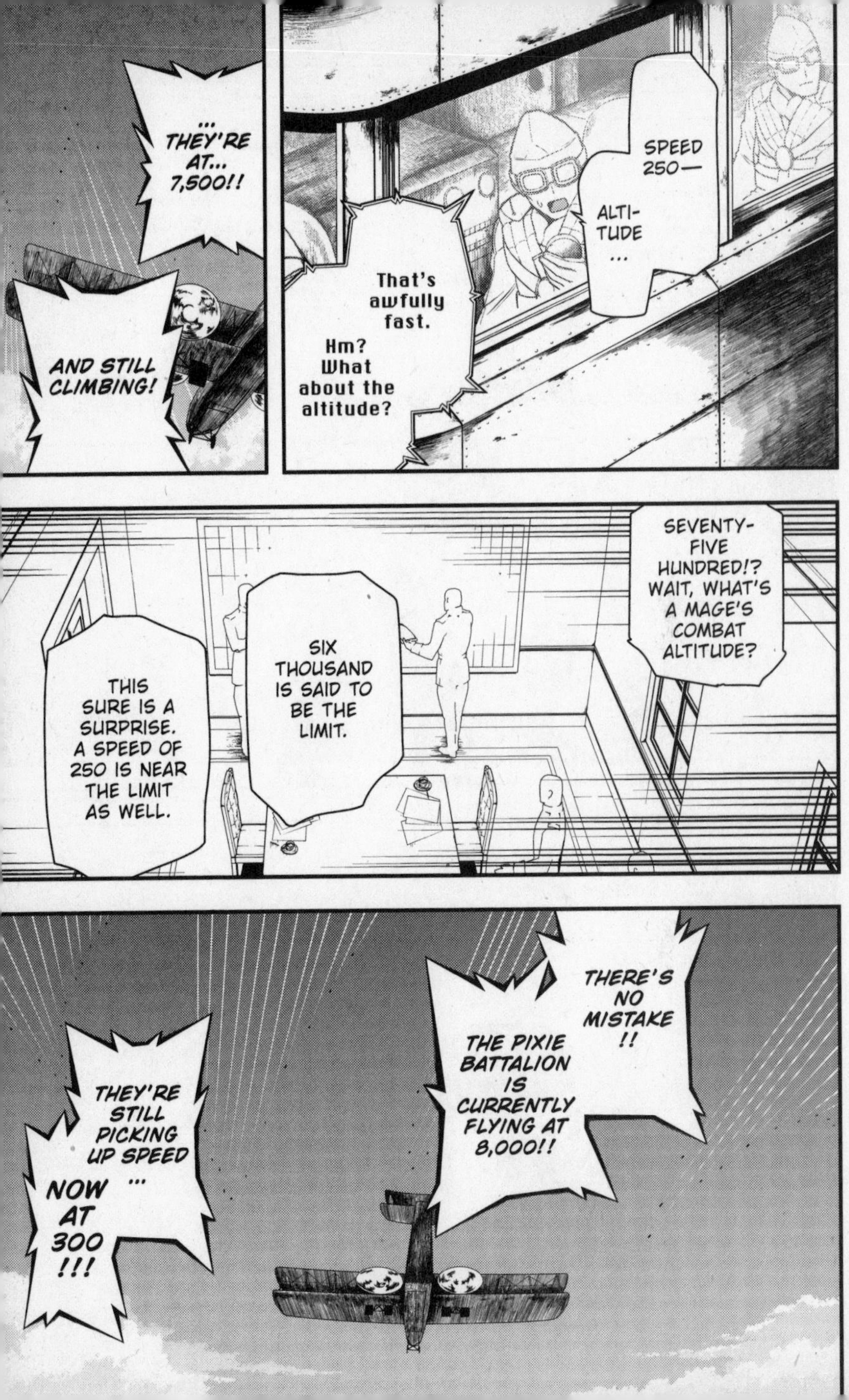
SPEED 250—
ALTI-TUDE ...
That's awfully fast.
Hm? What about the altitude?
... THEY'RE AT... 7,500!!
AND STILL CLIMBING!
SEVENTY-FIVE HUNDRED!? WAIT, WHAT'S A MAGE'S COMBAT ALTITUDE?
SIX THOUSAND IS SAID TO BE THE LIMIT.
THIS SURE IS A SURPRISE. A SPEED OF 250 IS NEAR THE LIMIT AS WELL.
THERE'S NO MISTAKE!!
THE PIXIE BATTALION IS CURRENTLY FLYING AT 8,000!!
THEY'RE STILL PICKING UP SPEED ...
NOW AT 300!!!

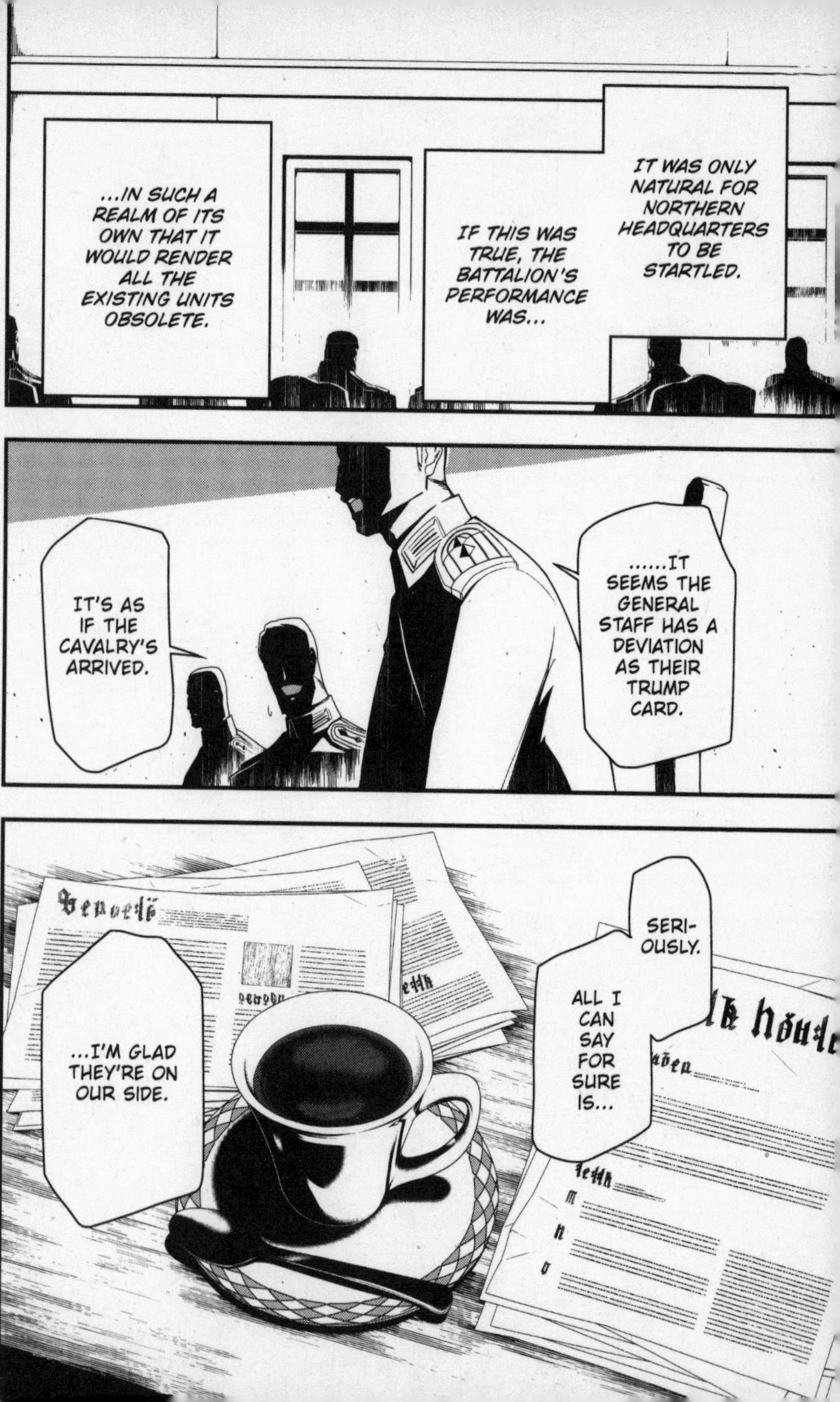
IT WAS ONLY NATURAL FOR NORTHERN HEADQUARTERS TO BE STARTLED.
IF THIS WAS TRUE, THE BATTALION'S PERFORMANCE WAS...
...IN SUCH A REALM OF ITS OWN THAT IT WOULD RENDER ALL THE EXISTING UNITS OBSOLETE.
......IT SEEMS THE GENERAL STAFF HAS A DEVIATION AS THEIR TRUMP CARD.
IT'S AS IF THE CAVALRY'S ARRIVED.
SERIOUSLY.
ALL I CAN SAY FOR SURE IS...
...I'M GLAD THEY'RE ON OUR SIDE.

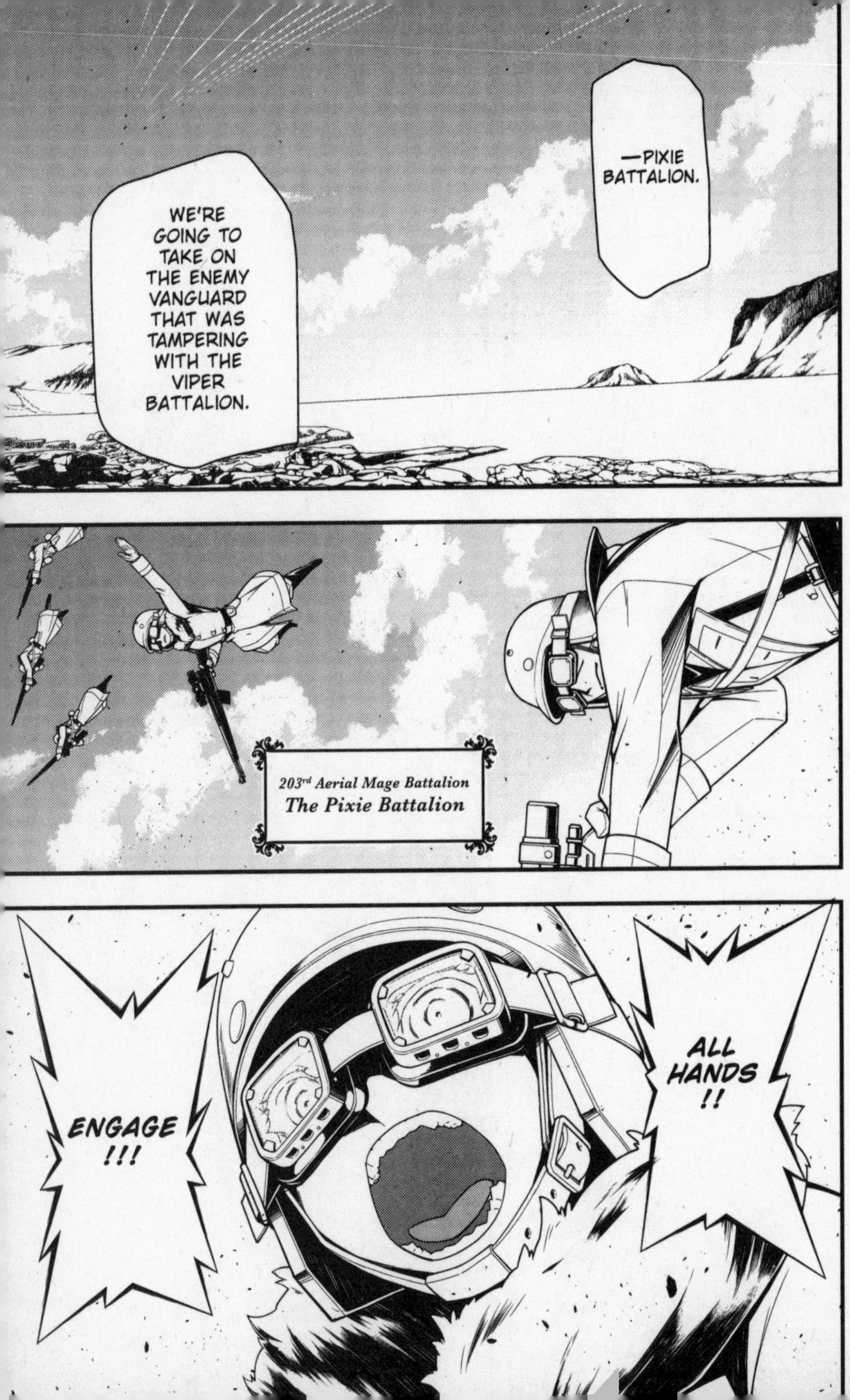
—PIXIE BATTALION.
WE'RE GOING TO TAKE ON THE ENEMY VANGUARD THAT WAS TAMPERING WITH THE VIPER BATTALION.
203rd Aerial Mage Battalion
The Pixie Battalion
ALL HANDS!!
ENGAGE!!!

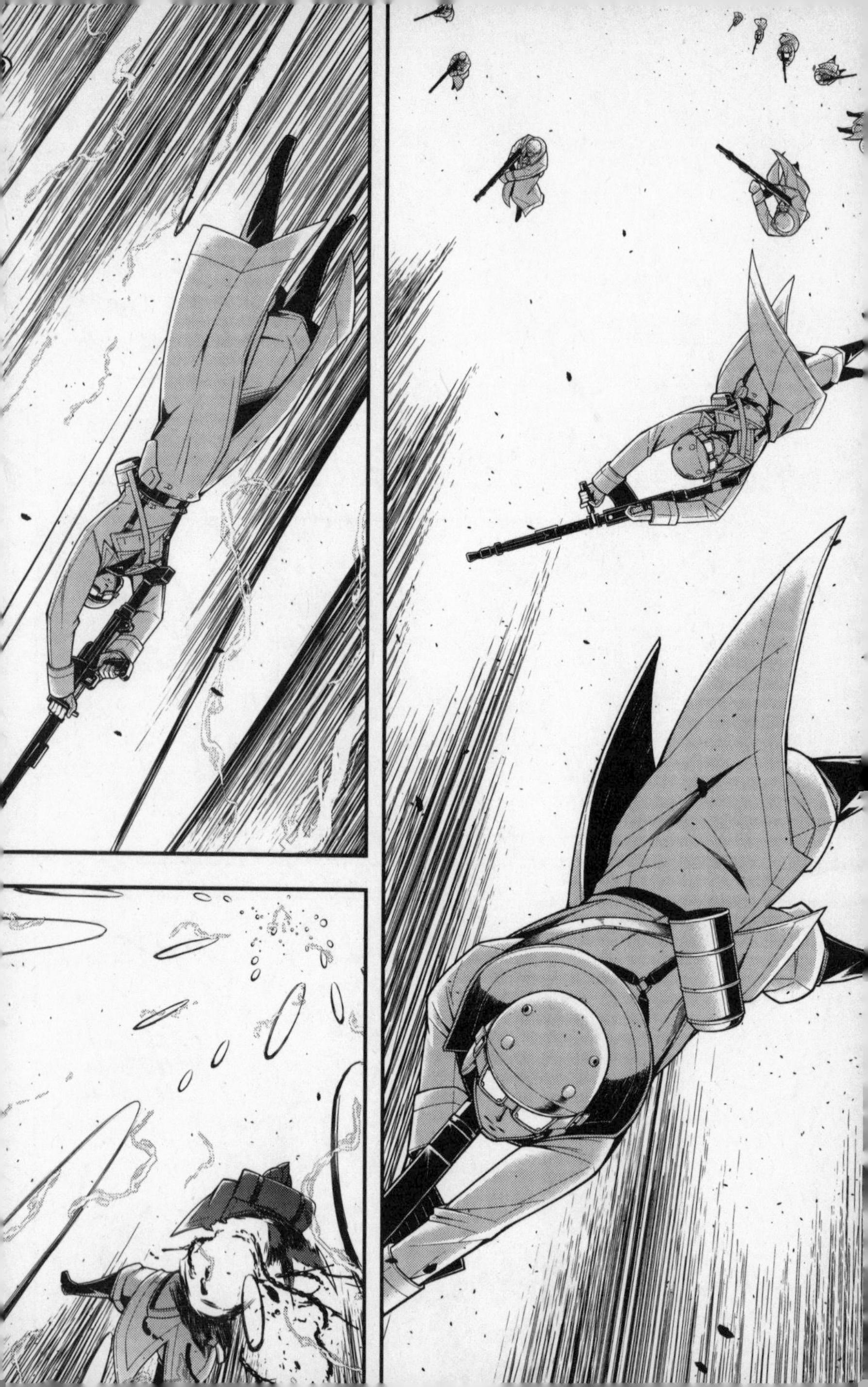

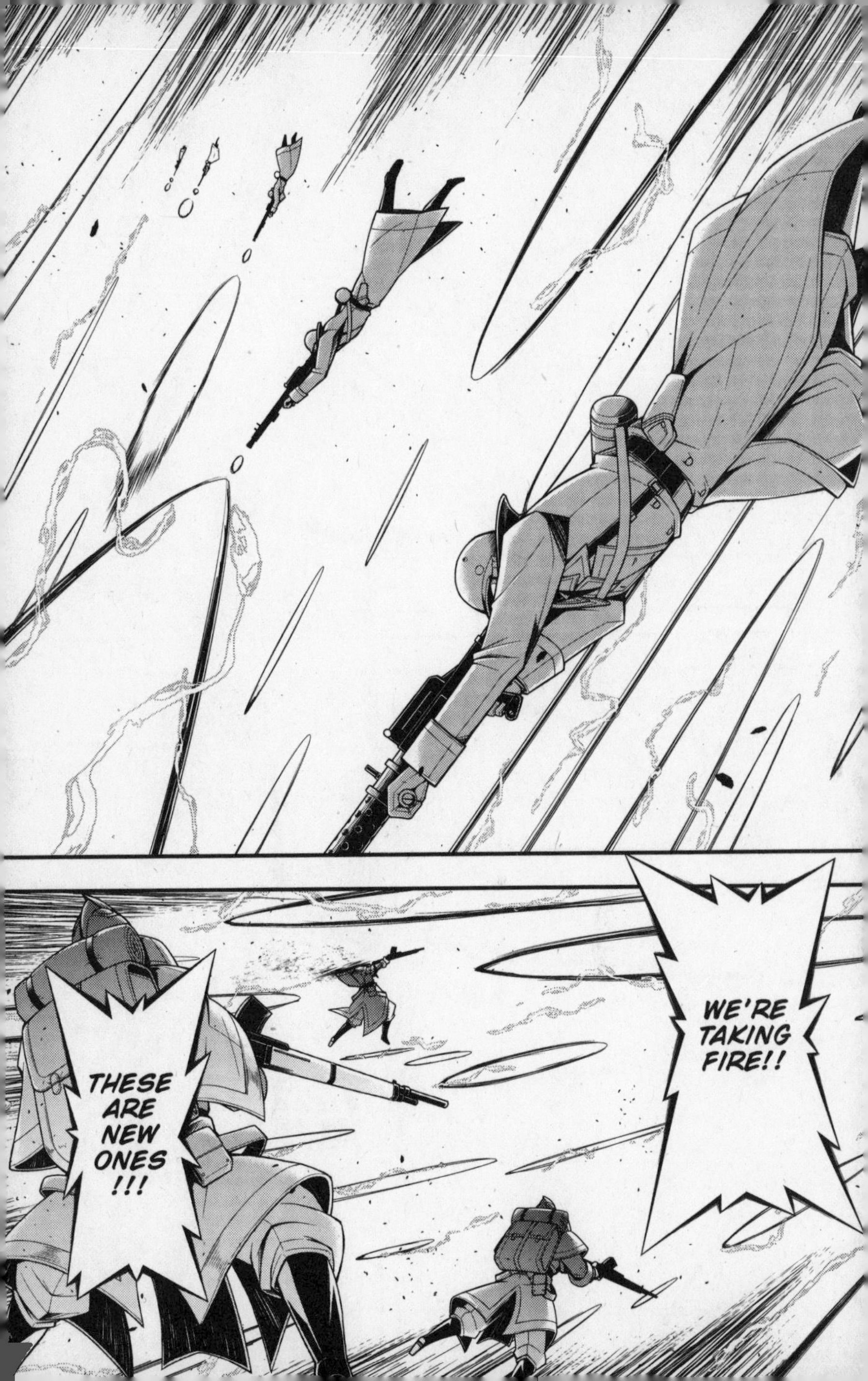
WE'RE TAKING FIRE!!
THESE ARE NEW ONES!!!

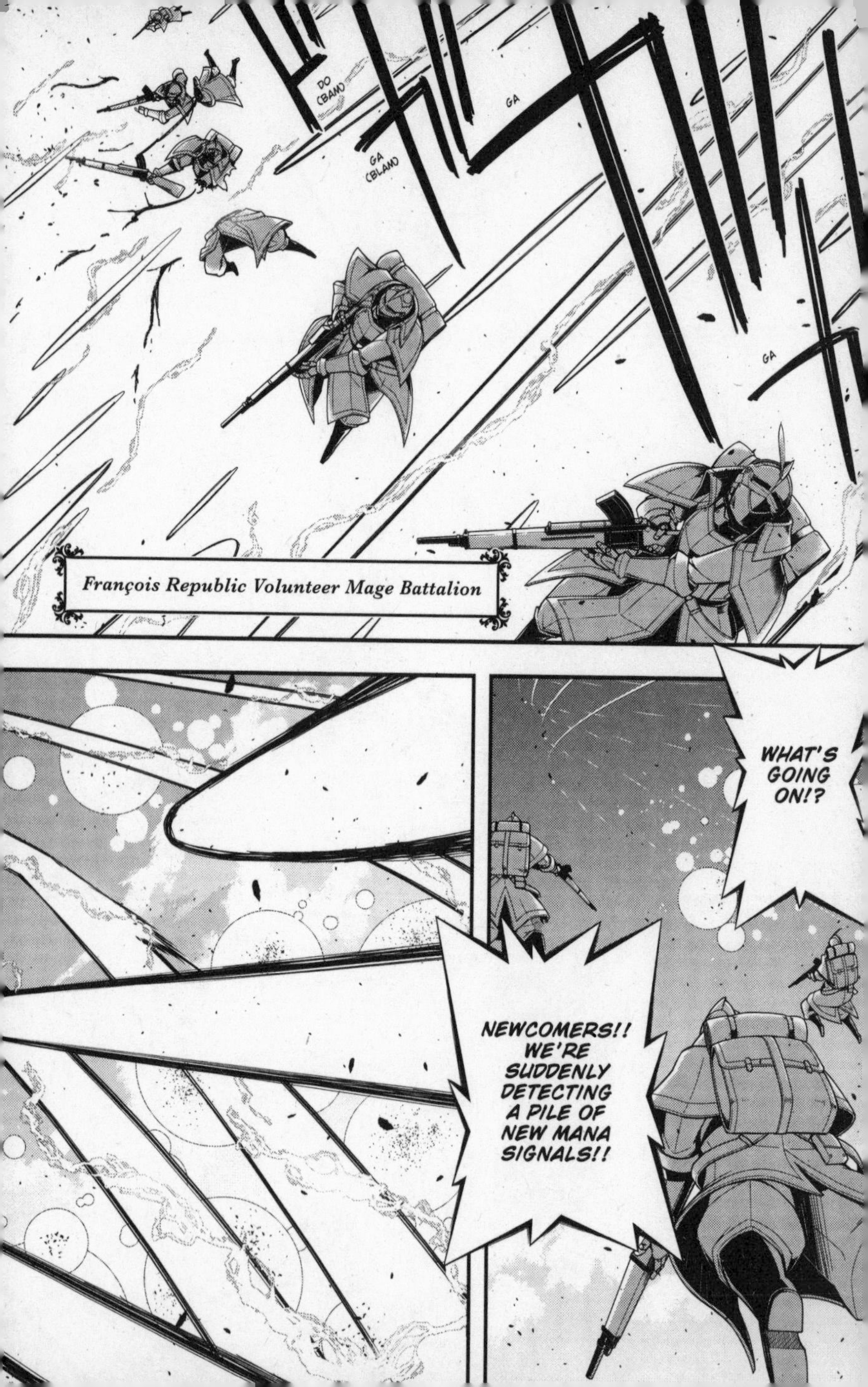
GA
GA
DO (BAM)
GA (BLAM)
François Republic Volunteer Mage Battalion
WHAT'S GOING ON!?
NEWCOMERS!! WE'RE SUDDENLY DETECTING A PILE OF NEW MANA SIGNALS!!

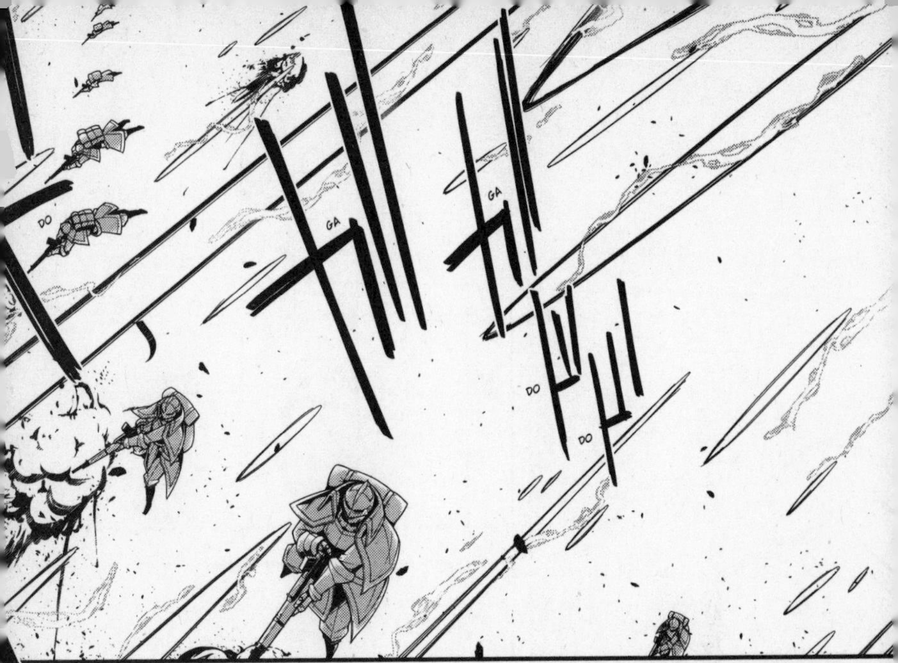
GA
DO
DO
GA
DO
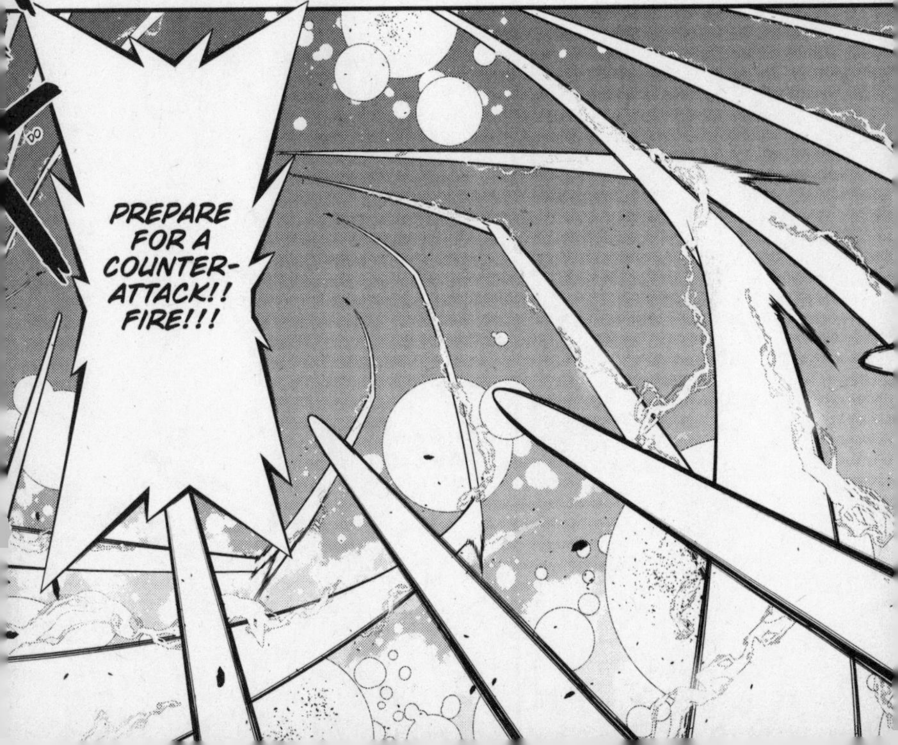
DO
PREPARE FOR A COUNTER-ATTACK!! FIRE!!!

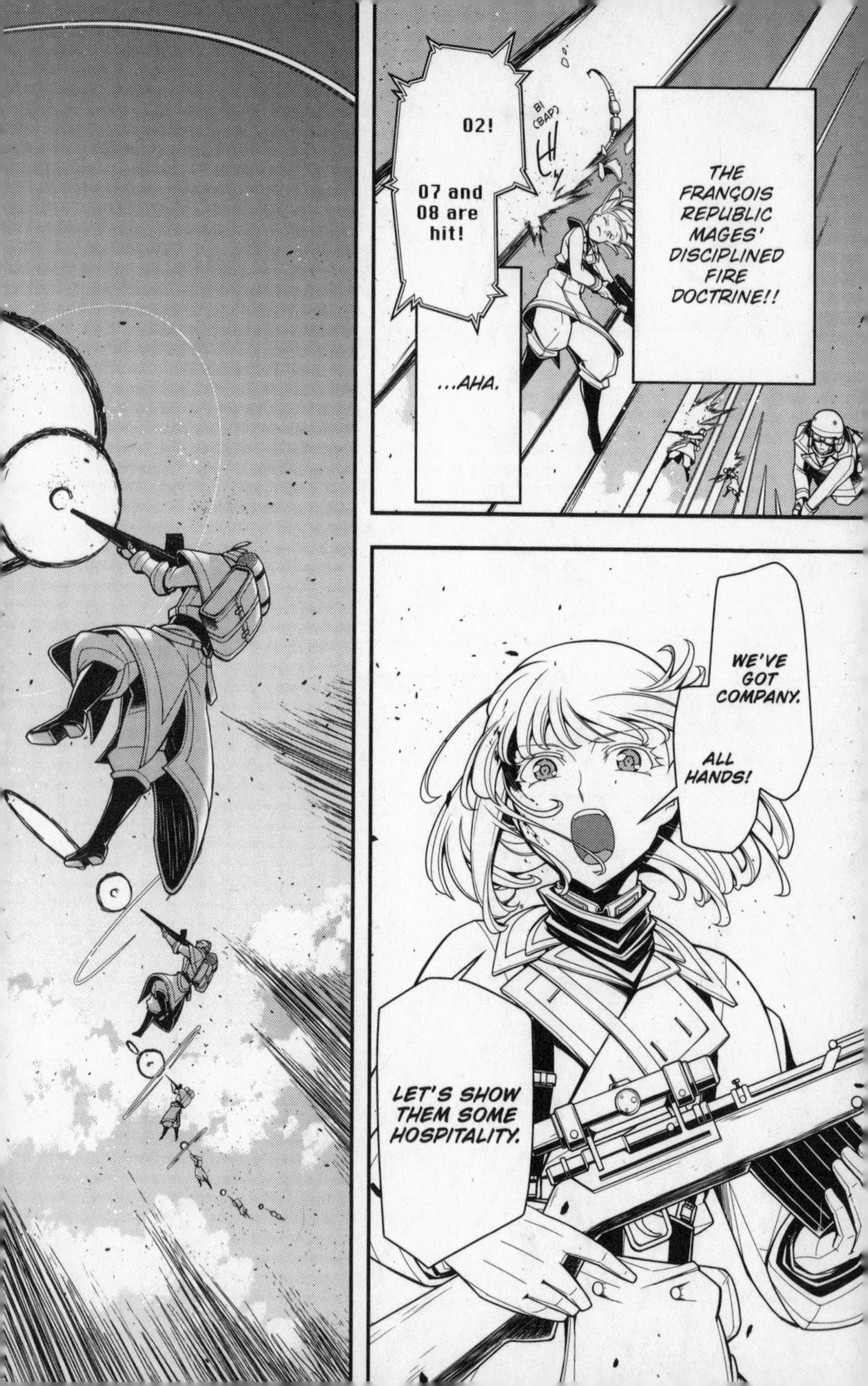
02!
07 and 08 are hit!
BI (BAP)
THE FRANÇOIS REPUBLIC MAGES' DISCIPLINED FIRE DOCTRINE!!
...AHA.
WE'VE GOT COMPANY.
ALL HANDS!
LET'S SHOW THEM SOME HOSPITALITY.

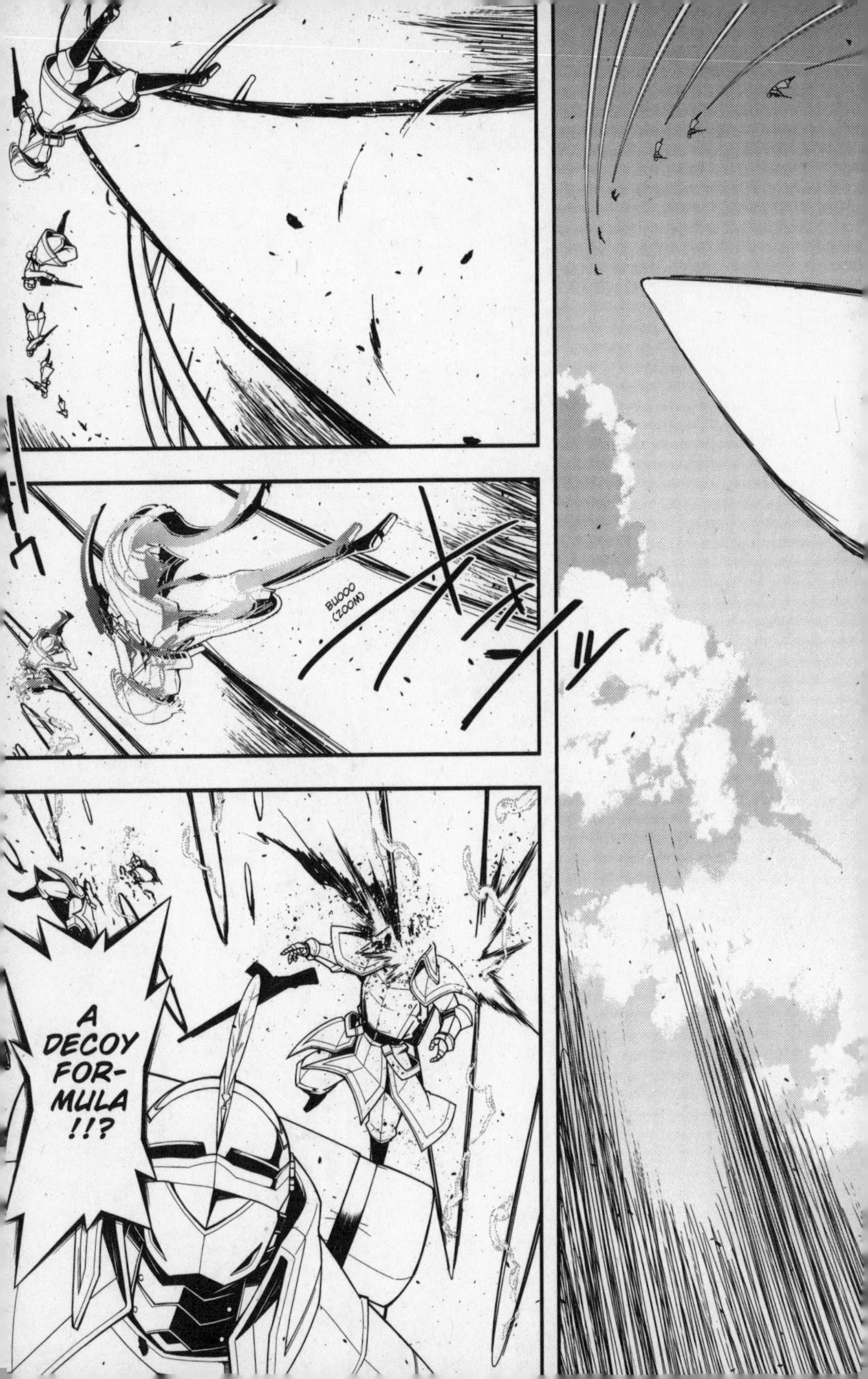
BUOOO
(ZOOM)
A DECOY FOR-MULA!!?

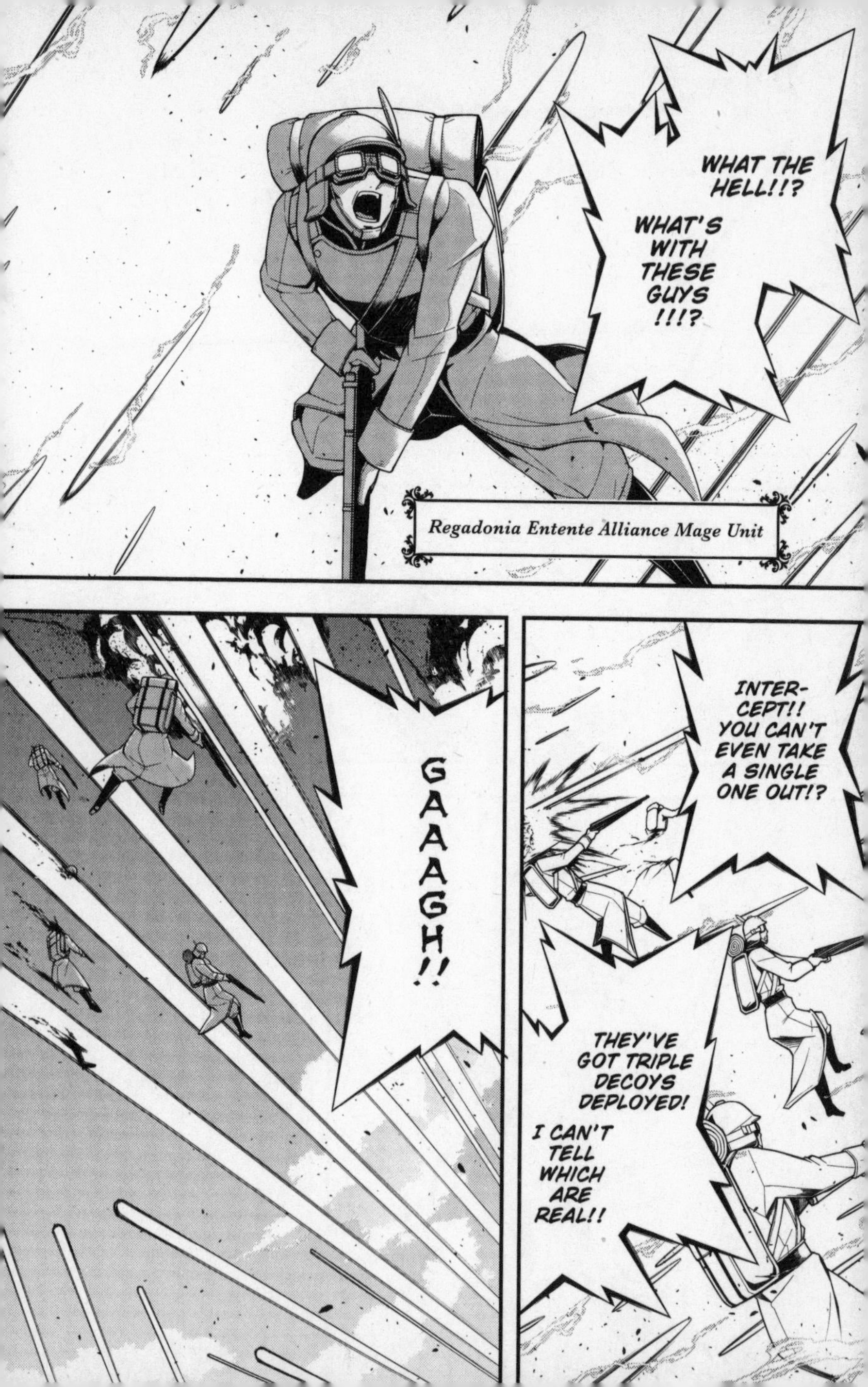
WHAT THE HELL!!?
WHAT'S WITH THESE GUYS!!!?
Regadonia Entente Alliance Mage Unit
INTERCEPT!! YOU CAN'T EVEN TAKE A SINGLE ONE OUT!?
THEY'VE GOT TRIPLE DECOYS DEPLOYED!
I CAN'T TELL WHICH ARE REAL!!
GAAAGH!!

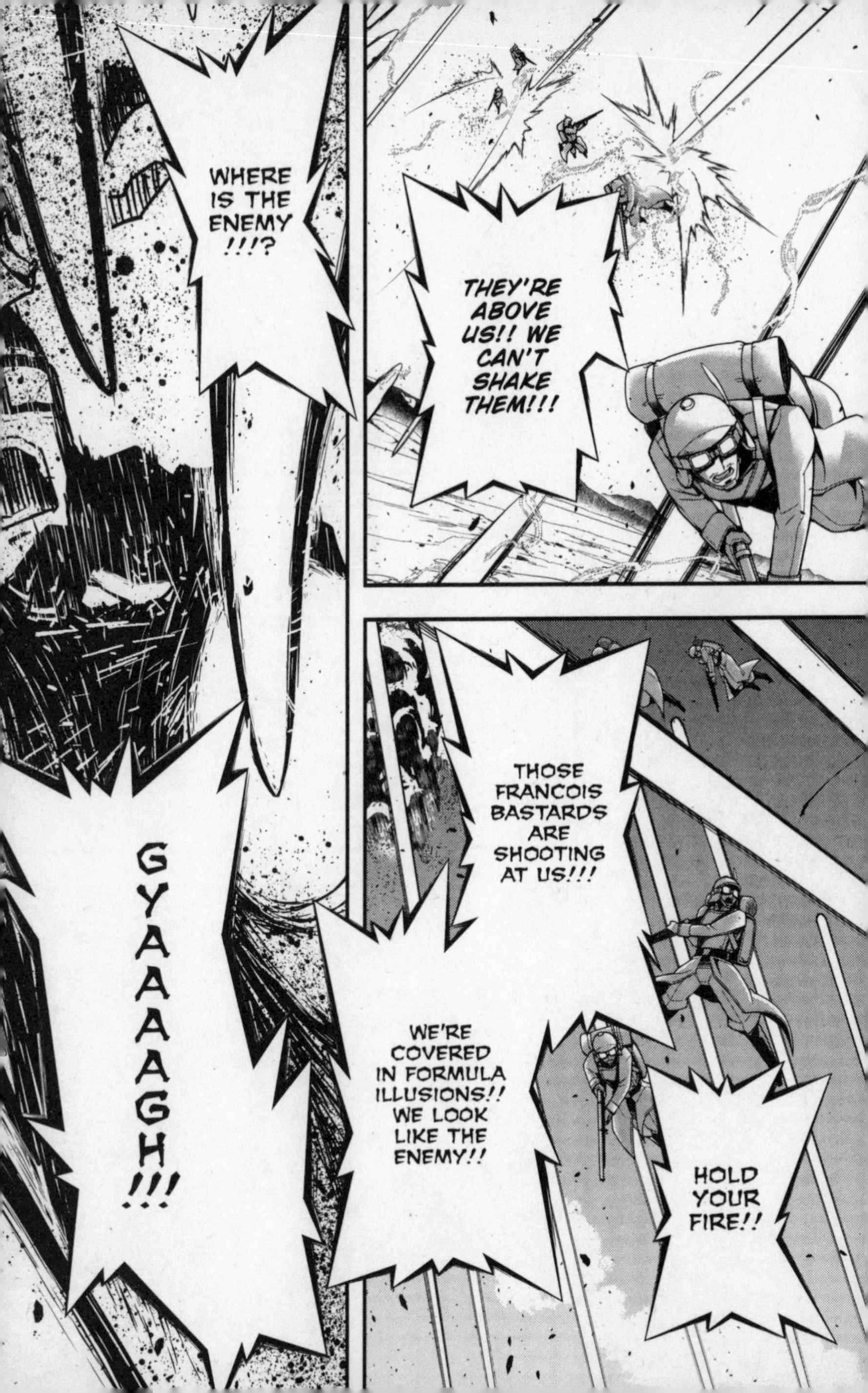
THEY'RE ABOVE US!! WE CAN'T SHAKE THEM!!!
THOSE FRANCOIS BASTARDS ARE SHOOTING AT US!!!
WE'RE COVERED IN FORMULA ILLUSIONS!! WE LOOK LIKE THE ENEMY!!
HOLD YOUR FIRE!!
WHERE IS THE ENEMY!!!?
GYAAAAGH!!!

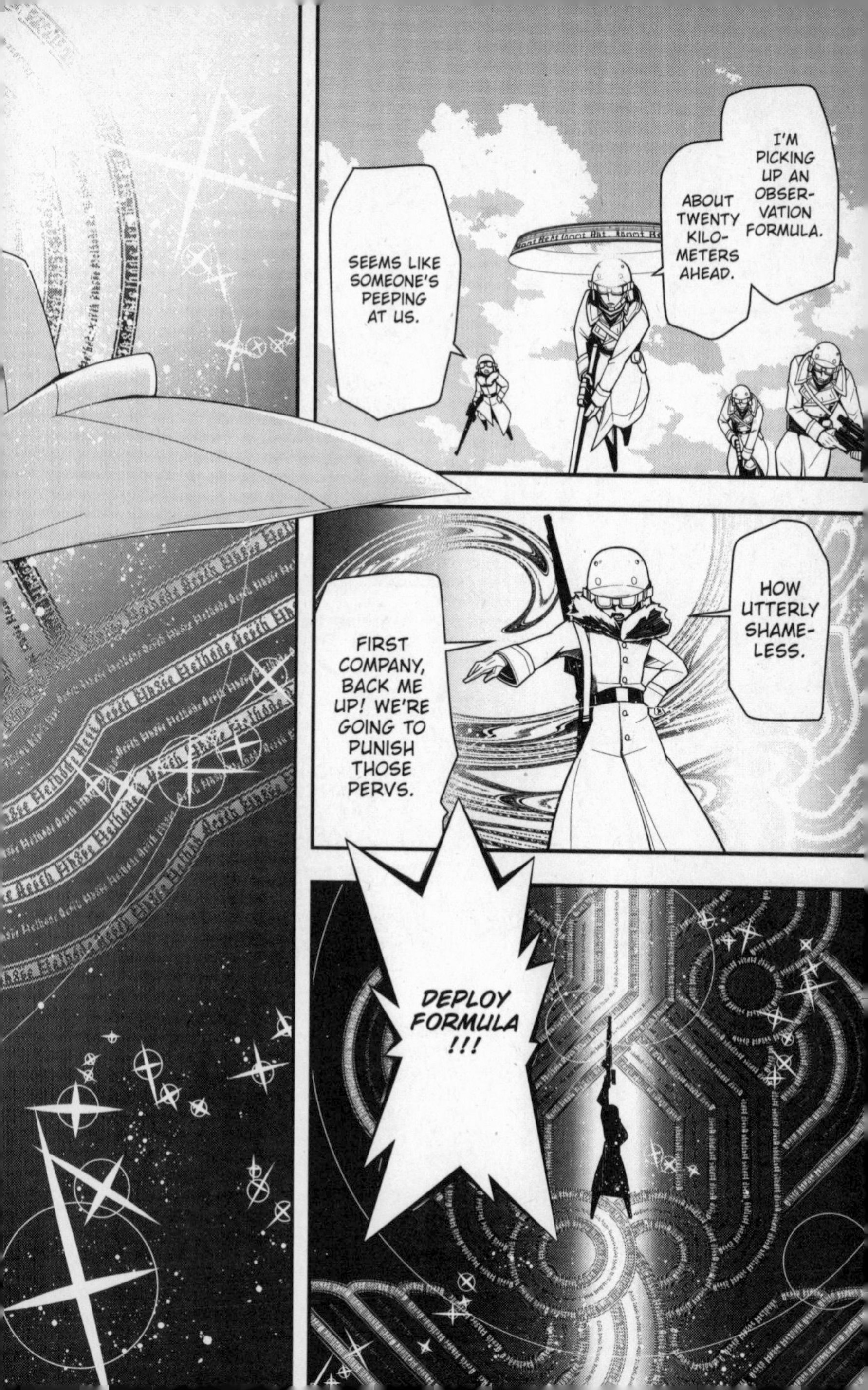
I'M PICKING UP AN OBSERVATION FORMULA.
ABOUT TWENTY KILOMETERS AHEAD.
SEEMS LIKE SOMEONE'S PEEPING AT US.
HOW UTTERLY SHAMELESS.
FIRST COMPANY, BACK ME UP! WE'RE GOING TO PUNISH THOSE PERVS.
DEPLOY FORMULA!!!

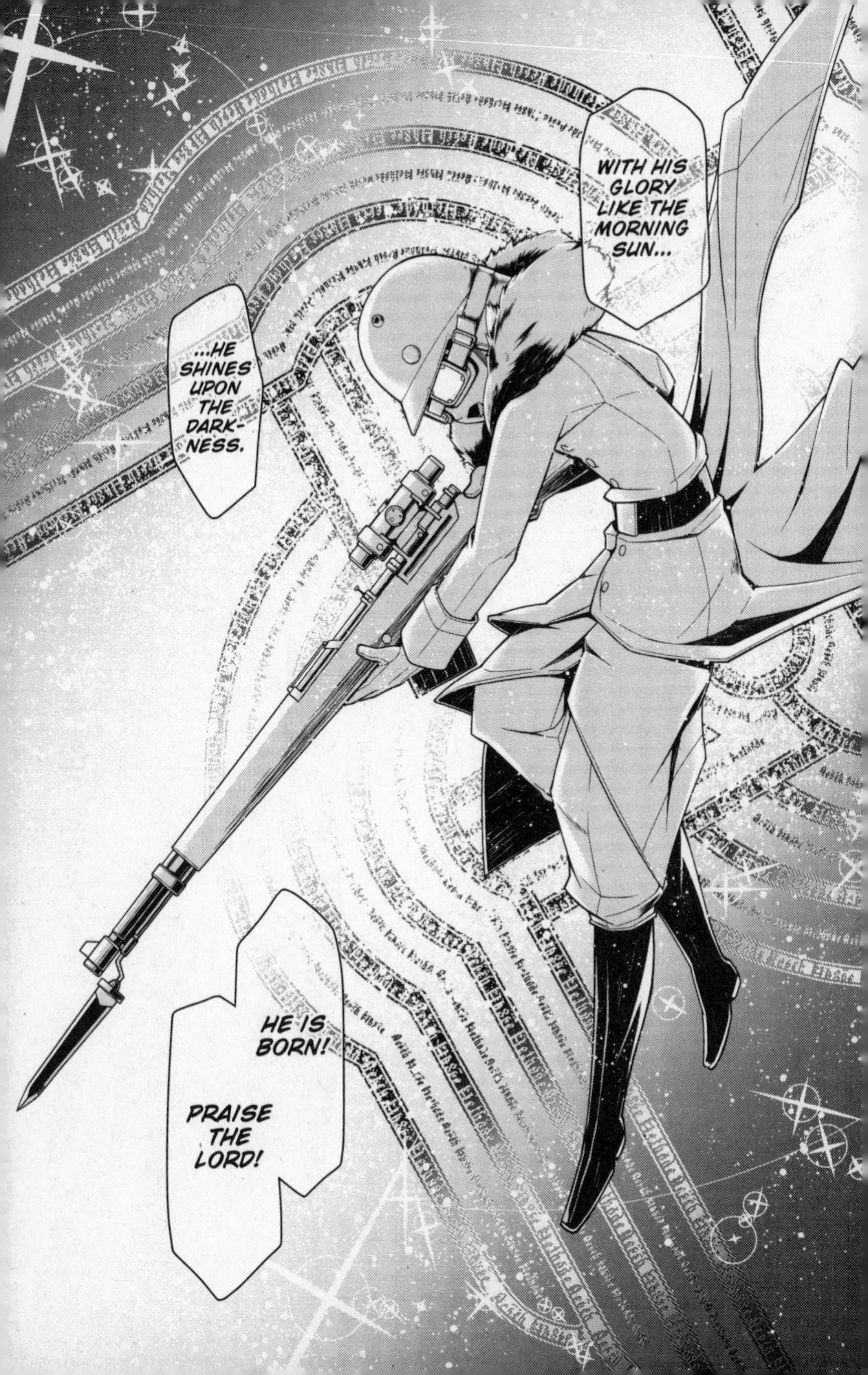
WITH HIS GLORY LIKE THE MORNING SUN...
...HE SHINES UPON THE DARK-NESS.
HE IS BORN!
PRAISE THE LORD!

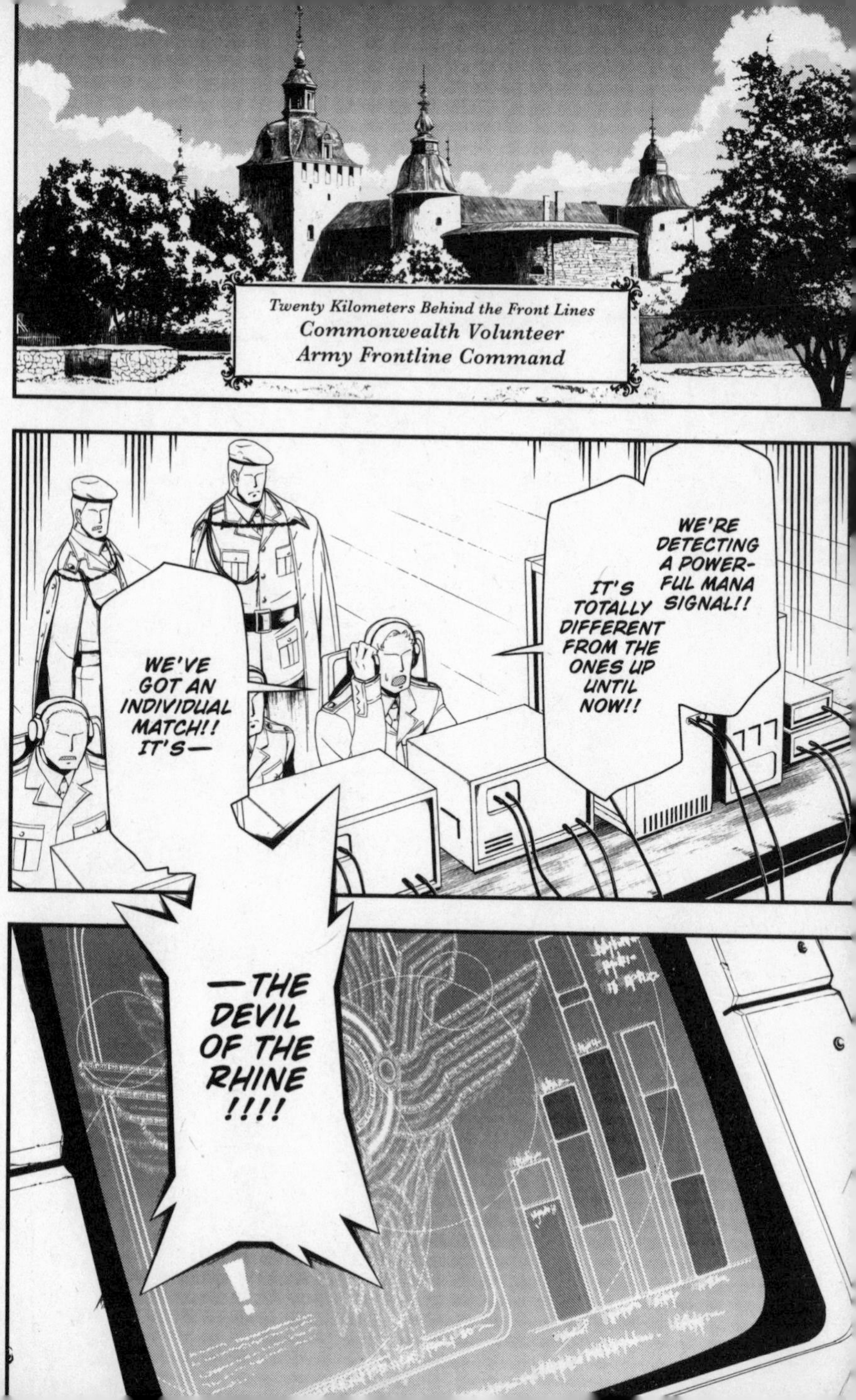
Twenty Kilometers Behind the Front Lines
Commonwealth Volunteer Army Frontline Command
WE'RE DETECTING A POWERFUL MANA SIGNAL!!
IT'S TOTALLY DIFFERENT FROM THE ONES UP UNTIL NOW!!
WE'VE GOT AN INDIVIDUAL MATCH!! IT'S—
—THE DEVIL OF THE RHINE!!!!

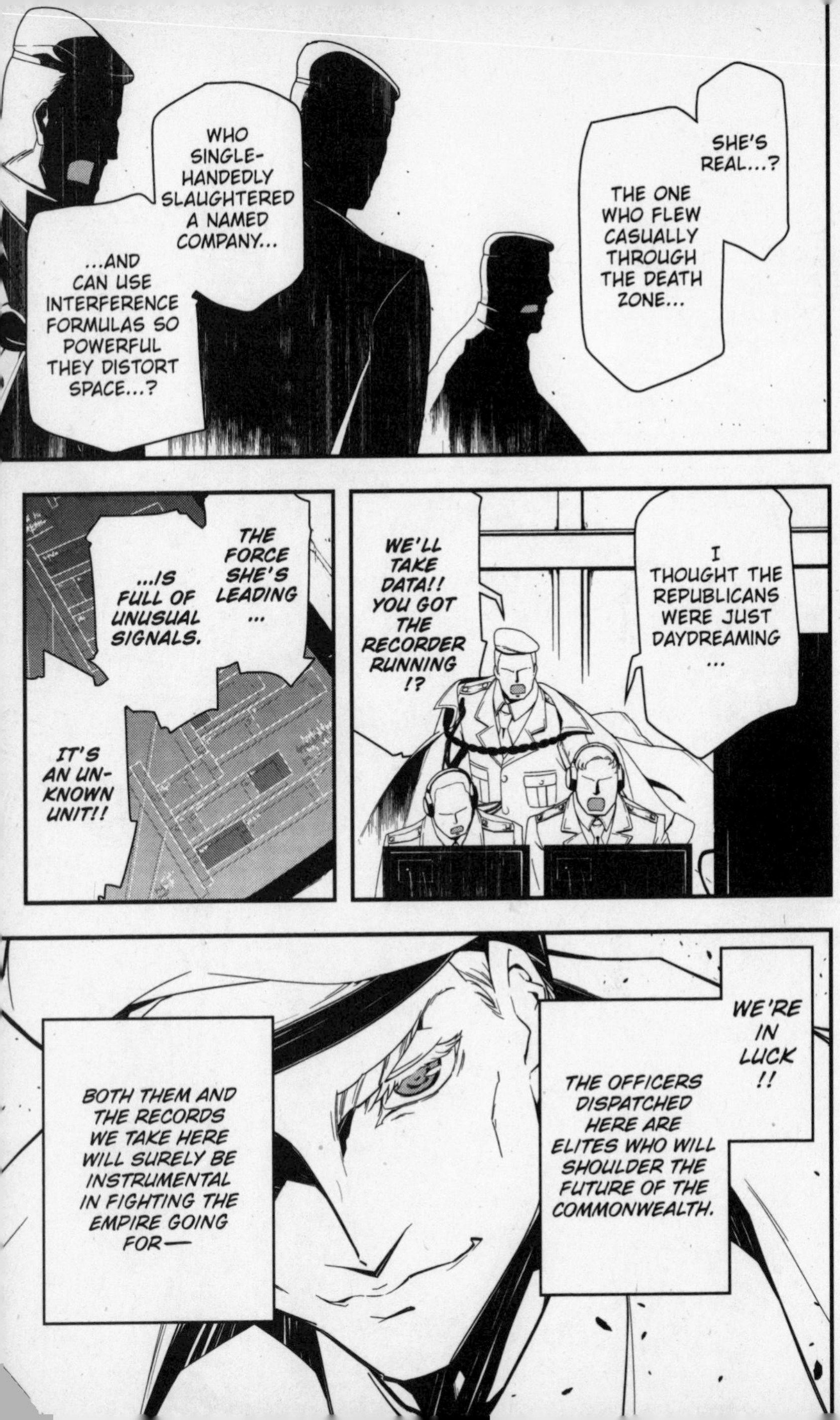
SHE'S REAL...?
THE ONE WHO FLEW CASUALLY THROUGH THE DEATH ZONE...
WHO SINGLE-HANDEDLY SLAUGHTERED A NAMED COMPANY...
...AND CAN USE INTERFERENCE FORMULAS SO POWERFUL THEY DISTORT SPACE...?
I THOUGHT THE REPUBLICANS WERE JUST DAYDREAMING...
WE'LL TAKE DATA!! YOU GOT THE RECORDER RUNNING!?
THE FORCE SHE'S LEADING...
...IS FULL OF UNUSUAL SIGNALS.
IT'S AN UNKNOWN UNIT!!
WE'RE IN LUCK!!
THE OFFICERS DISPATCHED HERE ARE ELITES WHO WILL SHOULDER THE FUTURE OF THE COMMONWEALTH.
BOTH THEM AND THE RECORDS WE TAKE HERE WILL SURELY BE INSTRUMENTAL IN FIGHTING THE EMPIRE GOING FOR—

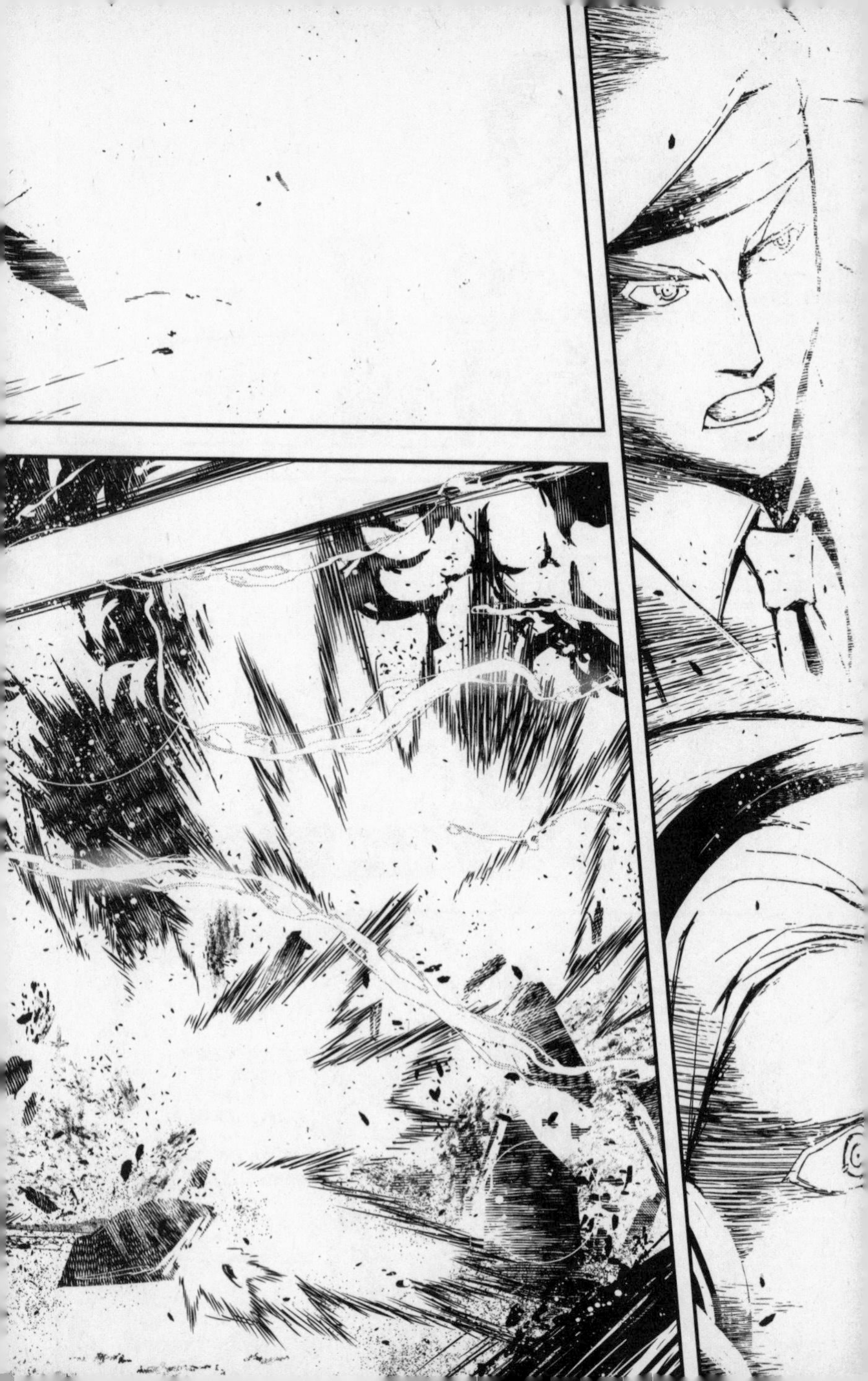

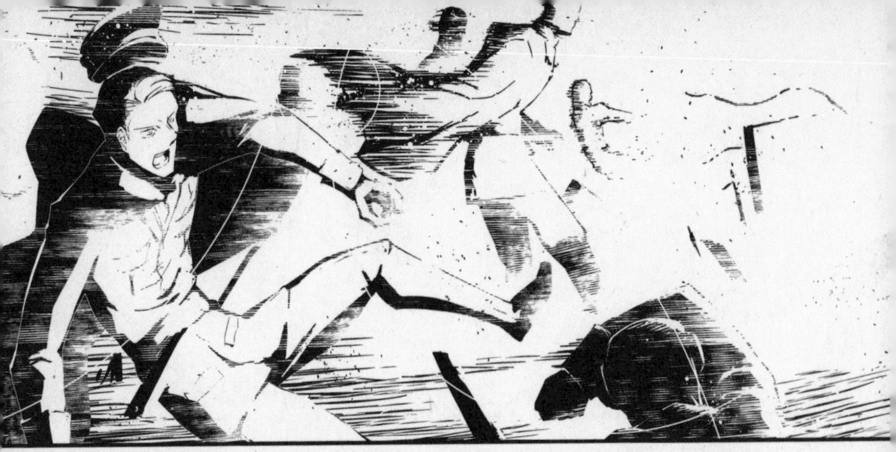

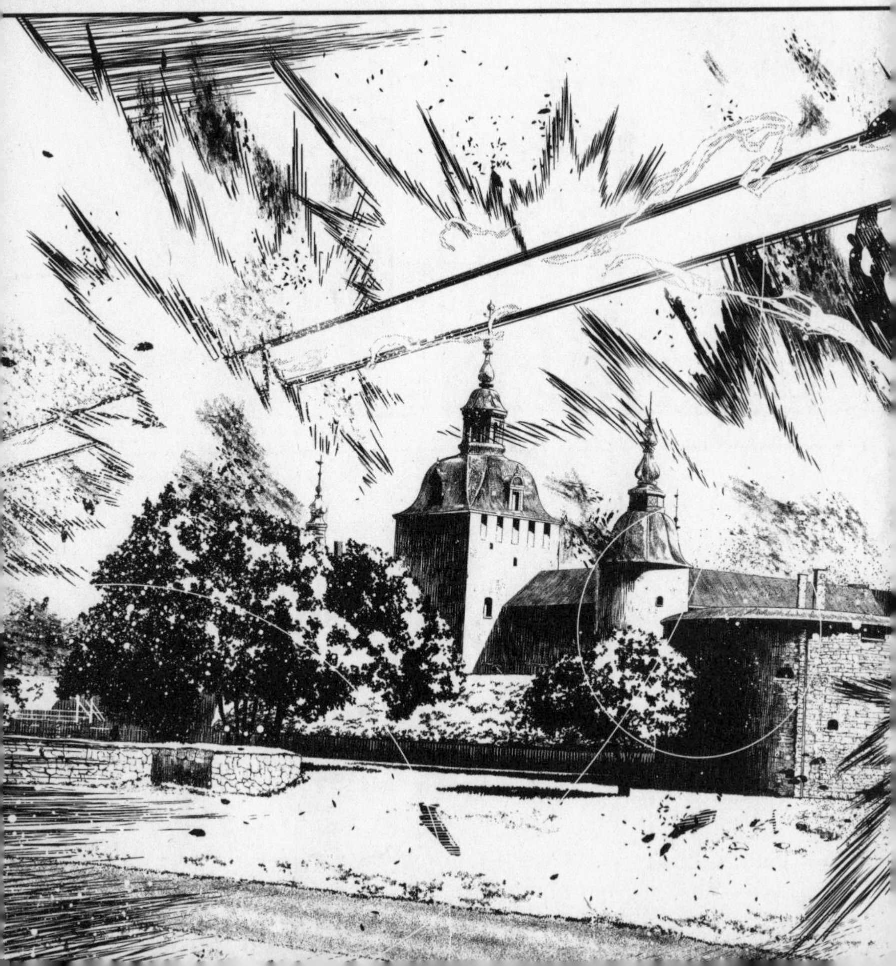

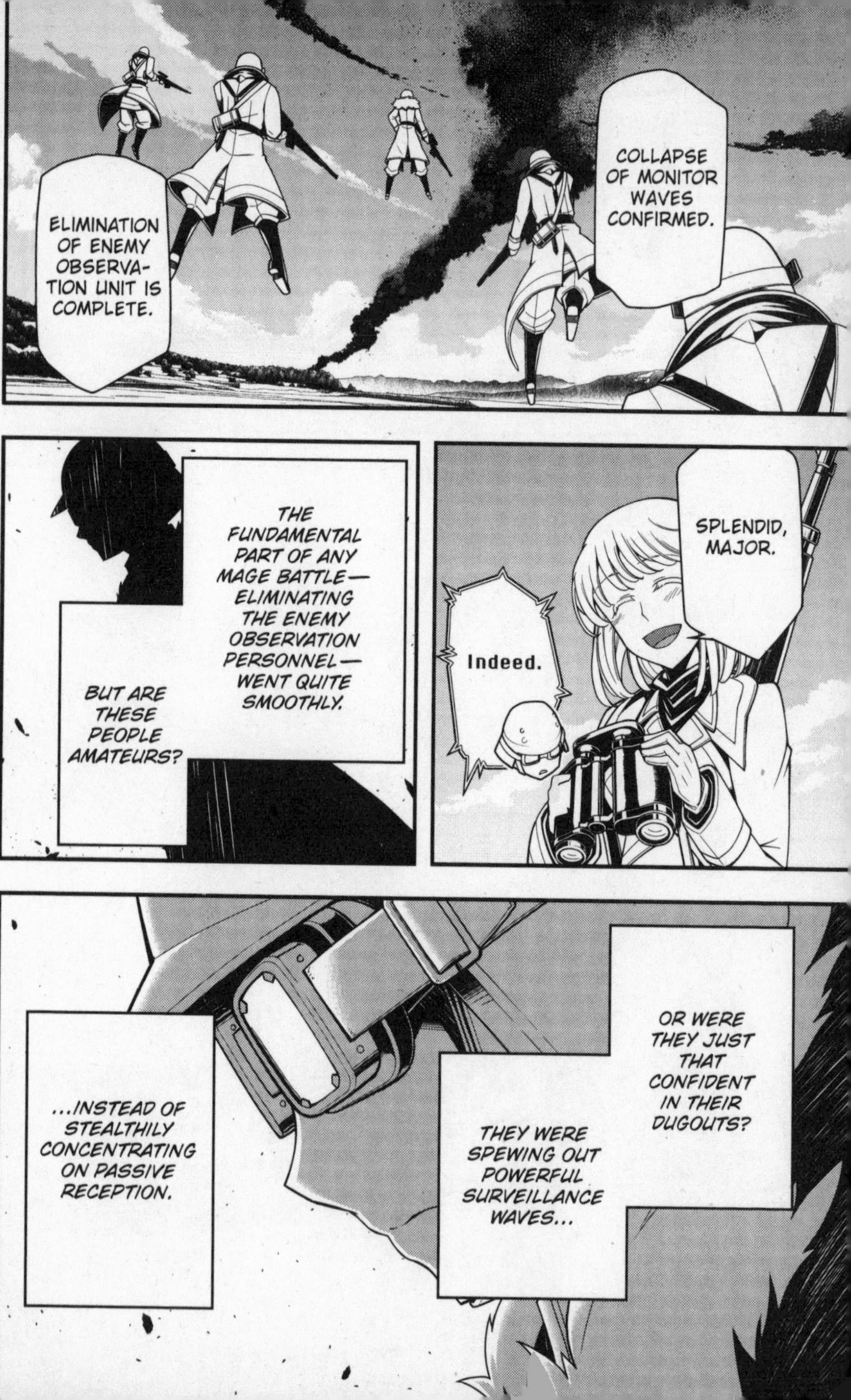
COLLAPSE OF MONITOR WAVES CONFIRMED.
ELIMINATION OF ENEMY OBSERVATION UNIT IS COMPLETE.
SPLENDID, MAJOR.
Indeed.
THE FUNDAMENTAL PART OF ANY MAGE BATTLE—ELIMINATING THE ENEMY OBSERVATION PERSONNEL—WENT QUITE SMOOTHLY.
BUT ARE THESE PEOPLE AMATEURS?
OR WERE THEY JUST THAT CONFIDENT IN THEIR DUGOUTS?
THEY WERE SPEWING OUT POWERFUL SURVEILLANCE WAVES...
...INSTEAD OF STEALTHILY CONCENTRATING ON PASSIVE RECEPTION.

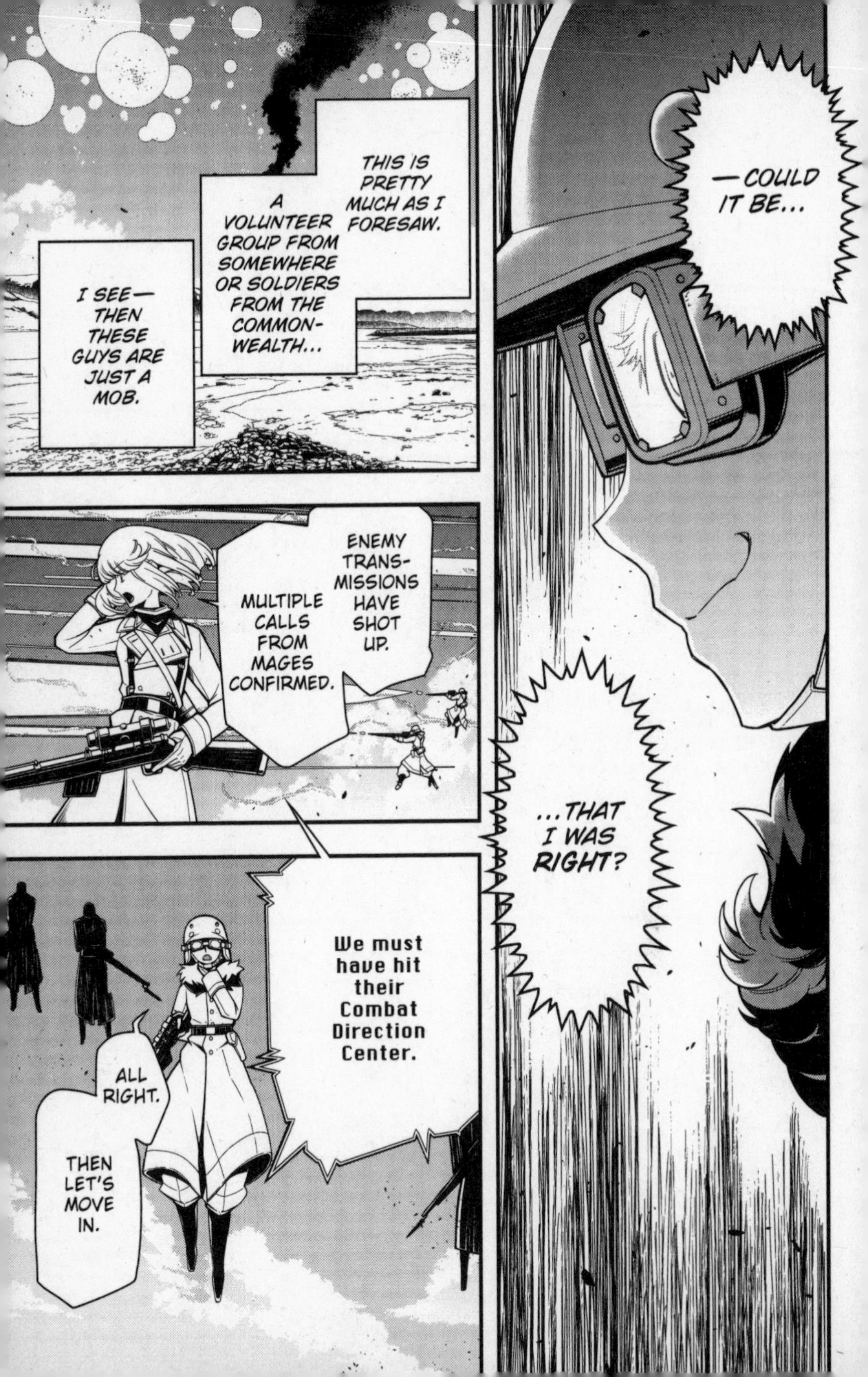
—COULD IT BE...
...THAT I WAS RIGHT?
THIS IS PRETTY MUCH AS I FORESAW.
A VOLUNTEER GROUP FROM SOMEWHERE OR SOLDIERS FROM THE COMMONWEALTH...
I SEE—THEN THESE GUYS ARE JUST A MOB.
ENEMY TRANSMISSIONS HAVE SHOT UP.
MULTIPLE CALLS FROM MAGES CONFIRMED.
We must have hit their Combat Direction Center.
ALL RIGHT.
THEN LET'S MOVE IN.

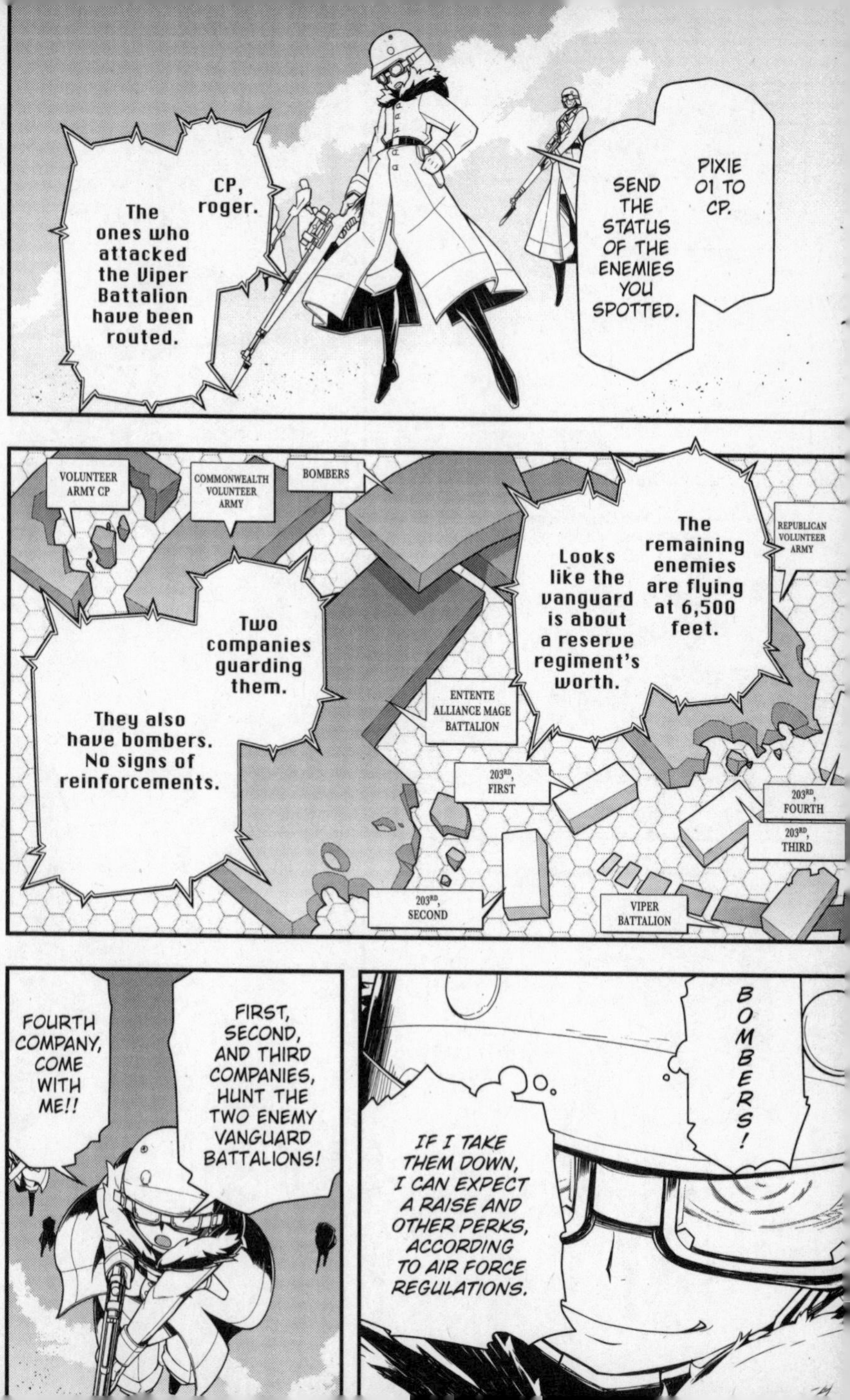
PIXIE 01 TO CP.
SEND THE STATUS OF THE ENEMIES YOU SPOTTED.
CP, roger.
The ones who attacked the Viper Battalion have been routed.
The remaining enemies are flying at 6,500 feet.
Looks like the vanguard is about a reserve regiment's worth.
Two companies guarding them.
They also have bombers. No signs of reinforcements.
REPUBLICAN VOLUNTEER ARMY
BOMBERS
COMMONWEALTH VOLUNTEER ARMY
VOLUNTEER ARMY CP
ENTENTE ALLIANCE MAGE BATTALION
203RD, FIRST
203RD, FOURTH
203RD, THIRD
VIPER BATTALION
203RD, SECOND
BOMBERS!
IF I TAKE THEM DOWN, I CAN EXPECT A RAISE AND OTHER PERKS, ACCORDING TO AIR FORCE REGULATIONS.
FIRST, SECOND, AND THIRD COMPANIES, HUNT THE TWO ENEMY VANGUARD BATTALIONS!
FOURTH COMPANY, COME WITH ME!!

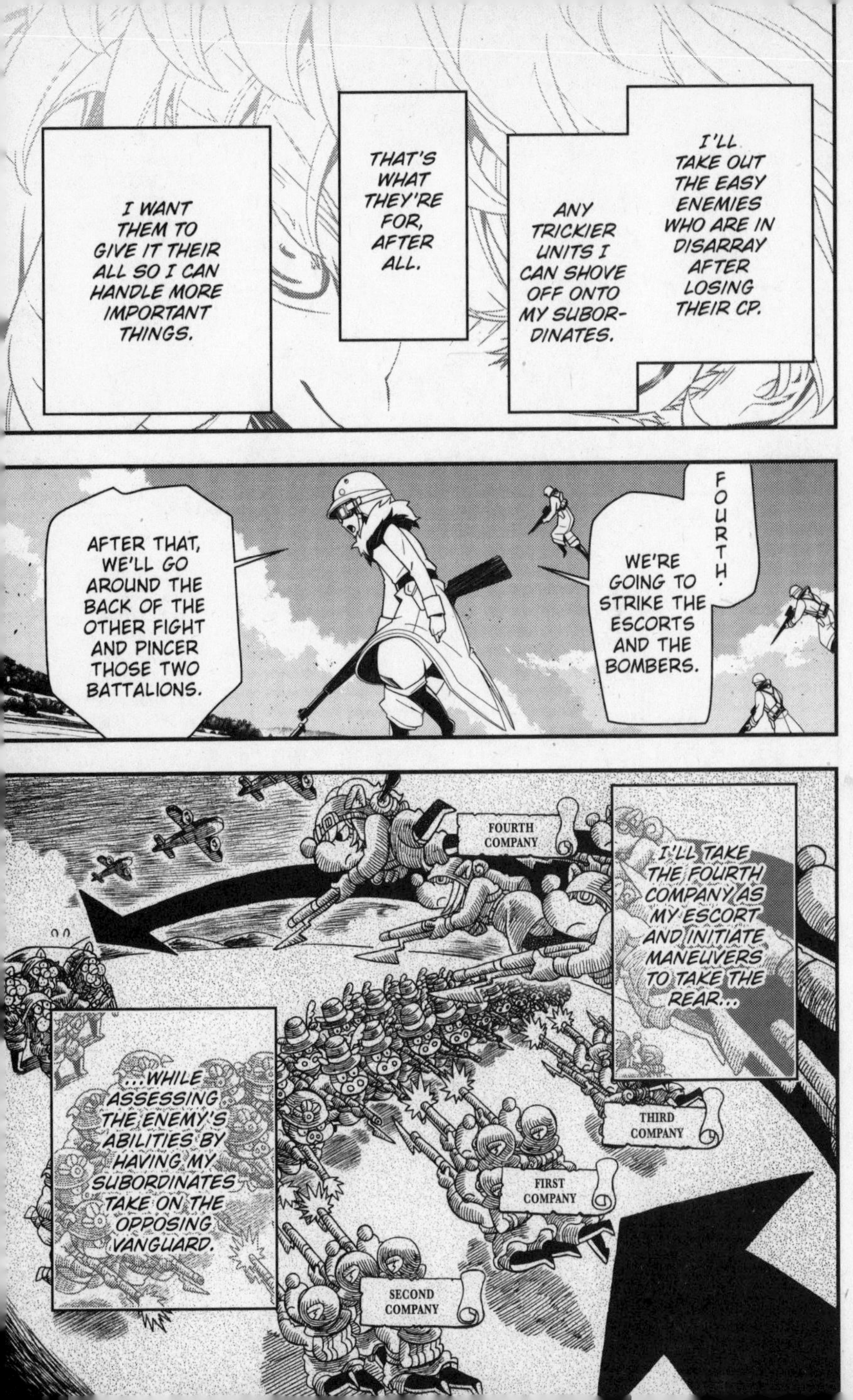
I'LL TAKE OUT THE EASY ENEMIES WHO ARE IN DISARRAY AFTER LOSING THEIR CP.
ANY TRICKIER UNITS I CAN SHOVE OFF ONTO MY SUBORDINATES.
THAT'S WHAT THEY'RE FOR, AFTER ALL.
I WANT THEM TO GIVE IT THEIR ALL SO I CAN HANDLE MORE IMPORTANT THINGS.
FOURTH.
WE'RE GOING TO STRIKE THE ESCORTS AND THE BOMBERS.
AFTER THAT, WE'LL GO AROUND THE BACK OF THE OTHER FIGHT AND PINCER THOSE TWO BATTALIONS.
I'LL TAKE THE FOURTH COMPANY AS MY ESCORT AND INITIATE MANEUVERS TO TAKE THE REAR...
FOURTH COMPANY
THIRD COMPANY
FIRST COMPANY
SECOND COMPANY
...WHILE ASSESSING THE ENEMY'S ABILITIES BY HAVING MY SUBORDINATES TAKE ON THE OPPOSING VANGUARD.

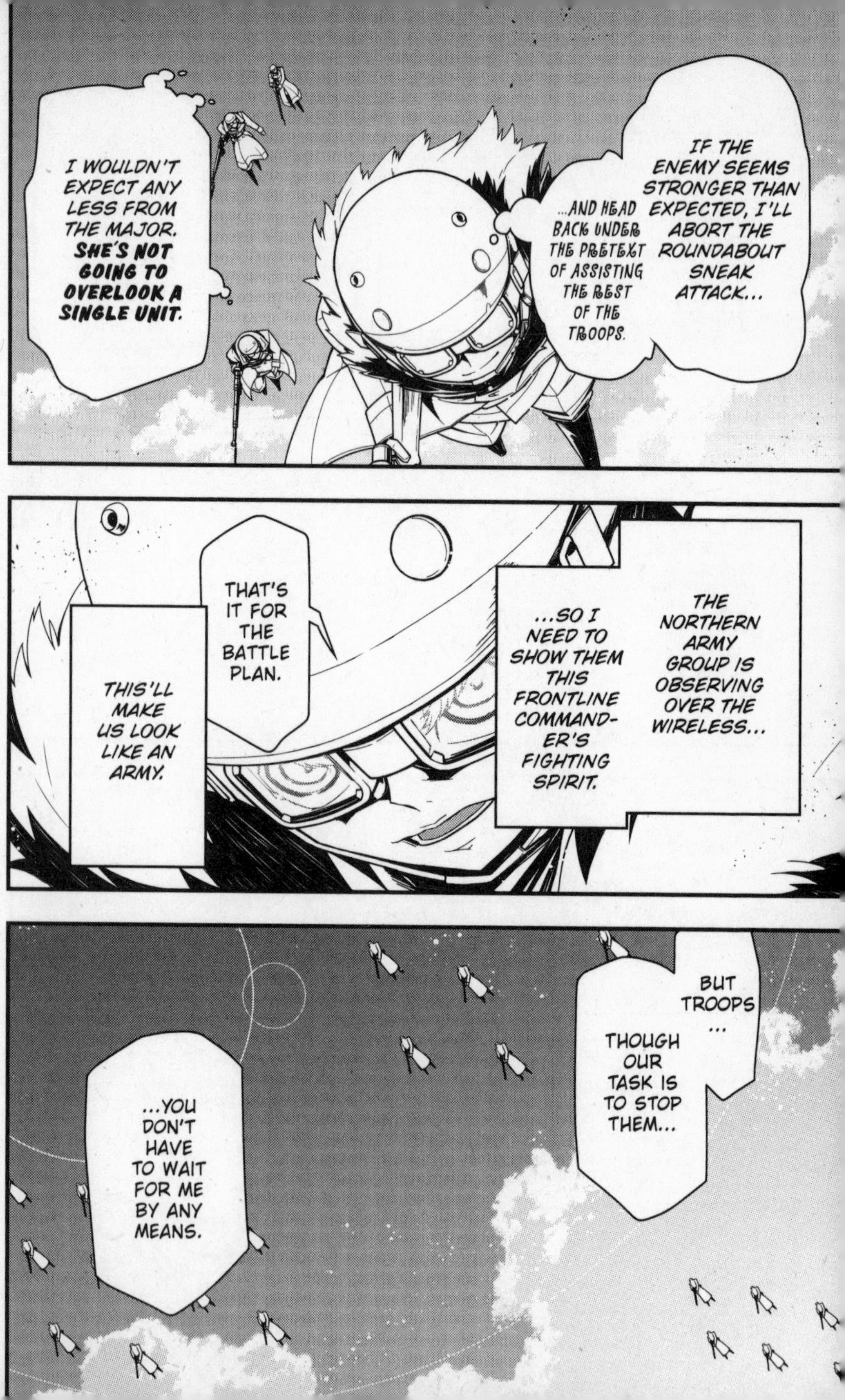
IF THE ENEMY SEEMS STRONGER THAN EXPECTED, I'LL ABORT THE ROUNDABOUT SNEAK ATTACK...
...AND HEAD BACK UNDER THE PRETEXT OF ASSISTING THE REST OF THE TROOPS.
I WOULDN'T EXPECT ANY LESS FROM THE MAJOR. SHE'S NOT GOING TO OVERLOOK A SINGLE UNIT.
THE NORTHERN ARMY GROUP IS OBSERVING OVER THE WIRELESS...
...SO I NEED TO SHOW THEM THIS FRONTLINE COMMANDER'S FIGHTING SPIRIT.
THAT'S IT FOR THE BATTLE PLAN.
THIS'LL MAKE US LOOK LIKE AN ARMY.
BUT TROOPS...
THOUGH OUR TASK IS TO STOP THEM...
...YOU DON'T HAVE TO WAIT FOR ME BY ANY MEANS.

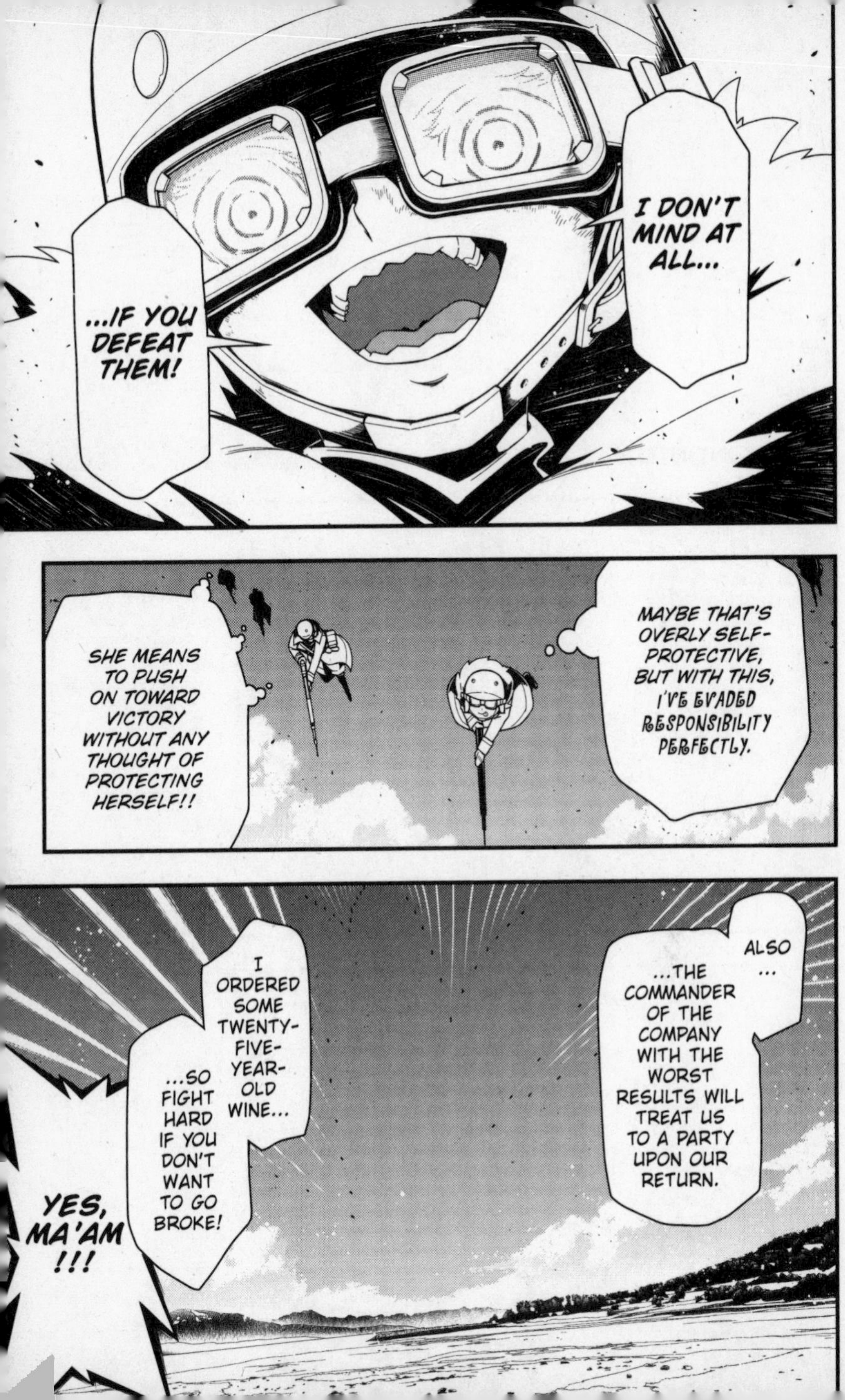
I DON'T MIND AT ALL...
...IF YOU DEFEAT THEM!
MAYBE THAT'S OVERLY SELF-PROTECTIVE, BUT WITH THIS, I'VE EVADED RESPONSIBILITY PERFECTLY.
SHE MEANS TO PUSH ON TOWARD VICTORY WITHOUT ANY THOUGHT OF PROTECTING HERSELF!!
ALSO...
...THE COMMANDER OF THE COMPANY WITH THE WORST RESULTS WILL TREAT US TO A PARTY UPON OUR RETURN.
I ORDERED SOME TWENTY-FIVE-YEAR-OLD WINE...
...SO FIGHT HARD IF YOU DON'T WANT TO GO BROKE!
YES, MA'AM!!!

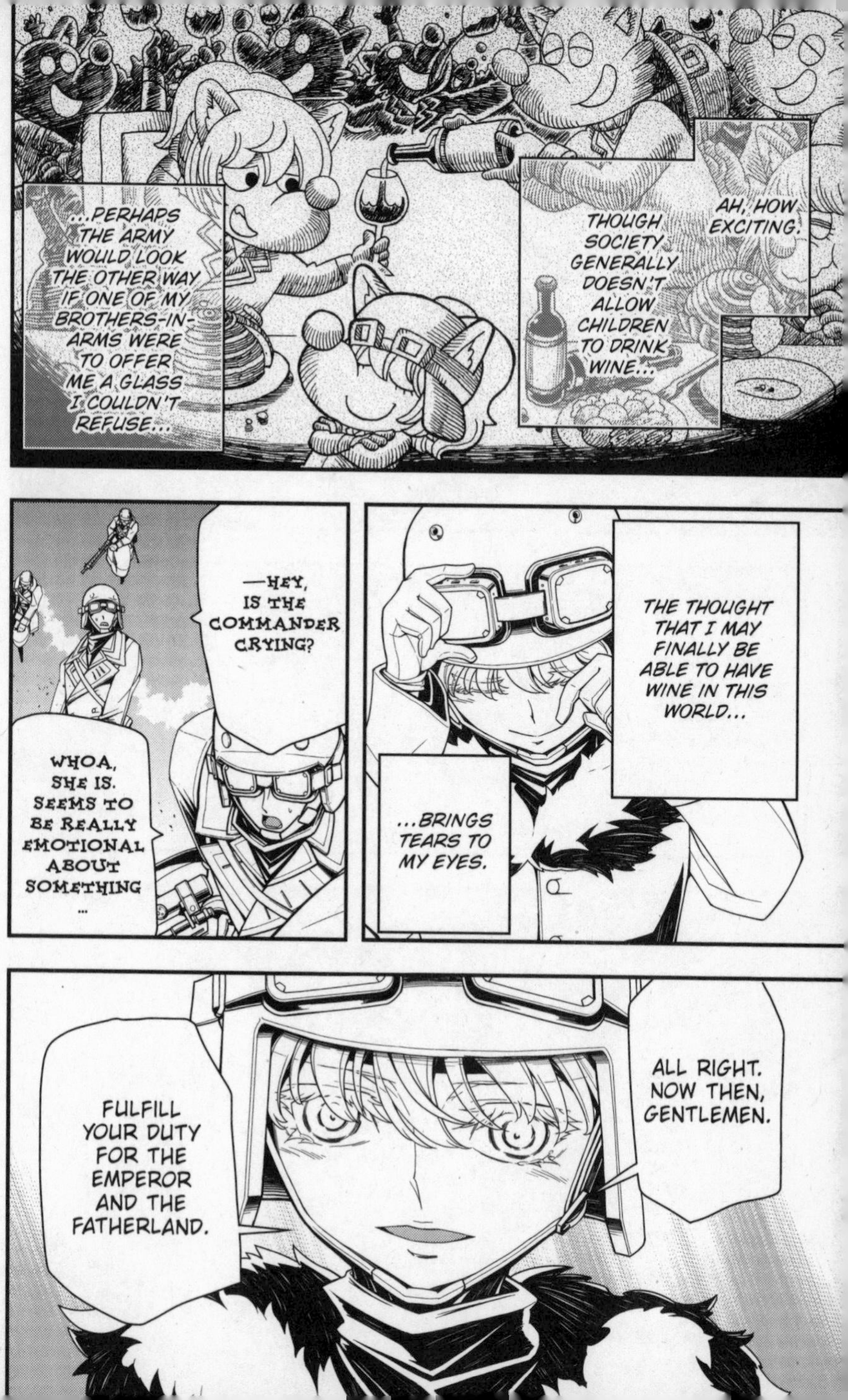
AH, HOW EXCITING.
THOUGH SOCIETY GENERALLY DOESN'T ALLOW CHILDREN TO DRINK WINE...
...PERHAPS THE ARMY WOULD LOOK THE OTHER WAY IF ONE OF MY BROTHERS-IN-ARMS WERE TO OFFER ME A GLASS I COULDN'T REFUSE...
THE THOUGHT THAT I MAY FINALLY BE ABLE TO HAVE WINE IN THIS WORLD...
...BRINGS TEARS TO MY EYES.
—HEY, IS THE COMMANDER CRYING?
WHOA, SHE IS. SEEMS TO BE REALLY EMOTIONAL ABOUT SOMETHING...
ALL RIGHT. NOW THEN, GENTLEMEN.
FULFILL YOUR DUTY FOR THE EMPEROR AND THE FATHERLAND.

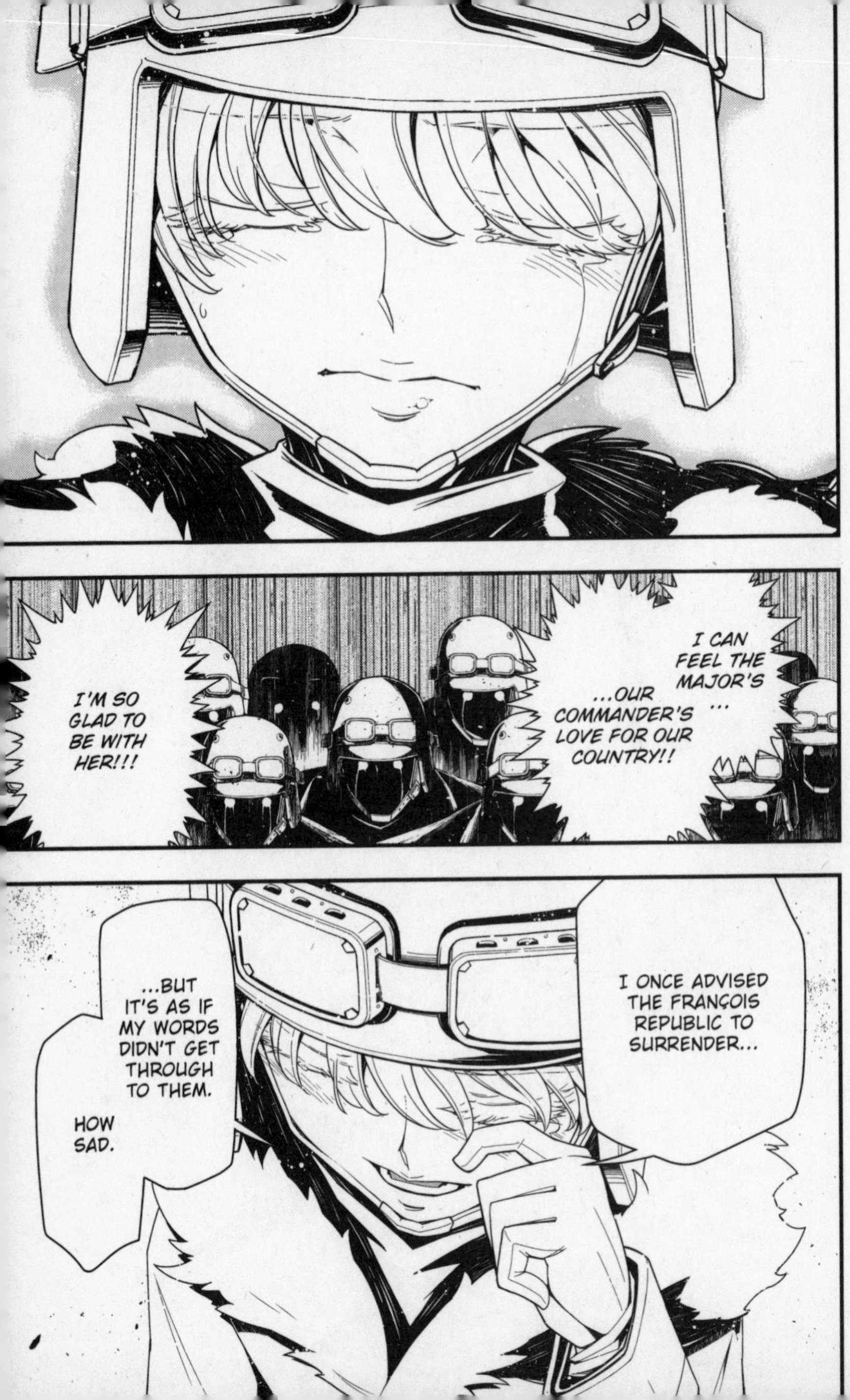
I CAN FEEL THE MAJOR'S ...
...OUR COMMANDER'S LOVE FOR OUR COUNTRY!!
I'M SO GLAD TO BE WITH HER!!!
I ONCE ADVISED THE FRANÇOIS REPUBLIC TO SURRENDER...
...BUT IT'S AS IF MY WORDS DIDN'T GET THROUGH TO THEM.
HOW SAD.

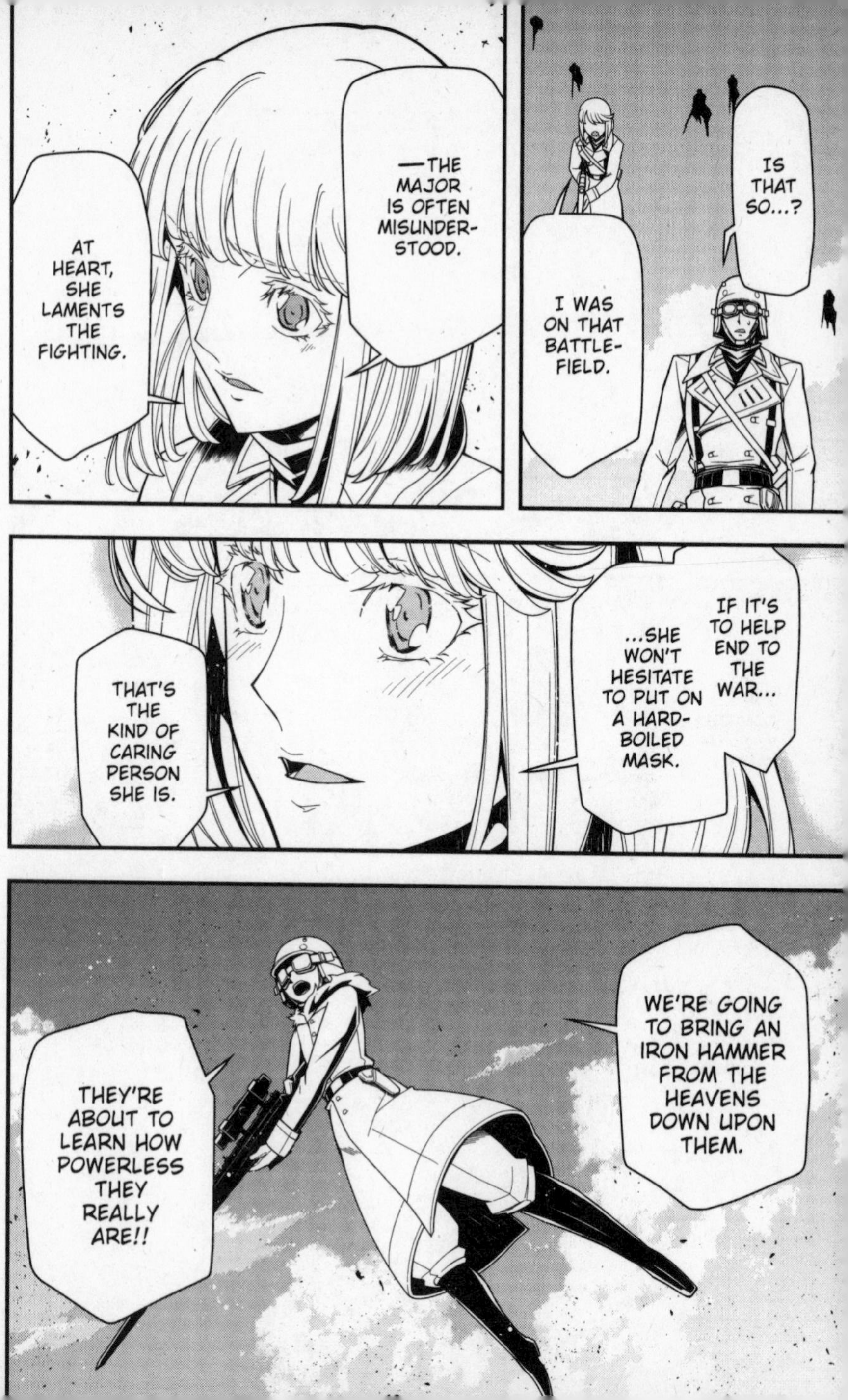
IS THAT SO...?
I WAS ON THAT BATTLE-FIELD.
—THE MAJOR IS OFTEN MISUNDER-STOOD.
AT HEART, SHE LAMENTS THE FIGHTING.
IF IT'S TO HELP END TO THE WAR...
...SHE WON'T HESITATE TO PUT ON A HARD-BOILED MASK.
THAT'S THE KIND OF CARING PERSON SHE IS.
WE'RE GOING TO BRING AN IRON HAMMER FROM THE HEAVENS DOWN UPON THEM.
THEY'RE ABOUT TO LEARN HOW POWERLESS THEY REALLY ARE!!

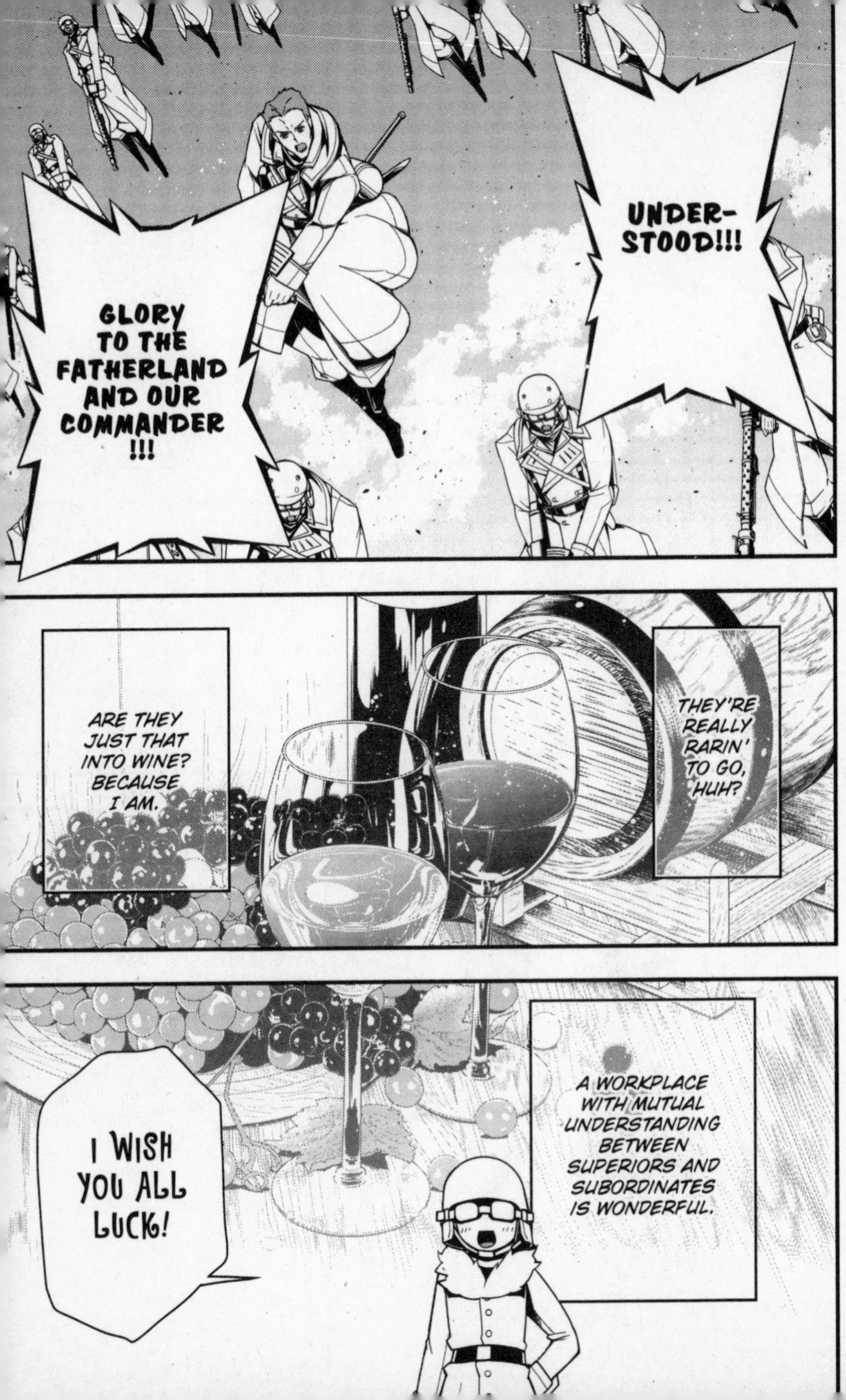
UNDERSTOOD!!!
GLORY TO THE FATHERLAND AND OUR COMMANDER!!!
THEY'RE REALLY RARIN' TO GO, HUH?
ARE THEY JUST THAT INTO WINE? BECAUSE I AM.
A WORKPLACE WITH MUTUAL UNDERSTANDING BETWEEN SUPERIORS AND SUBORDINATES IS WONDERFUL.
I WISH YOU ALL LUCK!

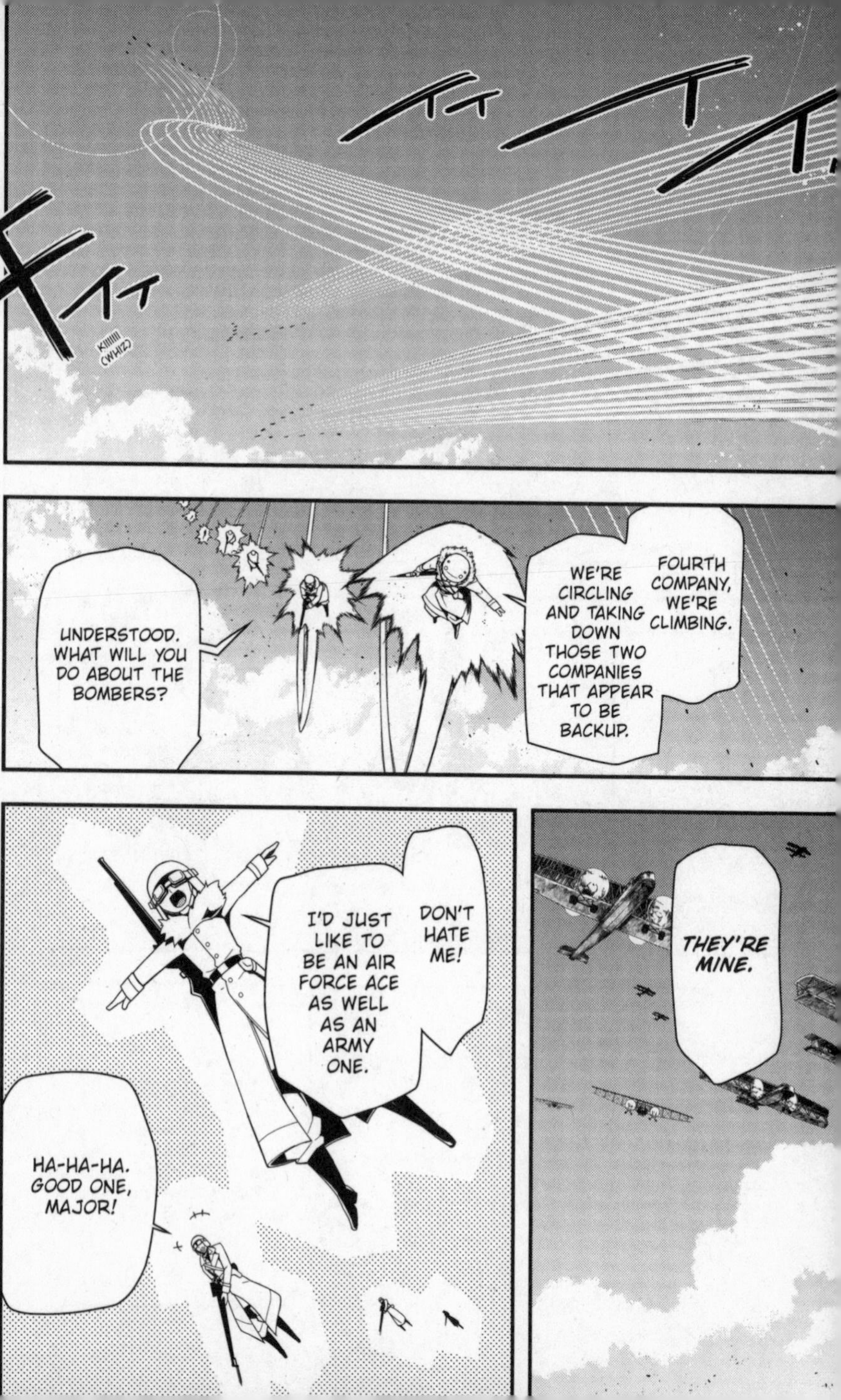
KIIIIII (WHIZ)
FOURTH COMPANY, WE'RE CLIMBING.
WE'RE CIRCLING AND TAKING DOWN THOSE TWO COMPANIES THAT APPEAR TO BE BACKUP.
UNDERSTOOD. WHAT WILL YOU DO ABOUT THE BOMBERS?
THEY'RE MINE.
DON'T HATE ME!
I'D JUST LIKE TO BE AN AIR FORCE ACE AS WELL AS AN ARMY ONE.
HA-HA-HA. GOOD ONE, MAJOR!

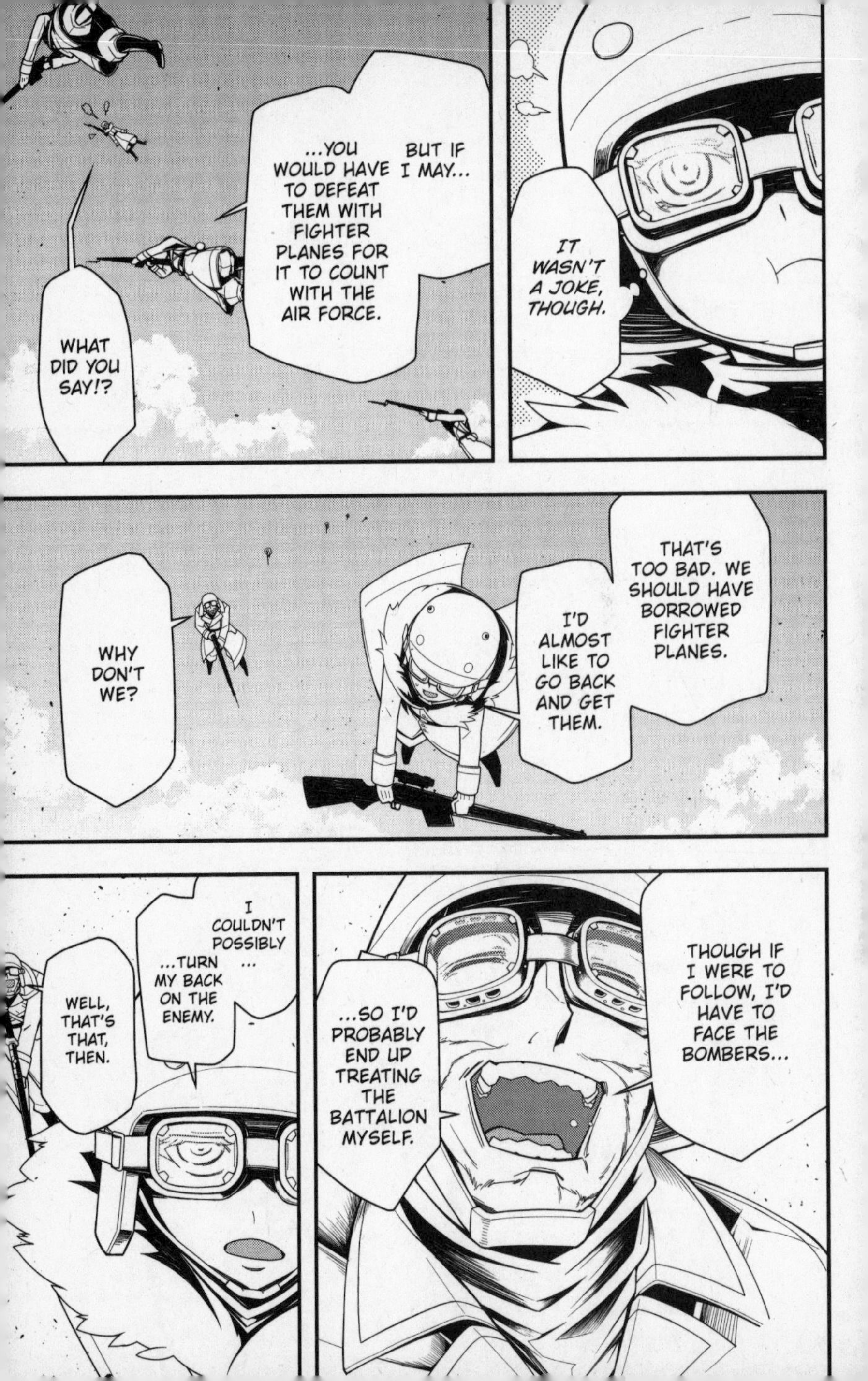
IT WASN'T A JOKE, THOUGH.
BUT IF I MAY...
...YOU WOULD HAVE TO DEFEAT THEM WITH FIGHTER PLANES FOR IT TO COUNT WITH THE AIR FORCE.
WHAT DID YOU SAY!?
THAT'S TOO BAD. WE SHOULD HAVE BORROWED FIGHTER PLANES.
I'D ALMOST LIKE TO GO BACK AND GET THEM.
WHY DON'T WE?
THOUGH IF I WERE TO FOLLOW, I'D HAVE TO FACE THE BOMBERS...
...SO I'D PROBABLY END UP TREATING THE BATTALION MYSELF.
I COULDN'T POSSIBLY ...
...TURN MY BACK ON THE ENEMY.
WELL, THAT'S THAT, THEN.

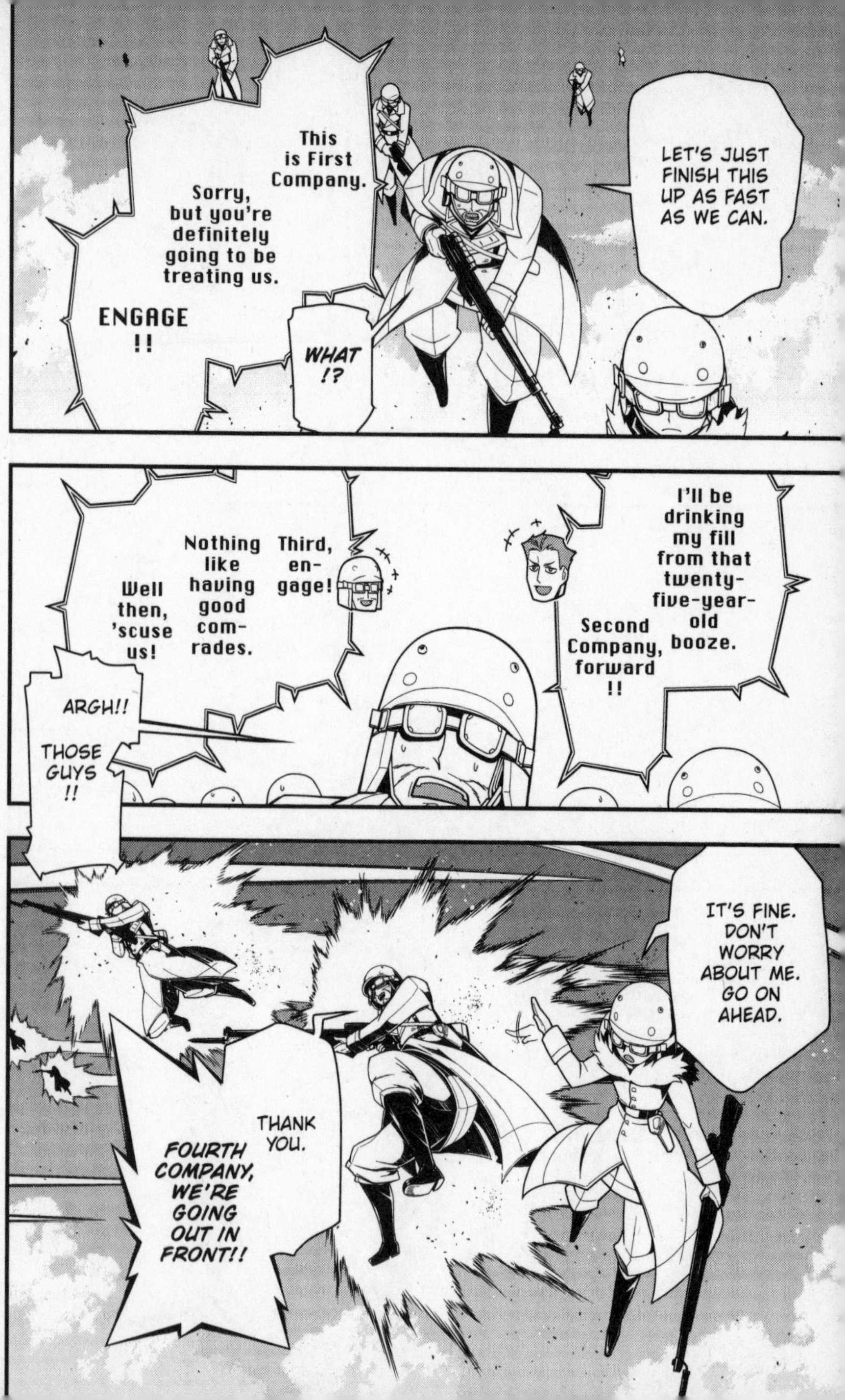
LET'S JUST FINISH THIS UP AS FAST AS WE CAN.
This is First Company.
Sorry, but you're definitely going to be treating us.
ENGAGE!!
WHAT!?
I'll be drinking my fill from that twenty-five-year-old booze.
Second Company, forward!!
Third, engage!
Nothing like having good comrades.
Well then, 'scuse us!
ARGH!!
THOSE GUYS!!
IT'S FINE. DON'T WORRY ABOUT ME. GO ON AHEAD.
THANK YOU.
FOURTH COMPANY, WE'RE GOING OUT IN FRONT!!

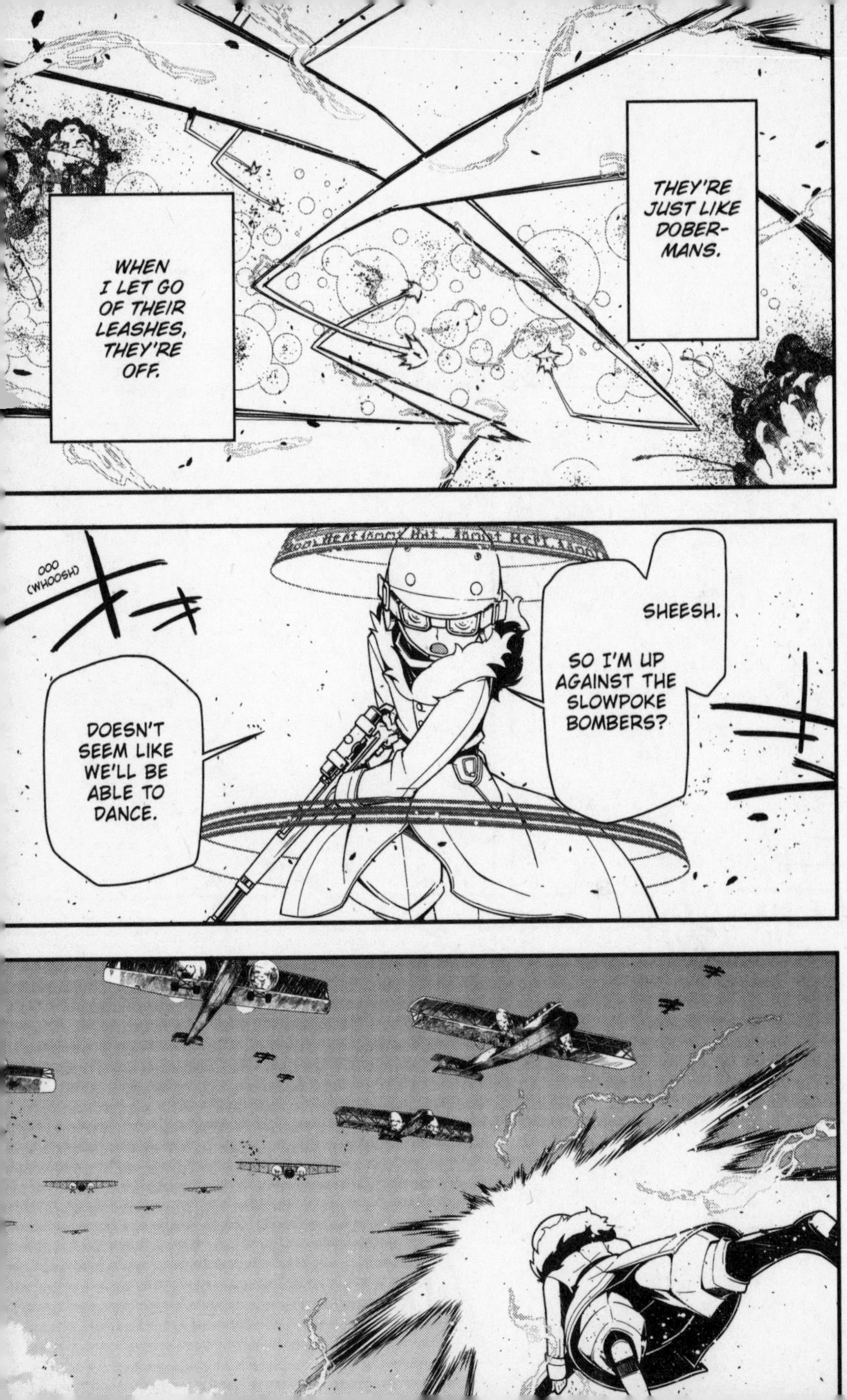
THEY'RE JUST LIKE DOBER-MANS.
WHEN I LET GO OF THEIR LEASHES, THEY'RE OFF.
SHEESH.
SO I'M UP AGAINST THE SLOWPOKE BOMBERS?
OOO (WHOOSH)
DOESN'T SEEM LIKE WE'LL BE ABLE TO DANCE.

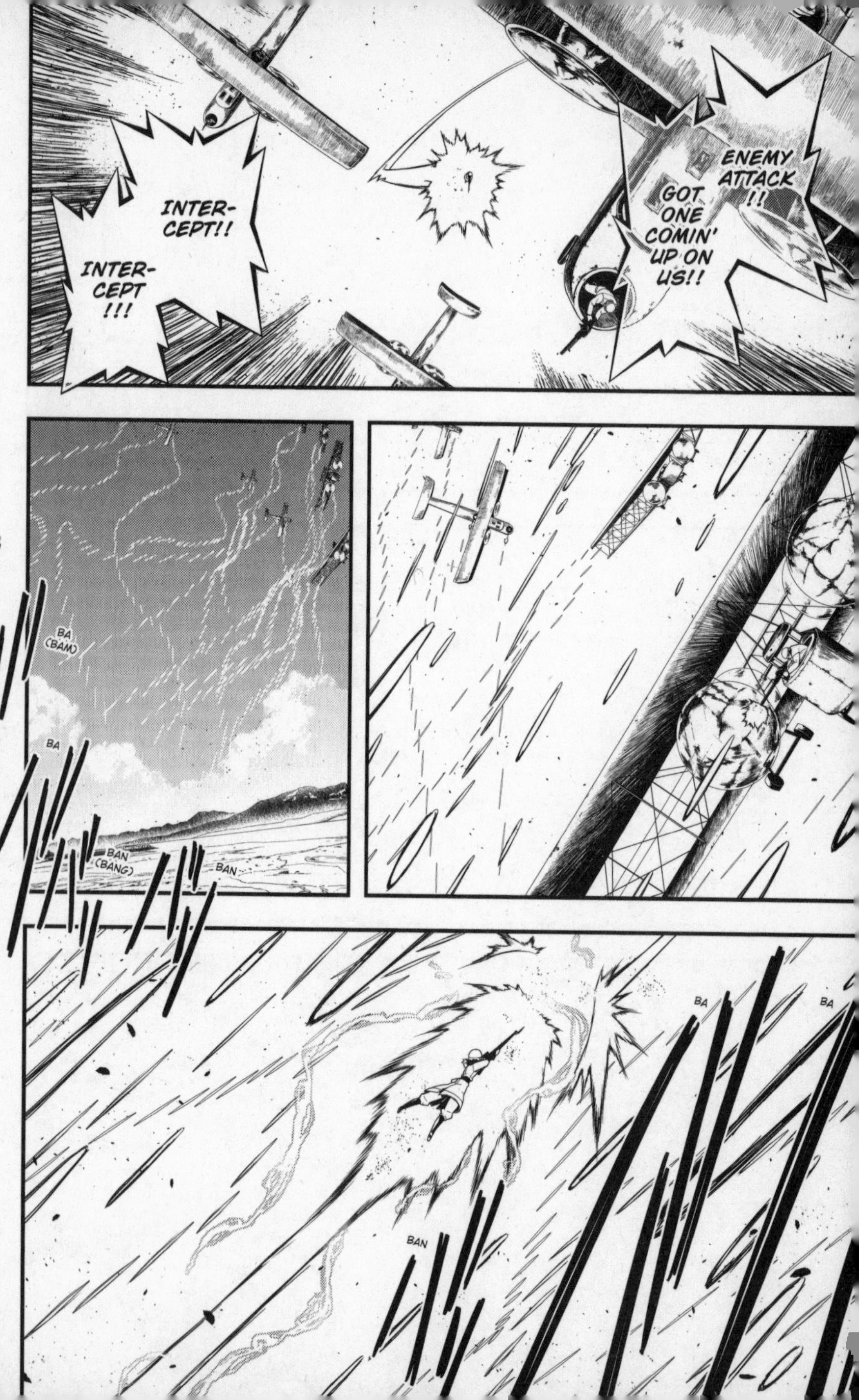
ENEMY ATTACK!!
GOT ONE COMIN' UP ON US!!
INTER-CEPT!!
INTER-CEPT!!!
BA (BAM)
BA
BAN (BANG)
BAN
BA
BA
BAN

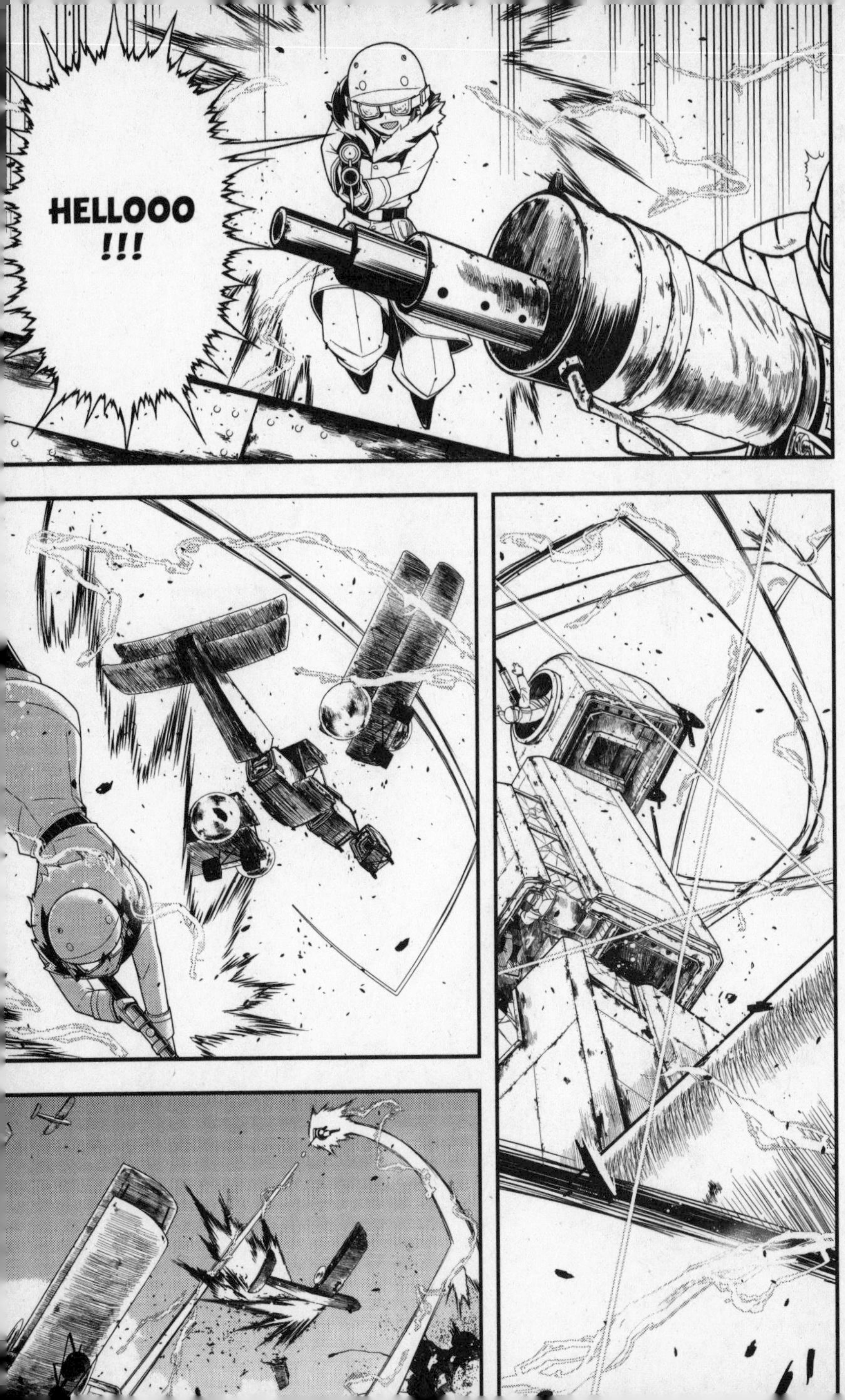
HELLOOO
!!!

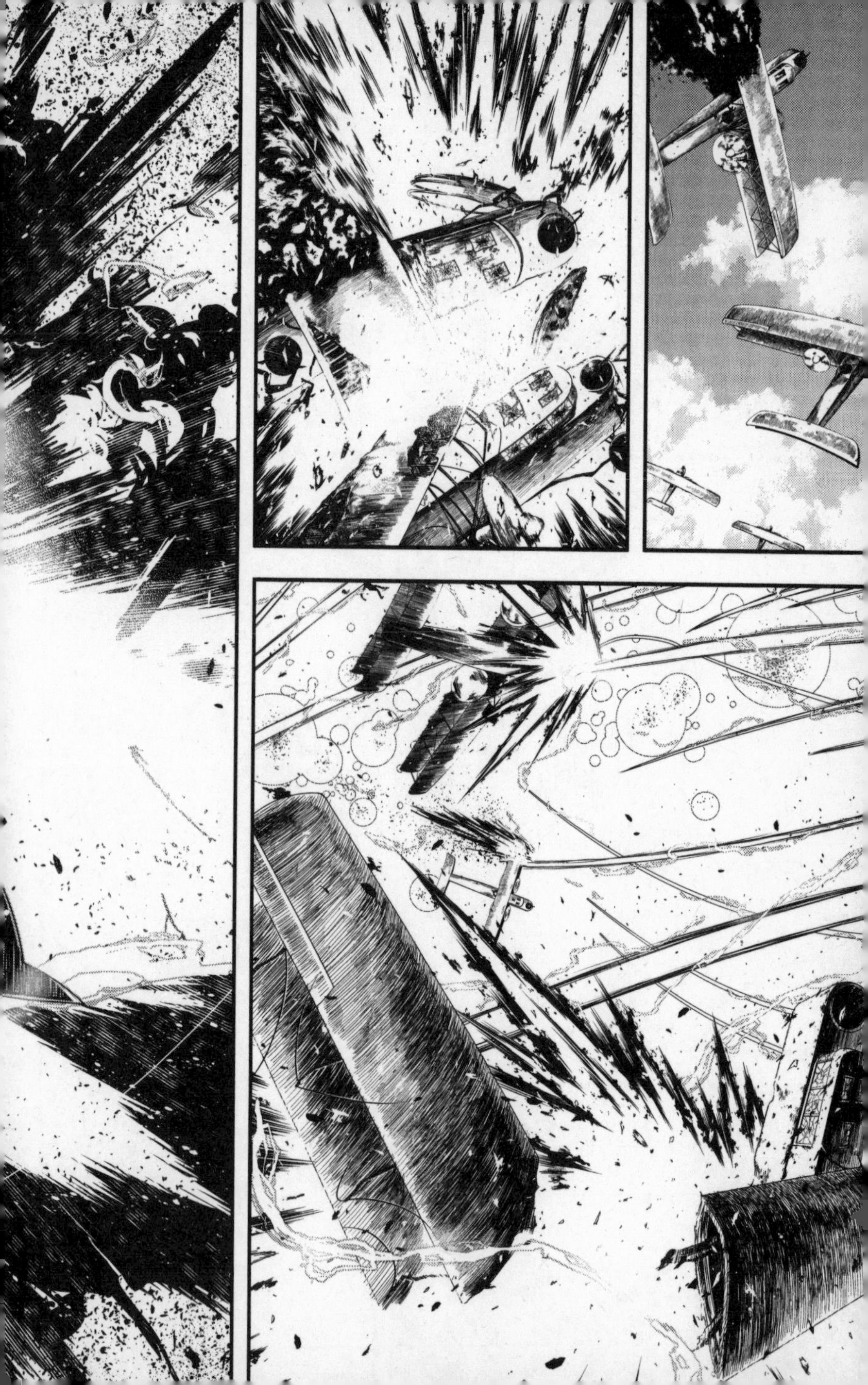

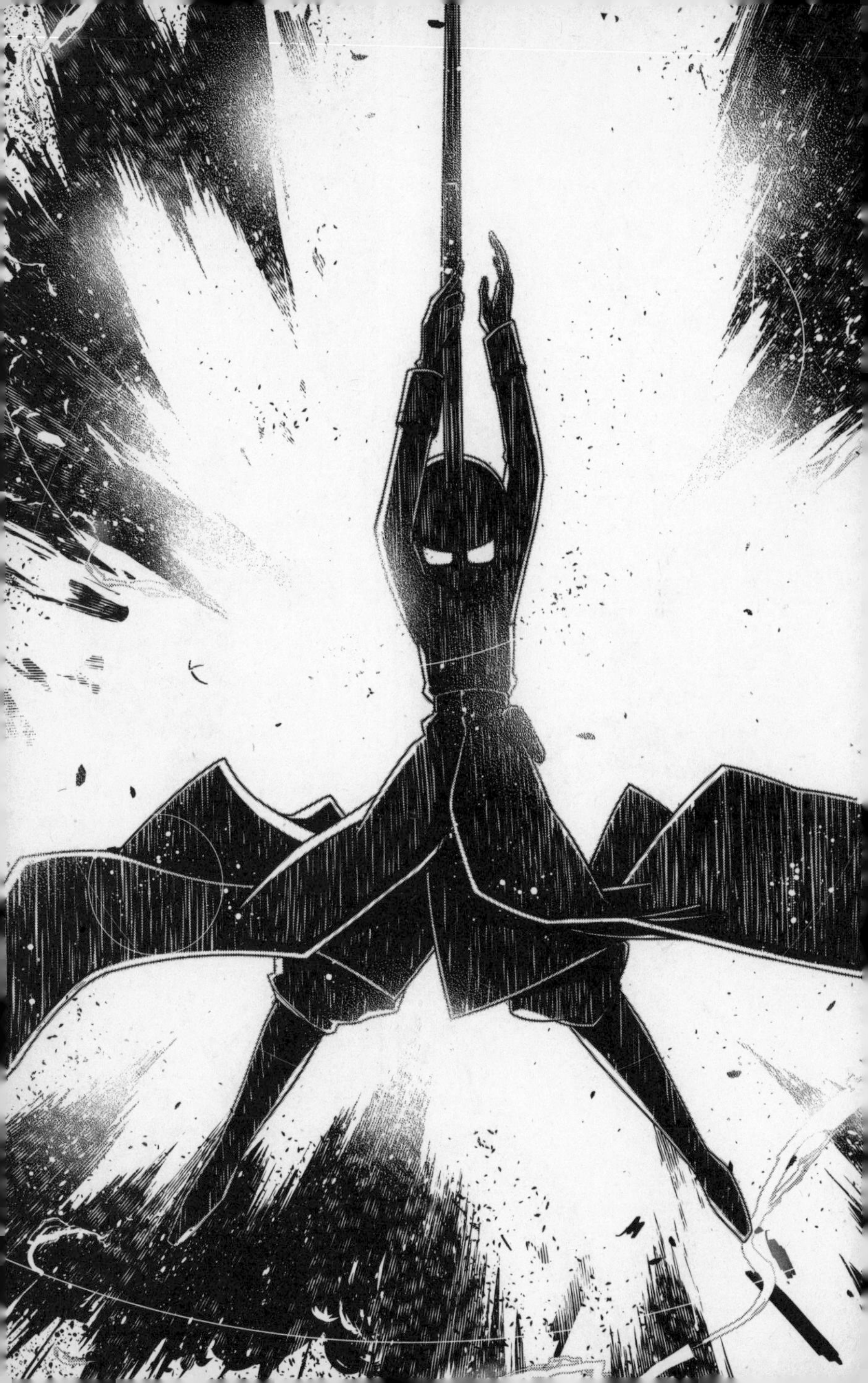

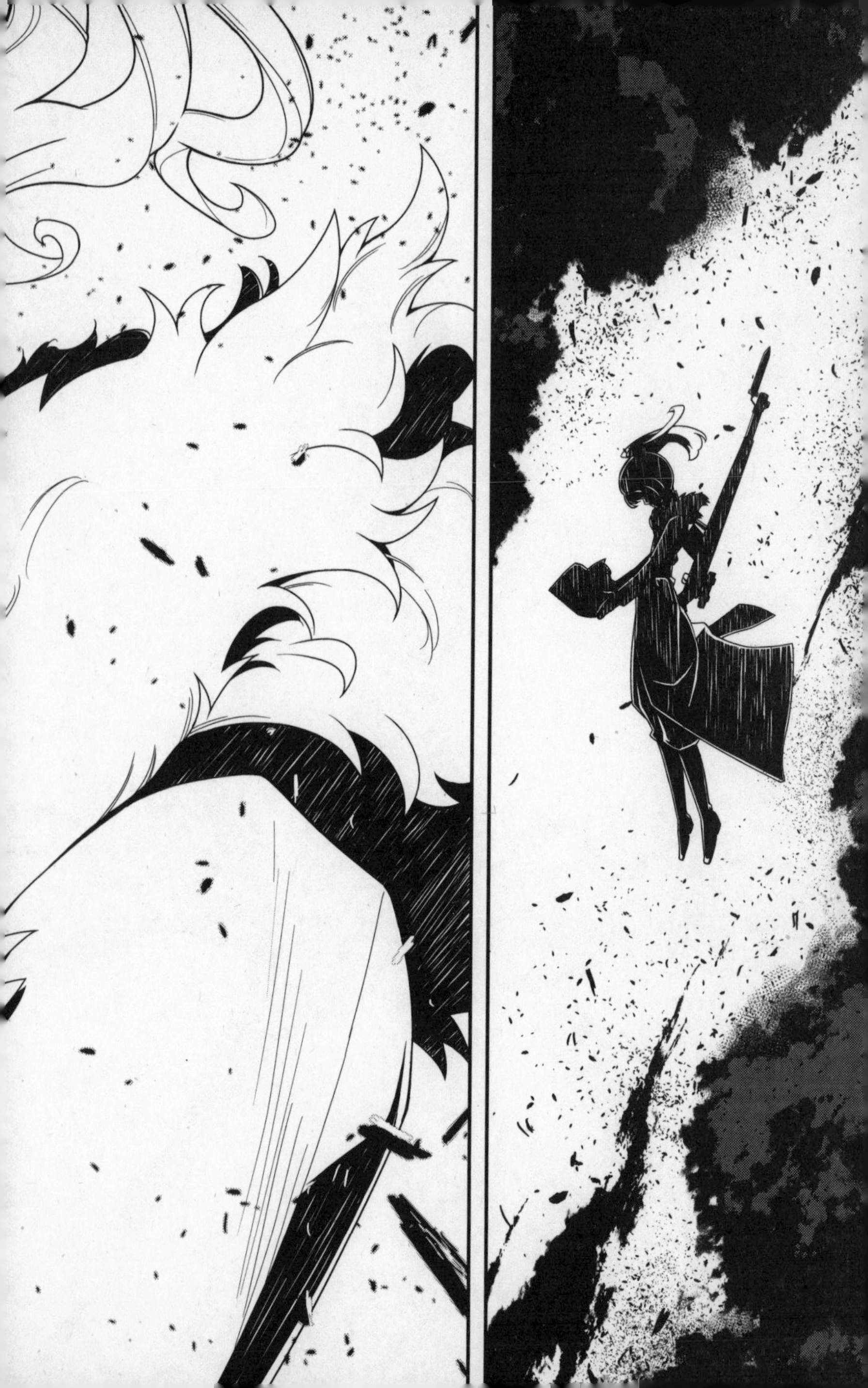

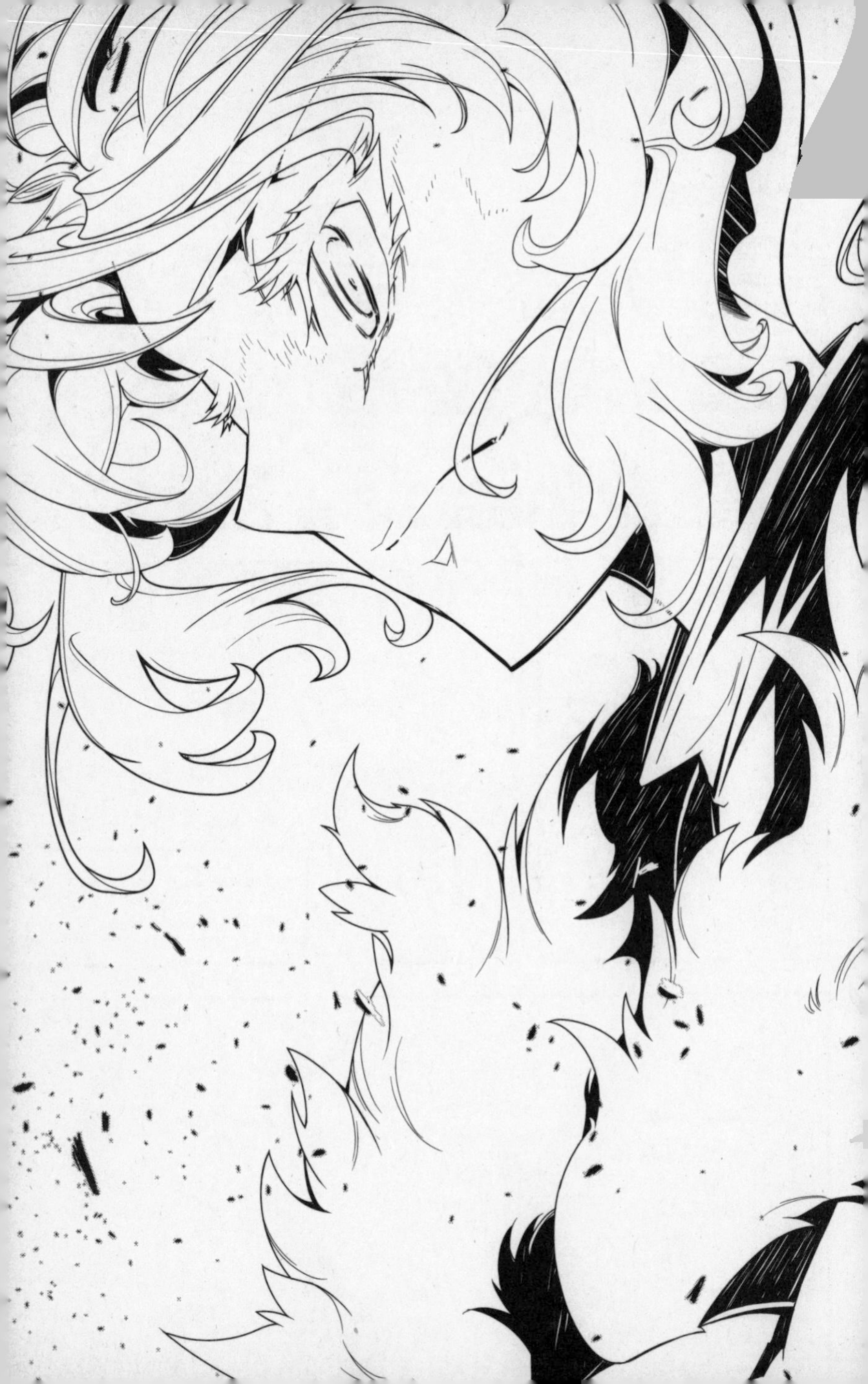

November 7, Unified Year 1925
Somewhere in the Entente Alliance

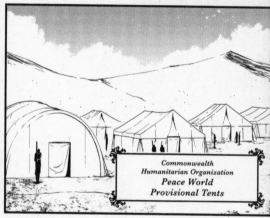

Commonwealth Humanitarian Organization
Peace World Provisional Tents

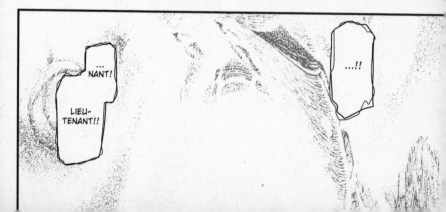

...NANT!

LIEU-TENANT!!

...!!

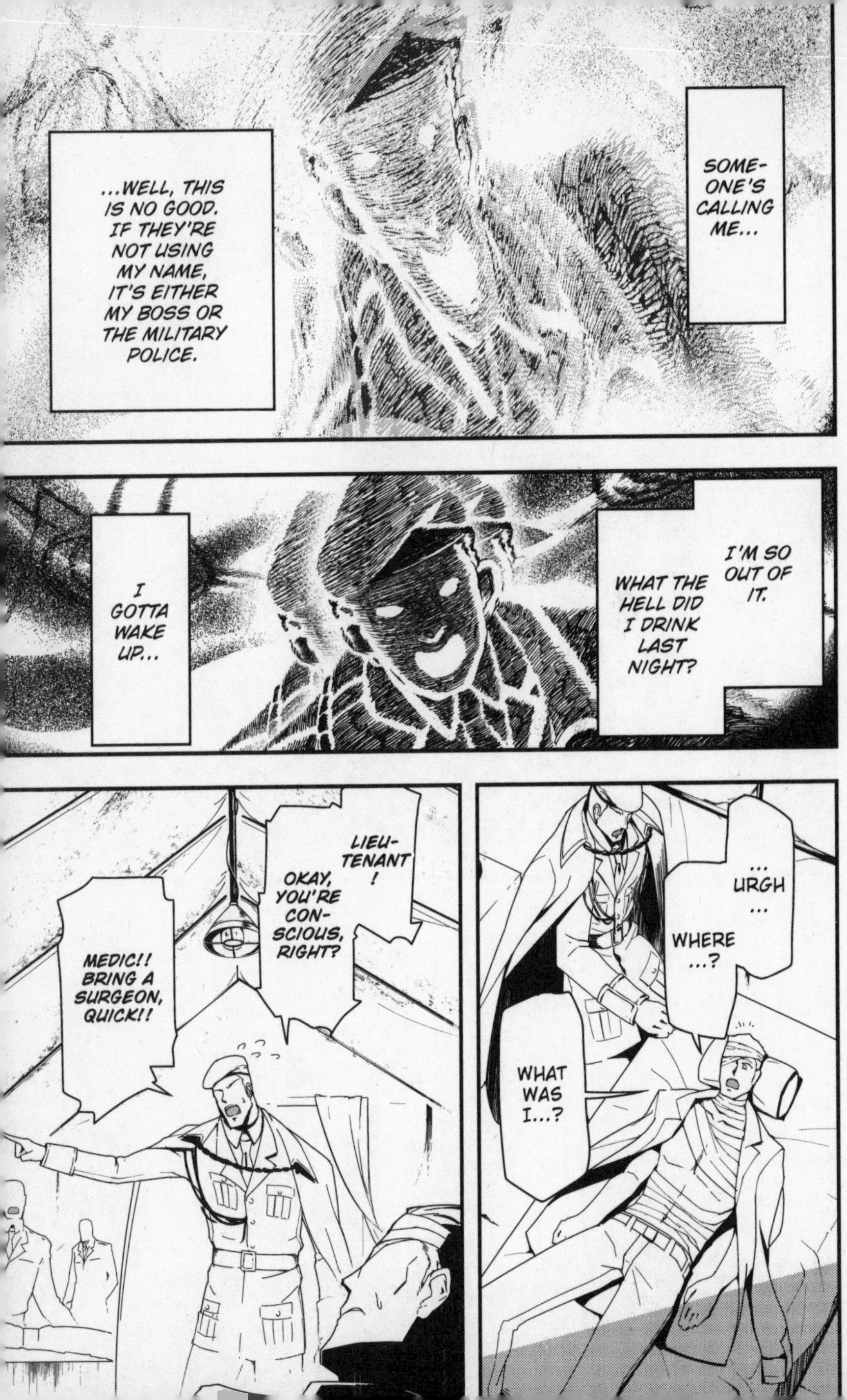
SOMEONE'S CALLING ME...
...WELL, THIS IS NO GOOD. IF THEY'RE NOT USING MY NAME, IT'S EITHER MY BOSS OR THE MILITARY POLICE.
I'M SO OUT OF IT.
WHAT THE HELL DID I DRINK LAST NIGHT?
I GOTTA WAKE UP...
...URGH...
WHERE...?
WHAT WAS I...?
LIEUTENANT!
OKAY, YOU'RE CONSCIOUS, RIGHT?
MEDIC!! BRING A SURGEON, QUICK!!

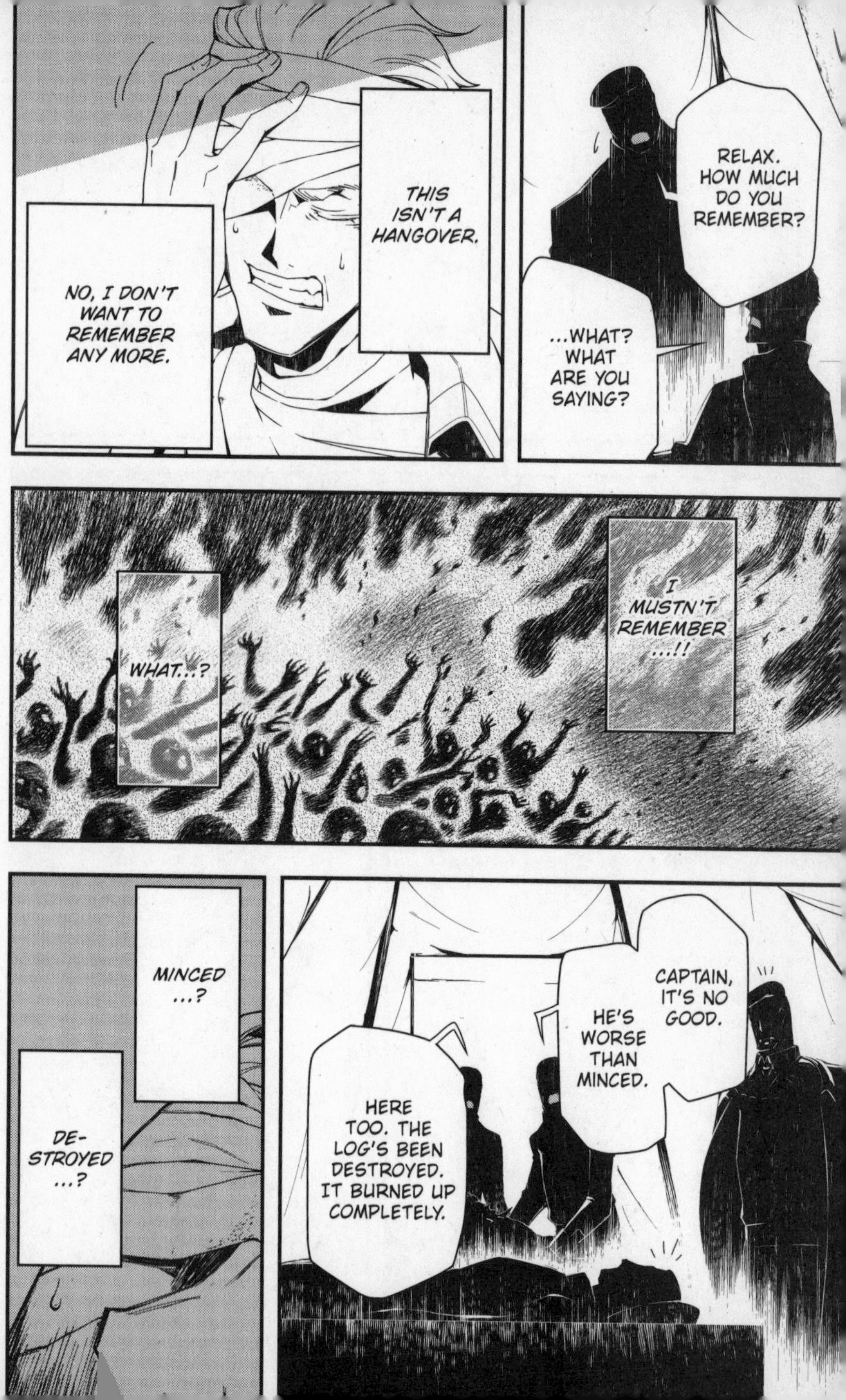
RELAX. HOW MUCH DO YOU REMEMBER?
...WHAT? WHAT ARE YOU SAYING?
THIS ISN'T A HANGOVER.
NO, I DON'T WANT TO REMEMBER ANY MORE.
I MUSTN'T REMEMBER ...!!
WHAT...?
CAPTAIN, IT'S NO GOOD.
HE'S WORSE THAN MINCED.
HERE TOO. THE LOG'S BEEN DESTROYED. IT BURNED UP COMPLETELY.
MINCED ...?
DE-STROYED ...?

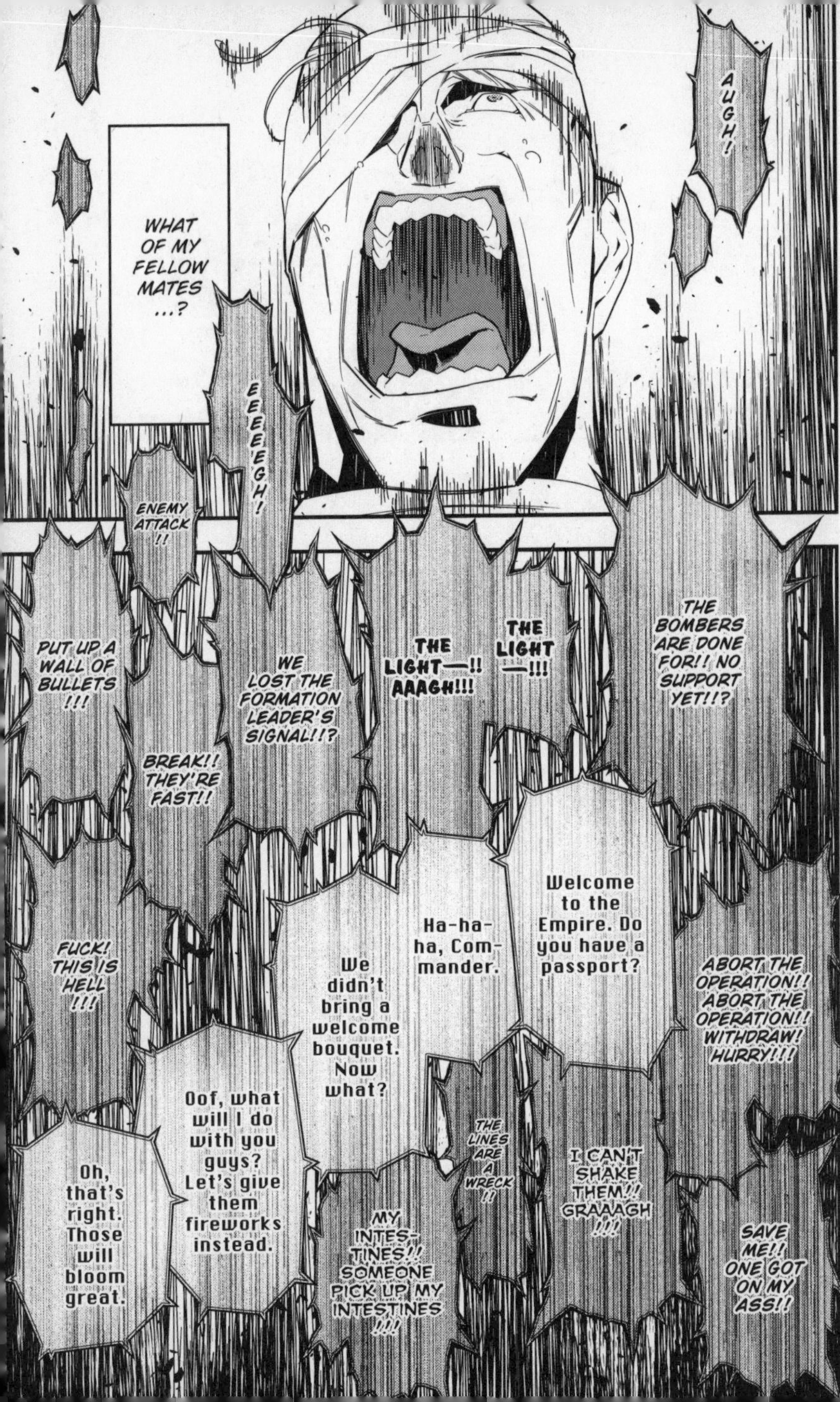
AUGH!
WHAT OF MY FELLOW MATES ...?
EEEEEEGH!
ENEMY ATTACK!!
THE BOMBERS ARE DONE FOR!! NO SUPPORT YET!!?
THE LIGHT—!!!
THE LIGHT—!! AAAGH!!!
WE LOST THE FORMATION LEADER'S SIGNAL!!?
PUT UP A WALL OF BULLETS!!!
BREAK!! THEY'RE FAST!!
Welcome to the Empire. Do you have a passport?
Ha-ha-ha, Commander.
ABORT THE OPERATION!! ABORT THE OPERATION!! WITHDRAW! HURRY!!!
We didn't bring a welcome bouquet. Now what?
FUCK! THIS IS HELL!!!
Oof, what will I do with you guys? Let's give them fireworks instead.
THE LINES ARE A WRECK!!
I CAN'T SHAKE THEM!! GRAAAGH!!!
SAVE ME!! ONE GOT ON MY ASS!!
MY INTESTINES!! SOMEONE PICK UP MY INTESTINES!!!
Oh, that's right. Those will bloom great.

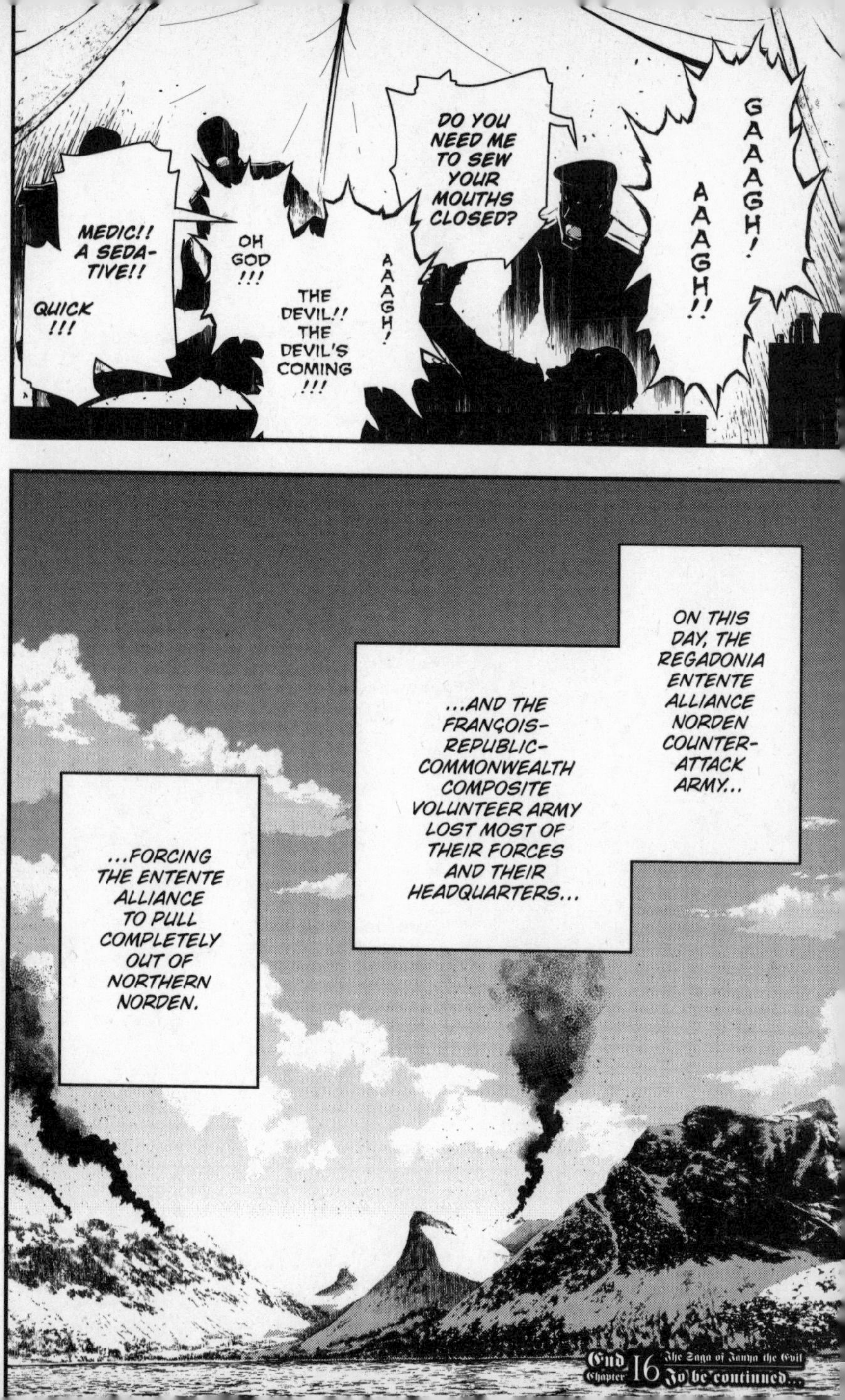
GAAAGH!
AAAGH!!
DO YOU NEED ME TO SEW YOUR MOUTHS CLOSED?
AAAGH!
THE DEVIL!! THE DEVIL'S COMING!!!
OH GOD!!!
MEDIC!! A SEDA-TIVE!!
QUICK!!!
ON THIS DAY, THE REGADONIA ENTENTE ALLIANCE NORDEN COUNTER-ATTACK ARMY...
...AND THE FRANÇOIS-REPUBLIC-COMMONWEALTH COMPOSITE VOLUNTEER ARMY LOST MOST OF THEIR FORCES AND THEIR HEADQUARTERS...
...FORCING THE ENTENTE ALLIANCE TO PULL COMPLETELY OUT OF NORTHERN NORDEN.
End Chapter 16 The Saga of Tanya the Evil
To be continued...

Glossary Chapter 19

Control Plane

A type of military plane that observes an air zone and organizes and analyzes information about the aircraft it finds.

When a plane is deemed hostile, the control plane judges the threat and priority levels and reports to nearby units and friendly bases. It also acts as air control for friendly aircraft.

Speed 300

This is in kmh. It was thought that the maximum speed for mages was around 250, so flying in formation at such a speed would take a tremendous amount of discipline. 300 kmh had just barely been achieved under experimental conditions, so no one thought it would be possible to engage in combat at such speed.

Cavalry

In broad terms, this refers to units mounted on horseback, but here it refers specifically to ground troops in the American Old West.

In Western movies, which portray the time period nostalgically, the cavalry often shows up when the people face a crisis and is seen as an ally of justice.

Of course, that's just part of the glorification of colonization and occupation in the name of "manifest destiny."

Disciplined Fire

When an entire unit fires on the same target at the same time. By firing on a single point from multiple directions, the number of hits can be increased.

Republican mages specialize in concentrating their fire, as opposed to the imperial mages' focus on individual quality, and they prioritize numbers and coordination; these factors have gotten them impressive results.

Glossary Chapter 20

Decoys

Used to lure in the enemy and draw off attacks.

The word was originally used for wooden birds used by hunters to attract birds of the same species who would recognize it as a friend. Now the term is also used in the military, but the effect is the opposite—they're used to make the enemy think they see their enemy in order to draw off their attacks.

Mages can create decoys with optical formulas, which are used in the following ways:

Luring: drawing attacks from the enemy to distract them from their true target.

Saturation: saturating their processing power by presenting them with more targets than they can fire on.

Detection: exposing the enemy position by getting them to fire on the decoy.

Combat Direction Center

Where control and leadership is carried out in each war area. Also called a "command post."

The command post is full of commanders and staff who use mana observation equipment and wireless communications to collect intel and give orders to each unit. On the communication network, their call sign is the location of the area plus "control." When the units call them, they often use the abbreviation "CP."

Quasi-Regiment

A formation that is treated as a regiment.

A regiment is the largest unit made up of troops all from the same branch. A mage regiment usually consists of seventy-two mages in six companies.

The force the 203rd went up against had a vanguard of two battalions. Since battalions are generally thirty-six mages in three companies, the headcount is the same as a regiment.

However, the one Entente Alliance mage battalion and two made up of Republican volunteer troops were undermanned, so the total was more like a quasi-regiment.

Humanitarian Organization "Peace World"

A charity group from the Commonwealth that goes to war zones and treats the sick and wounded based on the Convention for the Amelioration of the Condition of the Wounded and Sick in Armed Forces in the Field. However, their facilities are mostly set up in the countries of their allies, and in the Republic, it's next to Rhine headquarters. Although there's no doubt the idea is noble, you can't say they don't discriminate between countries.

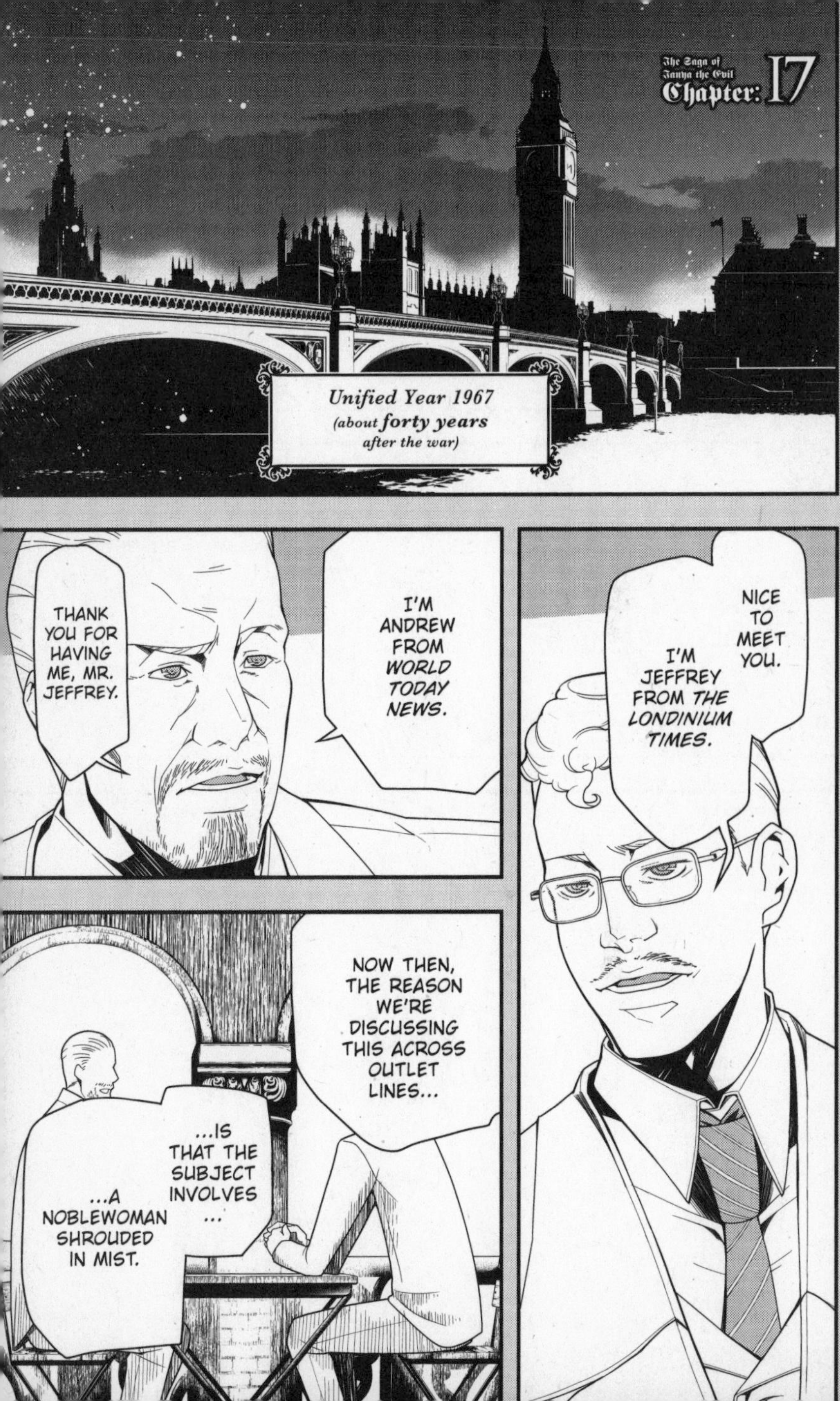
The Saga of Tanya the Evil
Chapter: 17
Unified Year 1967 (about forty years after the war)
NICE TO MEET YOU.
I'M JEFFREY FROM THE LONDINIUM TIMES.
I'M ANDREW FROM WORLD TODAY NEWS.
THANK YOU FOR HAVING ME, MR. JEFFREY.
NOW THEN, THE REASON WE'RE DISCUSSING THIS ACROSS OUTLET LINES...
...IS THAT THE SUBJECT INVOLVES...
...A NOBLEWOMAN SHROUDED IN MIST.

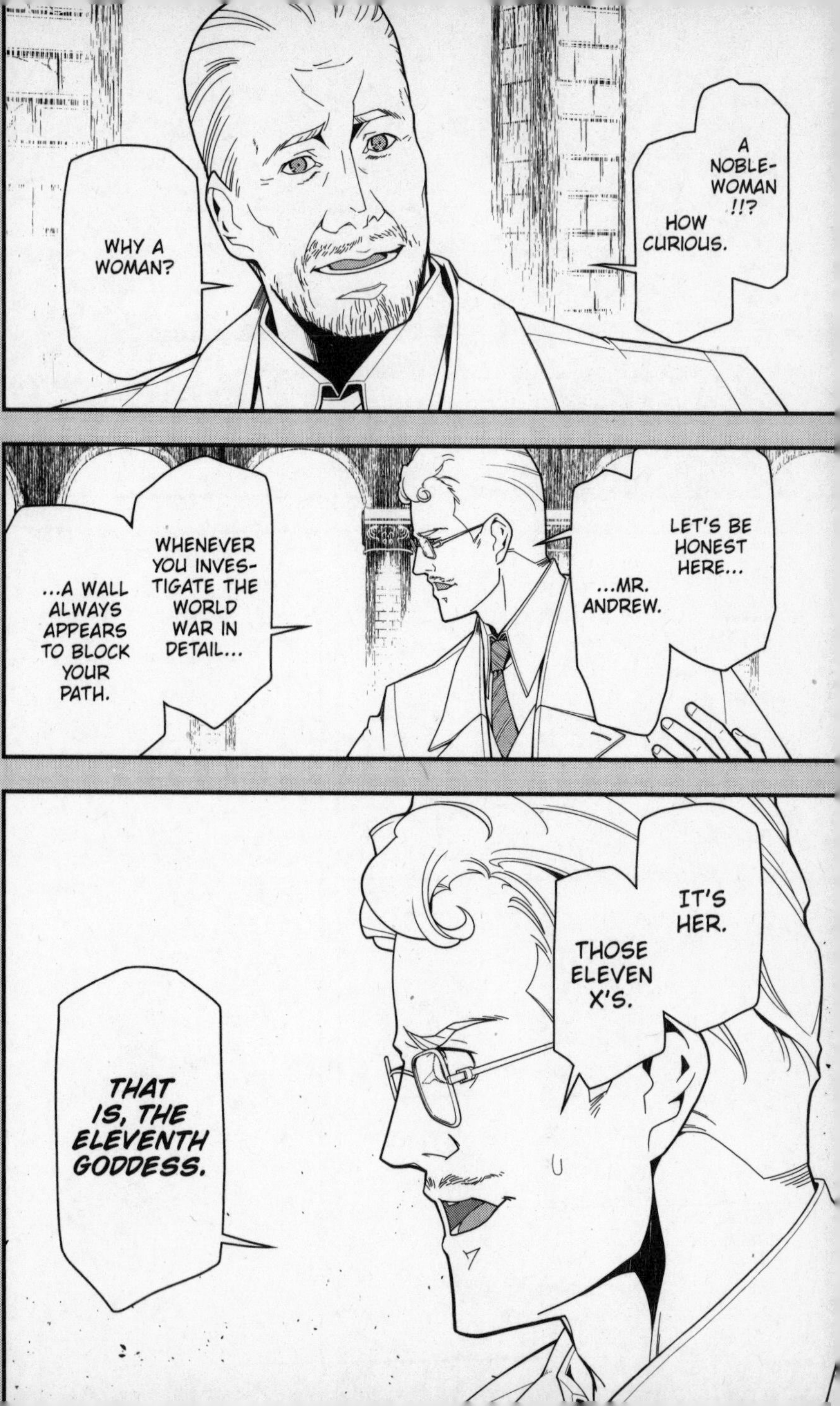
A NOBLE-WOMAN !!?
HOW CURIOUS.
WHY A WOMAN?
LET'S BE HONEST HERE...
...MR. ANDREW.
WHENEVER YOU INVES-TIGATE THE WORLD WAR IN DETAIL...
...A WALL ALWAYS APPEARS TO BLOCK YOUR PATH.
IT'S HER.
THOSE ELEVEN X'S.
THAT IS, THE ELEVENTH GODDESS.

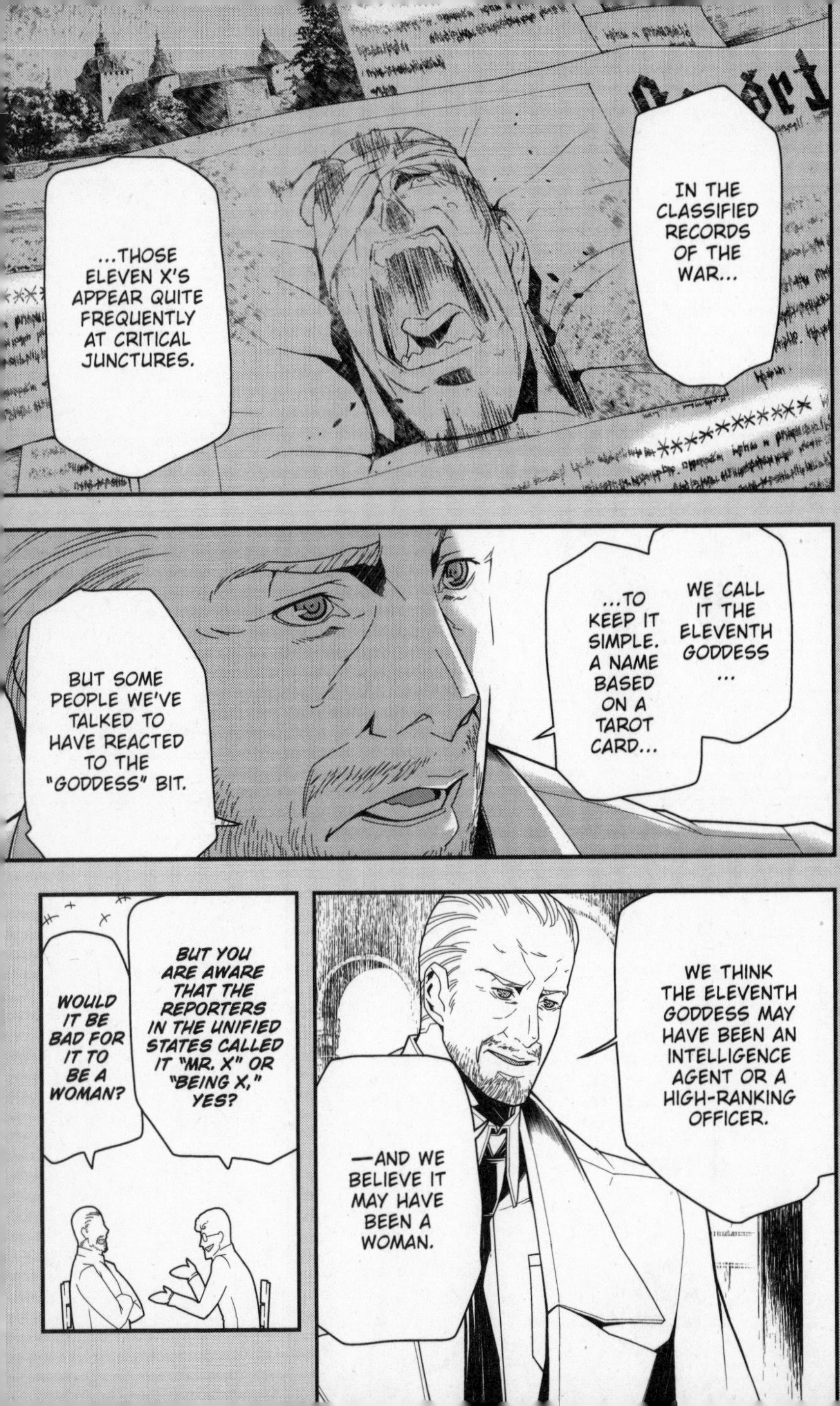
IN THE CLASSIFIED RECORDS OF THE WAR...
...THOSE ELEVEN X'S APPEAR QUITE FREQUENTLY AT CRITICAL JUNCTURES.
WE CALL IT THE ELEVENTH GODDESS...
...TO KEEP IT SIMPLE. A NAME BASED ON A TAROT CARD...
BUT SOME PEOPLE WE'VE TALKED TO HAVE REACTED TO THE "GODDESS" BIT.
WE THINK THE ELEVENTH GODDESS MAY HAVE BEEN AN INTELLIGENCE AGENT OR A HIGH-RANKING OFFICER.
—AND WE BELIEVE IT MAY HAVE BEEN A WOMAN.
BUT YOU ARE AWARE THAT THE REPORTERS IN THE UNIFIED STATES CALLED IT "MR. X" OR "BEING X," YES?
WOULD IT BE BAD FOR IT TO BE A WOMAN?

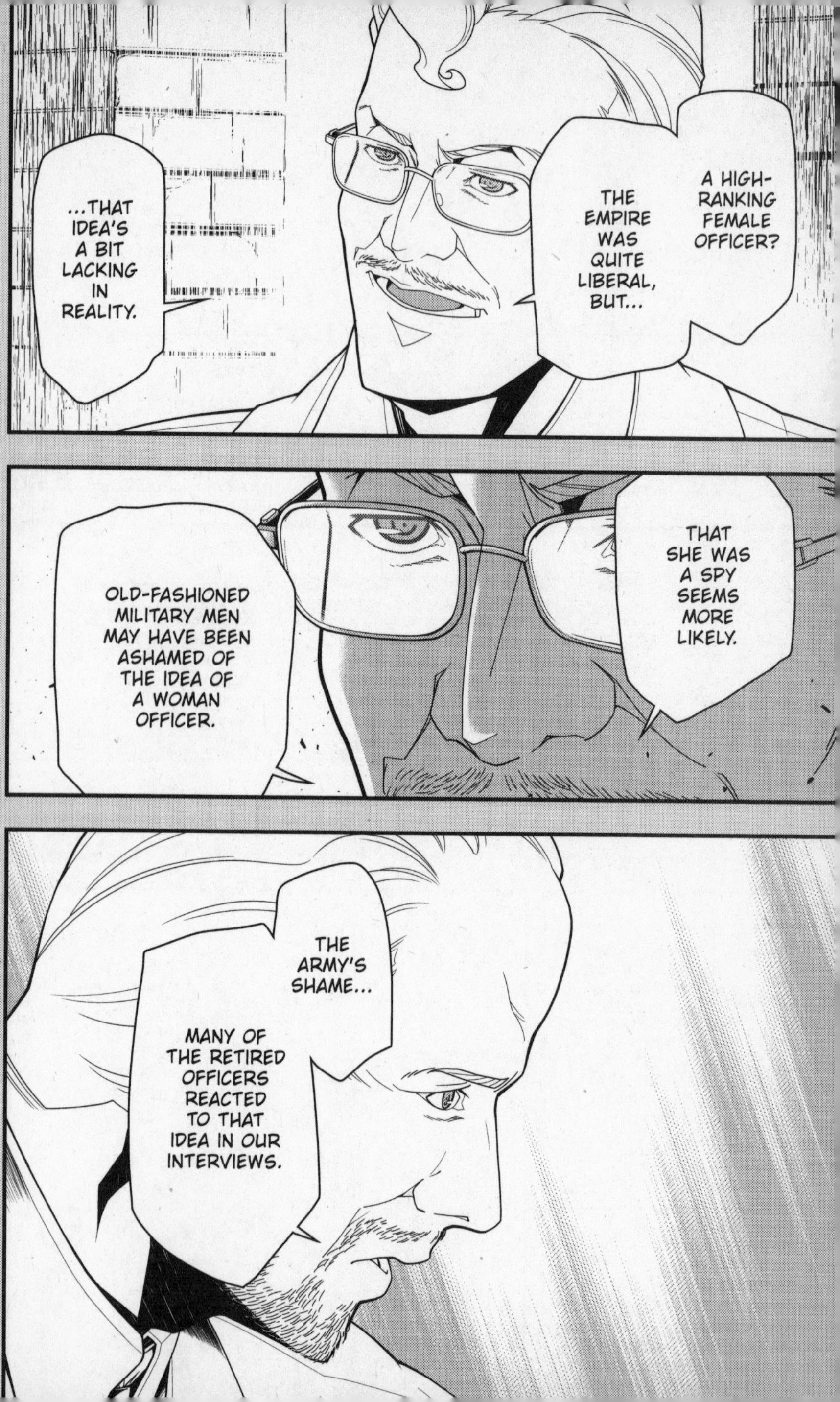
A HIGH-RANKING FEMALE OFFICER?
THE EMPIRE WAS QUITE LIBERAL, BUT...
...THAT IDEA'S A BIT LACKING IN REALITY.
THAT SHE WAS A SPY SEEMS MORE LIKELY.
OLD-FASHIONED MILITARY MEN MAY HAVE BEEN ASHAMED OF THE IDEA OF A WOMAN OFFICER.
THE ARMY'S SHAME...
MANY OF THE RETIRED OFFICERS REACTED TO THAT IDEA IN OUR INTERVIEWS.

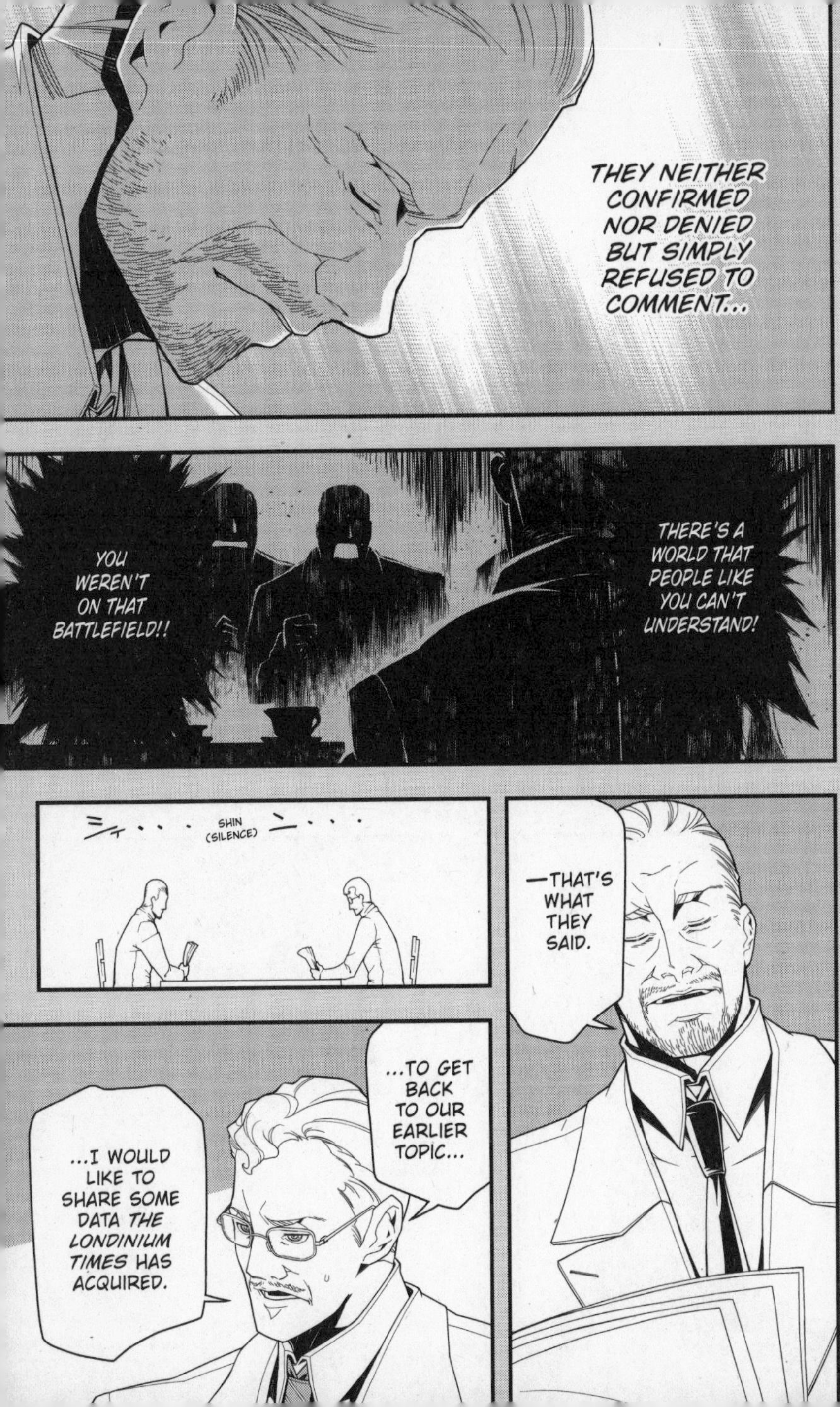
THEY NEITHER CONFIRMED NOR DENIED BUT SIMPLY REFUSED TO COMMENT...
THERE'S A WORLD THAT PEOPLE LIKE YOU CAN'T UNDERSTAND!
YOU WEREN'T ON THAT BATTLEFIELD!!
—THAT'S WHAT THEY SAID.
SHIN (SILENCE)
...TO GET BACK TO OUR EARLIER TOPIC...
...I WOULD LIKE TO SHARE SOME DATA THE LONDINIUM TIMES HAS ACQUIRED.

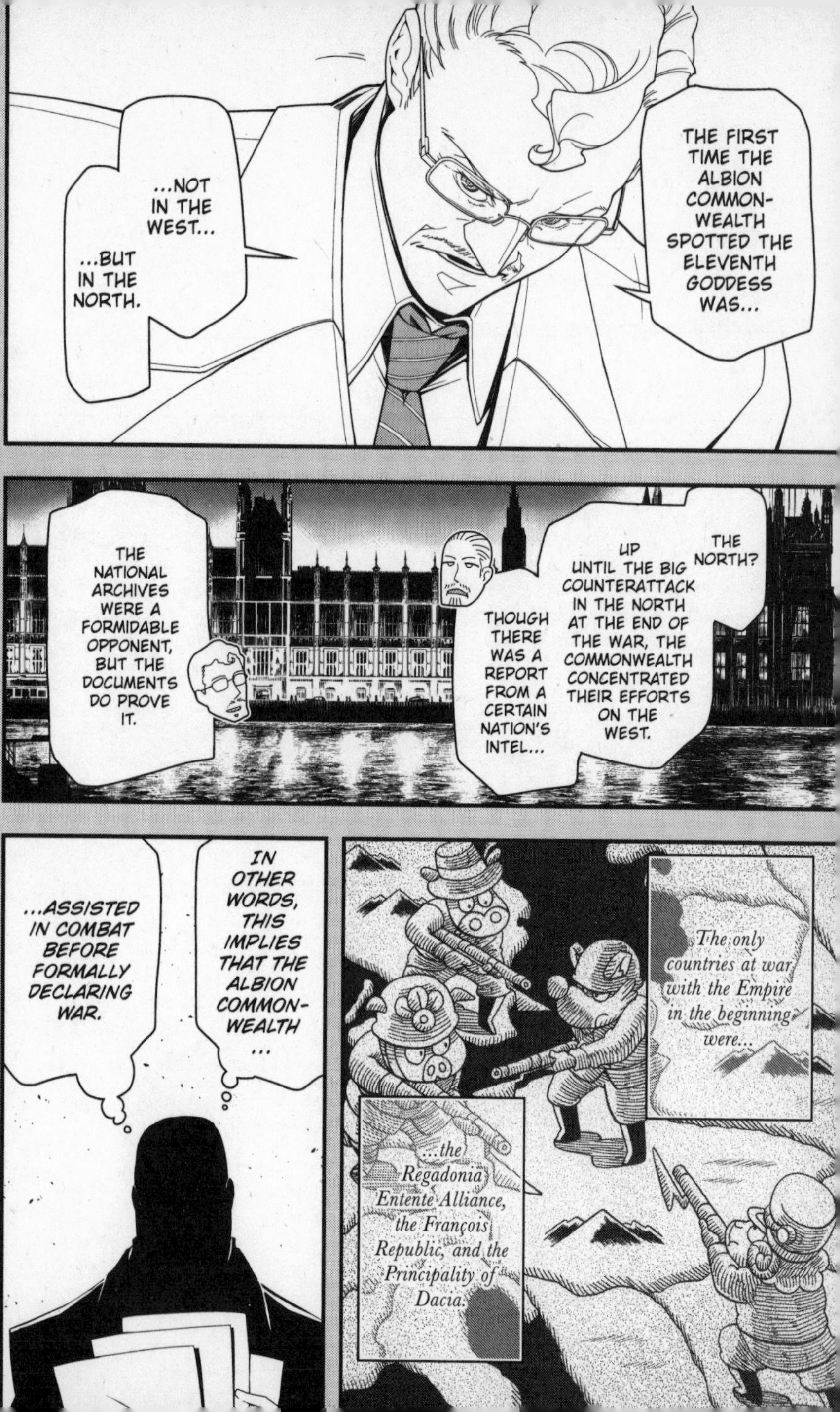
THE FIRST TIME THE ALBION COMMON-WEALTH SPOTTED THE ELEVENTH GODDESS WAS...
...NOT IN THE WEST...
...BUT IN THE NORTH.
THE NORTH?
UP UNTIL THE BIG COUNTERATTACK IN THE NORTH AT THE END OF THE WAR, THE COMMONWEALTH CONCENTRATED THEIR EFFORTS ON THE WEST.
THOUGH THERE WAS A REPORT FROM A CERTAIN NATION'S INTEL...
THE NATIONAL ARCHIVES WERE A FORMIDABLE OPPONENT, BUT THE DOCUMENTS DO PROVE IT.
The only countries at war with the Empire in the beginning were...
...the Regadonia Entente Alliance, the François Republic, and the Principality of Dacia.
IN OTHER WORDS, THIS IMPLIES THAT THE ALBION COMMON-WEALTH...
...ASSISTED IN COMBAT BEFORE FORMALLY DECLARING WAR.

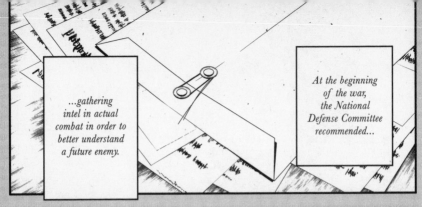

At the beginning of the war, the National Defense Committee recommended...
...gathering intel in actual combat in order to better understand a future enemy.
In response, a "volunteer army" consisting mainly of a small number of mage units...
...was dispatched to the Regadonia Entente Alliance.
IT MUST BE TRUE.
WHICH MEANS THAT THE COMMON-WEALTH, WHICH AT THE TIME WAS NEUTRAL...
...A REGIMENT OF AERIAL MAGES...
...FACED THE ELEVENTH GODDESS?

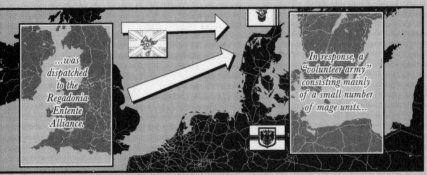

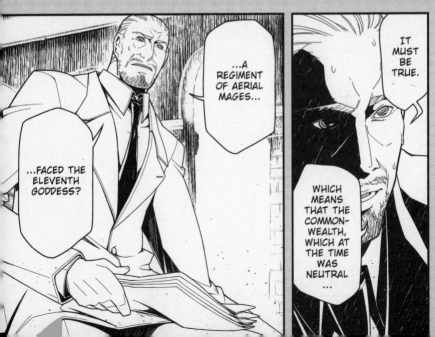

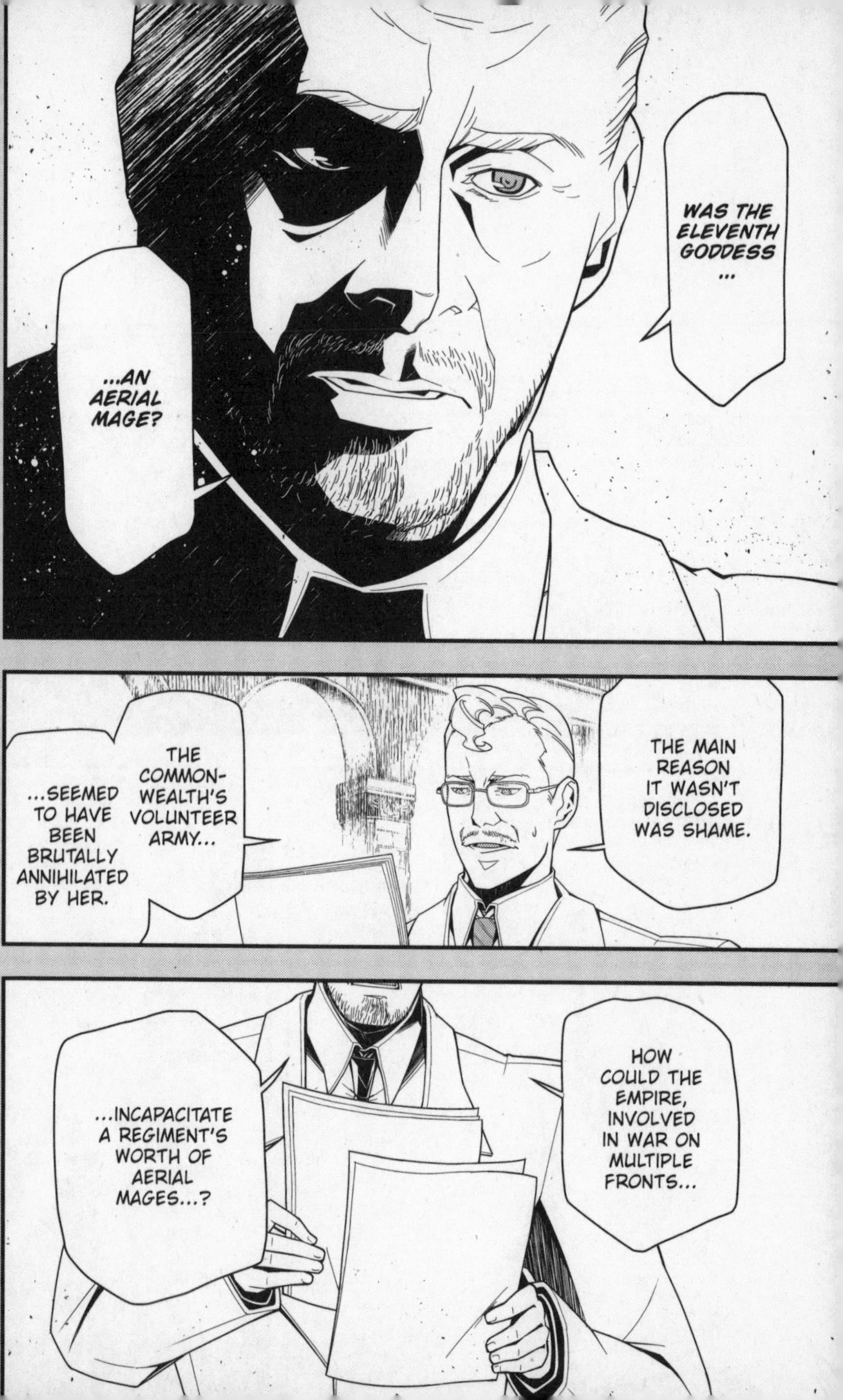
WAS THE ELEVENTH GODDESS...
...AN AERIAL MAGE?
THE MAIN REASON IT WASN'T DISCLOSED WAS SHAME.
THE COMMON-WEALTH'S VOLUNTEER ARMY...
...SEEMED TO HAVE BEEN BRUTALLY ANNIHILATED BY HER.
HOW COULD THE EMPIRE, INVOLVED IN WAR ON MULTIPLE FRONTS...
...INCAPACITATE A REGIMENT'S WORTH OF AERIAL MAGES...?

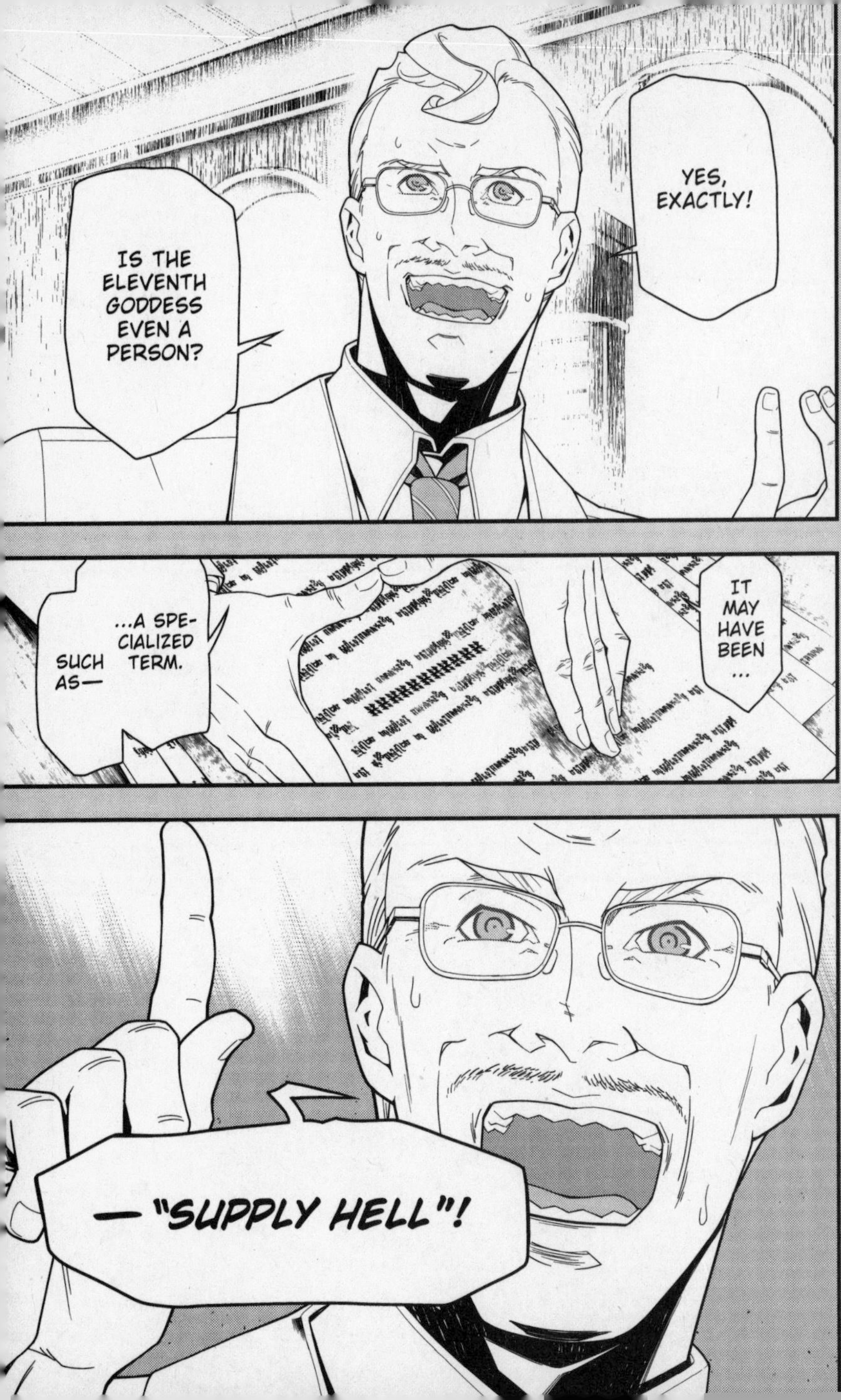
YES, EXACTLY!
IS THE ELEVENTH GODDESS EVEN A PERSON?
IT MAY HAVE BEEN...
...A SPE-CIALIZED TERM.
SUCH AS—
—"SUPPLY HELL"!

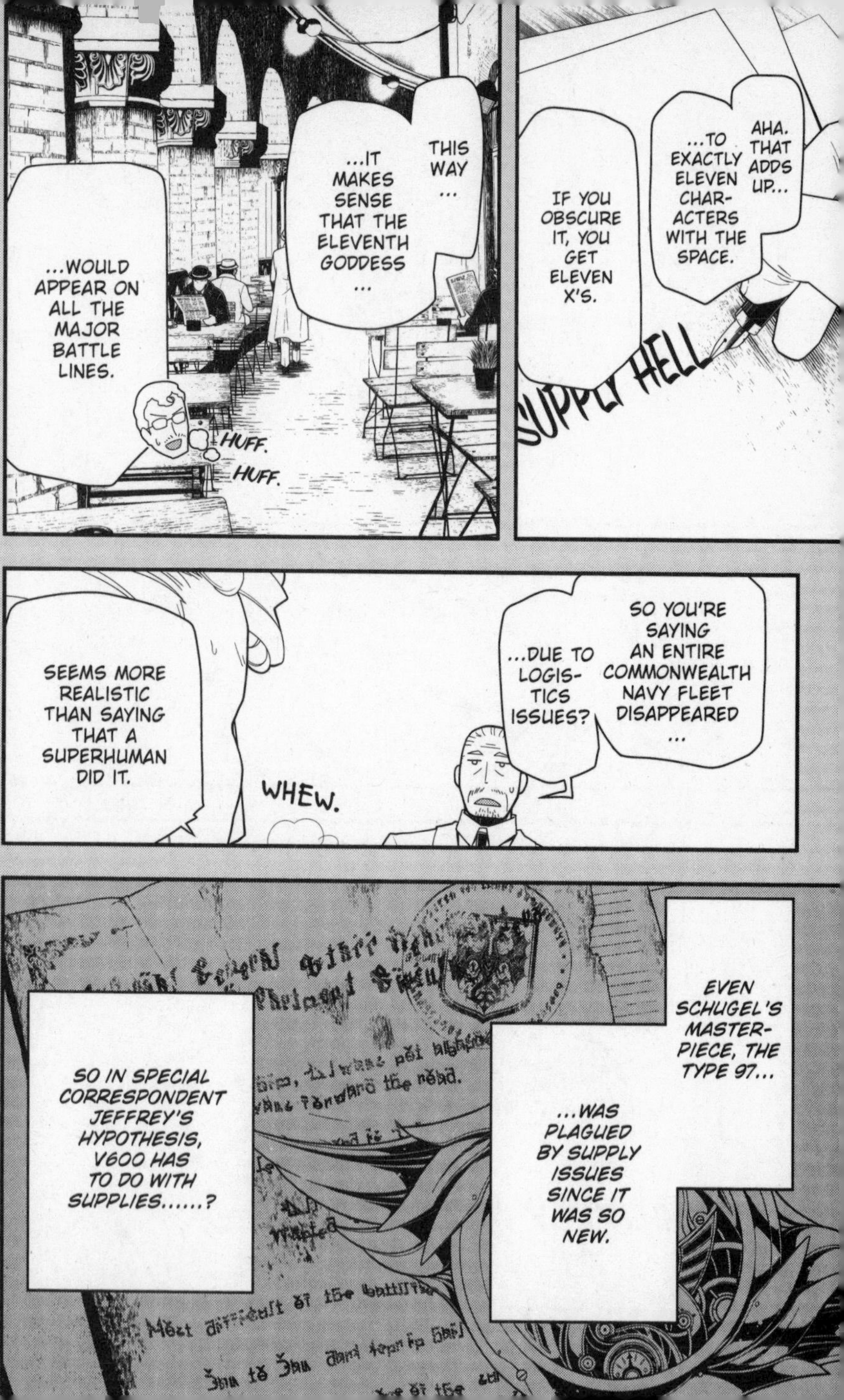
AHA. THAT ADDS UP...
...TO EXACTLY ELEVEN CHARACTERS WITH THE SPACE.
IF YOU OBSCURE IT, YOU GET ELEVEN X'S.
SUPPLY HELL
THIS WAY...
...IT MAKES SENSE THAT THE ELEVENTH GODDESS...
...WOULD APPEAR ON ALL THE MAJOR BATTLE LINES.
HUFF.
HUFF.
SO YOU'RE SAYING AN ENTIRE COMMONWEALTH NAVY FLEET DISAPPEARED...
...DUE TO LOGISTICS ISSUES?
SEEMS MORE REALISTIC THAN SAYING THAT A SUPERHUMAN DID IT.
WHEW.
EVEN SCHUGEL'S MASTERPIECE, THE TYPE 97...
...WAS PLAGUED BY SUPPLY ISSUES SINCE IT WAS SO NEW.
SO IN SPECIAL CORRESPONDENT JEFFREY'S HYPOTHESIS, V600 HAS TO DO WITH SUPPLIES......?

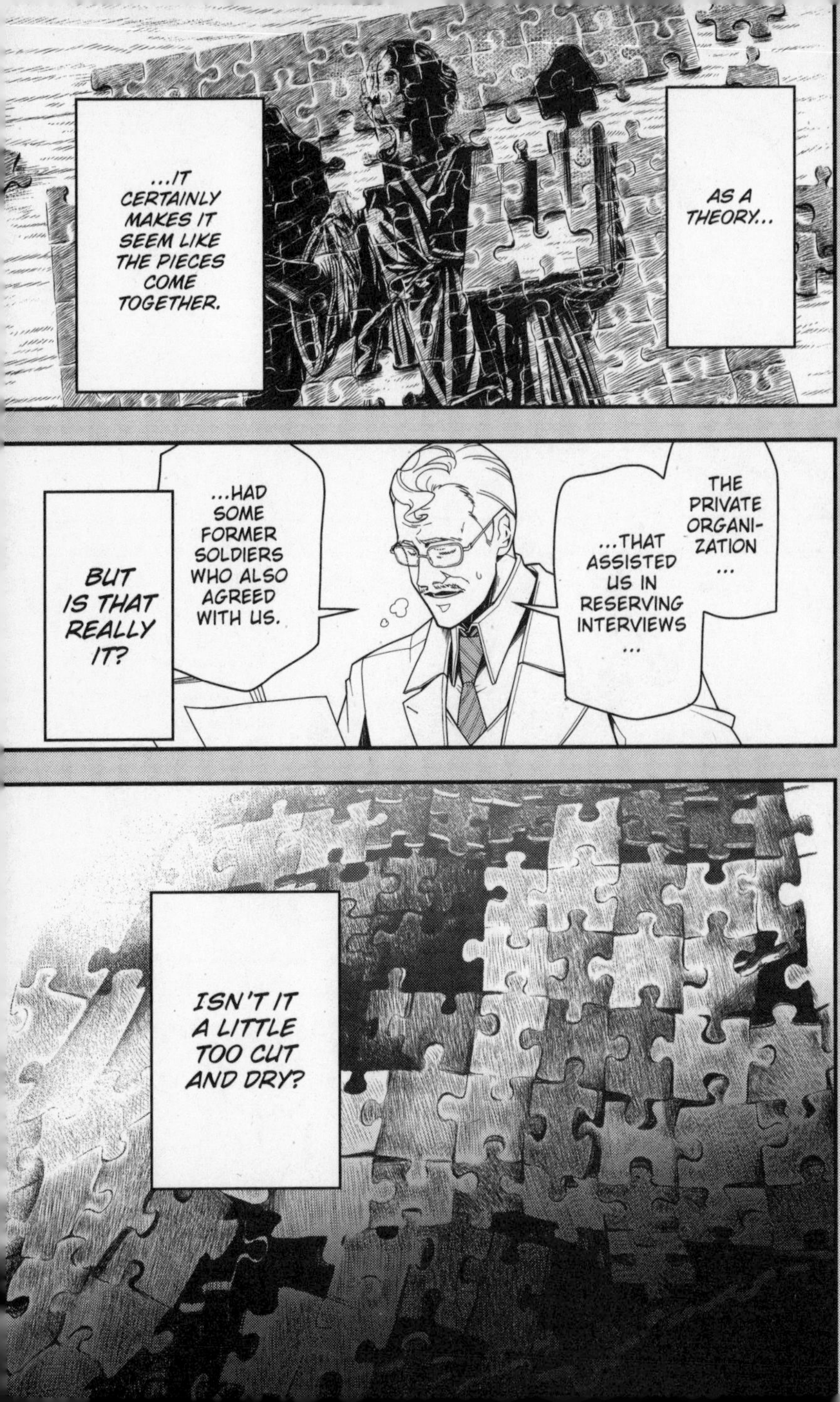
AS A THEORY...
...IT CERTAINLY MAKES IT SEEM LIKE THE PIECES COME TOGETHER.
THE PRIVATE ORGANIZATION ...
...THAT ASSISTED US IN RESERVING INTERVIEWS ...
...HAD SOME FORMER SOLDIERS WHO ALSO AGREED WITH US.
BUT IS THAT REALLY IT?
ISN'T IT A LITTLE TOO CUT AND DRY?

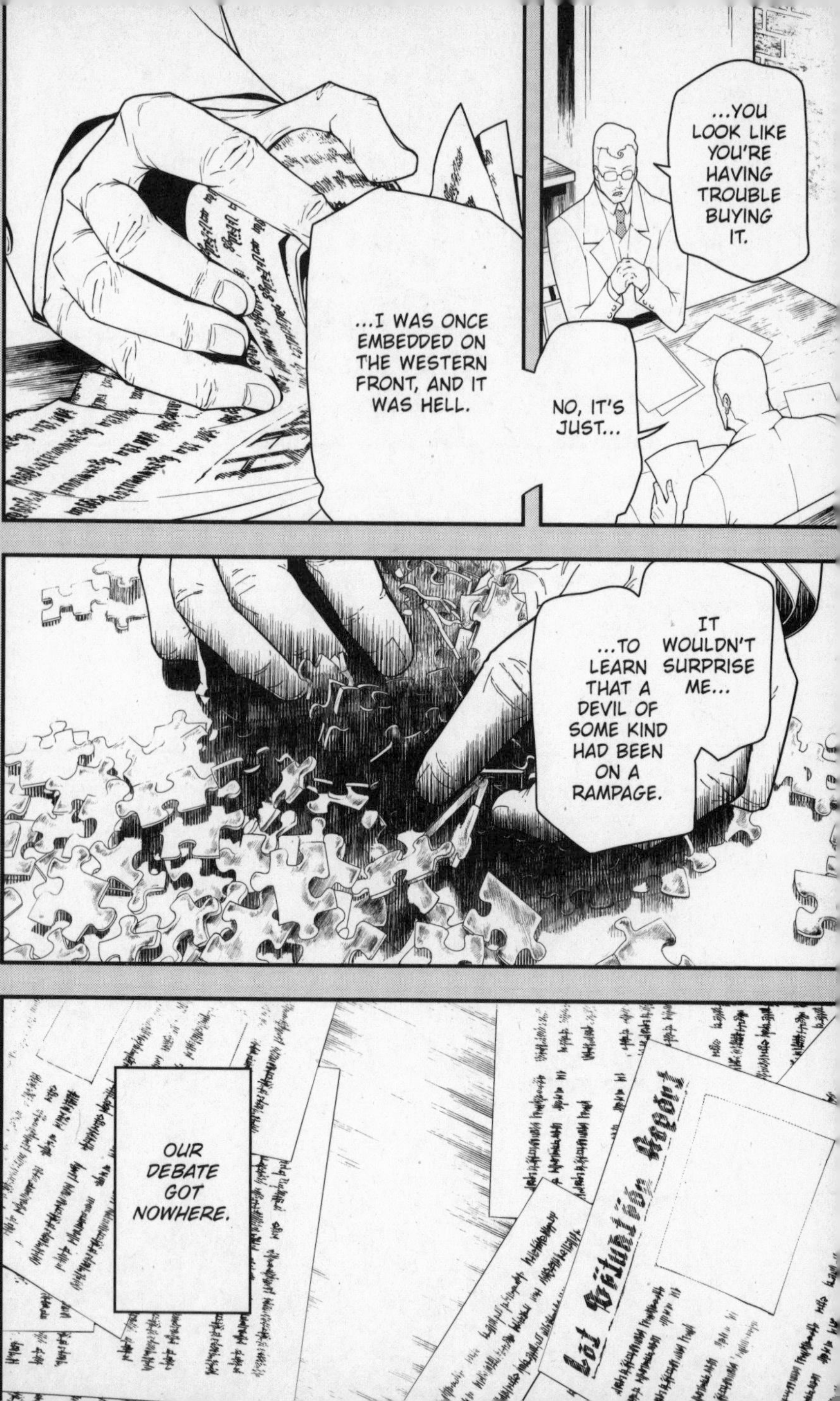
...YOU LOOK LIKE YOU'RE HAVING TROUBLE BUYING IT.
NO, IT'S JUST...
...I WAS ONCE EMBEDDED ON THE WESTERN FRONT, AND IT WAS HELL.
IT WOULDN'T SURPRISE ME...
...TO LEARN THAT A DEVIL OF SOME KIND HAD BEEN ON A RAMPAGE.
OUR DEBATE GOT NOWHERE.

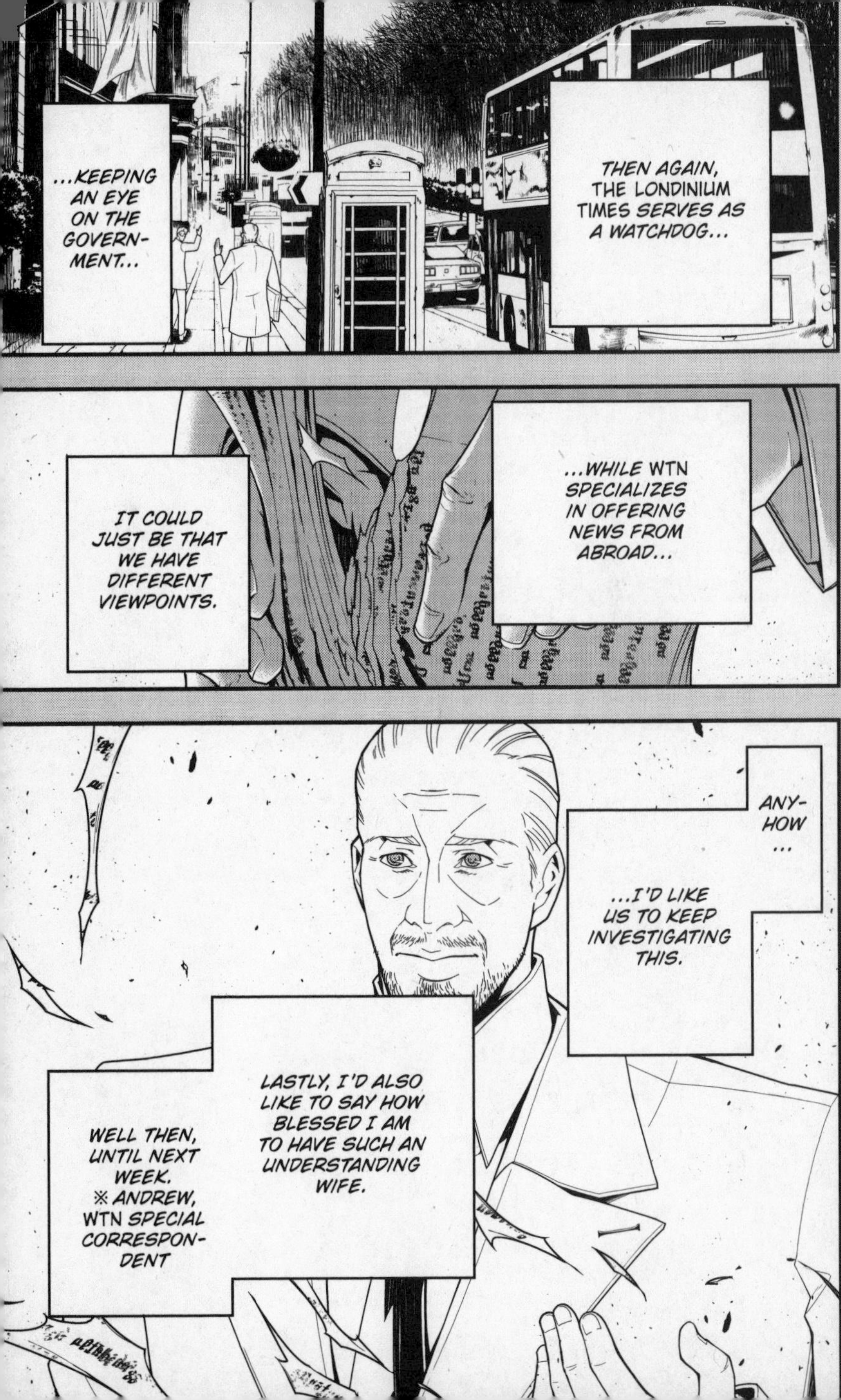
THEN AGAIN, THE LONDINIUM TIMES SERVES AS A WATCHDOG...
...KEEPING AN EYE ON THE GOVERN-MENT...
...WHILE WTN SPECIALIZES IN OFFERING NEWS FROM ABROAD...
IT COULD JUST BE THAT WE HAVE DIFFERENT VIEWPOINTS.
ANY-HOW...
...I'D LIKE US TO KEEP INVESTIGATING THIS.
LASTLY, I'D ALSO LIKE TO SAY HOW BLESSED I AM TO HAVE SUCH AN UNDERSTANDING WIFE.
WELL THEN, UNTIL NEXT WEEK.
※ ANDREW, WTN SPECIAL CORRESPON-DENT

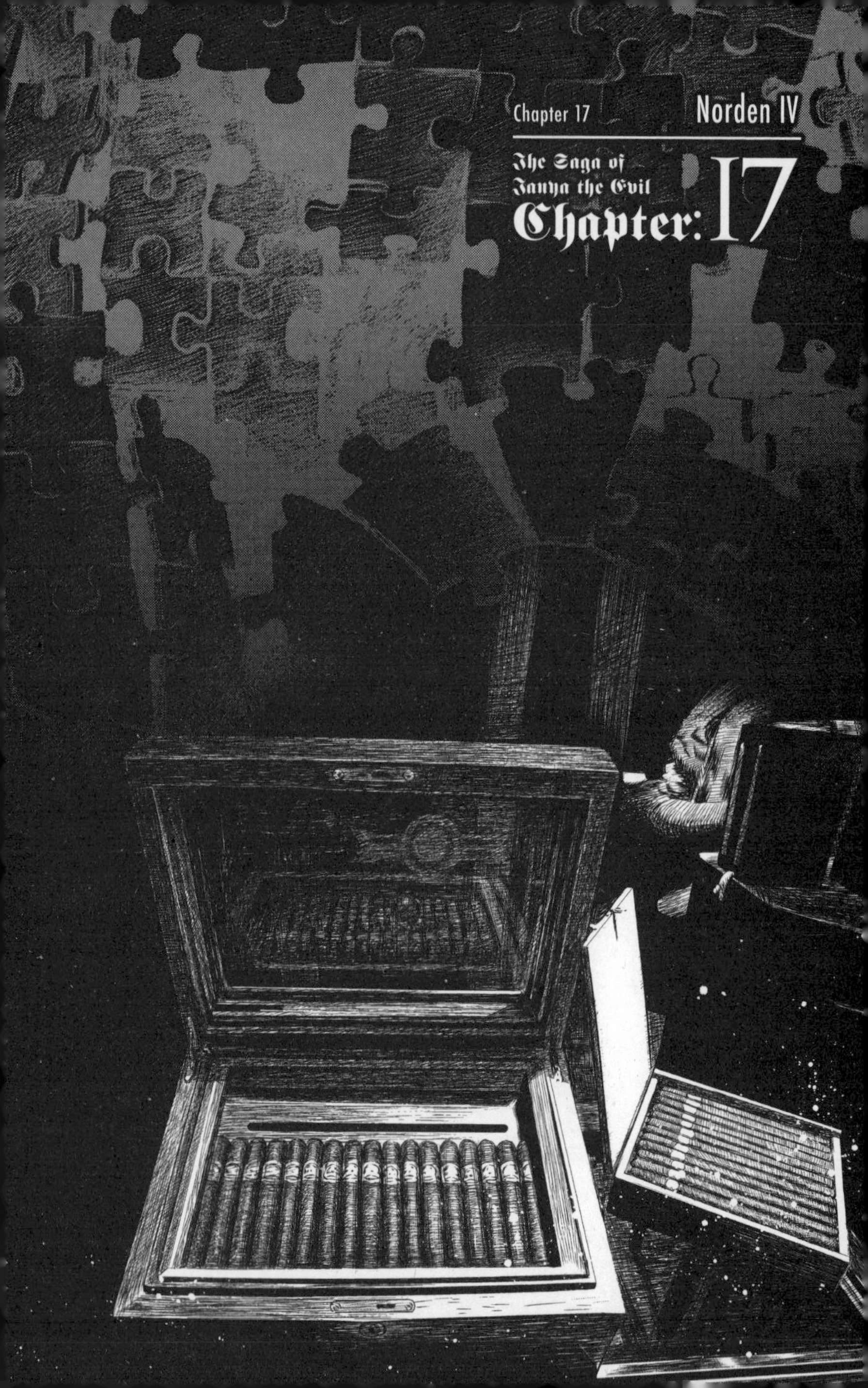
Chapter 17
Norden IV
The Saga of Tanya the Evil
Chapter: 17

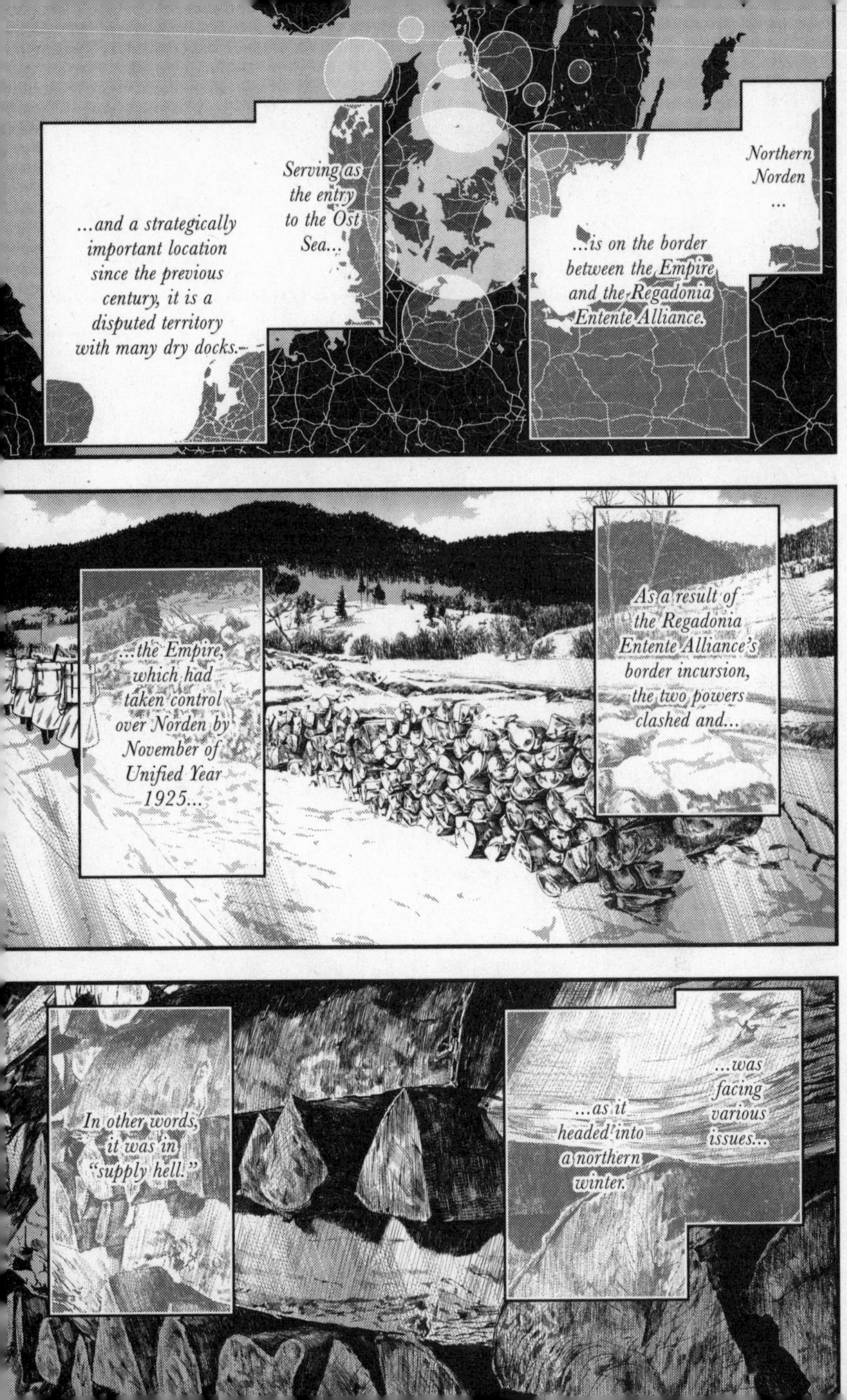
Northern Norden ...
...is on the border between the Empire and the Regadonia Entente Alliance.
Serving as the entry to the Ost Sea...
...and a strategically important location since the previous century, it is a disputed territory with many dry docks.
As a result of the Regadonia Entente Alliance's border incursion, the two powers clashed and...
...the Empire, which had taken control over Norden by November of Unified Year 1925...
...was facing various issues...
...as it headed into a northern winter.
In other words, it was in "supply hell."

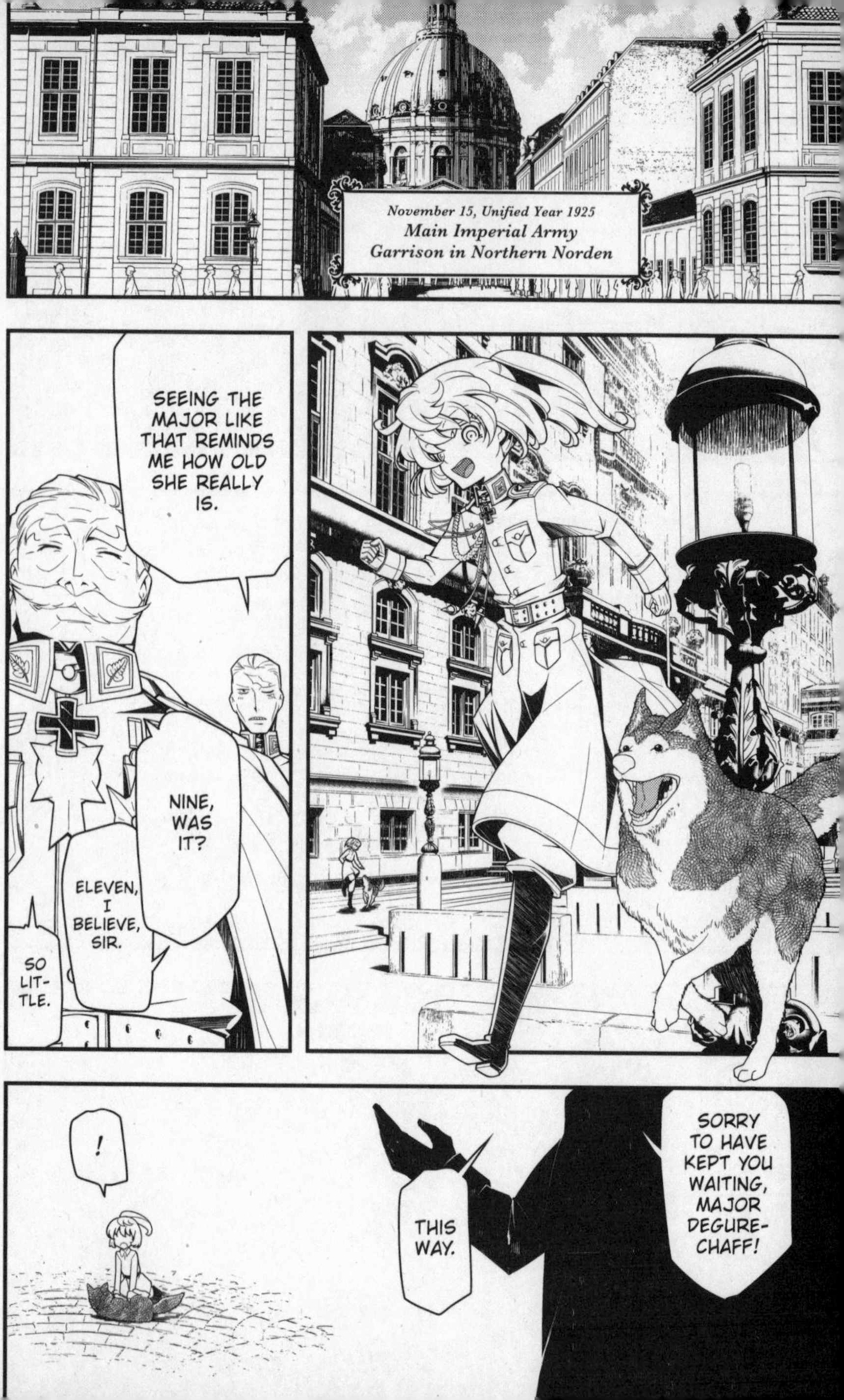
November 15, Unified Year 1925
Main Imperial Army Garrison in Northern Norden
SEEING THE MAJOR LIKE THAT REMINDS ME HOW OLD SHE REALLY IS.
NINE, WAS IT?
ELEVEN, I BELIEVE, SIR.
SO LIT-TLE.
SORRY TO HAVE KEPT YOU WAITING, MAJOR DEGURE-CHAFF!
THIS WAY.
!

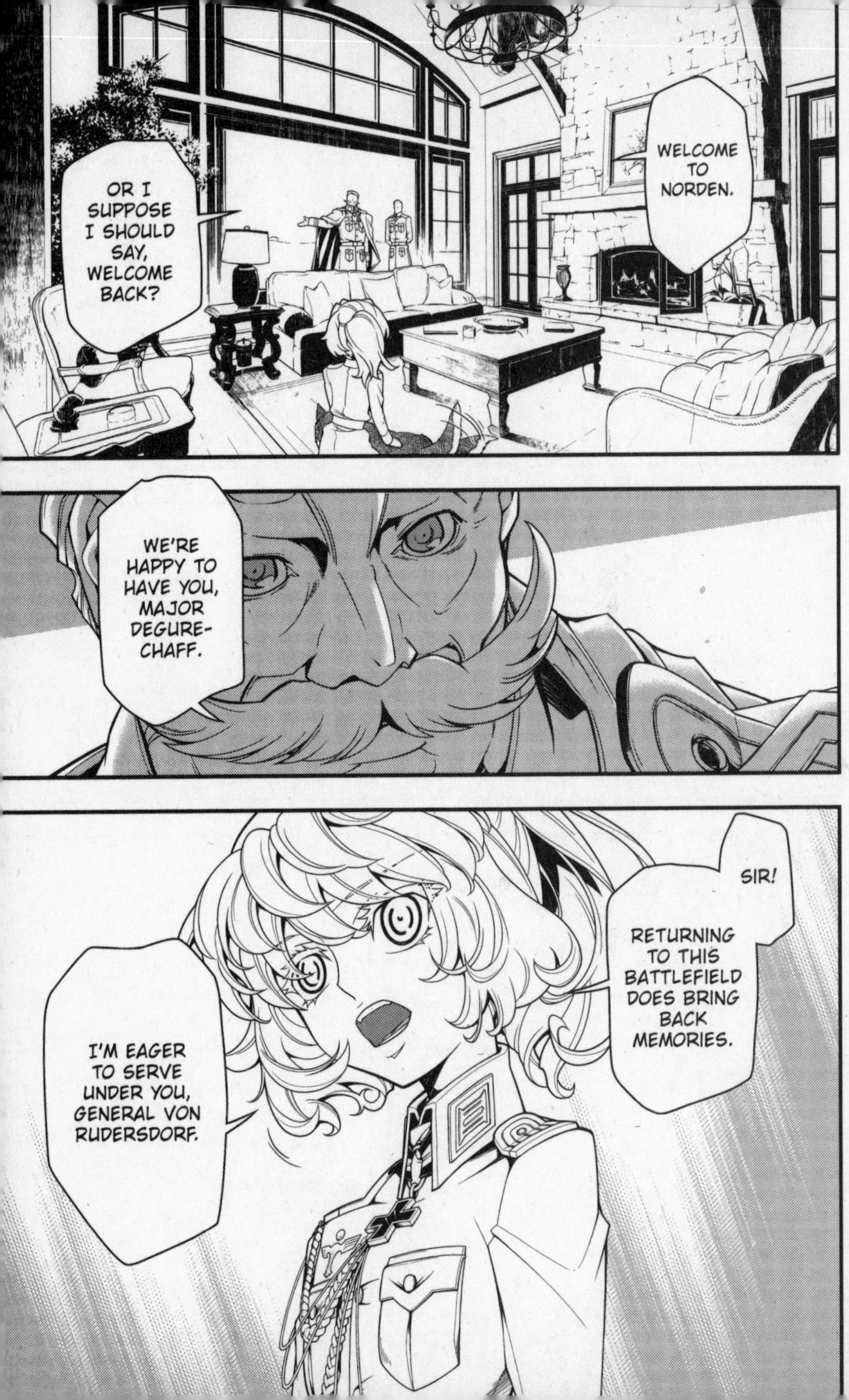
WELCOME TO NORDEN.
OR I SUPPOSE I SHOULD SAY, WELCOME BACK?
WE'RE HAPPY TO HAVE YOU, MAJOR DEGURE-CHAFF.
SIR!
RETURNING TO THIS BATTLEFIELD DOES BRING BACK MEMORIES.
I'M EAGER TO SERVE UNDER YOU, GENERAL VON RUDERSDORF.

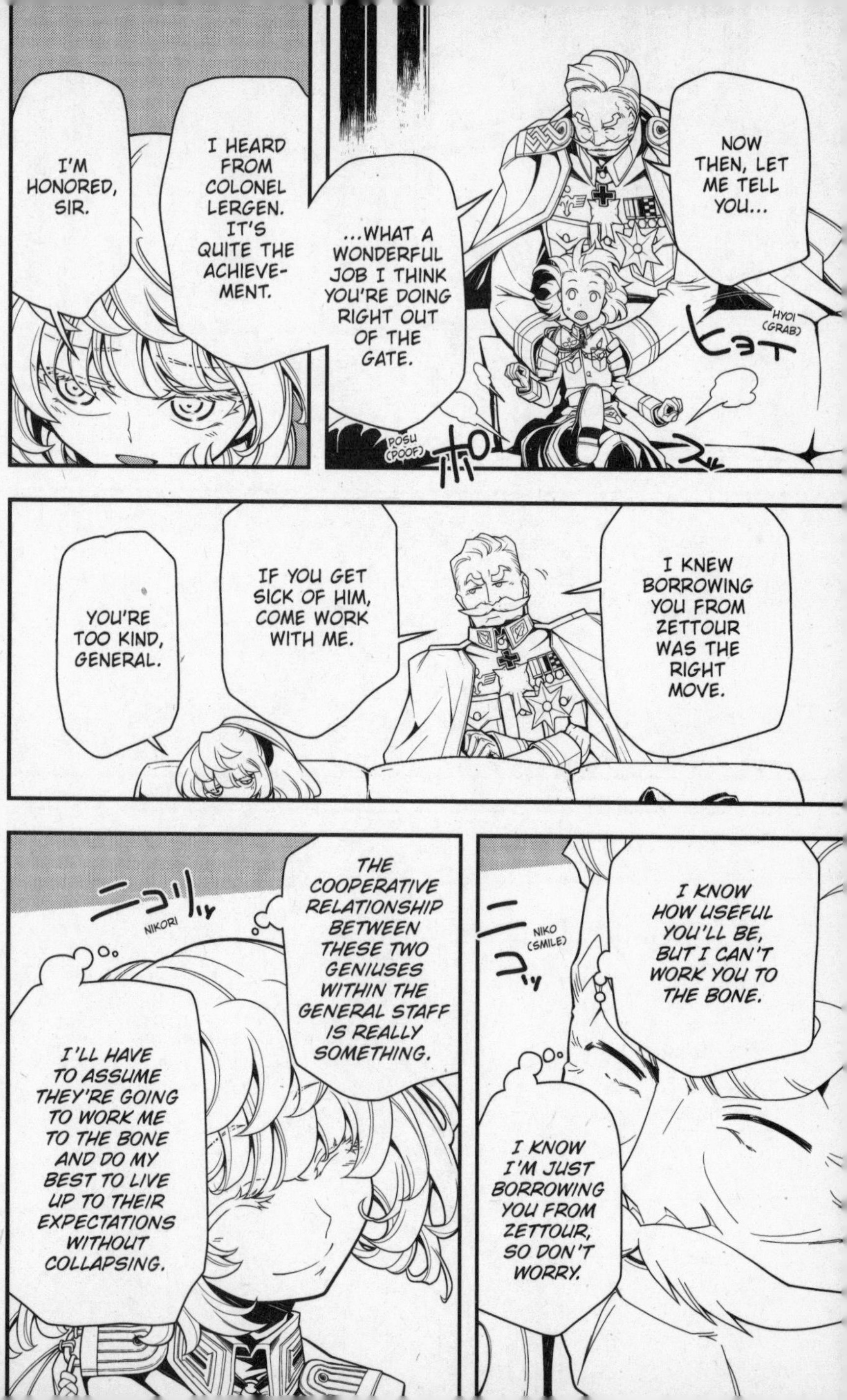
NOW THEN, LET ME TELL YOU...
HYOI (GRAB)
...WHAT A WONDERFUL JOB I THINK YOU'RE DOING RIGHT OUT OF THE GATE.
POSU (POOF)
I HEARD FROM COLONEL LERGEN. IT'S QUITE THE ACHIEVEMENT.
I'M HONORED, SIR.
I KNEW BORROWING YOU FROM ZETTOUR WAS THE RIGHT MOVE.
IF YOU GET SICK OF HIM, COME WORK WITH ME.
YOU'RE TOO KIND, GENERAL.
NIKO (SMILE)
I KNOW HOW USEFUL YOU'LL BE, BUT I CAN'T WORK YOU TO THE BONE.
I KNOW I'M JUST BORROWING YOU FROM ZETTOUR, SO DON'T WORRY.
NIKORI
THE COOPERATIVE RELATIONSHIP BETWEEN THESE TWO GENIUSES WITHIN THE GENERAL STAFF IS REALLY SOMETHING.
I'LL HAVE TO ASSUME THEY'RE GOING TO WORK ME TO THE BONE AND DO MY BEST TO LIVE UP TO THEIR EXPECTATIONS WITHOUT COLLAPSING.

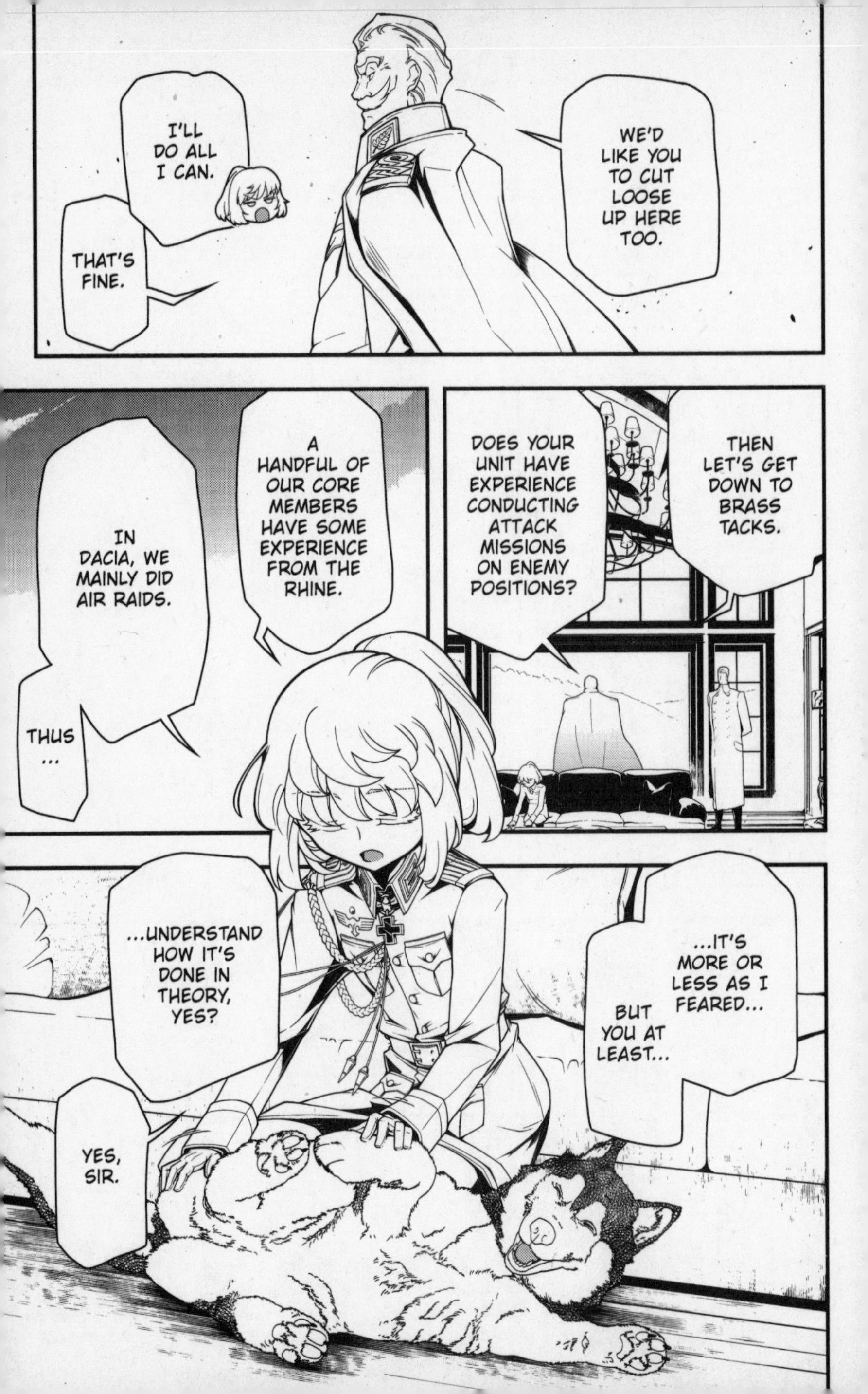
WE'D LIKE YOU TO CUT LOOSE UP HERE TOO.
I'LL DO ALL I CAN.
THAT'S FINE.
THEN LET'S GET DOWN TO BRASS TACKS.
DOES YOUR UNIT HAVE EXPERIENCE CONDUCTING ATTACK MISSIONS ON ENEMY POSITIONS?
A HANDFUL OF OUR CORE MEMBERS HAVE SOME EXPERIENCE FROM THE RHINE.
IN DACIA, WE MAINLY DID AIR RAIDS.
THUS ...
...IT'S MORE OR LESS AS I FEARED...
BUT YOU AT LEAST...
...UNDERSTAND HOW IT'S DONE IN THEORY, YES?
YES, SIR.

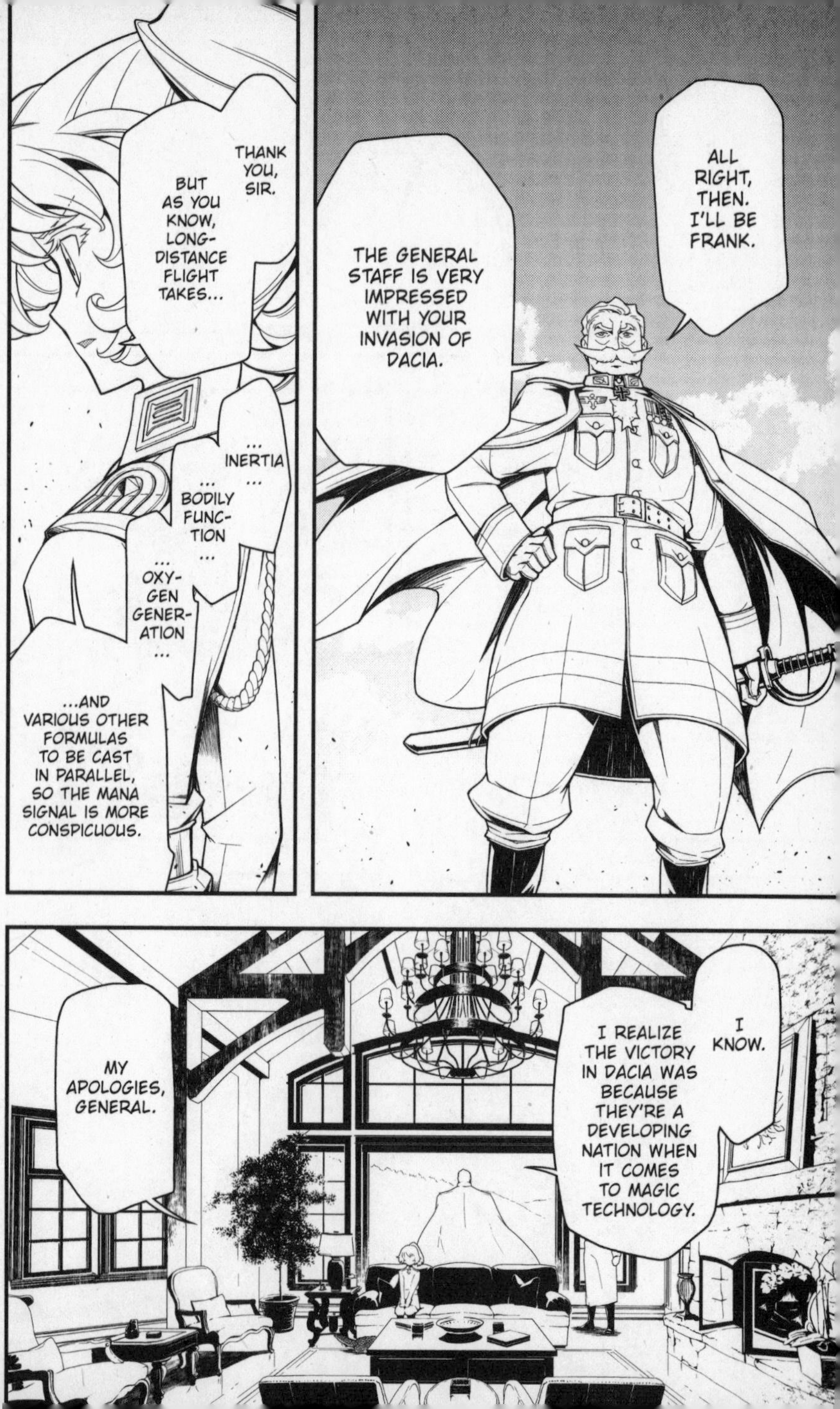
ALL RIGHT, THEN. I'LL BE FRANK.
THE GENERAL STAFF IS VERY IMPRESSED WITH YOUR INVASION OF DACIA.
THANK YOU, SIR.
BUT AS YOU KNOW, LONG-DISTANCE FLIGHT TAKES...
...INERTIA... ...BODILY FUNCTION... ...OXYGEN GENERATION...
...AND VARIOUS OTHER FORMULAS TO BE CAST IN PARALLEL, SO THE MANA SIGNAL IS MORE CONSPICUOUS.
I KNOW.
I REALIZE THE VICTORY IN DACIA WAS BECAUSE THEY'RE A DEVELOPING NATION WHEN IT COMES TO MAGIC TECHNOLOGY.
MY APOLOGIES, GENERAL.

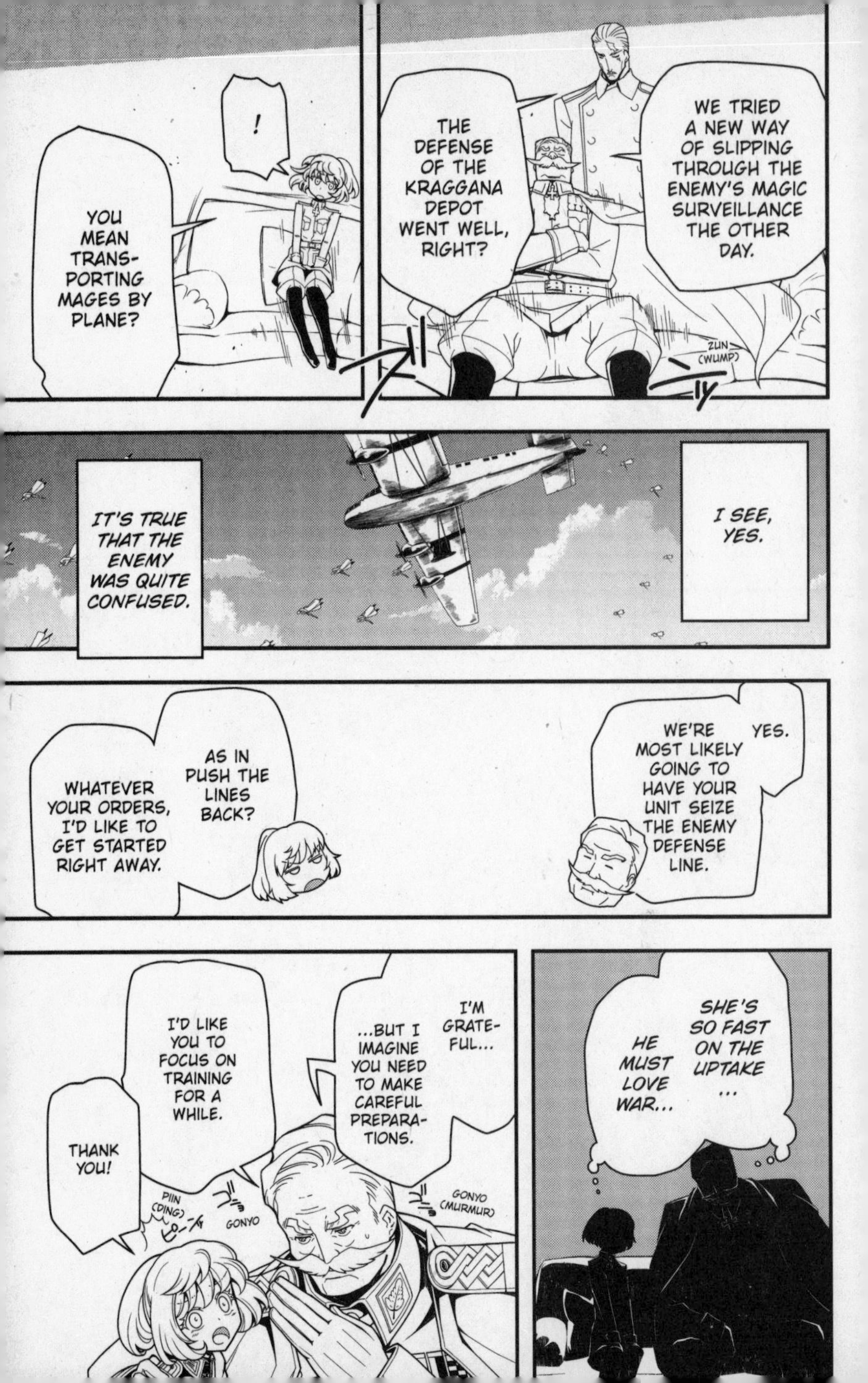
WE TRIED A NEW WAY OF SLIPPING THROUGH THE ENEMY'S MAGIC SURVEILLANCE THE OTHER DAY.
THE DEFENSE OF THE KRAGGANA DEPOT WENT WELL, RIGHT?
ZUN (WUMP)
!
YOU MEAN TRANS-PORTING MAGES BY PLANE?
I SEE, YES.
IT'S TRUE THAT THE ENEMY WAS QUITE CONFUSED.
YES.
WE'RE MOST LIKELY GOING TO HAVE YOUR UNIT SEIZE THE ENEMY DEFENSE LINE.
AS IN PUSH THE LINES BACK?
WHATEVER YOUR ORDERS, I'D LIKE TO GET STARTED RIGHT AWAY.
SHE'S SO FAST ON THE UPTAKE...
HE MUST LOVE WAR...
I'M GRATE-FUL...
...BUT I IMAGINE YOU NEED TO MAKE CAREFUL PREPARA-TIONS.
GONYO (MURMUR)
I'D LIKE YOU TO FOCUS ON TRAINING FOR A WHILE.
GONYO
PIIN (DING)
THANK YOU!

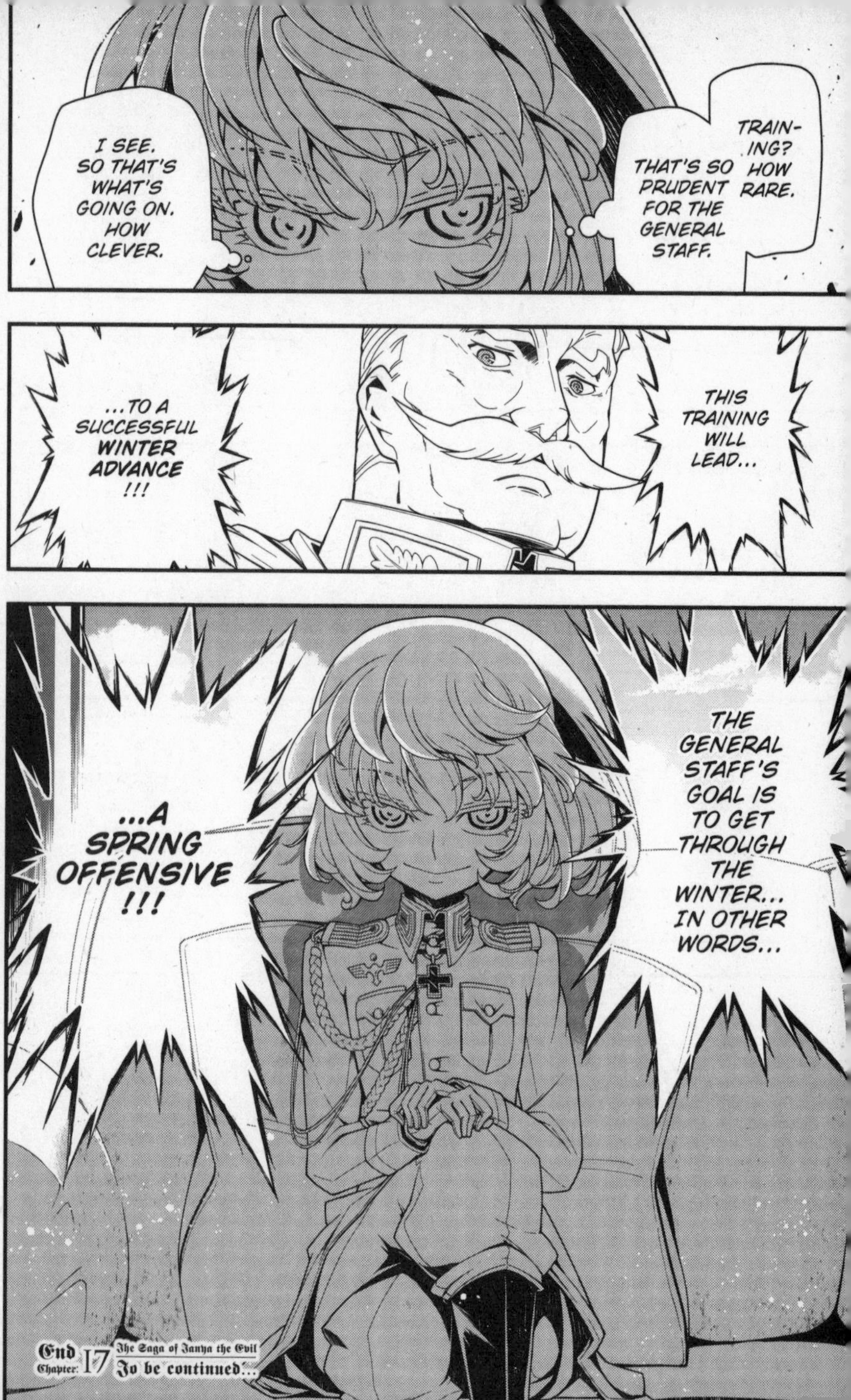
TRAINING? HOW RARE.
THAT'S SO PRUDENT FOR THE GENERAL STAFF.
I SEE. SO THAT'S WHAT'S GOING ON. HOW CLEVER.
THIS TRAINING WILL LEAD...
...TO A SUCCESSFUL WINTER ADVANCE!!!
THE GENERAL STAFF'S GOAL IS TO GET THROUGH THE WINTER... IN OTHER WORDS...
...A SPRING OFFENSIVE!!!
End Chapter: 17 The Saga of Tanya the Evil To be continued...

Glossary Chapter 21

Classified Documents

Papers that, for national strategy or military reasons, are kept secret. The contents include details of operations and written orders, schematics of weapons and information regarding their performance, notes on unit makeup and where they are stationed, and so on.

How secret something is depends on its classification. For example, some countries split them up as Top Secret, Secret, Confidential, and Restricted.

Once the war ends or there is no longer any reason for a document to be secret, it is sometimes declassified. In that case, democracies usually allow anyone to view them by following the proper procedure to file a release request.

Unlogistics

The negation of logistics. It's exactly eleven characters. The term was used in the original Japanese version of the volume to refer to a complete depletion of resources otherwise known as "supply hell."

Animal Therapy

As Degurechaff was petting the dog in the midst of her difficult work, she was probably subconsciously seeking comfort from the animal interaction.

It's well-known that interacting with animals like cats and dogs has soothing, relaxing effects. There have been efforts to apply that to soldiers for a long time; there are even records of a horseback-riding treatment from 400 BC where wounded soldiers would be put on a horse.

Some recuperation facilities for retired soldiers today have tried adopting treatments via animals. For instance, one clinic has a working farm where patients care for horses and other livestock and a park where they can interact with animals in a natural setting, which have assisted in the recovery of soldiers with emotional disturbances.

These treatments are called "animal therapy" and are used to resolve psychological issues. Mammals are most often employed, since they can empathize with human emotions on a higher level; apparently, dogs are particularly suitable because they pour out love unsparingly no matter what kind of person the patient is.

Degurechaff is often referred to as a "monster," so having a dog treat her as a regular human must have been tremendously comforting. Perhaps someone was kind enough to arrange their meeting.

Glossary Chapter 22

Volunteer Army

"Military volunteer" refers to neither drafted nationals nor mercenaries but soldiers who joined the war of their own volition. Volunteer armies are units formed mainly of military volunteers.

Although military volunteer participation is said to be personally motivated, it's not uncommon for a third country's regular military to move in and occupy territory while claiming to be a volunteer army. This technique is often employed when, due to political dynamics, a country can't openly join the war but wants to intervene for one reason or another.

Reasons for such action are varied. For example, they might want to swing the power balance between the warring countries in a manner that favors their own nation. Another could be that, for political reasons, they aren't able to form an alliance with one of the warring countries, but they hope it will win on the lines against another country. Using the battles as a testing ground for new tactics or equipment or for research is another possibility.

Culminating Point

The idea that, no matter how great an advantage your army has, there's a limit to how much attacking and advancing you can do.

When one side has an advantage over their enemy, they advance in order to rack up more achievements, but attacking will definitely wear their manpower down, and they'll be forced to split off more troops to guard the lengthening supply lines. The cons of advancing pile up and eventually overtake the gap that gave the advancing army the upper hand—and that is the limit. Pushing on without an understanding on where your limit is means giving up whatever advantage you had.

Commando Unit

Special units that are sent out with objectives such as performing sneak attacks, destroying supply lines, creating disturbances in the rear, and assassinating enemy commanders.

They are smaller units formed separately from the units engaged in battle, and since they perform penetrating raids with as little gear as possible, their role is similar to guerrilla troops. Sometimes they are called "guerrilla and commando units" as one entity, but unlike guerrilla units, which tend to be made up mainly of militia, commando units are considered to be elite members of the regular army.

This is a tangent, but the English-language slang "going commando" supposedly comes from a certain country's commando units' practice of not wearing underwear to save time on laundry.

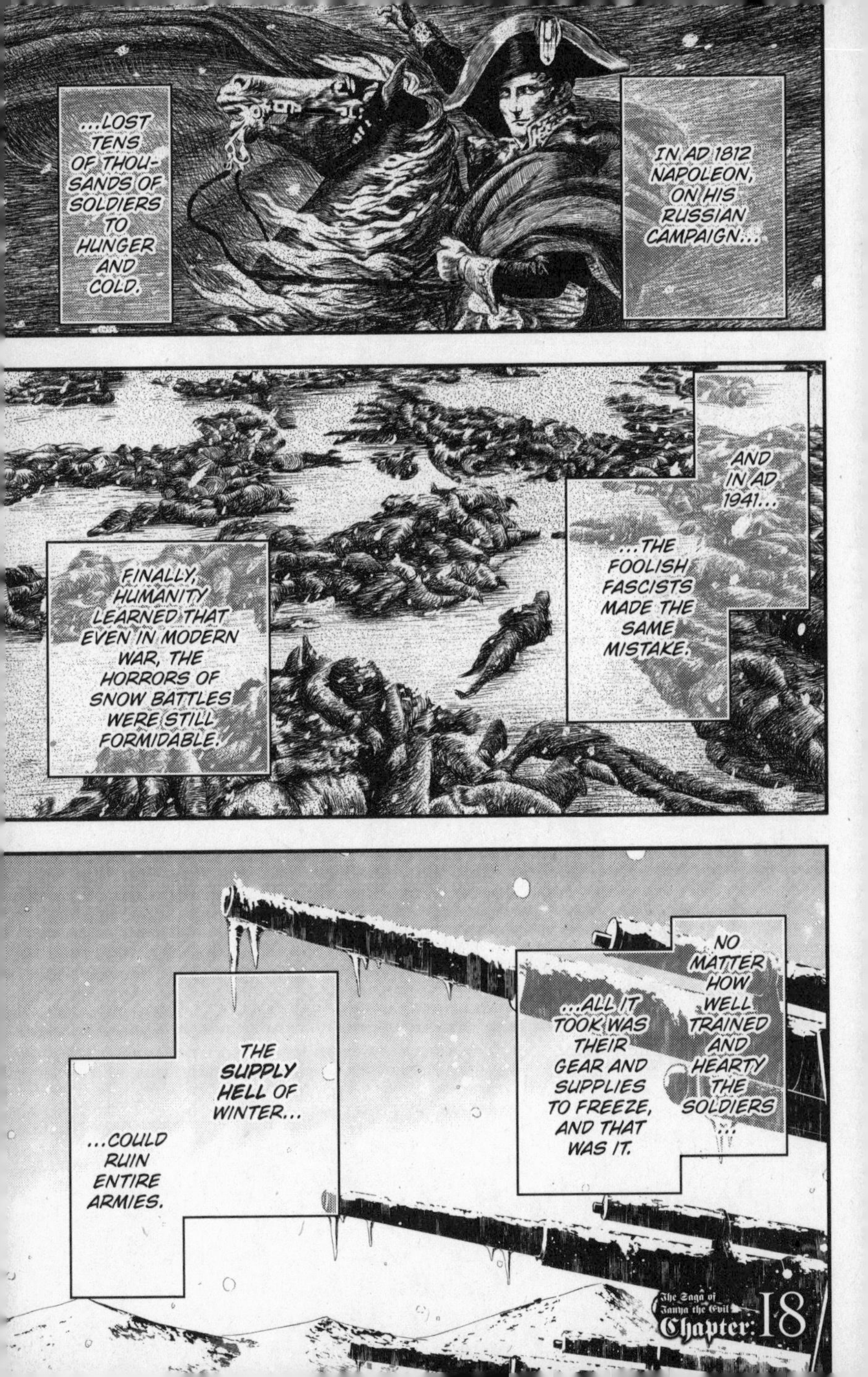
IN AD 1812 NAPOLEON, ON HIS RUSSIAN CAMPAIGN...
...LOST TENS OF THOUSANDS OF SOLDIERS TO HUNGER AND COLD.
AND IN AD 1941...
...THE FOOLISH FASCISTS MADE THE SAME MISTAKE.
FINALLY, HUMANITY LEARNED THAT EVEN IN MODERN WAR, THE HORRORS OF SNOW BATTLES WERE STILL FORMIDABLE.
NO MATTER HOW WELL TRAINED AND HEARTY THE SOLDIERS...
...ALL IT TOOK WAS THEIR GEAR AND SUPPLIES TO FREEZE, AND THAT WAS IT.
THE SUPPLY HELL OF WINTER...
...COULD RUIN ENTIRE ARMIES.
The Saga of Tanya the Evil
Chapter: 18

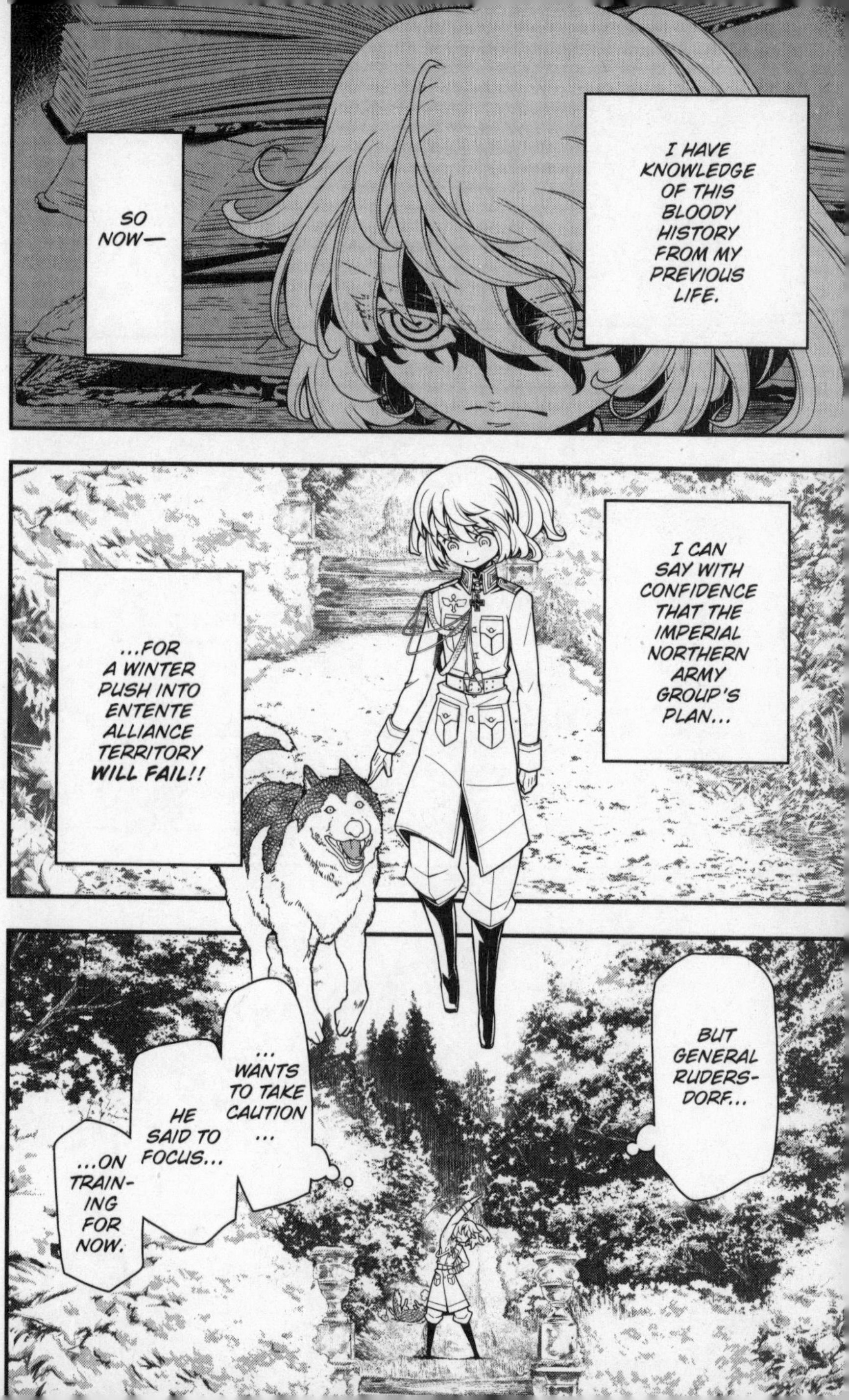
I HAVE KNOWLEDGE OF THIS BLOODY HISTORY FROM MY PREVIOUS LIFE.
SO NOW—
I CAN SAY WITH CONFIDENCE THAT THE IMPERIAL NORTHERN ARMY GROUP'S PLAN...
...FOR A WINTER PUSH INTO ENTENTE ALLIANCE TERRITORY **WILL FAIL!!**
BUT GENERAL RUDERS-DORF...
...WANTS TO TAKE CAUTION...
HE SAID TO FOCUS...
...ON TRAIN-ING FOR NOW.

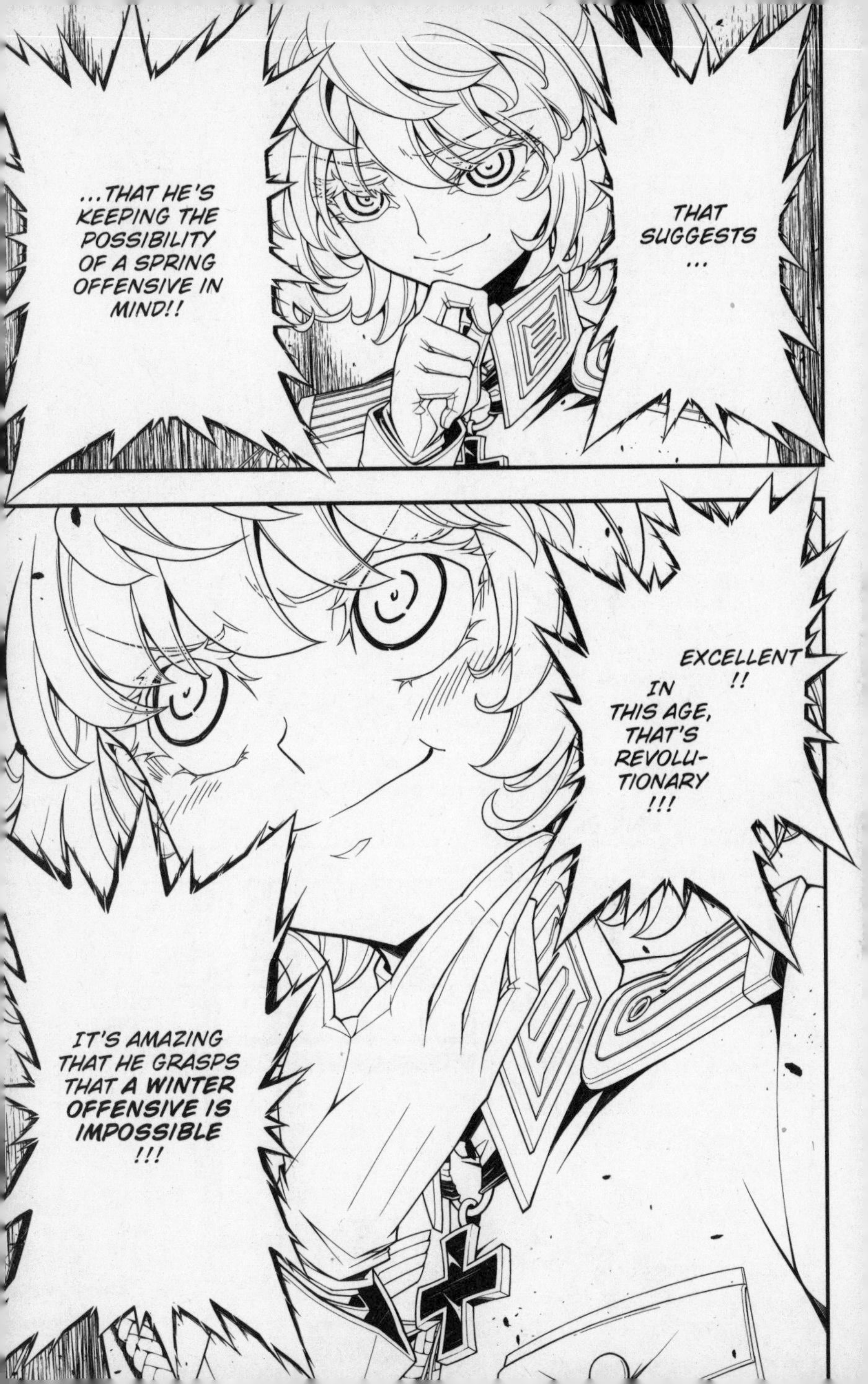
THAT SUGGESTS ...
...THAT HE'S KEEPING THE POSSIBILITY OF A SPRING OFFENSIVE IN MIND!!
EXCELLENT!!
IN THIS AGE, THAT'S REVOLUTIONARY!!!
IT'S AMAZING THAT HE GRASPS THAT A WINTER OFFENSIVE IS IMPOSSIBLE!!!

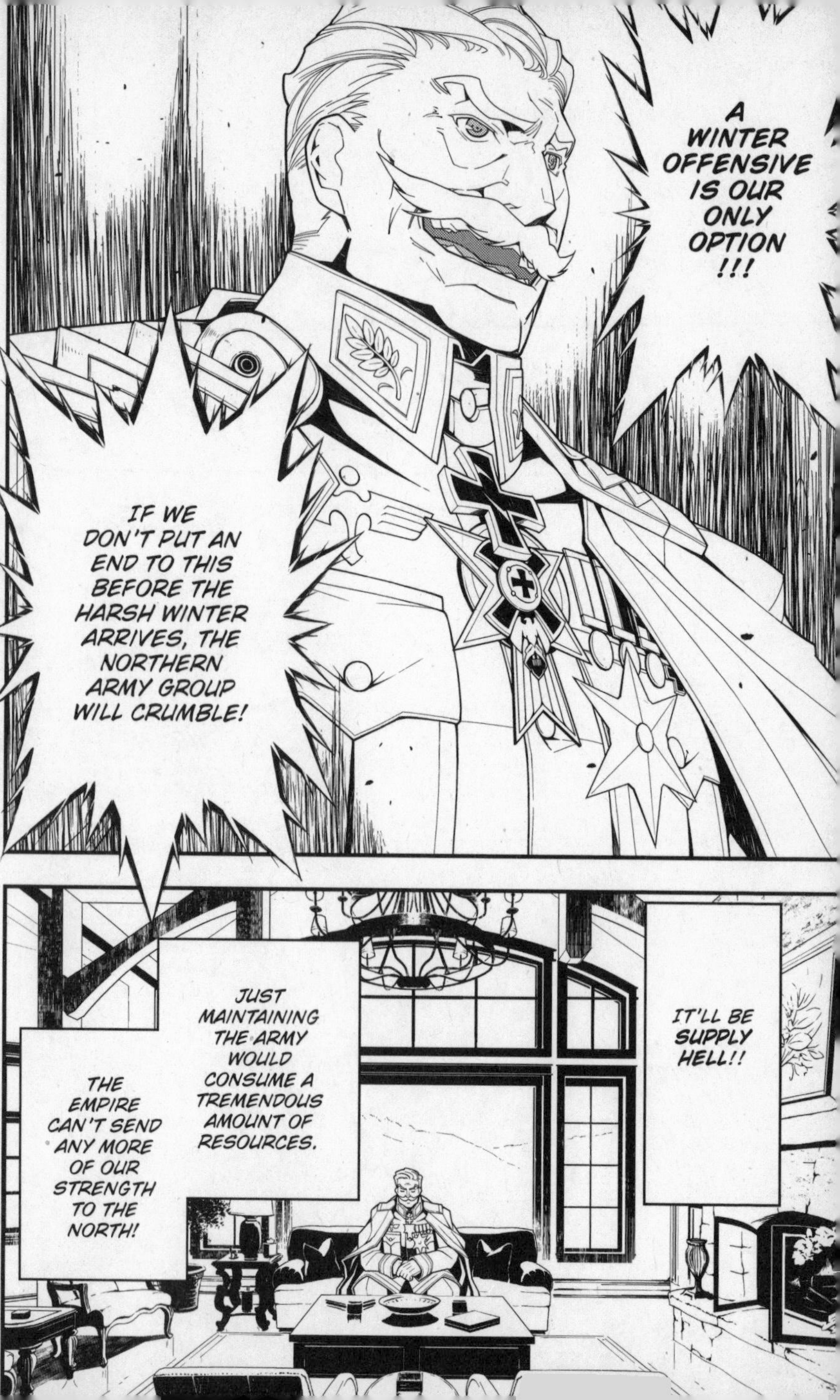
A WINTER OFFENSIVE IS OUR ONLY OPTION!!!
IF WE DON'T PUT AN END TO THIS BEFORE THE HARSH WINTER ARRIVES, THE NORTHERN ARMY GROUP WILL CRUMBLE!
IT'LL BE SUPPLY HELL!!
JUST MAINTAINING THE ARMY WOULD CONSUME A TREMENDOUS AMOUNT OF RESOURCES.
THE EMPIRE CAN'T SEND ANY MORE OF OUR STRENGTH TO THE NORTH!

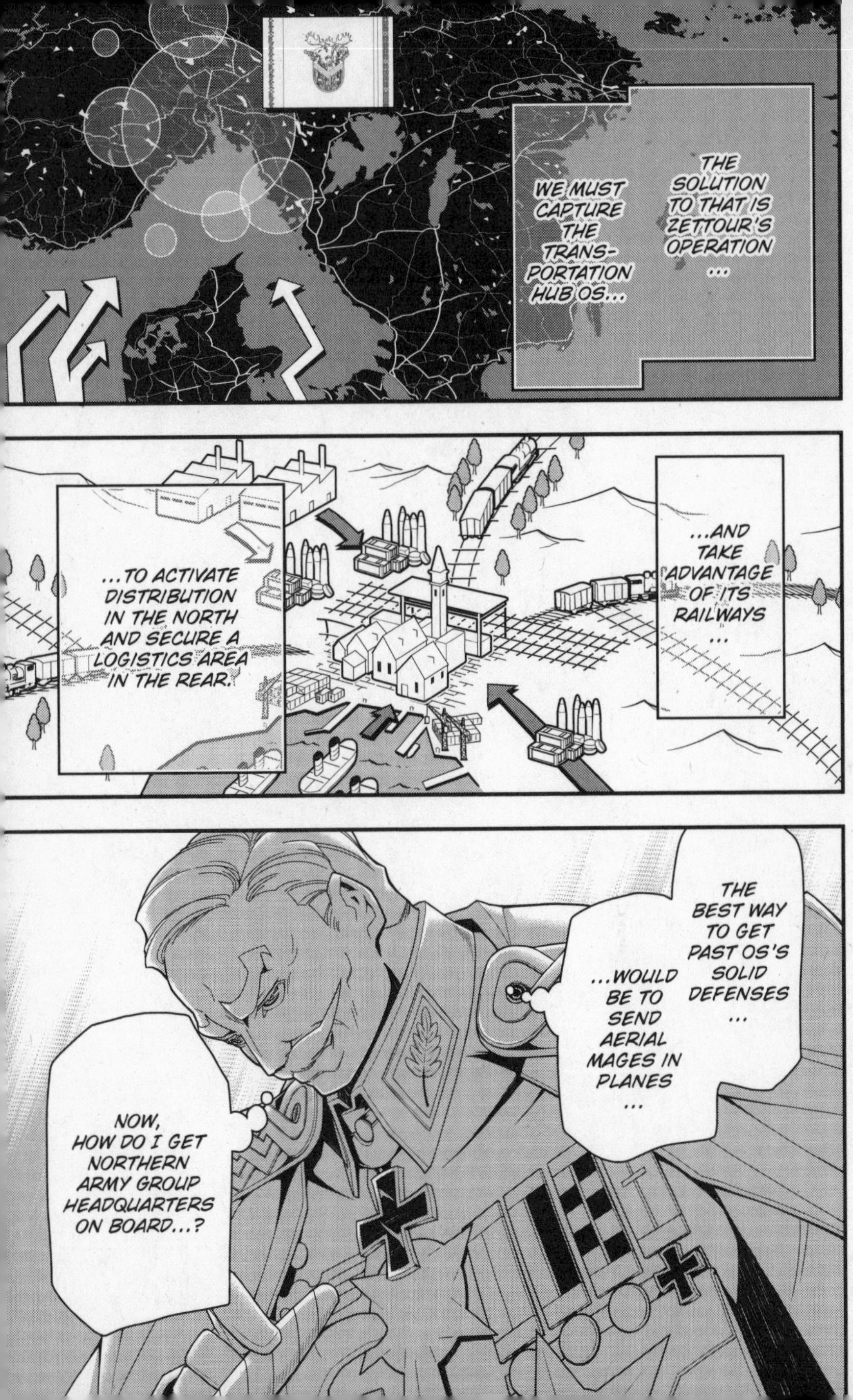
THE SOLUTION TO THAT IS ZETTOUR'S OPERATION...
WE MUST CAPTURE THE TRANS-PORTATION HUB OS...
...AND TAKE ADVANTAGE OF ITS RAILWAYS...
...TO ACTIVATE DISTRIBUTION IN THE NORTH AND SECURE A LOGISTICS AREA IN THE REAR.
THE BEST WAY TO GET PAST OS'S SOLID DEFENSES...
...WOULD BE TO SEND AERIAL MAGES IN PLANES...
NOW, HOW DO I GET NORTHERN ARMY GROUP HEADQUARTERS ON BOARD...?

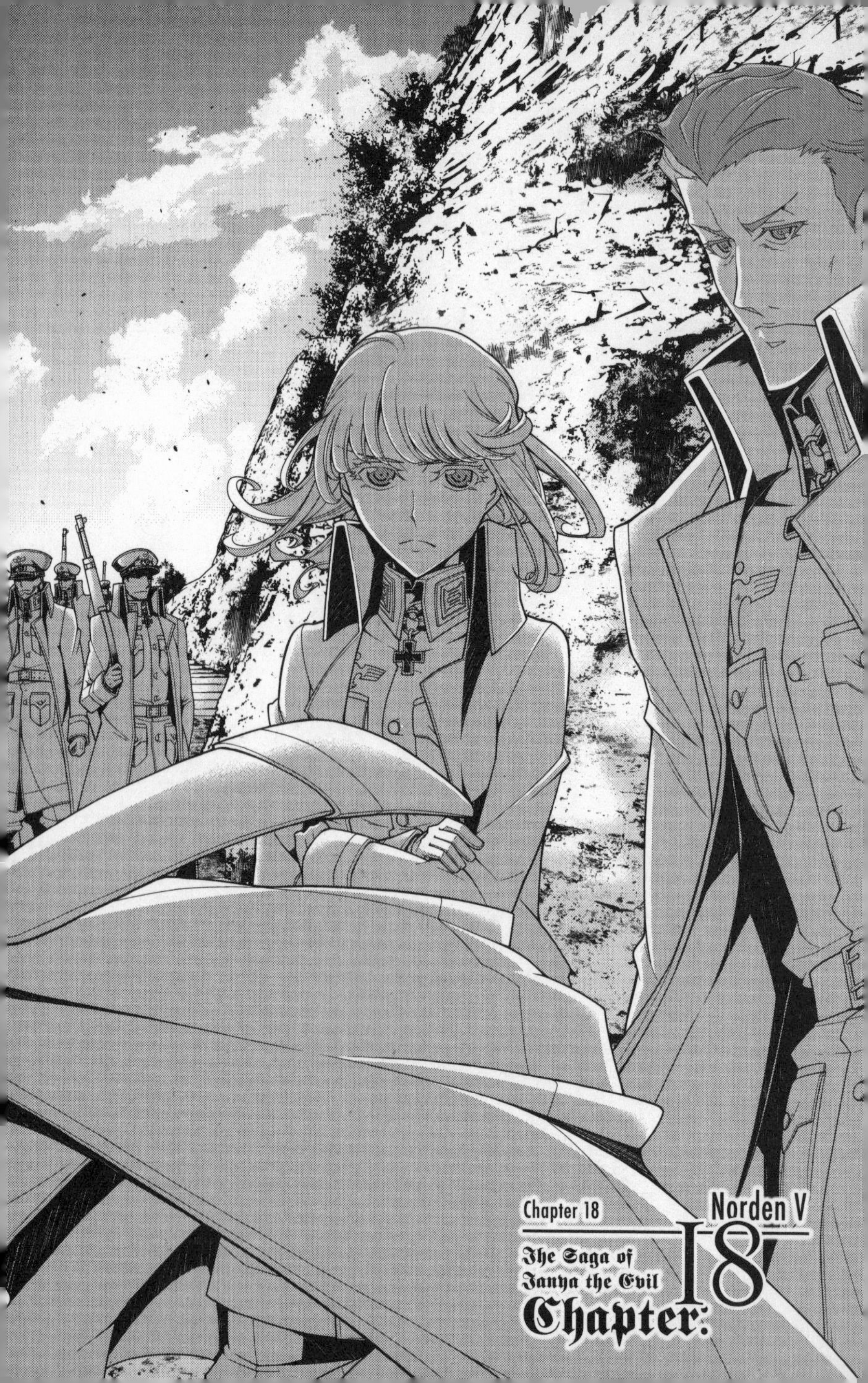
Chapter 18
Norden V
The Saga of Tanya the Evil
Chapter: 18

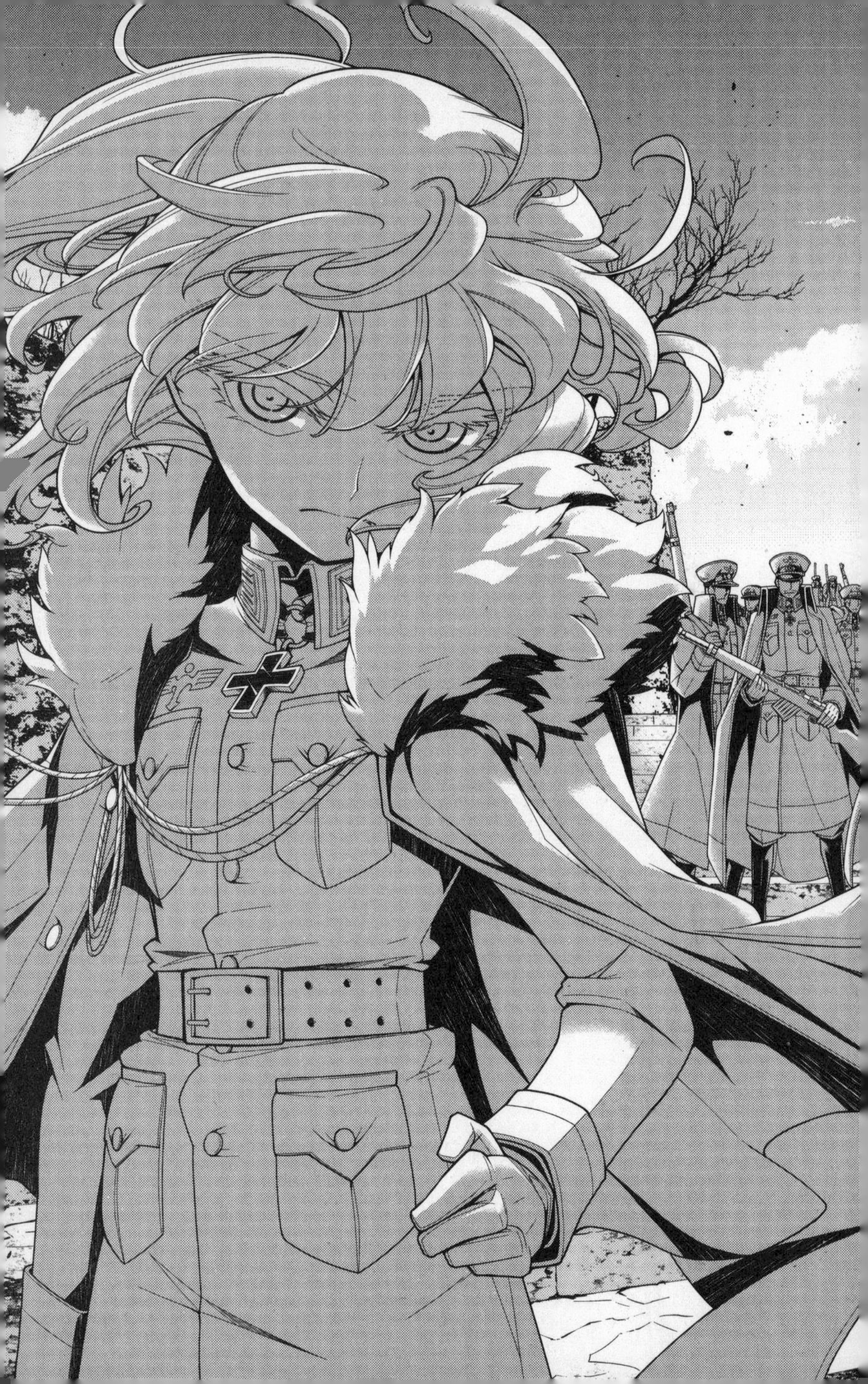

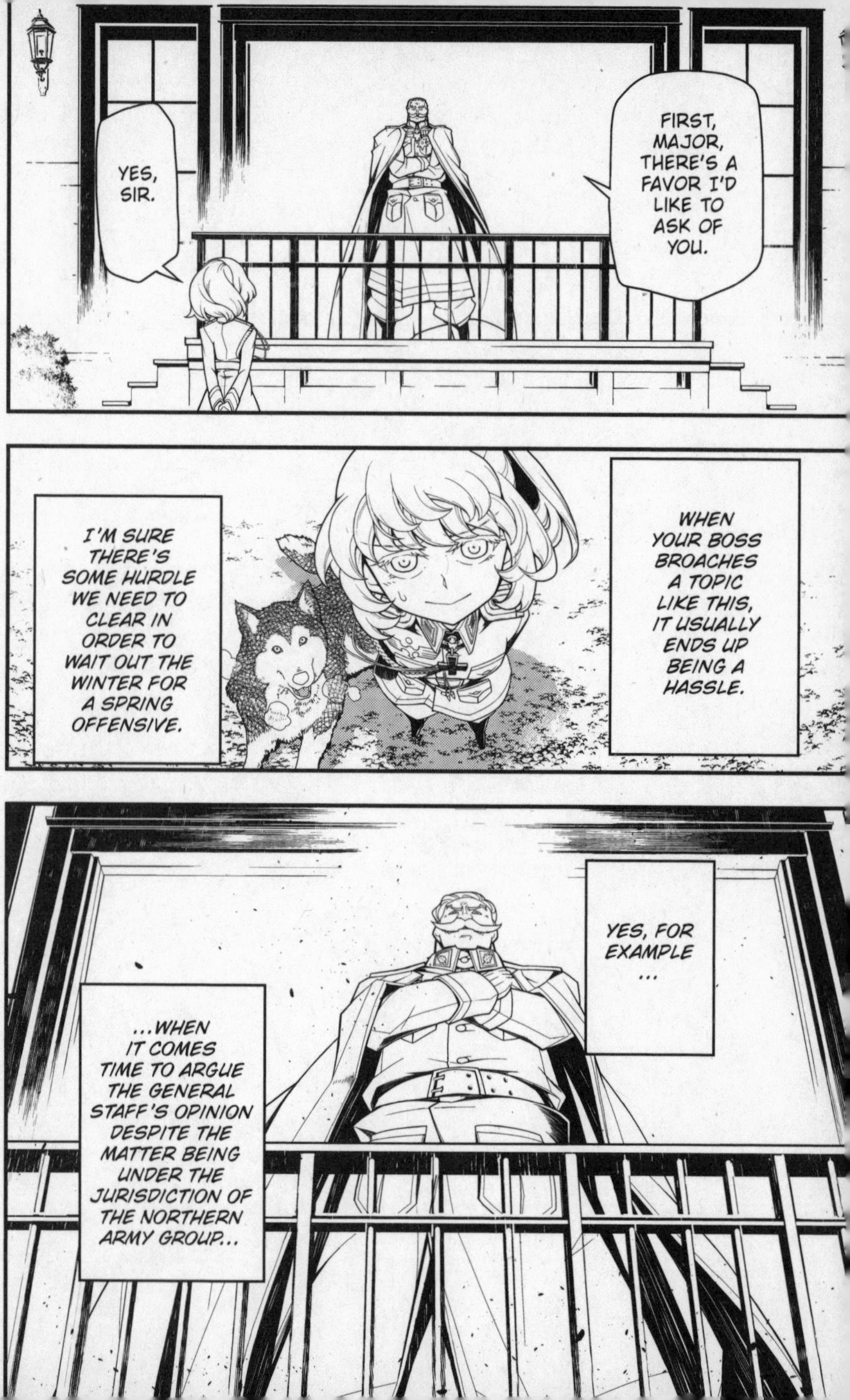
FIRST, MAJOR, THERE'S A FAVOR I'D LIKE TO ASK OF YOU.
YES, SIR.
WHEN YOUR BOSS BROACHES A TOPIC LIKE THIS, IT USUALLY ENDS UP BEING A HASSLE.
I'M SURE THERE'S SOME HURDLE WE NEED TO CLEAR IN ORDER TO WAIT OUT THE WINTER FOR A SPRING OFFENSIVE.
YES, FOR EXAMPLE ...
...WHEN IT COMES TIME TO ARGUE THE GENERAL STAFF'S OPINION DESPITE THE MATTER BEING UNDER THE JURISDICTION OF THE NORTHERN ARMY GROUP...

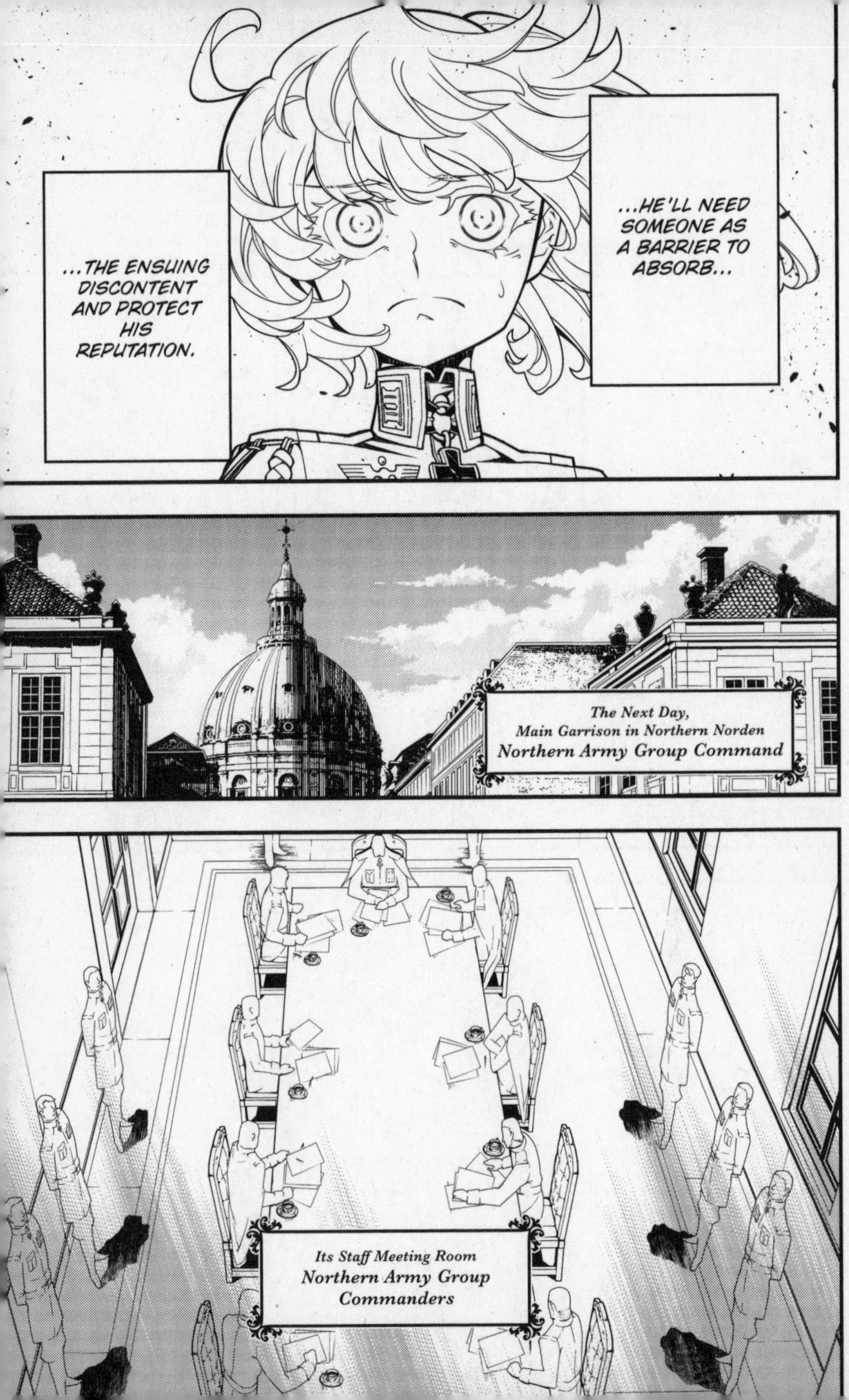
...HE'LL NEED SOMEONE AS A BARRIER TO ABSORB...
...THE ENSUING DISCONTENT AND PROTECT HIS REPUTATION.
The Next Day, Main Garrison in Northern Norden Northern Army Group Command
Its Staff Meeting Room Northern Army Group Commanders

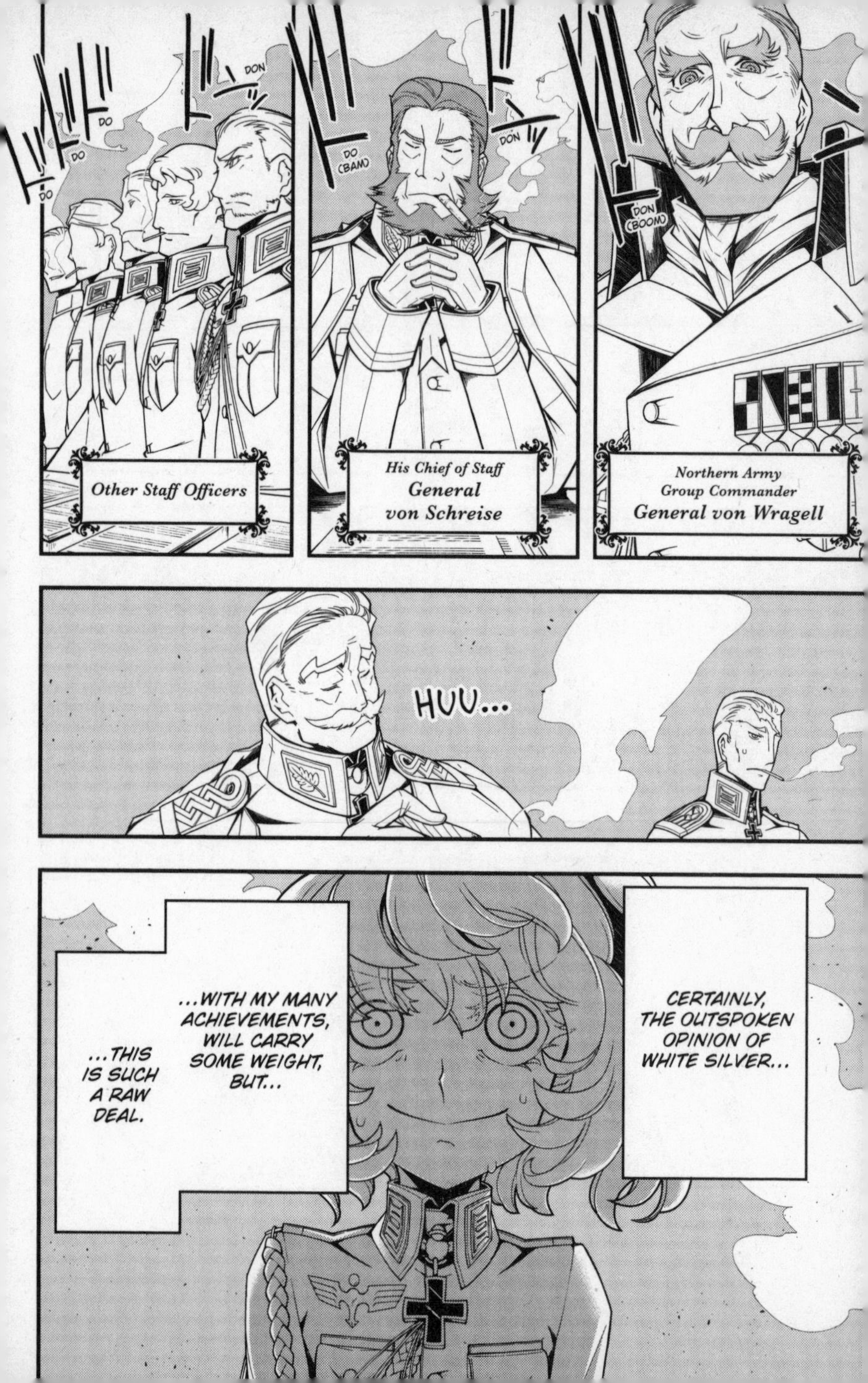
DON (BOOM)
Northern Army Group Commander General von Wragell
DON
DO (BAM)
His Chief of Staff General von Schreise
DON
DO
DO
DO
Other Staff Officers
HUU...
CERTAINLY, THE OUTSPOKEN OPINION OF WHITE SILVER...
...WITH MY MANY ACHIEVEMENTS, WILL CARRY SOME WEIGHT, BUT...
...THIS IS SUCH A RAW DEAL.

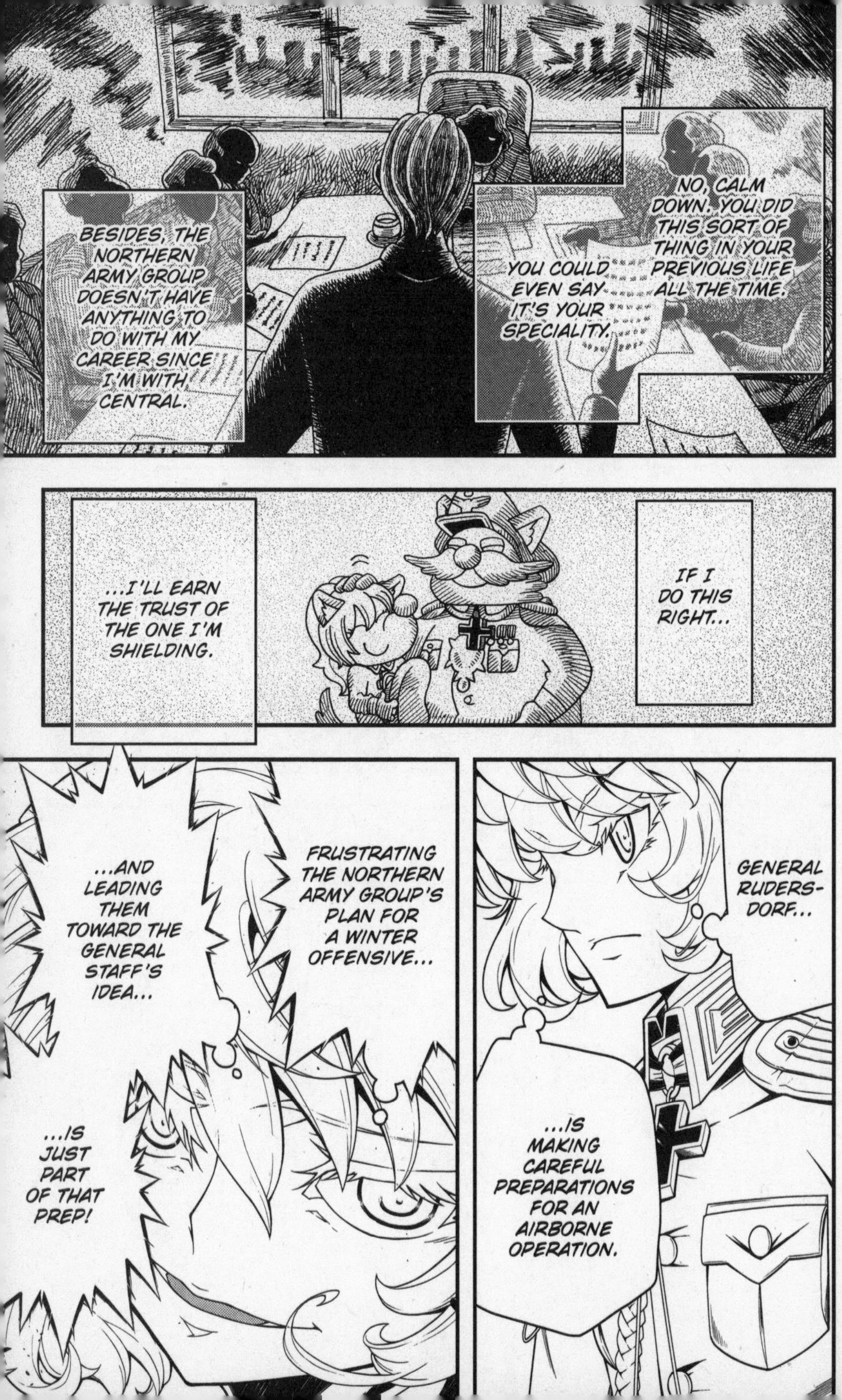
NO, CALM DOWN. YOU DID THIS SORT OF THING IN YOUR PREVIOUS LIFE ALL THE TIME.
YOU COULD EVEN SAY IT'S YOUR SPECIALITY.
BESIDES, THE NORTHERN ARMY GROUP DOESN'T HAVE ANYTHING TO DO WITH MY CAREER SINCE I'M WITH CENTRAL.
IF I DO THIS RIGHT...
...I'LL EARN THE TRUST OF THE ONE I'M SHIELDING.
GENERAL RUDERS-DORF...
...IS MAKING CAREFUL PREPARATIONS FOR AN AIRBORNE OPERATION.
FRUSTRATING THE NORTHERN ARMY GROUP'S PLAN FOR A WINTER OFFENSIVE...
...AND LEADING THEM TOWARD THE GENERAL STAFF'S IDEA...
...IS JUST PART OF THAT PREP!

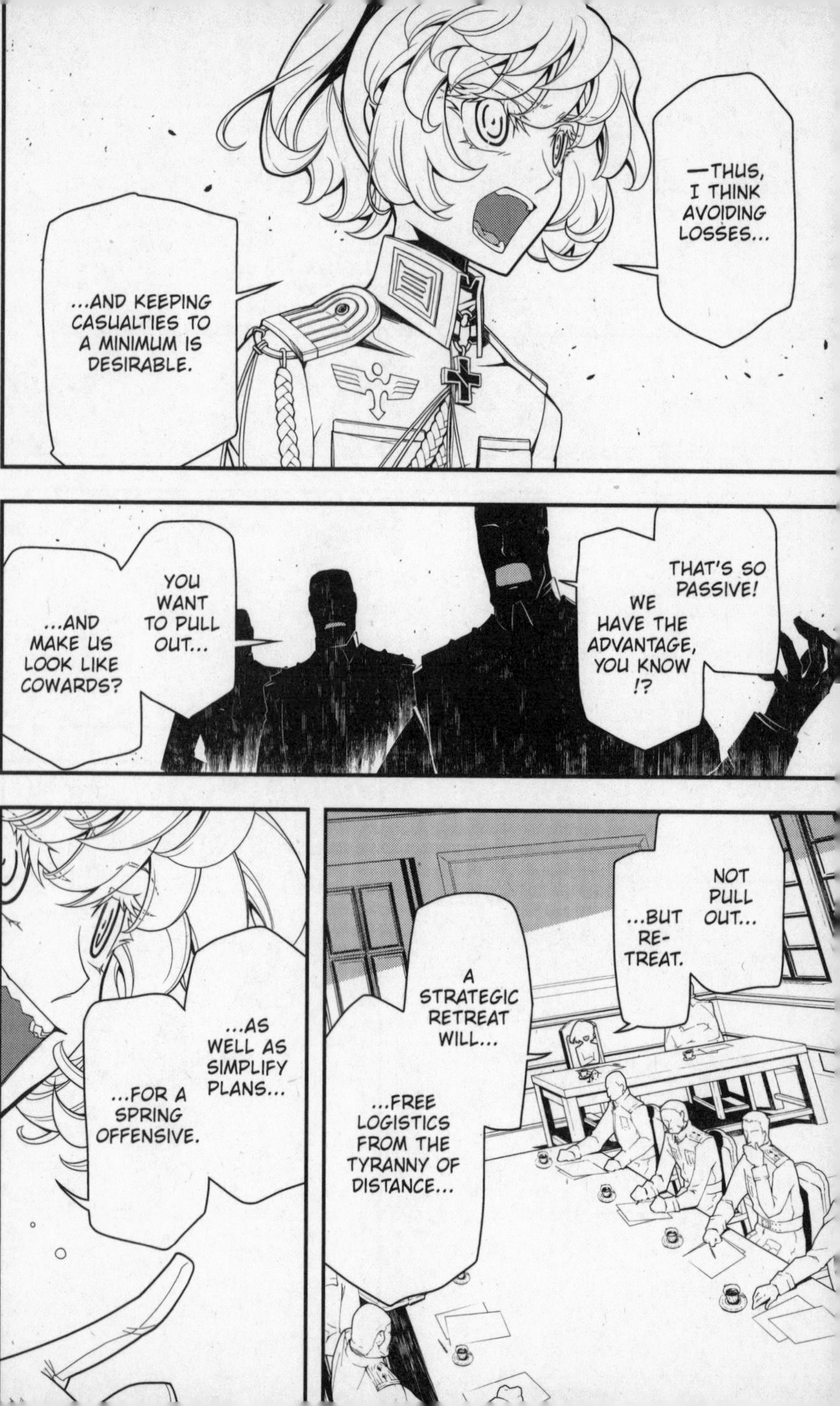
—THUS, I THINK AVOIDING LOSSES...
...AND KEEPING CASUALTIES TO A MINIMUM IS DESIRABLE.
THAT'S SO PASSIVE!
WE HAVE THE ADVANTAGE, YOU KNOW !?
YOU WANT TO PULL OUT...
...AND MAKE US LOOK LIKE COWARDS?
NOT PULL OUT...
...BUT RE-TREAT.
A STRATEGIC RETREAT WILL...
...FREE LOGISTICS FROM THE TYRANNY OF DISTANCE...
...AS WELL AS SIMPLIFY PLANS...
...FOR A SPRING OFFENSIVE.

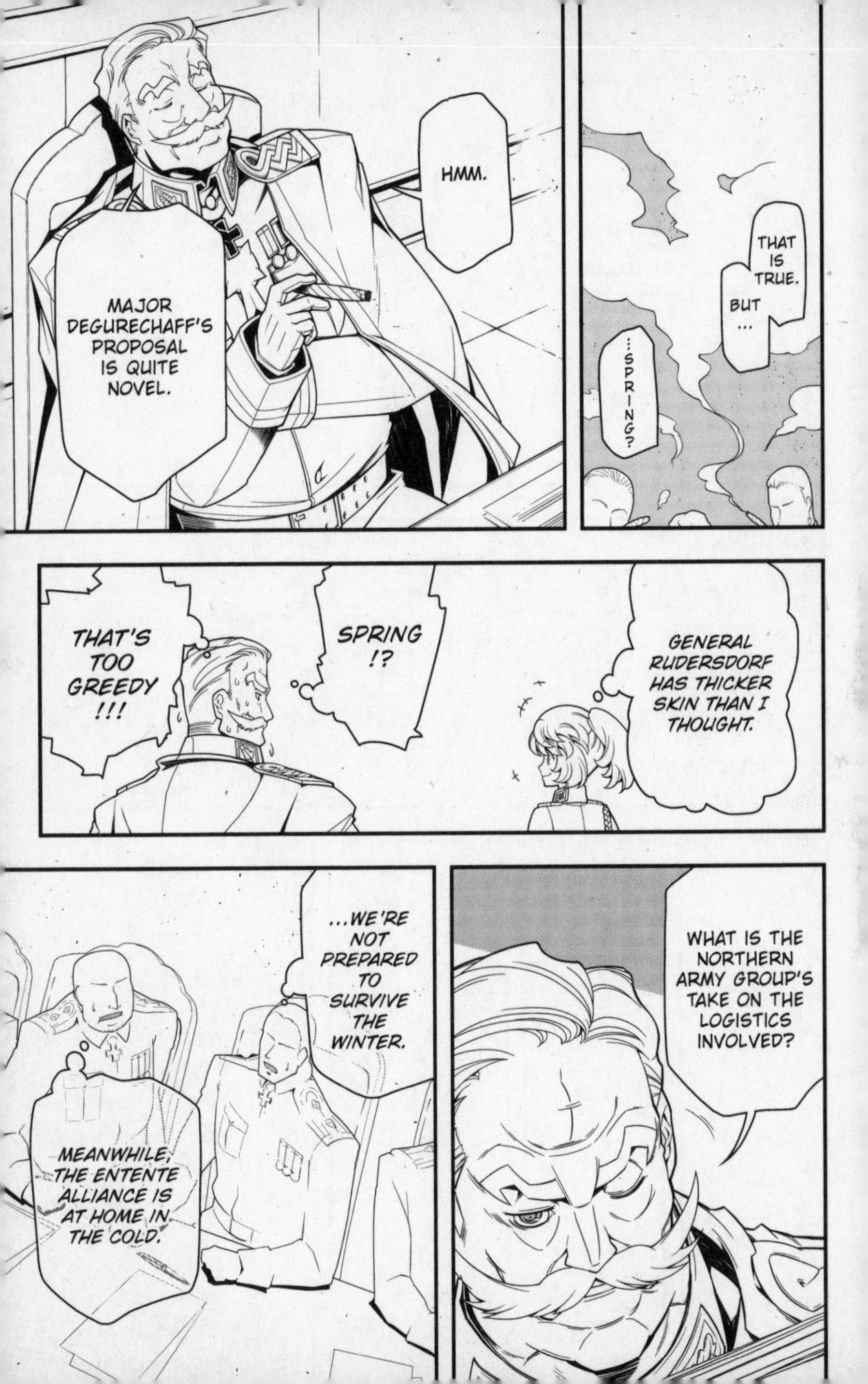
THAT IS TRUE.
BUT ...
...SPRING?
HMM.
MAJOR DEGURECHAFF'S PROPOSAL IS QUITE NOVEL.
GENERAL RUDERSDORF HAS THICKER SKIN THAN I THOUGHT.
SPRING !?
THAT'S TOO GREEDY !!!
WHAT IS THE NORTHERN ARMY GROUP'S TAKE ON THE LOGISTICS INVOLVED?
...WE'RE NOT PREPARED TO SURVIVE THE WINTER.
MEANWHILE, THE ENTENTE ALLIANCE IS AT HOME IN THE COLD.

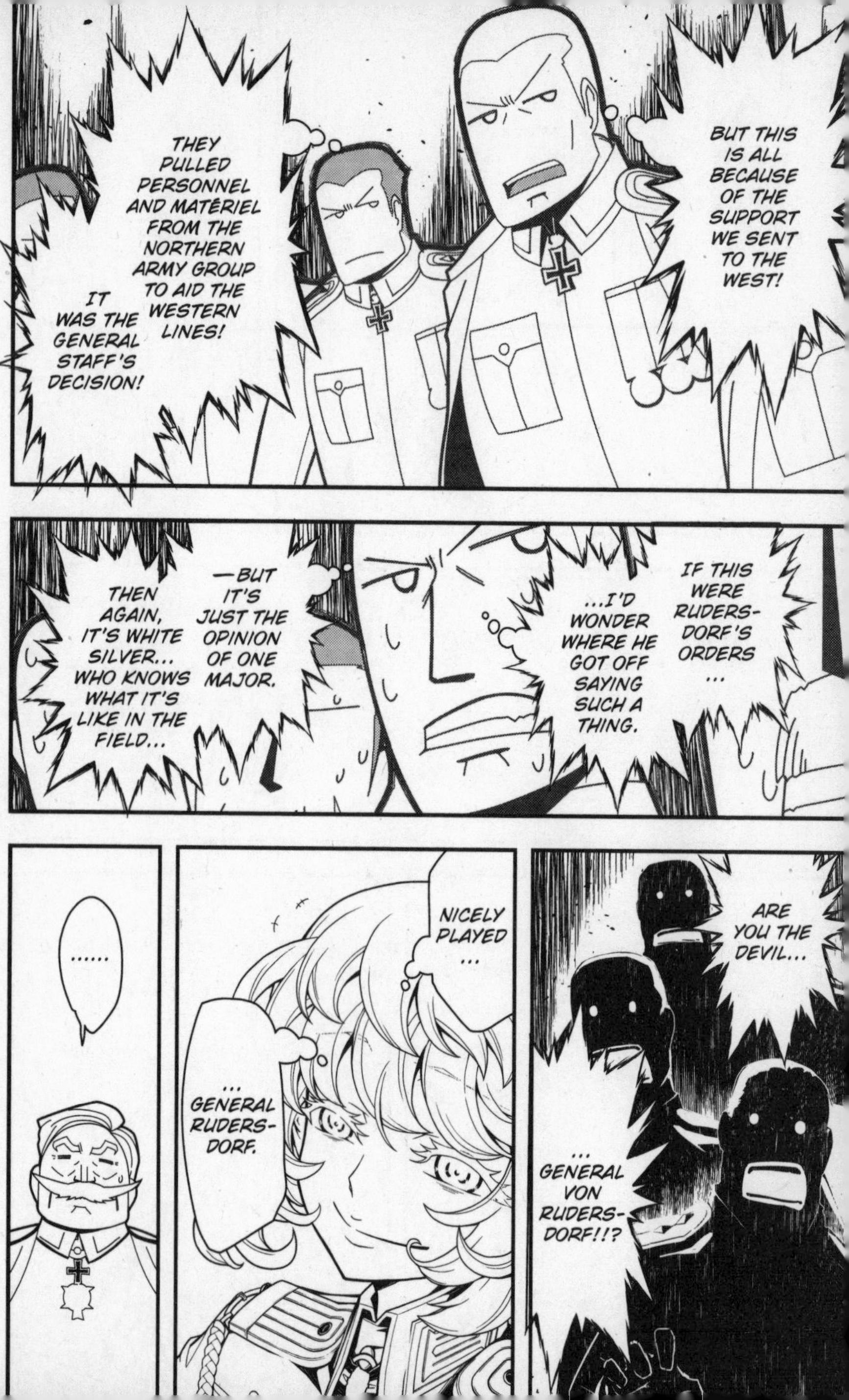
BUT THIS IS ALL BECAUSE OF THE SUPPORT WE SENT TO THE WEST!
THEY PULLED PERSONNEL AND MATÉRIEL FROM THE NORTHERN ARMY GROUP TO AID THE WESTERN LINES!
IT WAS THE GENERAL STAFF'S DECISION!
IF THIS WERE RUDERSDORF'S ORDERS...
...I'D WONDER WHERE HE GOT OFF SAYING SUCH A THING.
—BUT IT'S JUST THE OPINION OF ONE MAJOR.
THEN AGAIN, IT'S WHITE SILVER... WHO KNOWS WHAT IT'S LIKE IN THE FIELD...
ARE YOU THE DEVIL...
...GENERAL VON RUDERSDORF!!?
NICELY PLAYED...
...GENERAL RUDERSDORF.
......

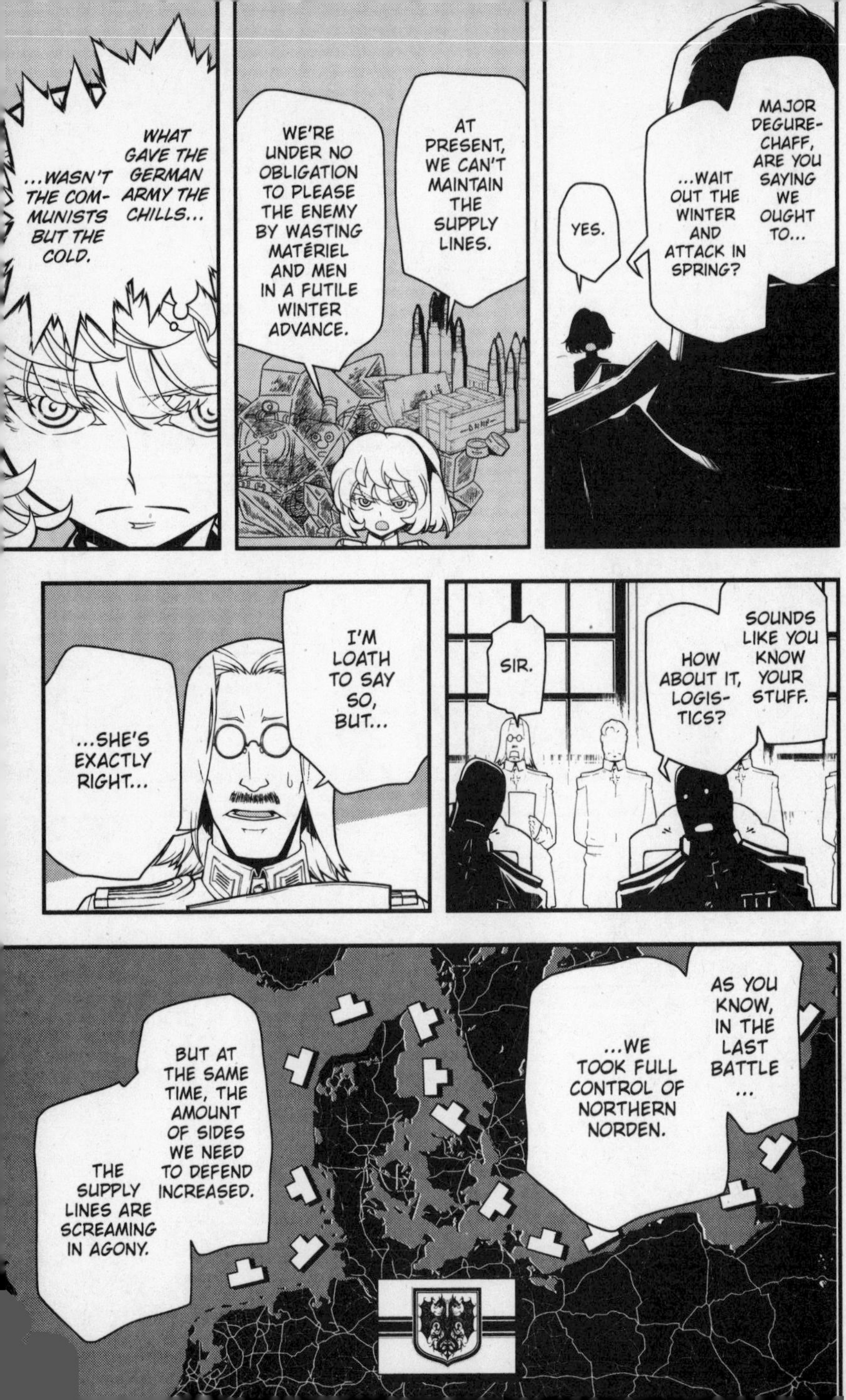
MAJOR DEGURECHAFF, ARE YOU SAYING WE OUGHT TO...
...WAIT OUT THE WINTER AND ATTACK IN SPRING?
YES.
AT PRESENT, WE CAN'T MAINTAIN THE SUPPLY LINES.
WE'RE UNDER NO OBLIGATION TO PLEASE THE ENEMY BY WASTING MATÉRIEL AND MEN IN A FUTILE WINTER ADVANCE.
WHAT GAVE THE GERMAN ARMY THE CHILLS...
...WASN'T THE COMMUNISTS BUT THE COLD.
SOUNDS LIKE YOU KNOW YOUR STUFF.
HOW ABOUT IT, LOGISTICS?
SIR.
I'M LOATH TO SAY SO, BUT...
...SHE'S EXACTLY RIGHT...
AS YOU KNOW, IN THE LAST BATTLE...
...WE TOOK FULL CONTROL OF NORTHERN NORDEN.
BUT AT THE SAME TIME, THE AMOUNT OF SIDES WE NEED TO DEFEND INCREASED.
THE SUPPLY LINES ARE SCREAMING IN AGONY.

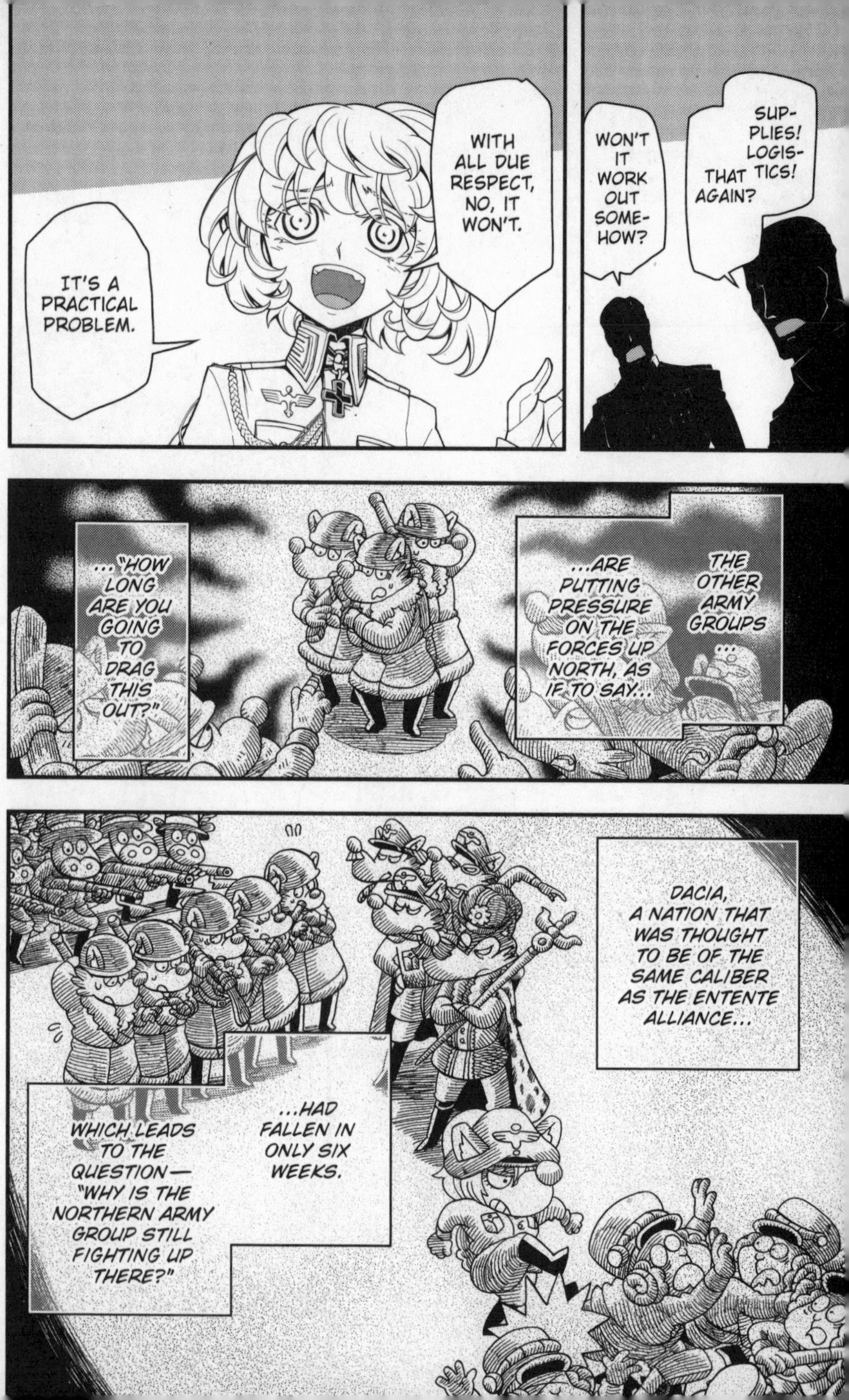
SUP-PLIES! LOGIS-TICS! THAT AGAIN?
WON'T IT WORK OUT SOME-HOW?
WITH ALL DUE RESPECT, NO, IT WON'T.
IT'S A PRACTICAL PROBLEM.
THE OTHER ARMY GROUPS
...ARE PUTTING PRESSURE ON THE FORCES UP NORTH, AS IF TO SAY...
..."HOW LONG ARE YOU GOING TO DRAG THIS OUT?"
DACIA, A NATION THAT WAS THOUGHT TO BE OF THE SAME CALIBER AS THE ENTENTE ALLIANCE...
...HAD FALLEN IN ONLY SIX WEEKS.
WHICH LEADS TO THE QUESTION— "WHY IS THE NORTHERN ARMY GROUP STILL FIGHTING UP THERE?"

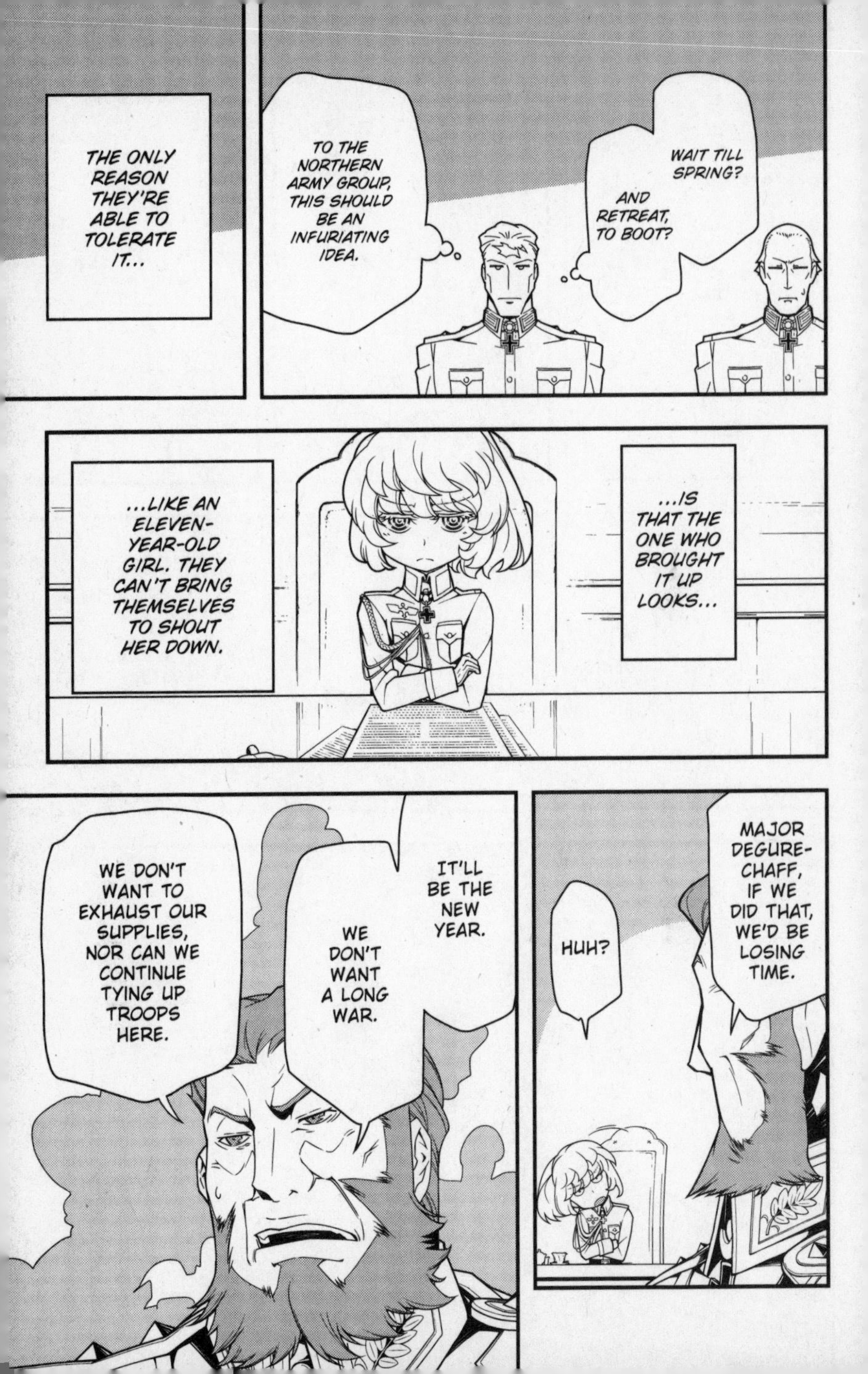
WAIT TILL SPRING?
AND RETREAT, TO BOOT?
TO THE NORTHERN ARMY GROUP, THIS SHOULD BE AN INFURIATING IDEA.
THE ONLY REASON THEY'RE ABLE TO TOLERATE IT...
...IS THAT THE ONE WHO BROUGHT IT UP LOOKS...
...LIKE AN ELEVEN-YEAR-OLD GIRL. THEY CAN'T BRING THEMSELVES TO SHOUT HER DOWN.
MAJOR DEGURE-CHAFF, IF WE DID THAT, WE'D BE LOSING TIME.
HUH?
IT'LL BE THE NEW YEAR.
WE DON'T WANT A LONG WAR.
WE DON'T WANT TO EXHAUST OUR SUPPLIES, NOR CAN WE CONTINUE TYING UP TROOPS HERE.

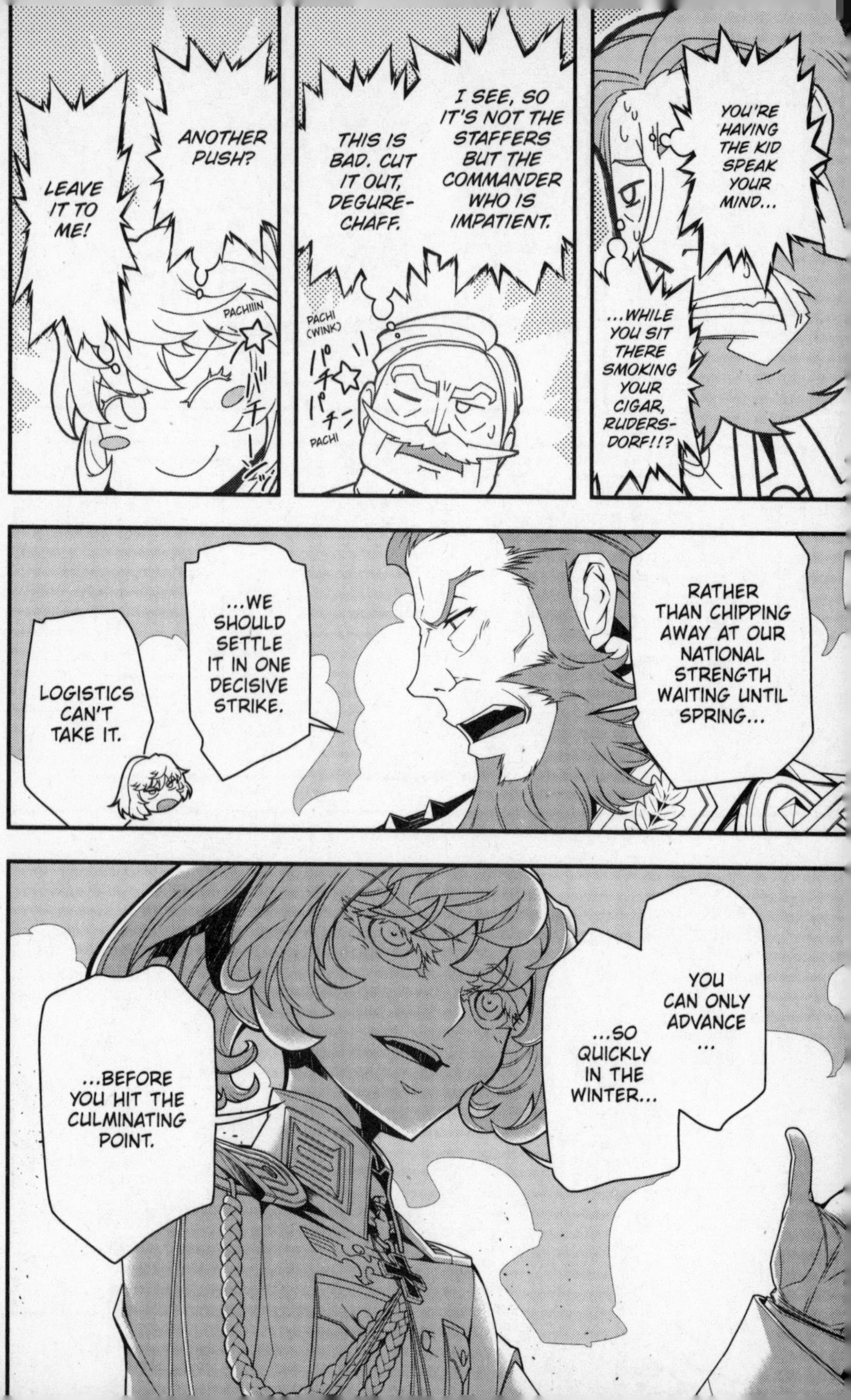
YOU'RE HAVING THE KID SPEAK YOUR MIND...
...WHILE YOU SIT THERE SMOKING YOUR CIGAR, RUDERSDORF!!?
I SEE, SO IT'S NOT THE STAFFERS BUT THE COMMANDER WHO IS IMPATIENT.
THIS IS BAD. CUT IT OUT, DEGURECHAFF.
PACHI (WINK)
PACHI
ANOTHER PUSH?
LEAVE IT TO ME!
PACHIIIN
RATHER THAN CHIPPING AWAY AT OUR NATIONAL STRENGTH WAITING UNTIL SPRING...
...WE SHOULD SETTLE IT IN ONE DECISIVE STRIKE.
LOGISTICS CAN'T TAKE IT.
YOU CAN ONLY ADVANCE...
...SO QUICKLY IN THE WINTER...
...BEFORE YOU HIT THE CULMINATING POINT.

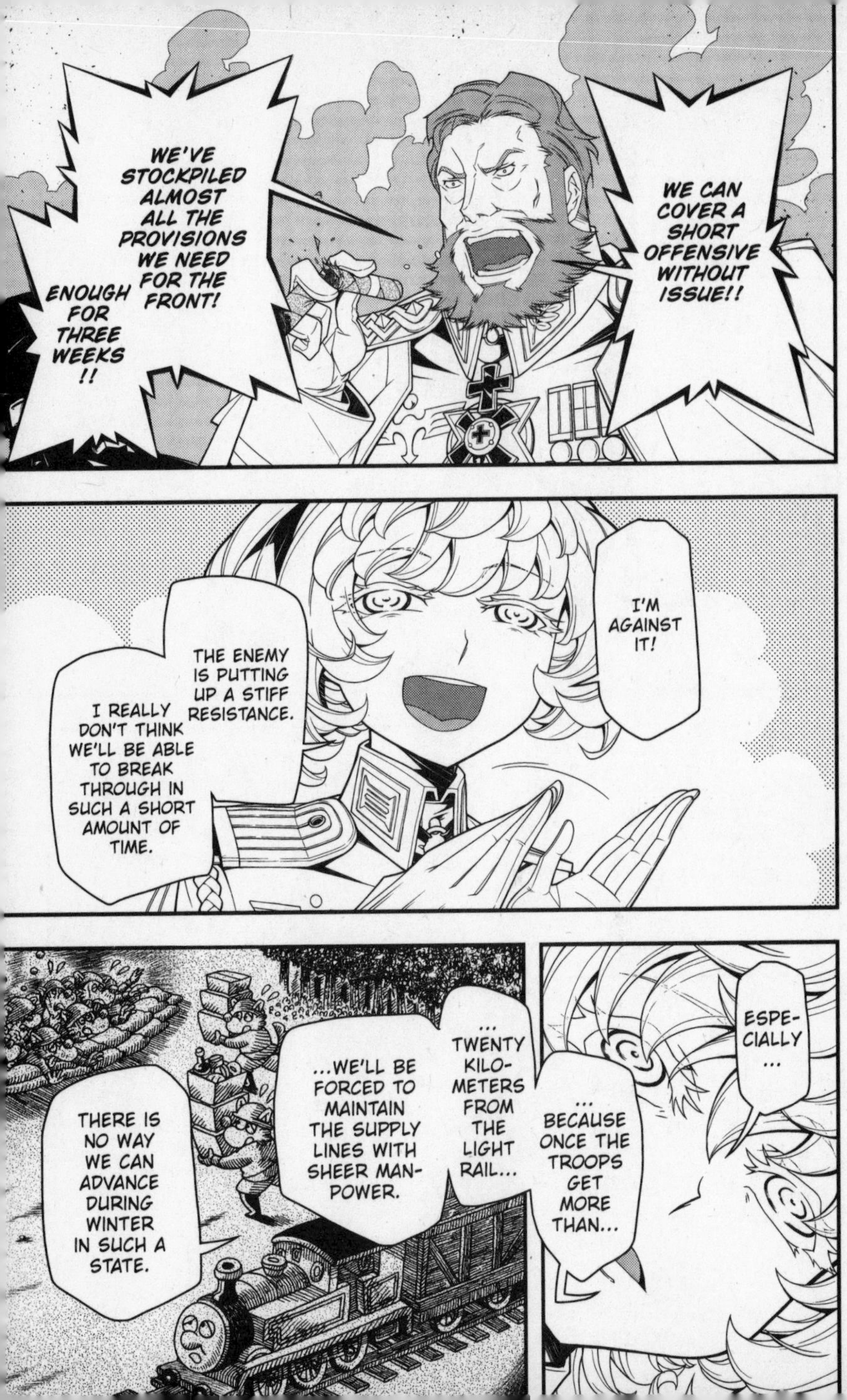
WE CAN COVER A SHORT OFFENSIVE WITHOUT ISSUE!!
WE'VE STOCKPILED ALMOST ALL THE PROVISIONS WE NEED FOR THE FRONT!
ENOUGH FOR THREE WEEKS!!
I'M AGAINST IT!
THE ENEMY IS PUTTING UP A STIFF RESISTANCE.
I REALLY DON'T THINK WE'LL BE ABLE TO BREAK THROUGH IN SUCH A SHORT AMOUNT OF TIME.
ESPE-CIALLY...
...BECAUSE ONCE THE TROOPS GET MORE THAN...
...TWENTY KILO-METERS FROM THE LIGHT RAIL...
...WE'LL BE FORCED TO MAINTAIN THE SUPPLY LINES WITH SHEER MAN-POWER.
THERE IS NO WAY WE CAN ADVANCE DURING WINTER IN SUCH A STATE.

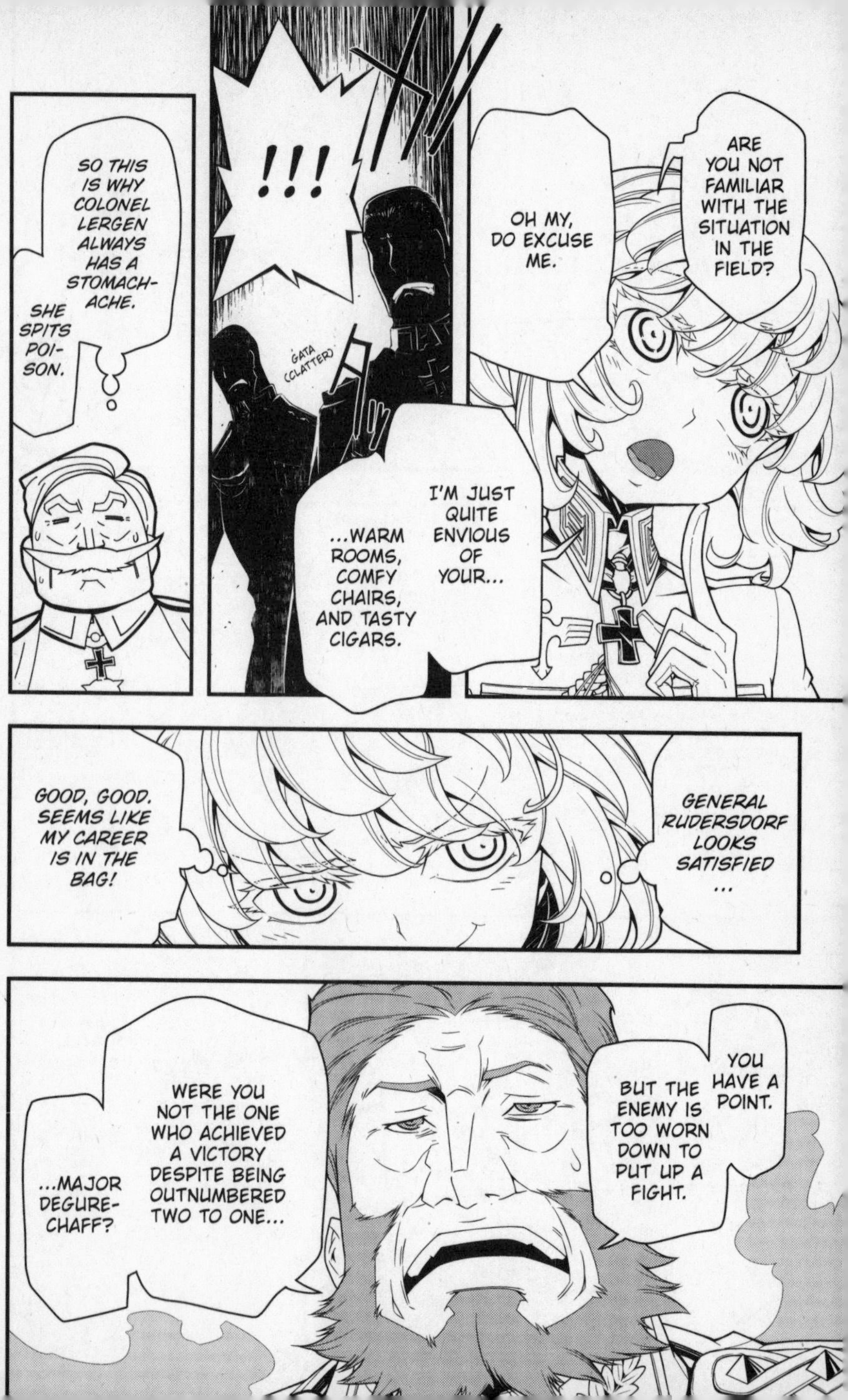
ARE YOU NOT FAMILIAR WITH THE SITUATION IN THE FIELD?
OH MY, DO EXCUSE ME.
I'M JUST QUITE ENVIOUS OF YOUR...
...WARM ROOMS, COMFY CHAIRS, AND TASTY CIGARS.
!!!
GATA (CLATTER)
SO THIS IS WHY COLONEL LERGEN ALWAYS HAS A STOMACH-ACHE.
SHE SPITS POI-SON.
GENERAL RUDERSDORF LOOKS SATISFIED ...
GOOD, GOOD. SEEMS LIKE MY CAREER IS IN THE BAG!
YOU HAVE A POINT.
BUT THE ENEMY IS TOO WORN DOWN TO PUT UP A FIGHT.
WERE YOU NOT THE ONE WHO ACHIEVED A VICTORY DESPITE BEING OUTNUMBERED TWO TO ONE...
...MAJOR DEGURE-CHAFF?

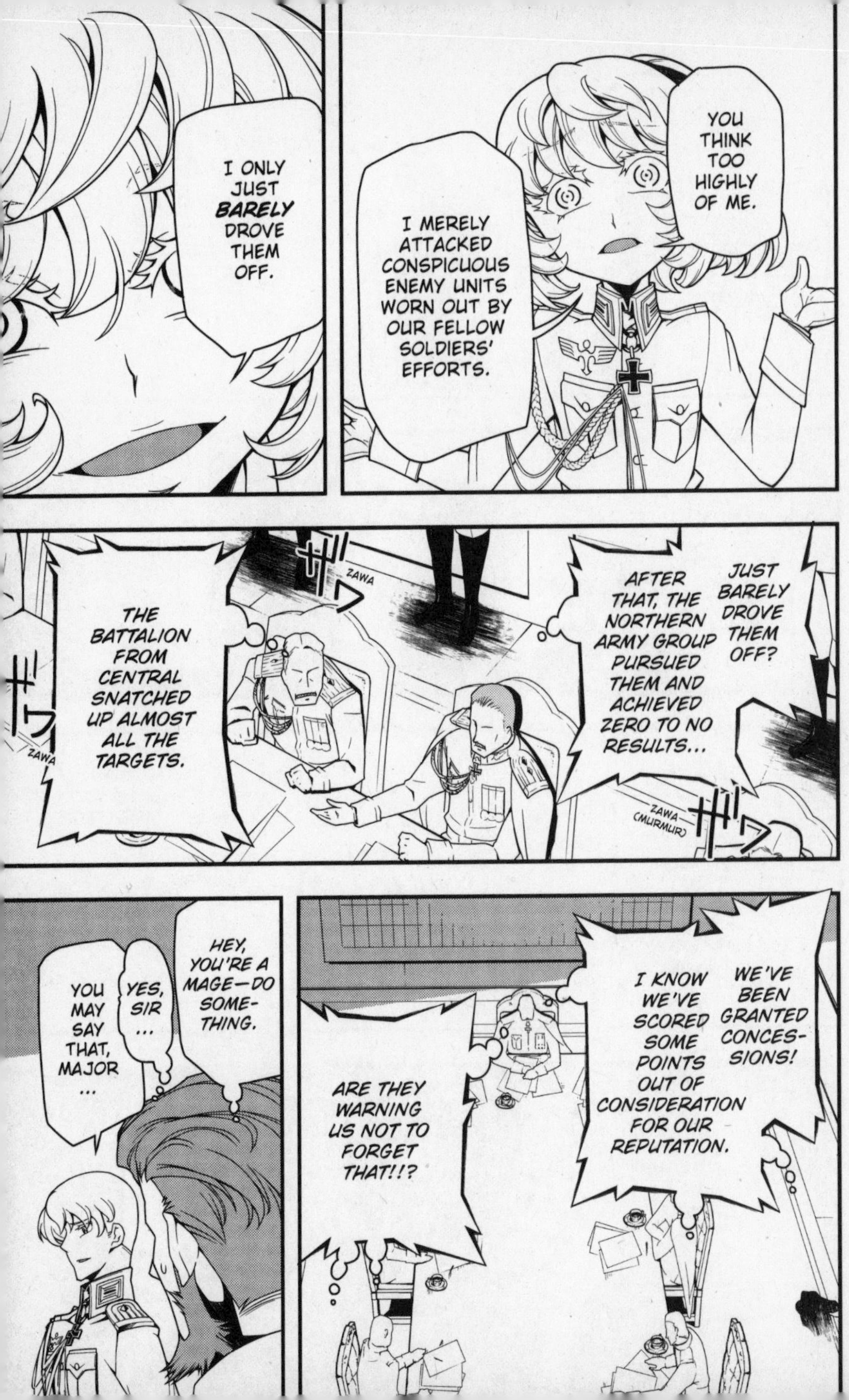
YOU THINK TOO HIGHLY OF ME.
I MERELY ATTACKED CONSPICUOUS ENEMY UNITS WORN OUT BY OUR FELLOW SOLDIERS' EFFORTS.
I ONLY JUST BARELY DROVE THEM OFF.
JUST BARELY DROVE THEM OFF?
AFTER THAT, THE NORTHERN ARMY GROUP PURSUED THEM AND ACHIEVED ZERO TO NO RESULTS...
ZAWA (MURMUR)
ZAWA
THE BATTALION FROM CENTRAL SNATCHED UP ALMOST ALL THE TARGETS.
ZAWA
WE'VE BEEN GRANTED CONCESSIONS!
I KNOW WE'VE SCORED SOME POINTS OUT OF CONSIDERATION FOR OUR REPUTATION.
ARE THEY WARNING US NOT TO FORGET THAT!!?
HEY, YOU'RE A MAGE—DO SOMETHING.
YES, SIR...
YOU MAY SAY THAT, MAJOR...

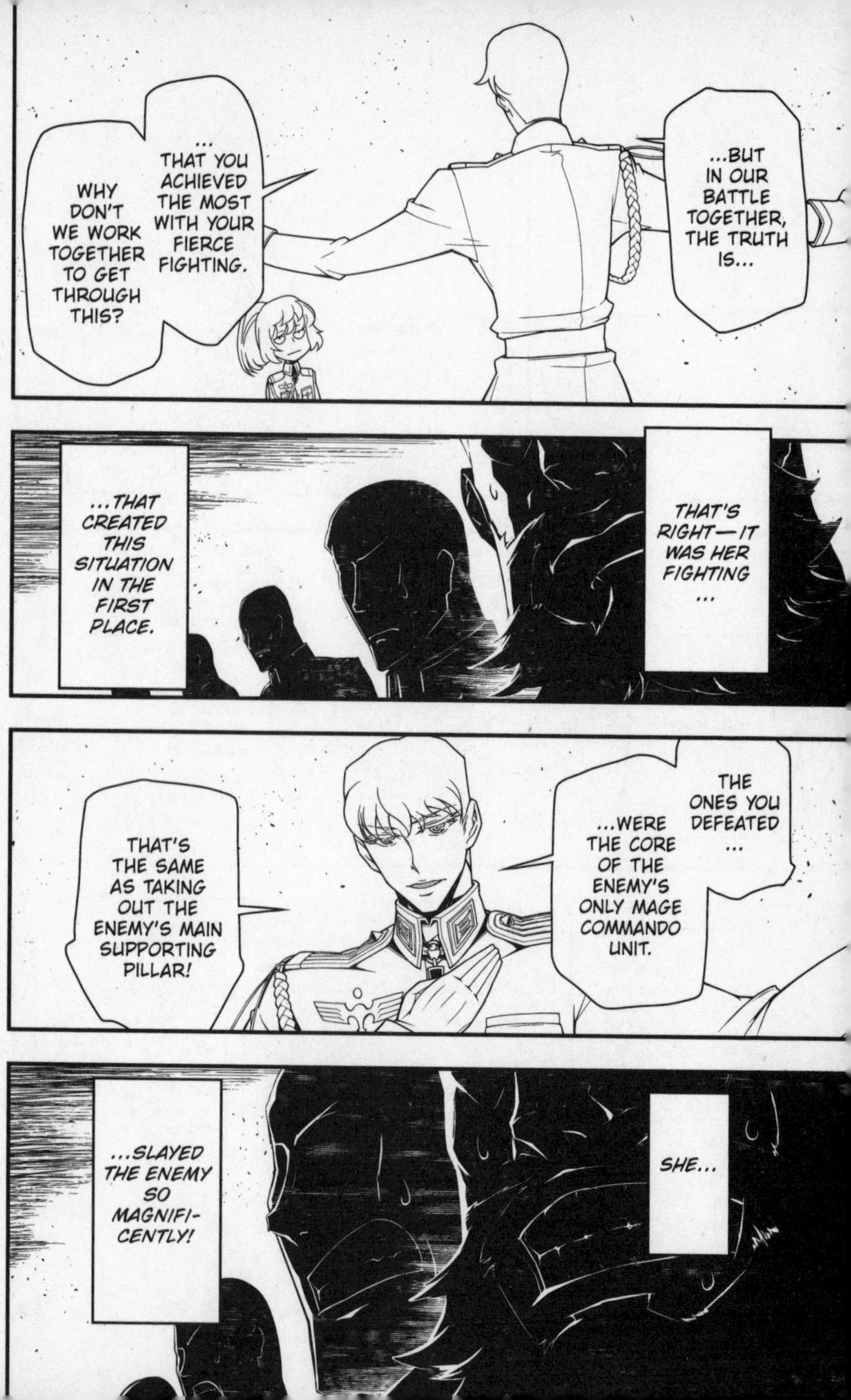
...BUT IN OUR BATTLE TOGETHER, THE TRUTH IS...
... THAT YOU ACHIEVED THE MOST WITH YOUR FIERCE FIGHTING.
WHY DON'T WE WORK TOGETHER TO GET THROUGH THIS?
THAT'S RIGHT—IT WAS HER FIGHTING ...
...THAT CREATED THIS SITUATION IN THE FIRST PLACE.
THE ONES YOU DEFEATED ...
...WERE THE CORE OF THE ENEMY'S ONLY MAGE COMMANDO UNIT.
THAT'S THE SAME AS TAKING OUT THE ENEMY'S MAIN SUPPORTING PILLAR!
SHE...
...SLAYED THE ENEMY SO MAGNIFI-CENTLY!

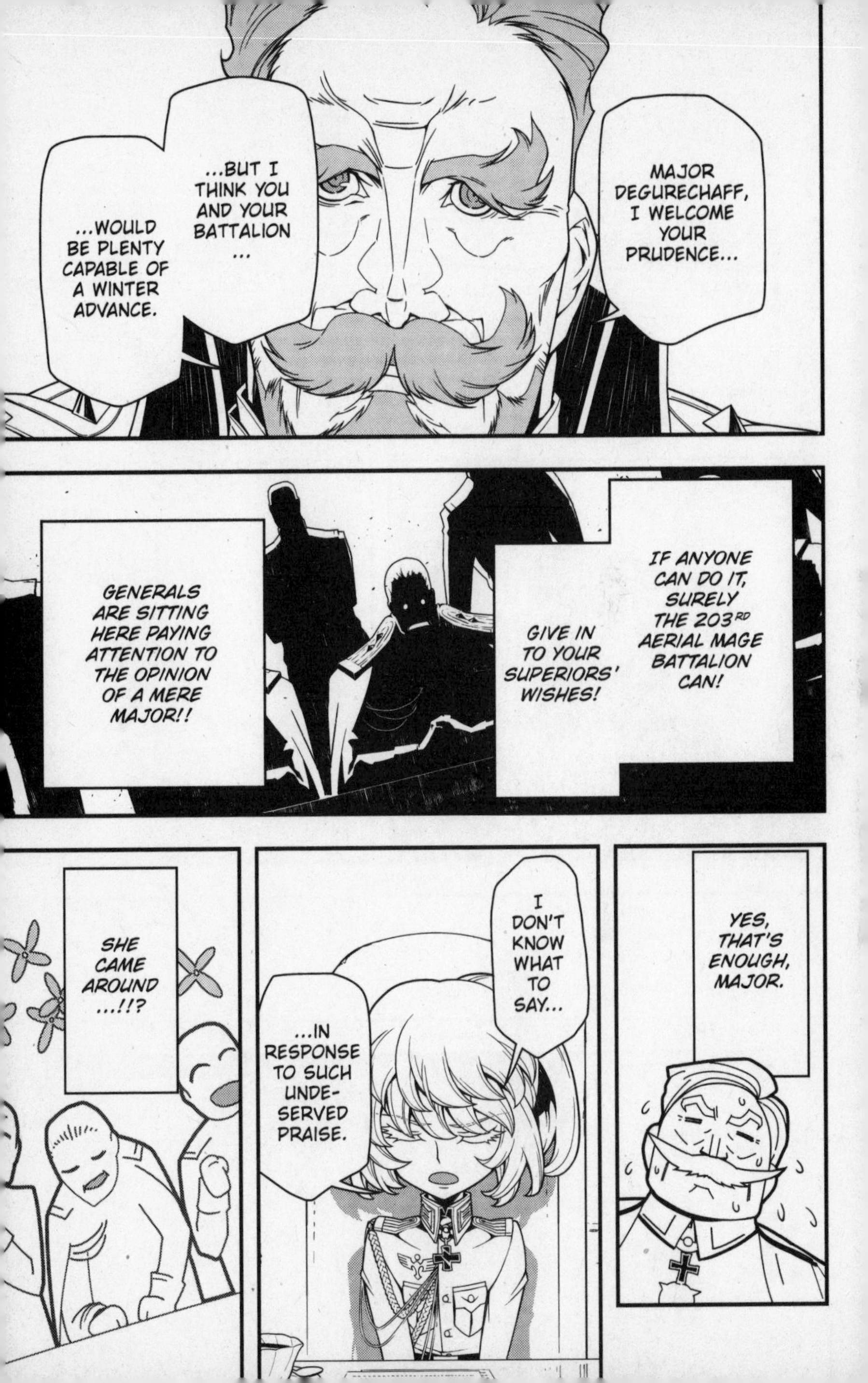
MAJOR DEGURECHAFF, I WELCOME YOUR PRUDENCE...
...BUT I THINK YOU AND YOUR BATTALION ...
...WOULD BE PLENTY CAPABLE OF A WINTER ADVANCE.
IF ANYONE CAN DO IT, SURELY THE 203RD AERIAL MAGE BATTALION CAN!
GIVE IN TO YOUR SUPERIORS' WISHES!
GENERALS ARE SITTING HERE PAYING ATTENTION TO THE OPINION OF A MERE MAJOR!!
YES, THAT'S ENOUGH, MAJOR.
I DON'T KNOW WHAT TO SAY...
...IN RESPONSE TO SUCH UNDE-SERVED PRAISE.
SHE CAME AROUND ...!!?

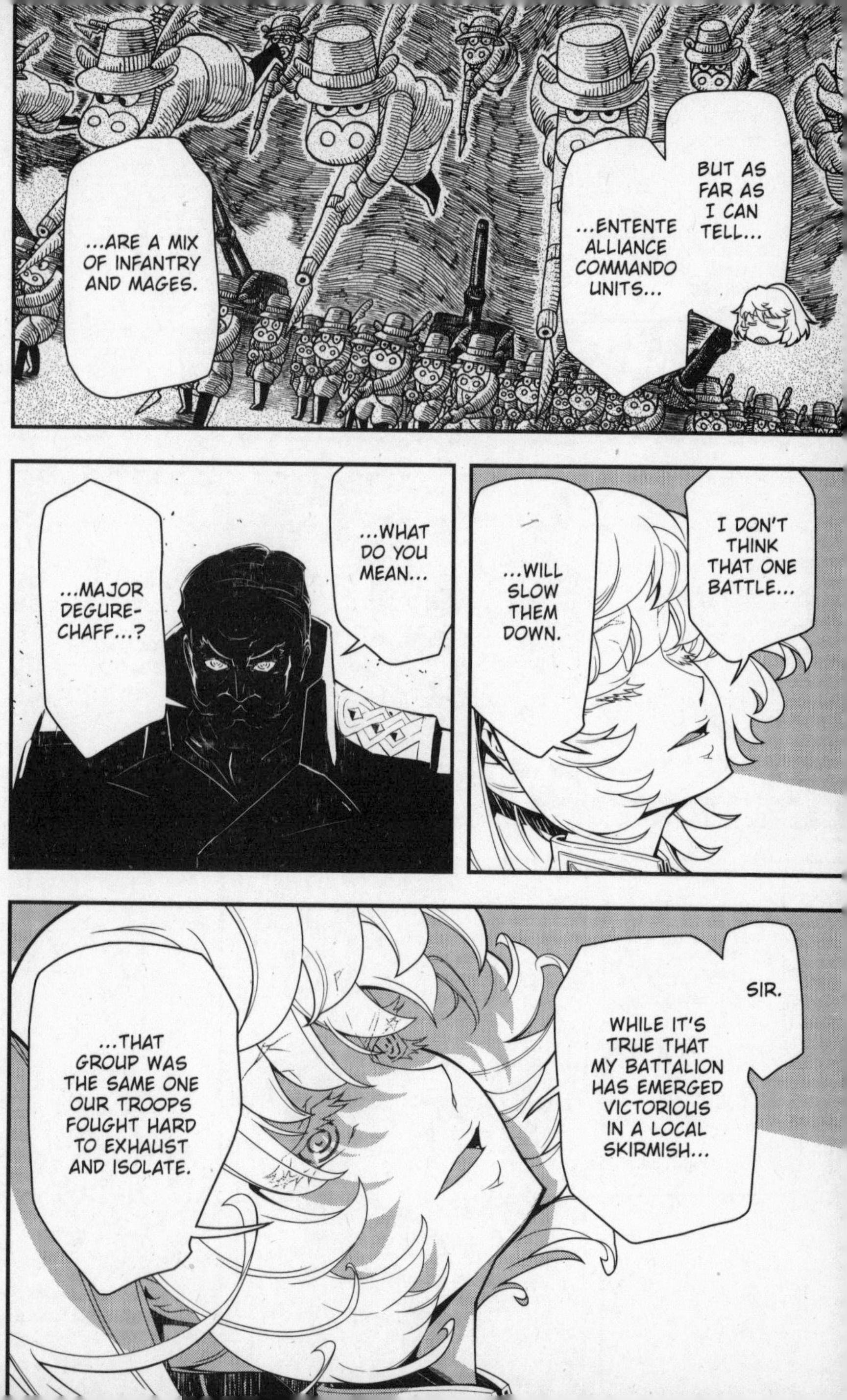
BUT AS FAR AS I CAN TELL...
...ENTENTE ALLIANCE COMMANDO UNITS...
...ARE A MIX OF INFANTRY AND MAGES.
I DON'T THINK THAT ONE BATTLE...
...WILL SLOW THEM DOWN.
...WHAT DO YOU MEAN...
...MAJOR DEGURE-CHAFF...?
SIR.
WHILE IT'S TRUE THAT MY BATTALION HAS EMERGED VICTORIOUS IN A LOCAL SKIRMISH...
...THAT GROUP WAS THE SAME ONE OUR TROOPS FOUGHT HARD TO EXHAUST AND ISOLATE.

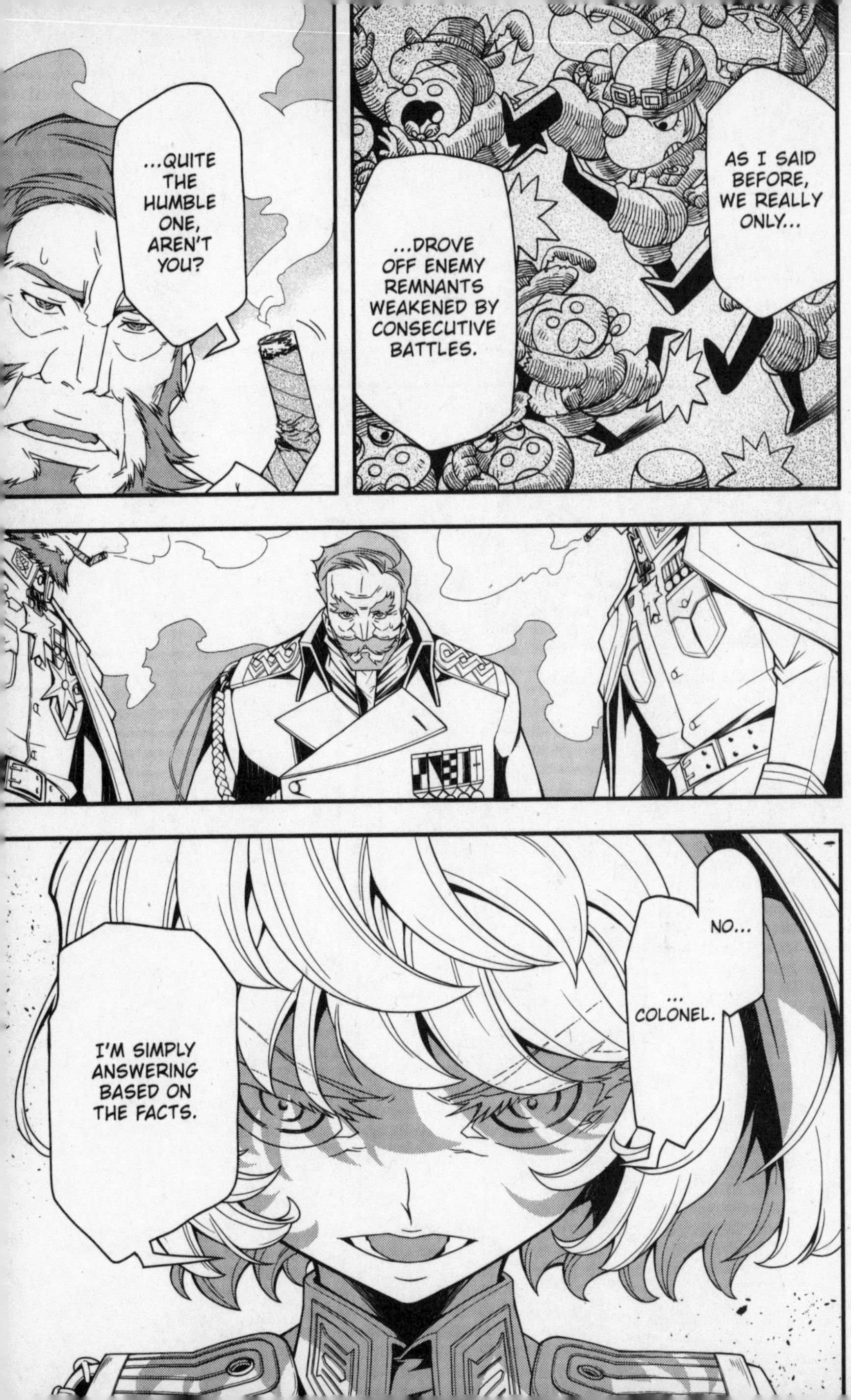
AS I SAID BEFORE, WE REALLY ONLY...
...DROVE OFF ENEMY REMNANTS WEAKENED BY CONSECUTIVE BATTLES.
...QUITE THE HUMBLE ONE, AREN'T YOU?
NO...
...COLONEL.
I'M SIMPLY ANSWERING BASED ON THE FACTS.

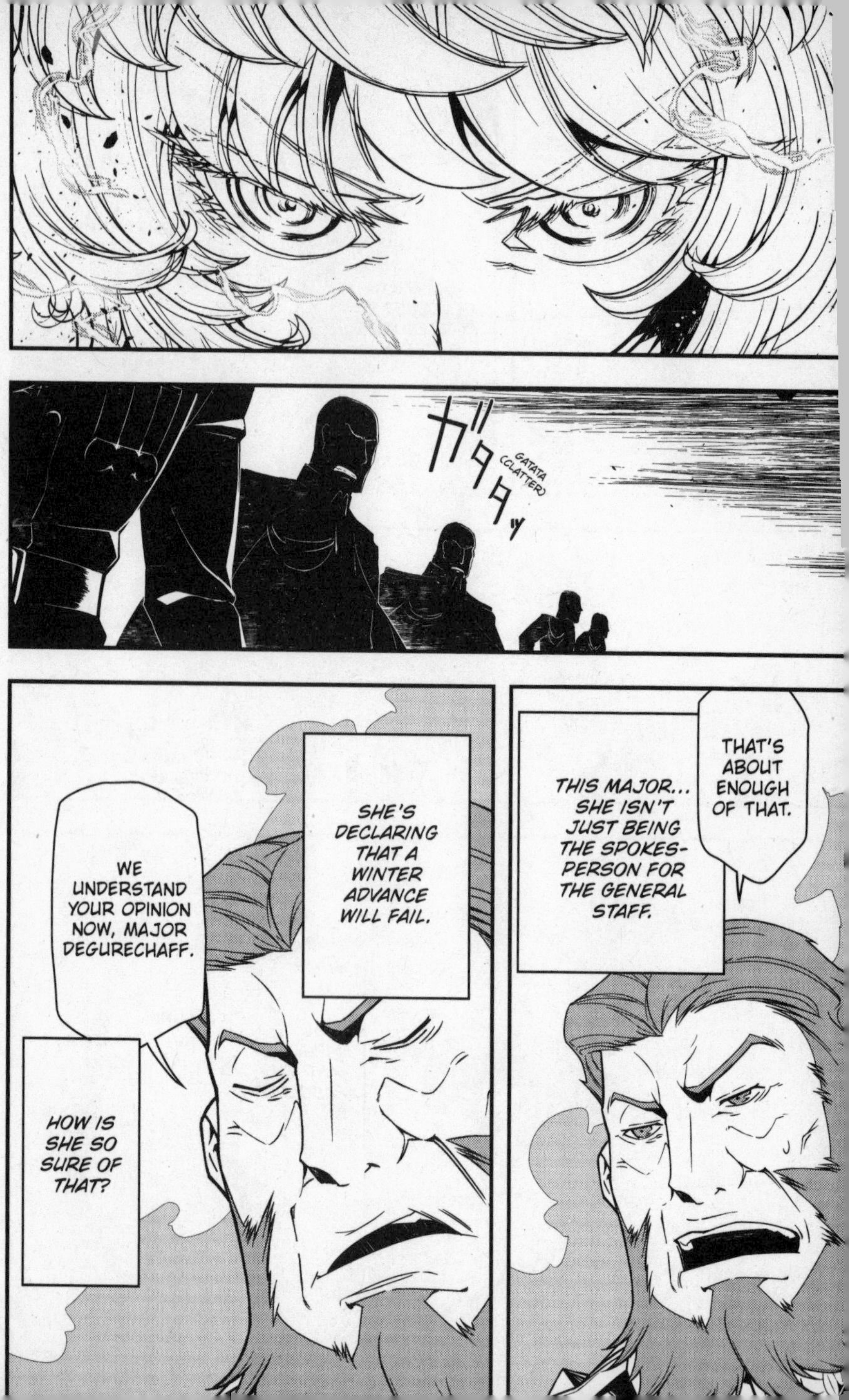
ガタタッ
GATATA (CLATTER)
THAT'S ABOUT ENOUGH OF THAT.
THIS MAJOR... SHE ISN'T JUST BEING THE SPOKESPERSON FOR THE GENERAL STAFF.
SHE'S DECLARING THAT A WINTER ADVANCE WILL FAIL.
WE UNDERSTAND YOUR OPINION NOW, MAJOR DEGURECHAFF.
HOW IS SHE SO SURE OF THAT?

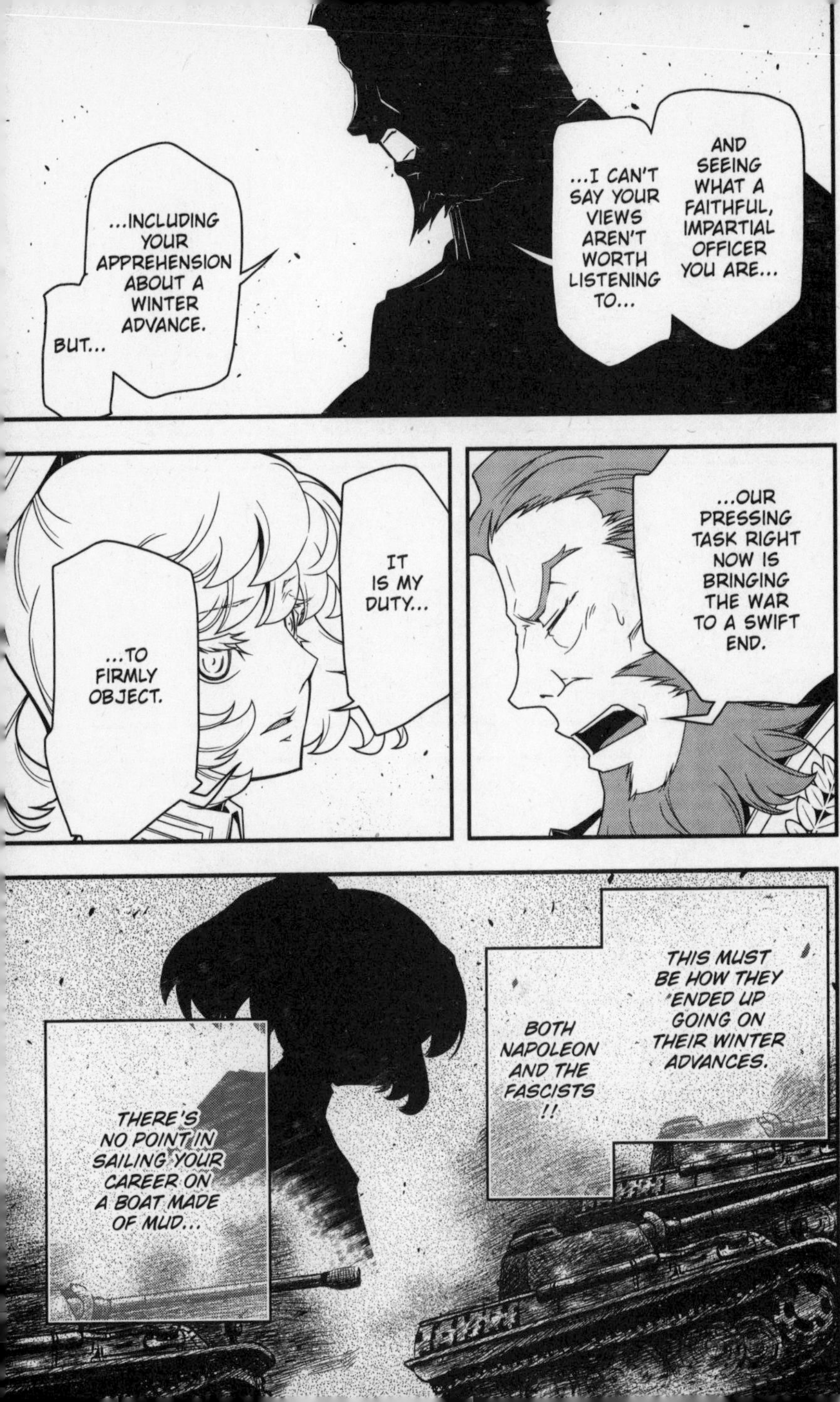
AND SEEING WHAT A FAITHFUL, IMPARTIAL OFFICER YOU ARE...
...I CAN'T SAY YOUR VIEWS AREN'T WORTH LISTENING TO...
...INCLUDING YOUR APPREHENSION ABOUT A WINTER ADVANCE.
BUT...
...OUR PRESSING TASK RIGHT NOW IS BRINGING THE WAR TO A SWIFT END.
IT IS MY DUTY...
...TO FIRMLY OBJECT.
THIS MUST BE HOW THEY ENDED UP GOING ON THEIR WINTER ADVANCES.
BOTH NAPOLEON AND THE FASCISTS!!
THERE'S NO POINT IN SAILING YOUR CAREER ON A BOAT MADE OF MUD...

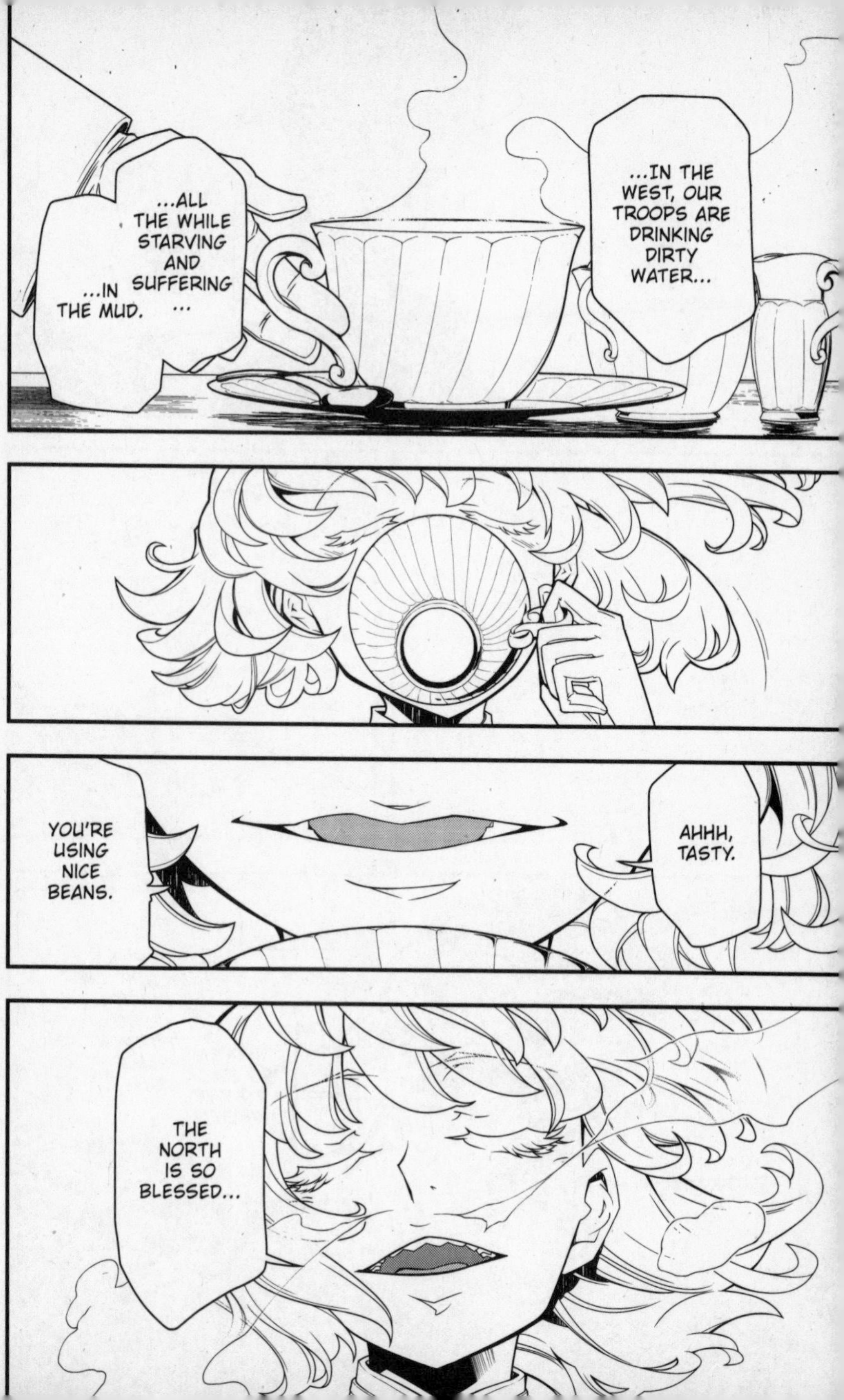
...IN THE WEST, OUR TROOPS ARE DRINKING DIRTY WATER...
...ALL THE WHILE STARVING AND SUFFERING...
...IN THE MUD.
AHHH, TASTY.
YOU'RE USING NICE BEANS.
THE NORTH IS SO BLESSED...

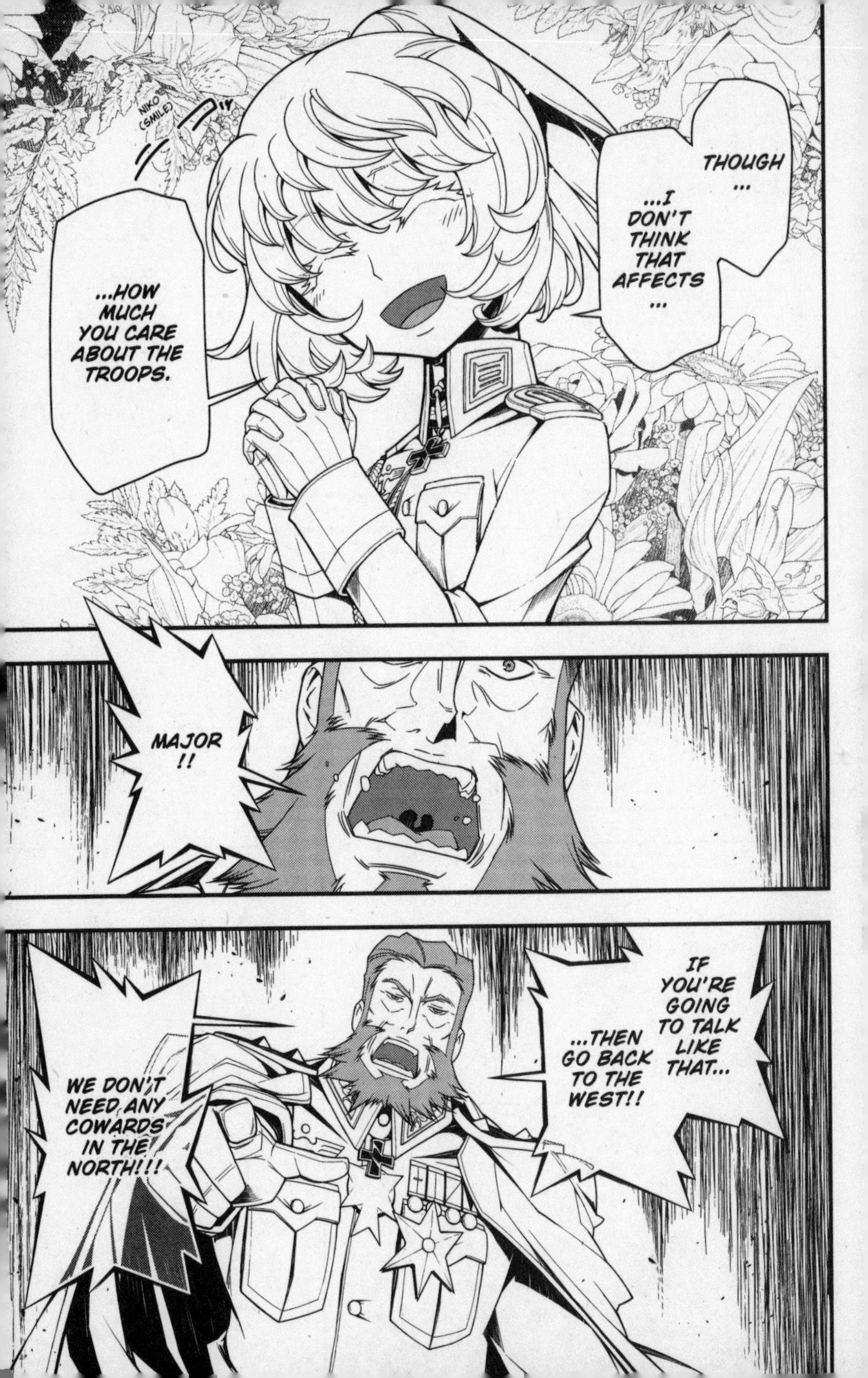
THOUGH...
...I DON'T THINK THAT AFFECTS...
NIKO (SMILE)
...HOW MUCH YOU CARE ABOUT THE TROOPS.
MAJOR!!
IF YOU'RE GOING TO TALK LIKE THAT...
...THEN GO BACK TO THE WEST!!
WE DON'T NEED ANY COWARDS IN THE NORTH!!!

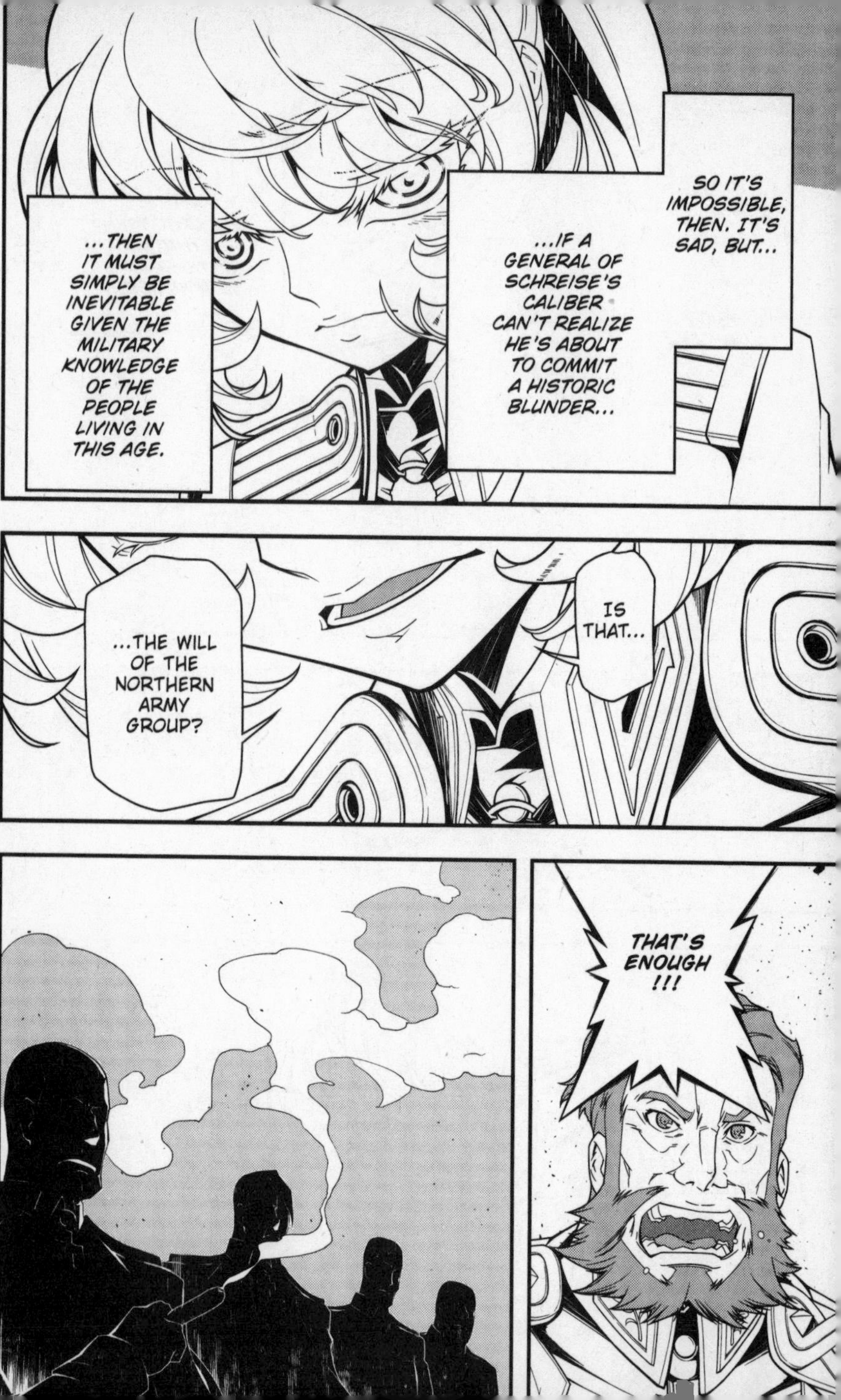
SO IT'S IMPOSSIBLE, THEN. IT'S SAD, BUT...
...IF A GENERAL OF SCHREISE'S CALIBER CAN'T REALIZE HE'S ABOUT TO COMMIT A HISTORIC BLUNDER...
...THEN IT MUST SIMPLY BE INEVITABLE GIVEN THE MILITARY KNOWLEDGE OF THE PEOPLE LIVING IN THIS AGE.
IS THAT...
...THE WILL OF THE NORTHERN ARMY GROUP?
THAT'S ENOUGH!!!

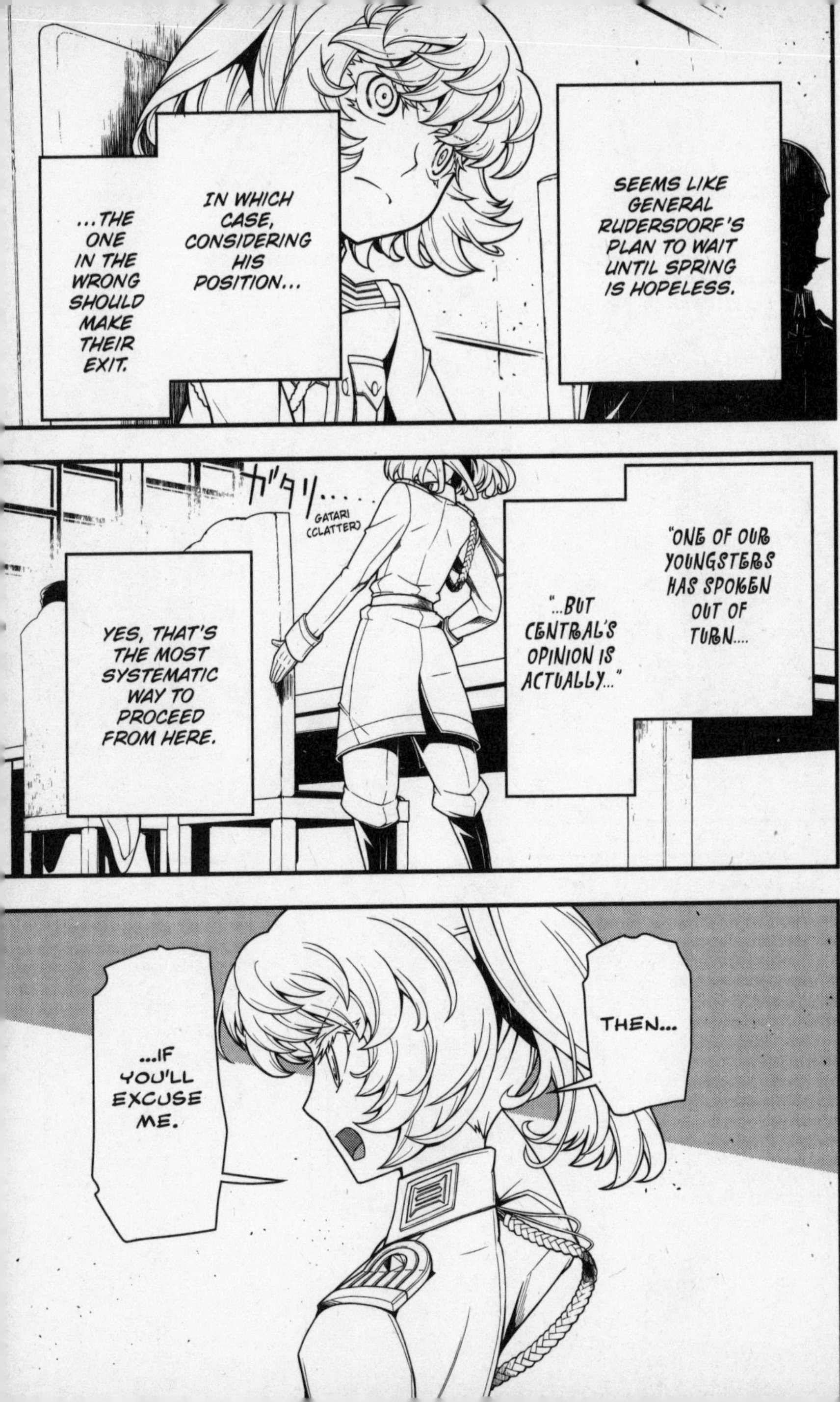
SEEMS LIKE GENERAL RUDERSDORF'S PLAN TO WAIT UNTIL SPRING IS HOPELESS.
IN WHICH CASE, CONSIDERING HIS POSITION...
...THE ONE IN THE WRONG SHOULD MAKE THEIR EXIT.
"ONE OF OUR YOUNGSTERS HAS SPOKEN OUT OF TURN....
"...BUT CENTRAL'S OPINION IS ACTUALLY..."
ガタリ……
GATARI (CLATTER)
YES, THAT'S THE MOST SYSTEMATIC WAY TO PROCEED FROM HERE.
THEN...
...IF YOU'LL EXCUSE ME.

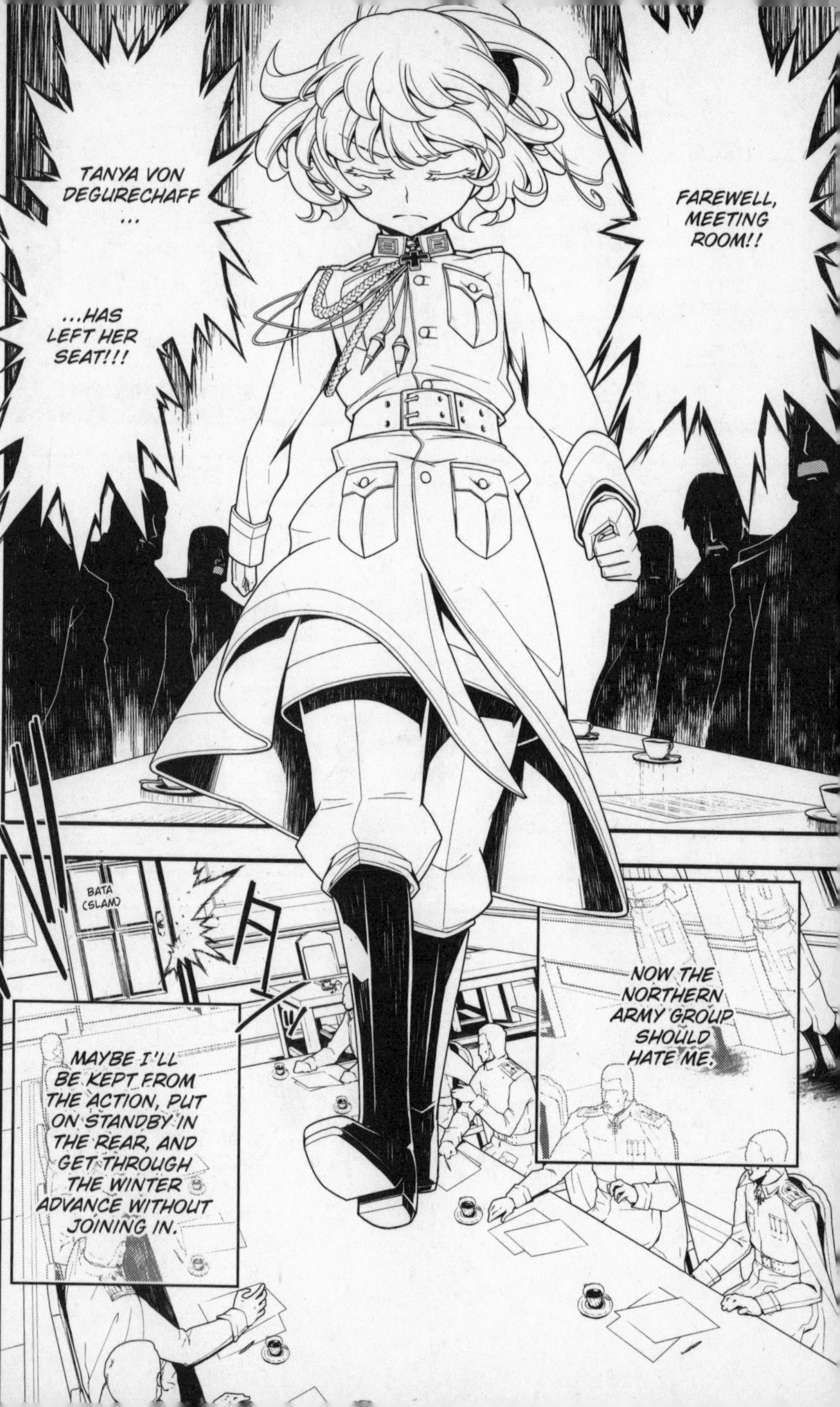
FAREWELL, MEETING ROOM!!
TANYA VON DEGURECHAFF ...
...HAS LEFT HER SEAT!!!
NOW THE NORTHERN ARMY GROUP SHOULD HATE ME.
BATA (SLAM)
MAYBE I'LL BE KEPT FROM THE ACTION, PUT ON STANDBY IN THE REAR, AND GET THROUGH THE WINTER ADVANCE WITHOUT JOINING IN.

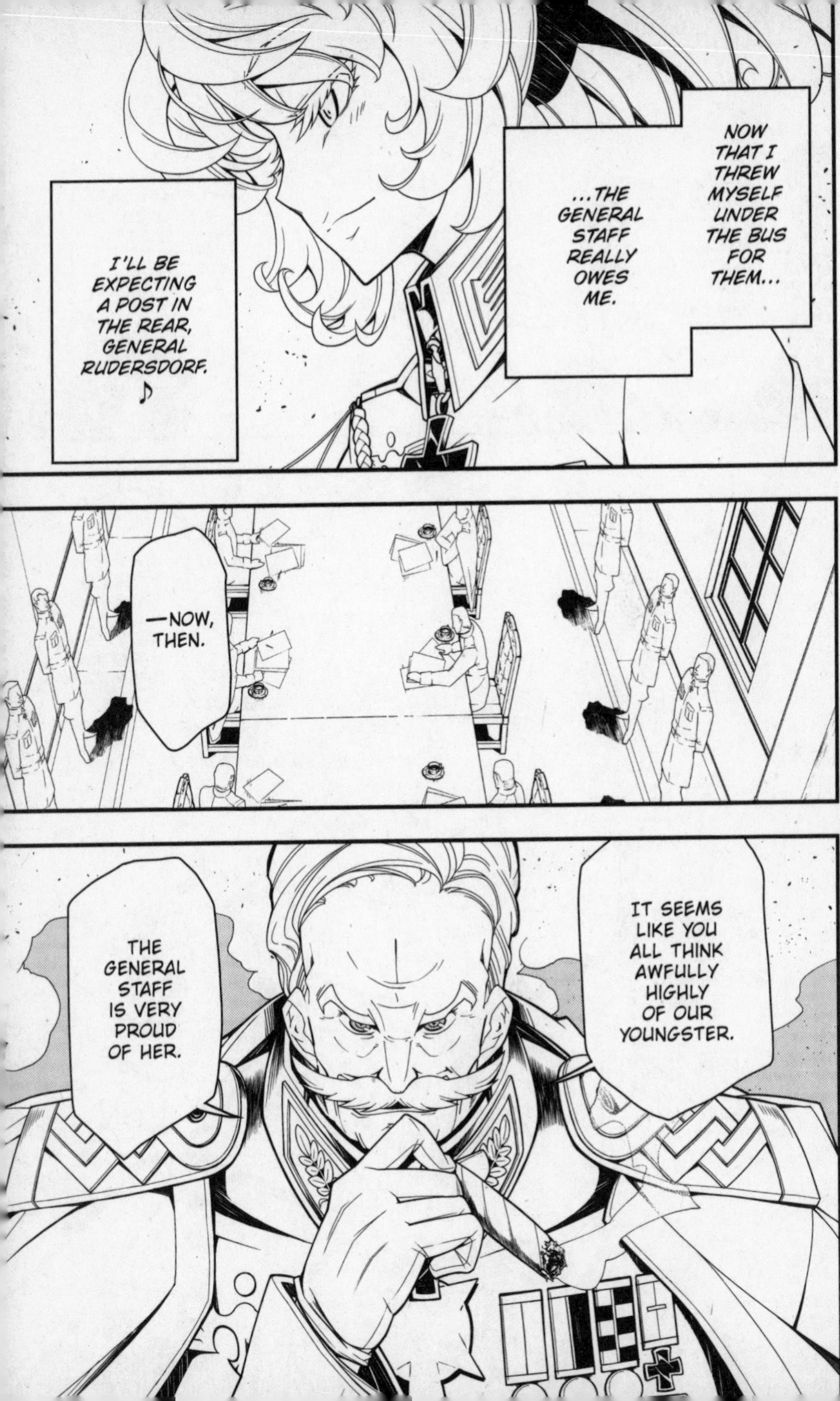
NOW THAT I THREW MYSELF UNDER THE BUS FOR THEM...
...THE GENERAL STAFF REALLY OWES ME.
I'LL BE EXPECTING A POST IN THE REAR, GENERAL RUDERSDORF. ♪
—NOW, THEN.
IT SEEMS LIKE YOU ALL THINK AWFULLY HIGHLY OF OUR YOUNGSTER.
THE GENERAL STAFF IS VERY PROUD OF HER.

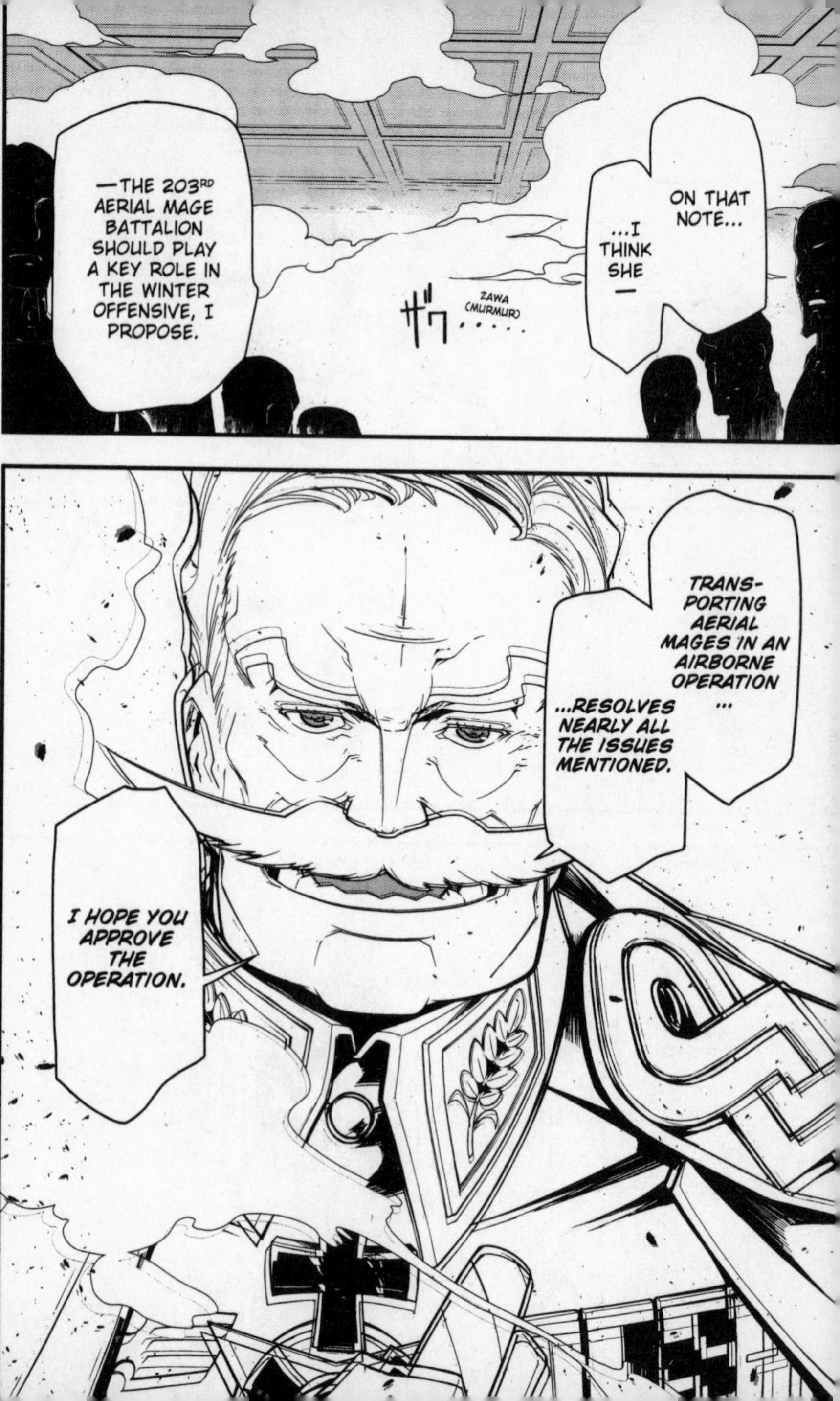
ON THAT NOTE...
...I THINK SHE—
ザワ
ZAWA (MURMUR)
—THE 203RD AERIAL MAGE BATTALION SHOULD PLAY A KEY ROLE IN THE WINTER OFFENSIVE, I PROPOSE.
TRANS-PORTING AERIAL MAGES IN AN AIRBORNE OPERATION...
...RESOLVES NEARLY ALL THE ISSUES MENTIONED.
I HOPE YOU APPROVE THE OPERATION.

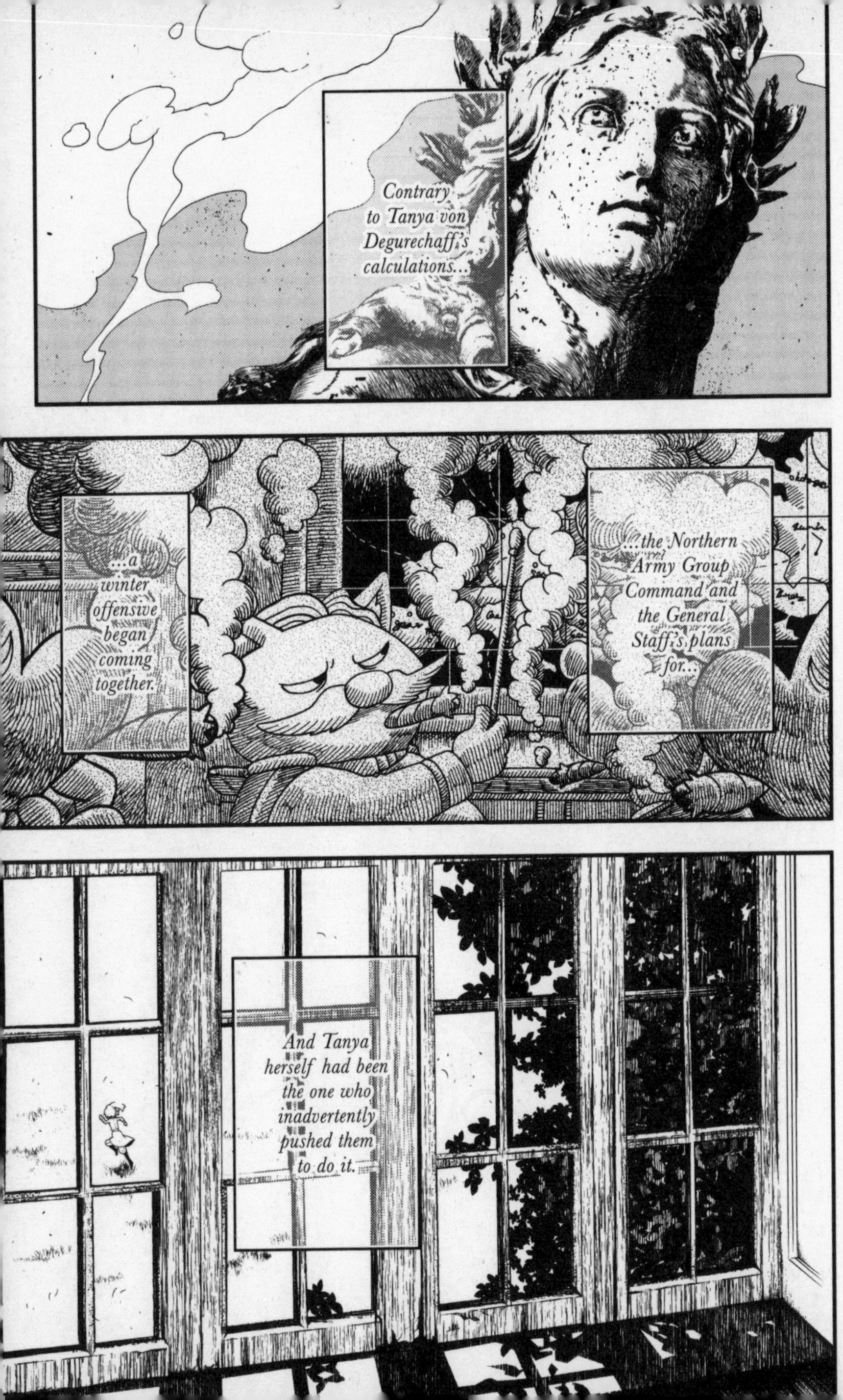
Contrary to Tanya von Degurechaff's calculations...
...the Northern Army Group Command and the General Staff's plans for...
...a winter offensive began coming together.
And Tanya herself had been the one who inadvertently pushed them to do it.

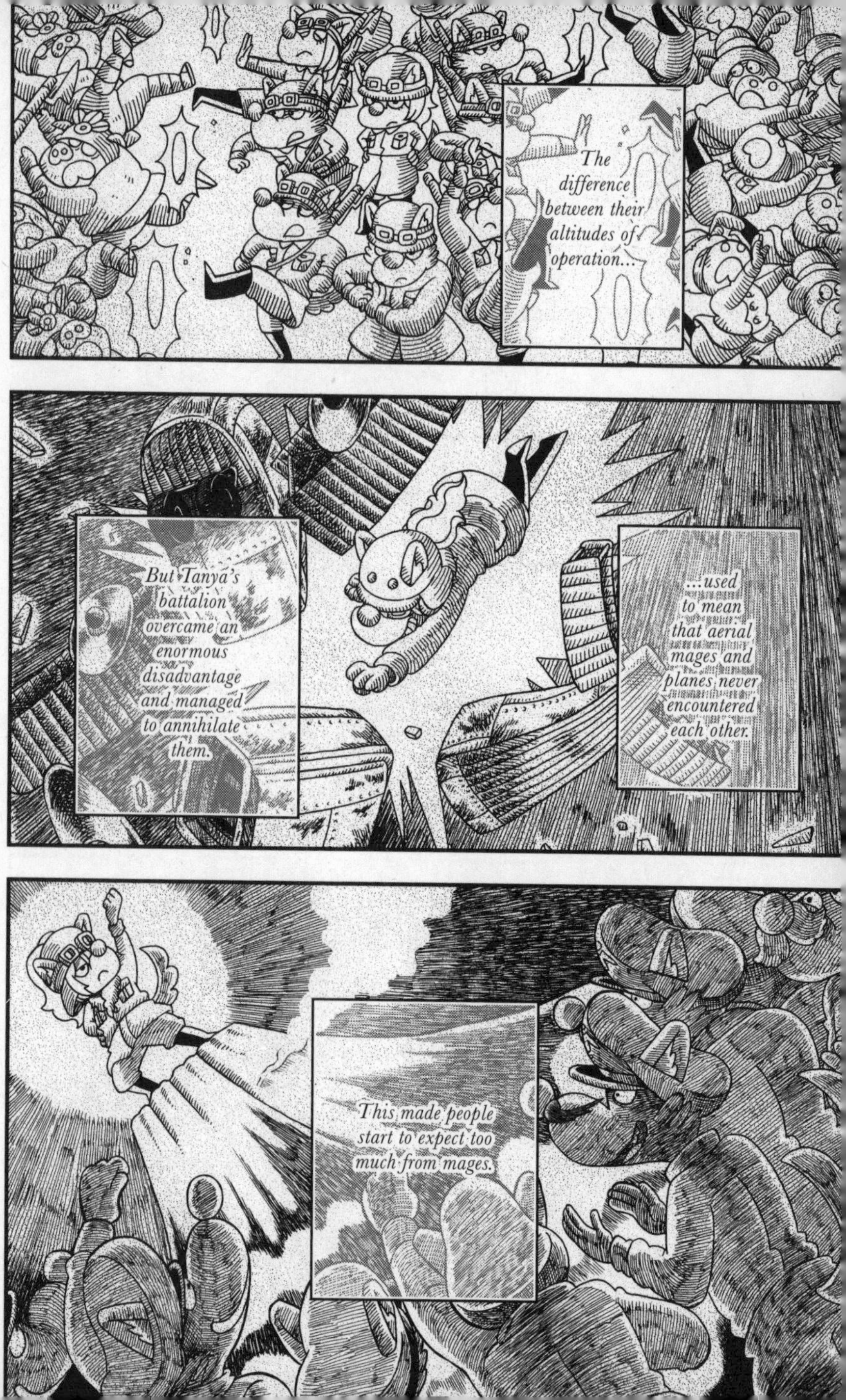
The difference between their altitudes of operation...
...used to mean that aerial mages and planes never encountered each other.
But Tanya's battalion overcame an enormous disadvantage and managed to annihilate them.
This made people start to expect too much from mages.

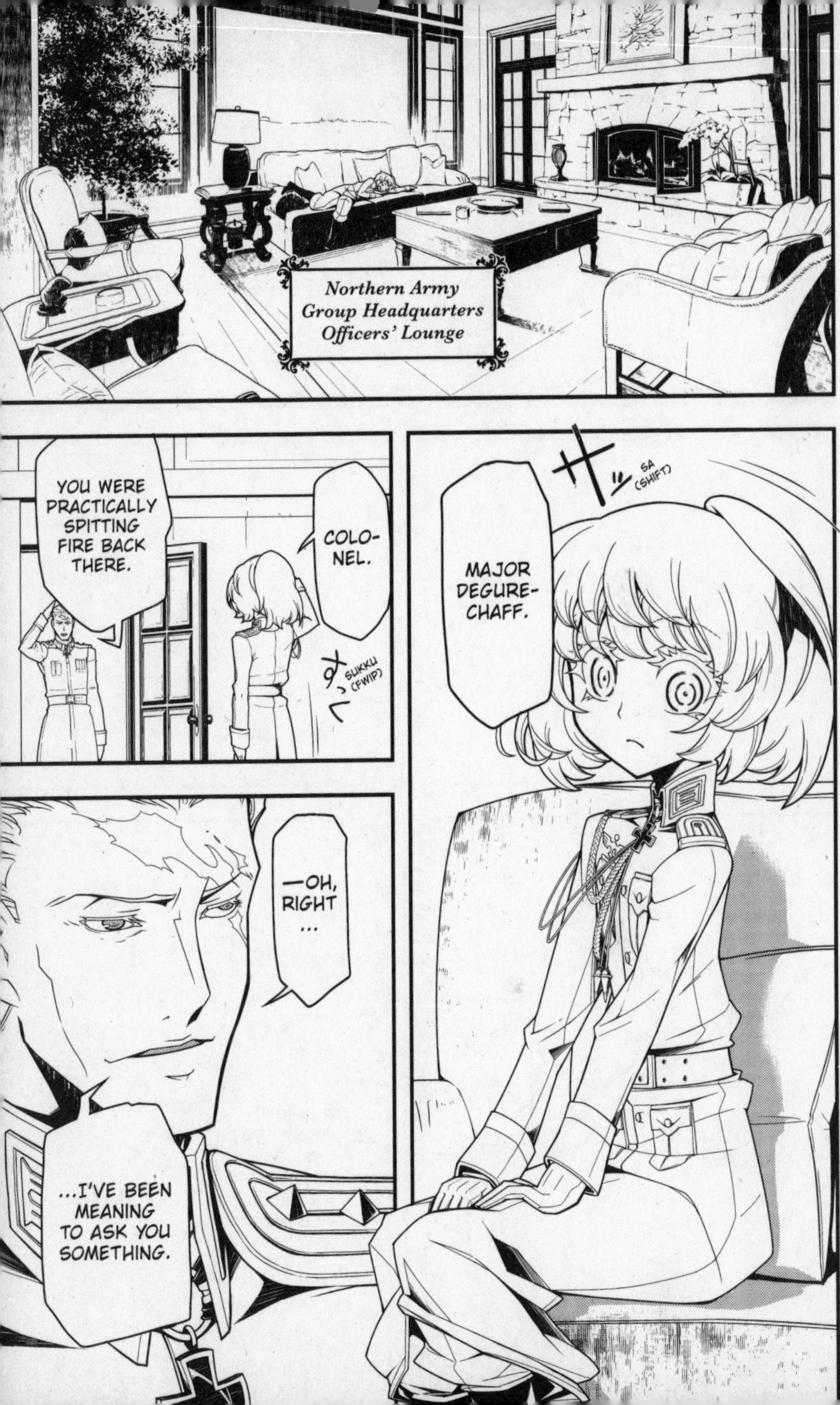
Northern Army
Group Headquarters
Officers' Lounge
MAJOR DEGURE-CHAFF.
SA (SHIFT)
COLO-NEL.
SUKKU (FWIP)
YOU WERE PRACTICALLY SPITTING FIRE BACK THERE.
—OH, RIGHT ...
...I'VE BEEN MEANING TO ASK YOU SOMETHING.

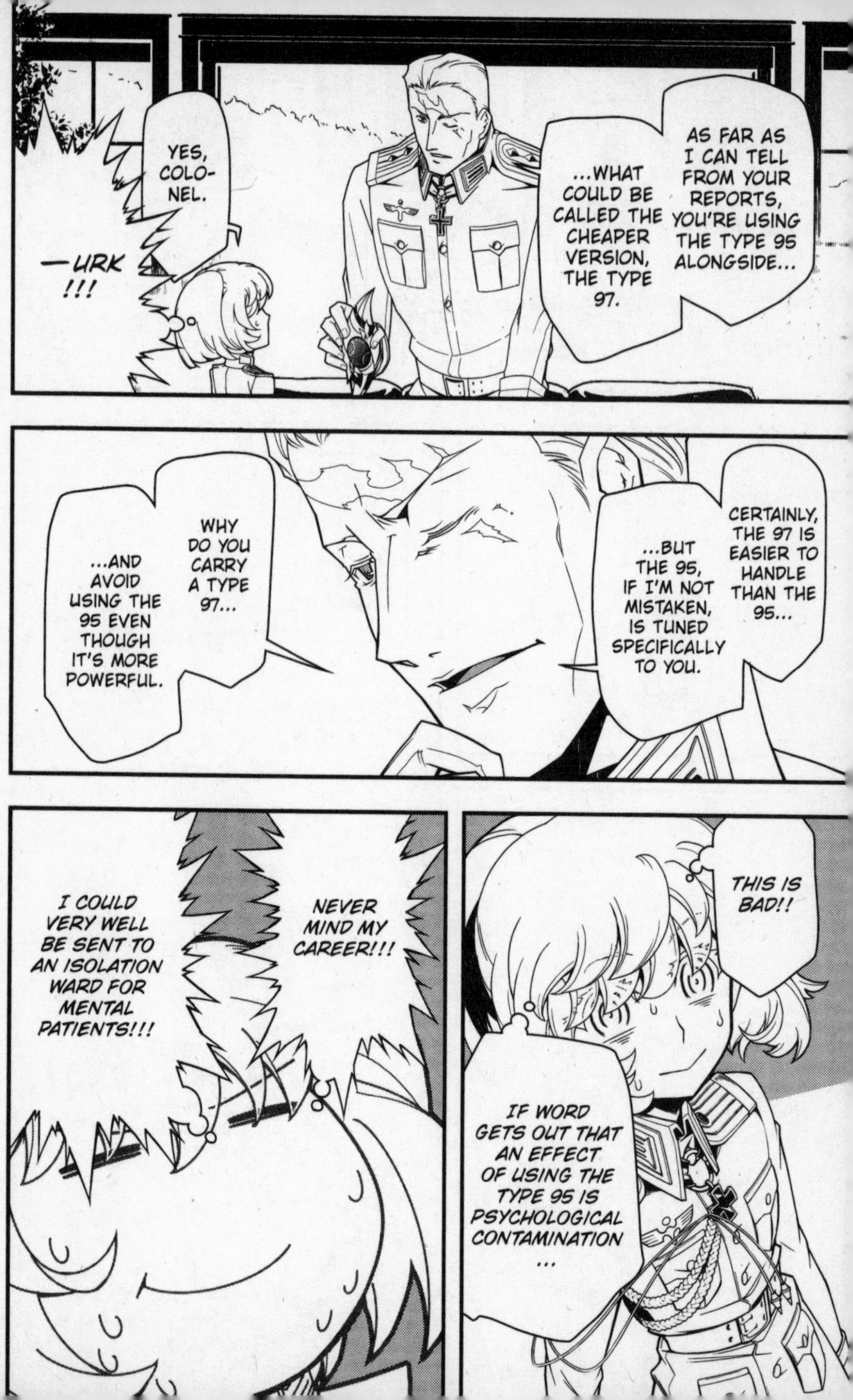
AS FAR AS I CAN TELL FROM YOUR REPORTS, YOU'RE USING THE TYPE 95 ALONGSIDE...
...WHAT COULD BE CALLED THE CHEAPER VERSION, THE TYPE 97.
YES, COLONEL.
—URK!!!
CERTAINLY, THE 97 IS EASIER TO HANDLE THAN THE 95...
...BUT THE 95, IF I'M NOT MISTAKEN, IS TUNED SPECIFICALLY TO YOU.
WHY DO YOU CARRY A TYPE 97...
...AND AVOID USING THE 95 EVEN THOUGH IT'S MORE POWERFUL.
THIS IS BAD!!
IF WORD GETS OUT THAT AN EFFECT OF USING THE TYPE 95 IS PSYCHOLOGICAL CONTAMINATION...
NEVER MIND MY CAREER!!!
I COULD VERY WELL BE SENT TO AN ISOLATION WARD FOR MENTAL PATIENTS!!!

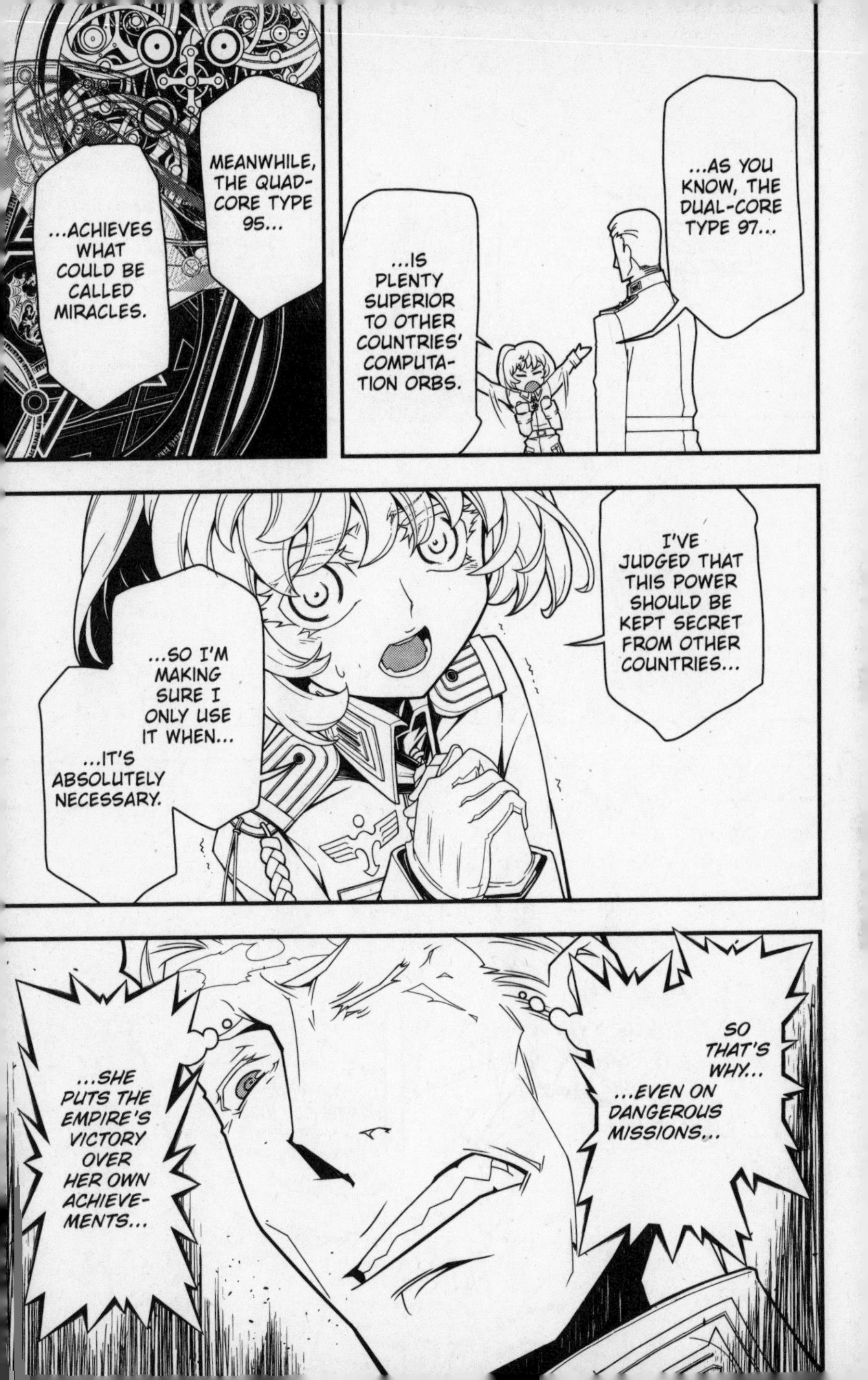
...AS YOU KNOW, THE DUAL-CORE TYPE 97...
...IS PLENTY SUPERIOR TO OTHER COUNTRIES' COMPUTATION ORBS.
MEANWHILE, THE QUAD-CORE TYPE 95...
...ACHIEVES WHAT COULD BE CALLED MIRACLES.
I'VE JUDGED THAT THIS POWER SHOULD BE KEPT SECRET FROM OTHER COUNTRIES...
...SO I'M MAKING SURE I ONLY USE IT WHEN...
...IT'S ABSOLUTELY NECESSARY.
SO THAT'S WHY...
...EVEN ON DANGEROUS MISSIONS...
...SHE PUTS THE EMPIRE'S VICTORY OVER HER OWN ACHIEVEMENTS...

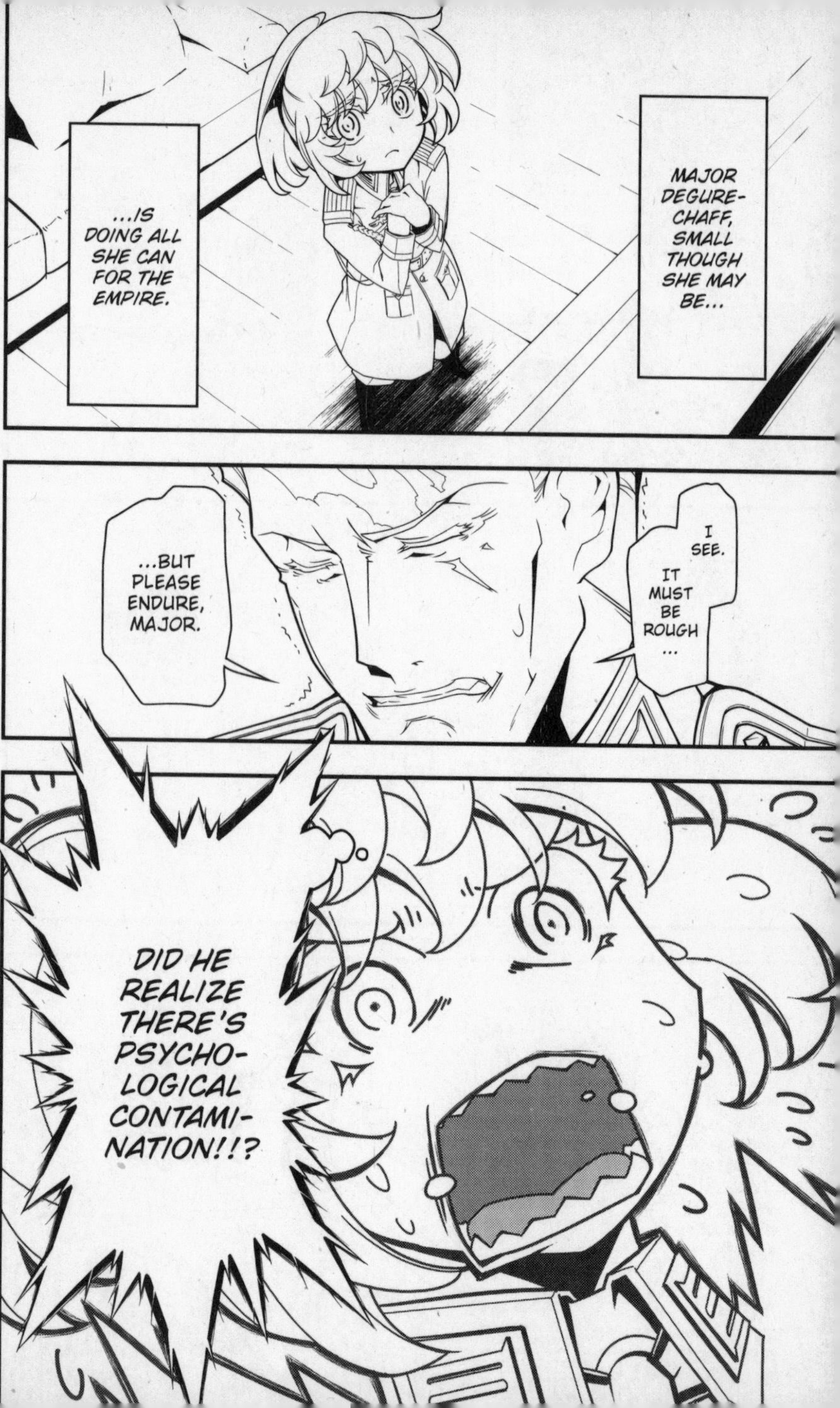
MAJOR DEGURE-CHAFF, SMALL THOUGH SHE MAY BE...
...IS DOING ALL SHE CAN FOR THE EMPIRE.
I SEE. IT MUST BE ROUGH...
...BUT PLEASE ENDURE, MAJOR.
DID HE REALIZE THERE'S PSYCHO-LOGICAL CONTAMI-NATION!!?

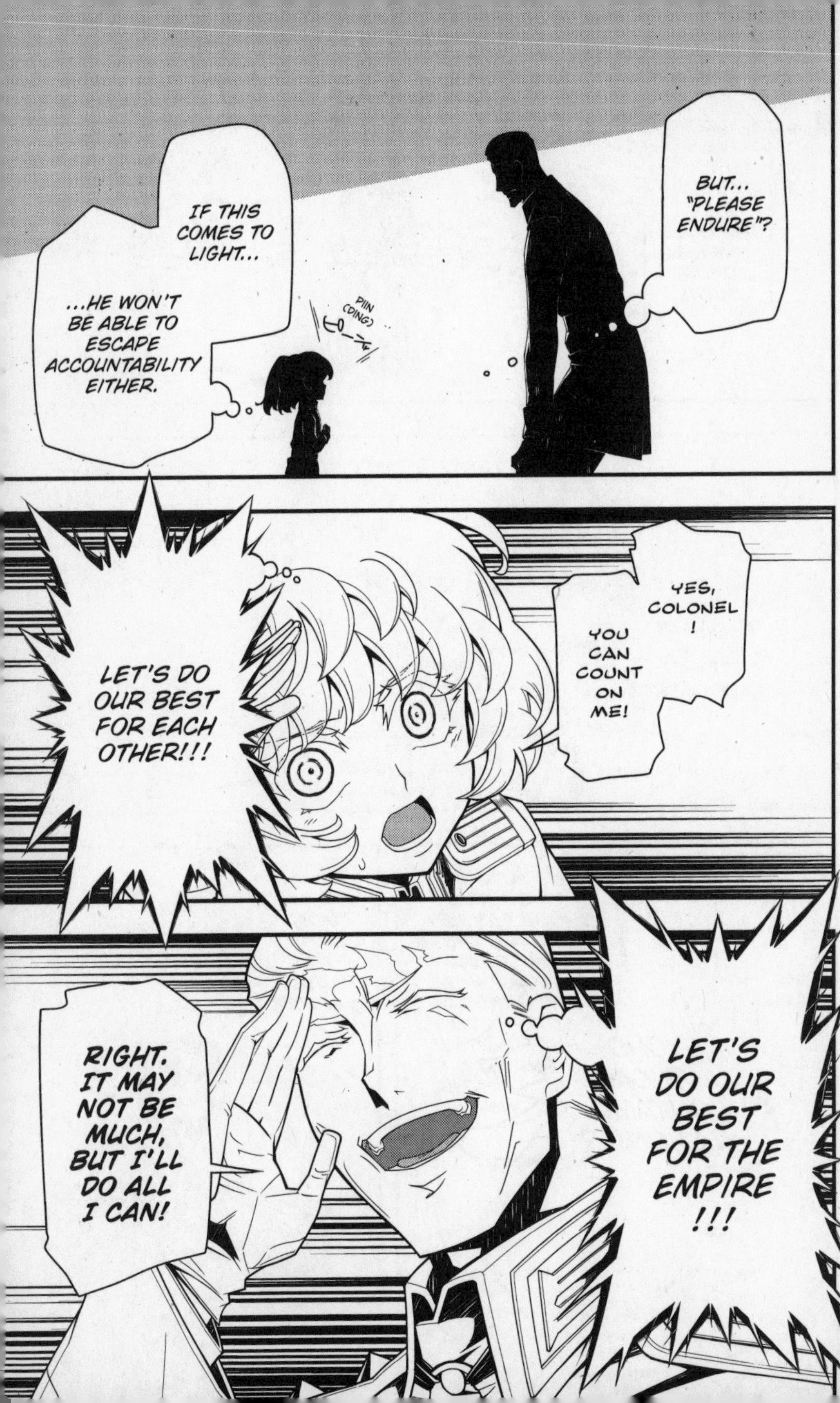
BUT... "PLEASE ENDURE"?
PIIN (DING)
IF THIS COMES TO LIGHT...
...HE WON'T BE ABLE TO ESCAPE ACCOUNTABILITY EITHER.
YES, COLONEL!
YOU CAN COUNT ON ME!
LET'S DO OUR BEST FOR EACH OTHER!!!
LET'S DO OUR BEST FOR THE EMPIRE!!!
RIGHT. IT MAY NOT BE MUCH, BUT I'LL DO ALL I CAN!

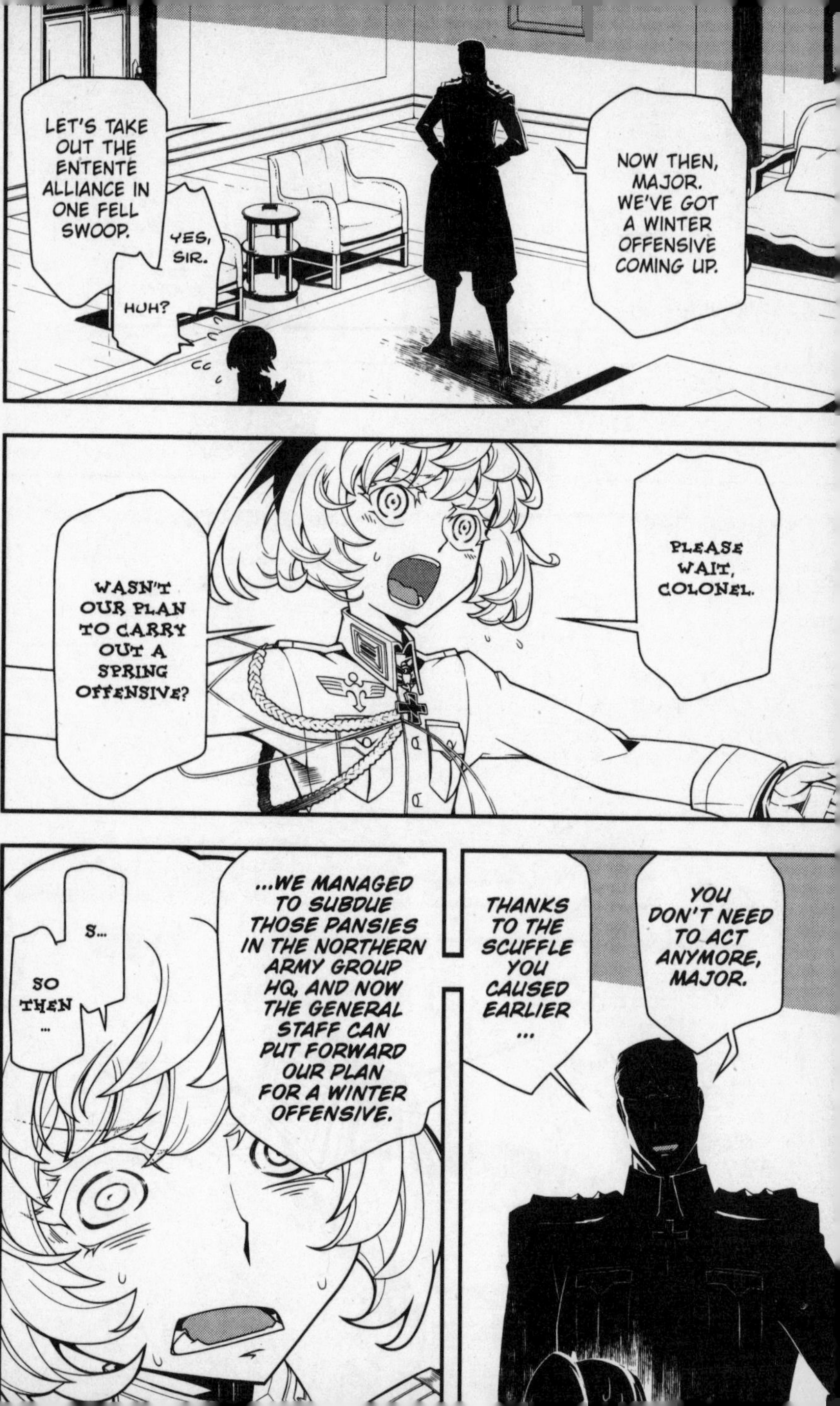
NOW THEN, MAJOR. WE'VE GOT A WINTER OFFENSIVE COMING UP.
LET'S TAKE OUT THE ENTENTE ALLIANCE IN ONE FELL SWOOP.
YES, SIR.
HUH?
PLEASE WAIT, COLONEL.
WASN'T OUR PLAN TO CARRY OUT A SPRING OFFENSIVE?
YOU DON'T NEED TO ACT ANYMORE, MAJOR.
THANKS TO THE SCUFFLE YOU CAUSED EARLIER...
...WE MANAGED TO SUBDUE THOSE PANSIES IN THE NORTHERN ARMY GROUP HQ, AND NOW THE GENERAL STAFF CAN PUT FORWARD OUR PLAN FOR A WINTER OFFENSIVE.
S...
SO THEN...

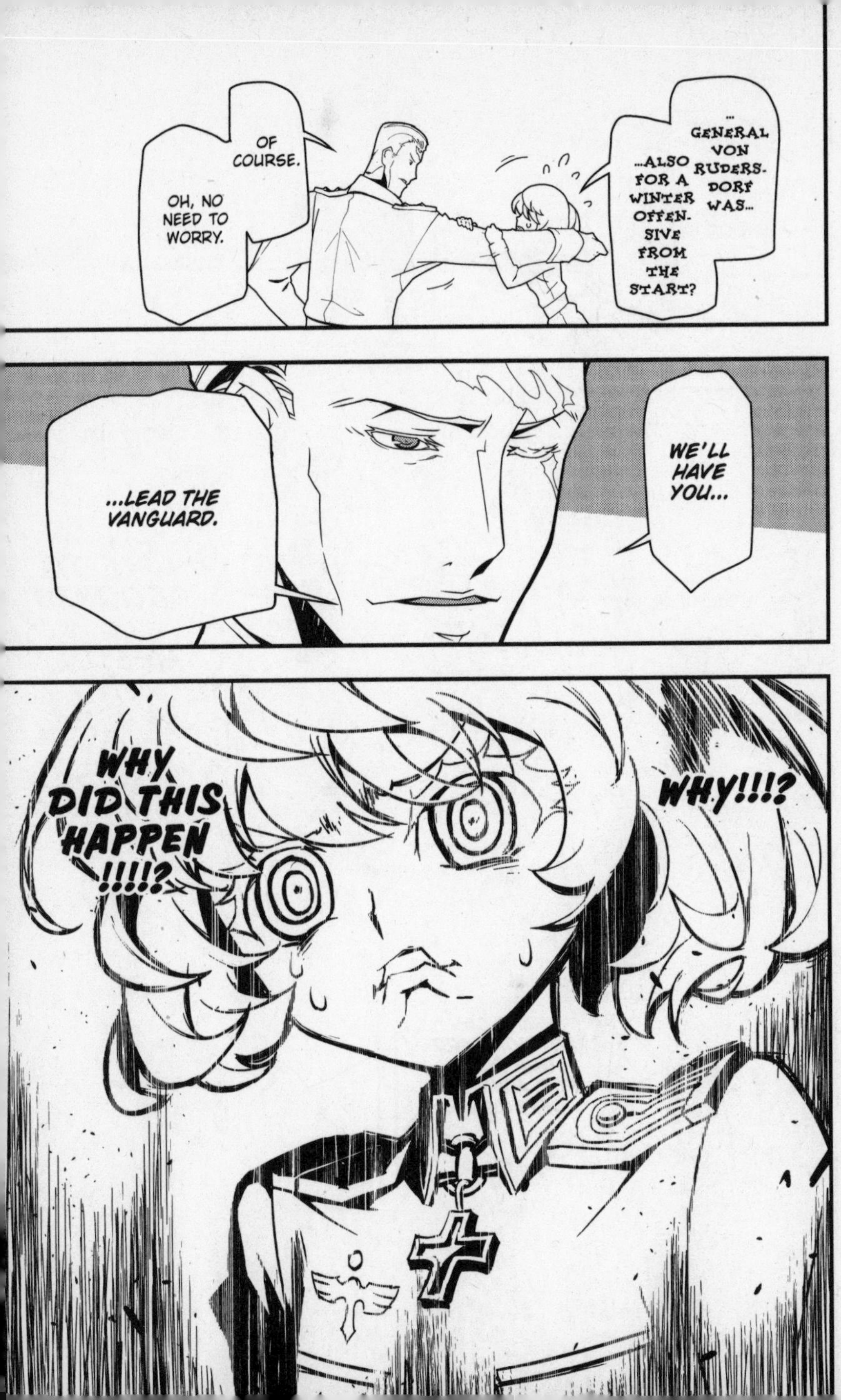
...GENERAL VON RUDERS-DORF WAS... ...ALSO FOR A WINTER OFFEN-SIVE FROM THE START?
OF COURSE.
OH, NO NEED TO WORRY.
WE'LL HAVE YOU...
...LEAD THE VANGUARD.
WHY!!!?
WHY DID THIS HAPPEN!!!!?

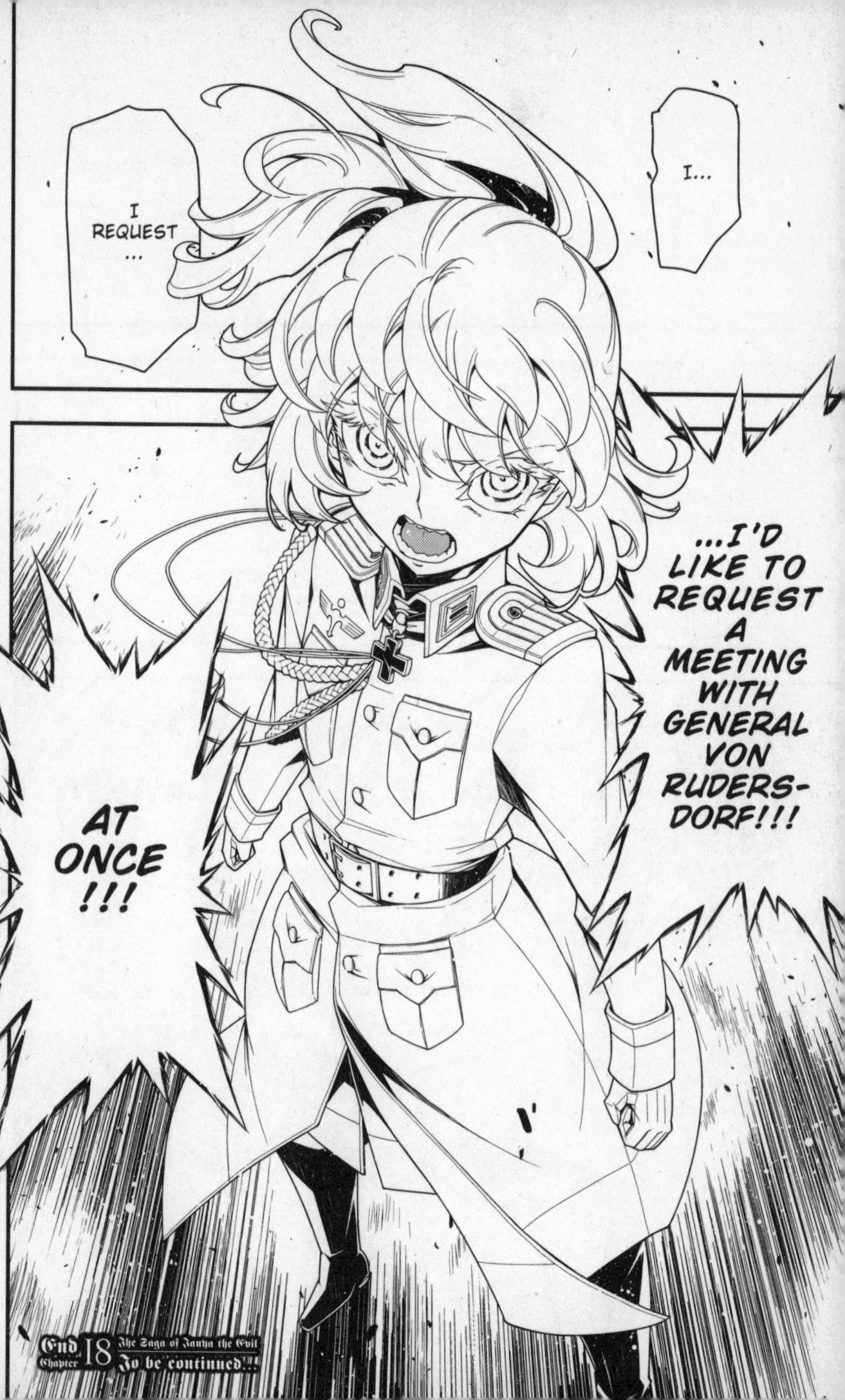

I...
I REQUEST ...
...I'D LIKE TO REQUEST A MEETING WITH GENERAL VON RUDERS-DORF!!!
AT ONCE!!!
End Chapter 18 The Saga of Tanya the Evil To be continued...

The Saga of
Tanya the Evil

06

Original Story: Carlo Zen   Art: Chika Tojo
Character Design: Shinobu Shinotsuki

Special Thanks

Carlo Zen

Shinobu Shinotsuki

Takamaru

KURI

Miira

Yamatatsu

Agatha

Kuuko

Mizuhara Yuuki

THE SAGA OF TANYA THE EVIL 06

ORIGINAL STORY: Carlo Zen

ART: Chika Tojo ✚ CHARACTER DESIGN: Shinobu Shinotsuki

Translation: Emily Balistrieri ✚ Lettering: Rochelle Gancio

This book is a work of fiction. Names, characters, places, and incidents are the product of the author's imagination or are used fictitiously. Any resemblance to actual events, locales, or persons, living or dead, is coincidental.

YOUJO SENKI Vol. 6
©Chika TOJO 2017
©2013 Carlo ZEN
First published in Japan in 2017 by KADOKAWA CORPORATION, Tokyo.
English translation rights arranged with KADOKAWA CORPORATION, Tokyo through TUTTLE-MORI AGENCY, INC., Tokyo.

English translation © 2019 by Yen Press, LLC

Yen Press
1290 Avenue of the Americas
New York, NY 10104

Visit us at yenpress.com
facebook.com/yenpress
twitter.com/yenpress
yenpress.tumblr.com
instagram.com/yenpress

First Yen Press Edition: April 2019

Yen Press is an imprint of Yen Press, LLC.
The Yen Press name and logo are trademarks of Yen Press, LLC.

The publisher is not responsible for websites (or their content) that are not owned by the publisher.

Library of Congress Control Number: 2017954161

ISBNs: 978-1-9753-0413-3 (paperback)
978-1-9753-5776-4 (ebook)

10 9 8 7 6 5 4 3 2 1

WOR

Printed in the United States of America